Landscape Origins

of the

Wye Valley

Landscape Origins

of the

Wye Valley

edited by

Heather Hurley

The River Wye Preservation Trust in association with Logaston Press

LOGASTON PRESS
Little Logaston, Logaston,
Woonton, Almeley, Herefordshire HR3 6QH
logastonpress.co.uk

First published by The River Wye Preservation Trust in association with Logaston Press 2008
(www.rwpt.net)
Text copyright author(s) of each chapter as stated 2008
Illustrations copyright as credited in Sources 2008

ISBN
978 1 904396 96 3 (hardback)
978 1 904396 97 0 (paperback)

Set in Times New Roman by Logaston Press
and printed and bound by
Bell & Bain. Ltd., Glasgow

Front cover illustration: *View from Capler Hill looking south-west*

Contents

Ballingham churchyard

Foreword

Areas of Outstanding Natural Beauty are a real gift for us all. They need cherishing, valuing but also understanding if we are to delight in them fully and care for them for the future.

The River Wye Preservation Trust (RWPT) has drawn together a group of local specialists and volunteers to gain a better understanding of an important section of the River Wye. They have sought to understand the history of the agriculture, woodland, settlement and economy of this beautiful stretch of the valley, drawing on historical mapping, documents, identification of archaeological sites and present knowledge. The result is a fascinating, authoritative and immensely attractive landscape history of the project area.

I should like to pay tribute to the expertise, energy, and enthusiasm with which so many people approached this project, and without which it would never have been possible. Also, my thanks go to the Herefordshire Rivers Leader+ programme, together with our other funders, and the partnership with the local communities which has also been essential for the success of this innovative work.

May the book encourage us all to enjoy and appreciate the Wye Valley even more and understand better the richness of heritage entrusted to us.

+ Anthony, Hereford
(President of the River Wye Preservation Trust)
May 2008

The study area on Taylor's map of 1754

Acknowledgements

The Landscape Origins of the Wye Valley project was developed by the River Wye Preservation Trust and its committee, under the chairmanship of Simon Dereham. The project team acknowledge with gratitude the financial support from the Herefordshire Rivers LEADER+ programme, the Heritage Lottery Fund, and the Wye Valley AONB Unit.

The project owes its success to the enthusiasm and involvement of many volunteers, supporters and specialists. Thanks are due to Huw Sherlock and his team at Archenfield Archaeology for excavation, training in field-walking, digital cartographic techniques, and identifying and processing finds. The project is grateful for the use of their facilities at Caplor Farm and for creating and maintaining the project website. The archaeological research is continuing with specialist reports so far by Alan Jacobs (pottery), Alvaro Mora-Ottomano (prehistoric flints) and Ian Baxter (animal bone). This material will be published in due course.

Particular thanks to Philip Watkins, for allowing the project to undertake the archaeological excavation at Gillow Farm. Also to the owners of Caplor, Caradoc, Pengethley, Aramstone, Llanfrother, Dockhill Well, The Firs, Lower Penalt, and Fawley Court farms; and the owners of Trilloes Court Wood and Wilton Castle, for allowing access to study the landscape and carry out archaeological work.

Martin and Ann Roseveare of ArchaeoPhysica Ltd., Mark Bowden, Nicky Smith and Lisa Moffett of English Heritage, Helen Stace of Natural England, Adam Buckley, George Nash, Keith Ray, and Derek Siveter are all thanked for their expertise. Many thanks are also due to Chris Musson, Elwyn Brooke, Jan Scudamore, John Williams, Julian Partridge, Kim Brooker, Maria Ball, Tim Ward, and to the late David Bick and Doreen Ruck who all kindly allowed their archives, photographs and maps to be digitally recorded for the use of the project.

Research for the the whole project leading up to this book would not have been possible without the help received from Rhys Griffith at the Herefordshire Record Office, Rosalind Caird at the Hereford Cathedral Library, Robin Hill at Hereford City Library, and from staff at Hereford and Monmouth Museums, the National Library of Wales, Gloucester Record Office, the National Archives, the National Monuments Record, and Herefordshire Archaeology. Lastly thanks to Andy Johnson, Ron and Jennifer Shoesmith and Karen Stout of Logaston Press for guidance and advice in producing this book, and lastly special thanks to Ron Shoesmith for his editorial assistance.

Project Steering Group Members

Catherine Fookes, Wye Valley AONB Office
Daphne Wyatt, Ross-on-Wye and District Civic Society
David Lovelace, River Wye Preservation Trust
Derek Wareham, Leader+
Gareth Williams, Caplor Farm
Janet Lomas, Farming and Wildlife Advisory Group
Patrick Darling, Wye Salmon Fisheries Association
Rhys Griffith, Herefordshire Record Office
Simon Dereham, River Wye Preservation Trust
Stuart Thomas, Herefordshire Council
Virginia Morgan, Council for the Protection of Rural England

Volunteers and Supporters

Adrian Harvey, King's Caple
Alan Parslow, Wilton Castle
Alice Hurley, Hoarwithy
Alwyn O'Hare, Ross,
Angela Williams, King's Caple
Ann Colman, Ross
Bernard & Cherry Newton, Hereford
Bernice Baker, Redbrook
Brian Thomas, King's Caple
Caroline Hands, Overdine Farm,
Caroline Stratford, Pencoyd
Charlotte Baron
Chris Parker, Bristol
Chris Peacock, Hentland
Chris Robertson, *Ross Gazette*
Daphne Rutter, Hoarwithy
Daphne Wyatt, Hoarwithy
David Clark, Fownhope
David Clarke, Fownhope
David Laws, Brockhampton
Debbie Shipp, Chippenham
Dede Liss, Newent
Diana Adams
Diane Gilbert, Sellack
Don Punnett, Ross Sub-Aqua Club
Doreen Ruck, Garway
Eileen O'Haire, Newent
Elaine and Paul Baron
Elaine Goddard, Much Birch
Elwyn Brooke, King's Caple
Fenny Smith, Ross
Frank Betambeau, Bishopstone
Frank Davis, Harewood
Gabrielle Hanson-Smith, Brockhampton
Gerald Dawe, Hereford
Henry & Sue Connor, Hereford
Hilary and Alistair Ross, Hoarwithy
Ian Brough, Brockhampton
Ian Gwynne, Ross
Ian Hughes, King's Caple
James Anthony, Hereford
Janet Cooper, Ross
Joe Weaver, Yatton
John Davies, Wormelow

John Goodrich, Bridstow
John Haines, Sellack
John Hudson, Brockhampton
John Parry, Ross
John Price, Bridstow
John Wilmore, Dormington
Jon Hurley, Hoarwithy
Judith Smith, Hereford
Kate Wollen, Ledbury
Katherine Andrew, Hereford Museum
Les Phillips, Hoarwithy
Lindsay Gilbert, Sellack
Lyn Cobley, Ingestone
Margot Miller, Fownhope
Mark & Janet Robinson, Hay on Wye
Mike Harper, Ledbury
Neil Stockdale
Nicky Hopwood, Brockhampton
Norma Rudge, Sellack
Paul Lyons, Hereford
Paul Newman, Phocle Green
Peter Day, How Caple
Peter and Joanna Huyton, Hoarwithy
Philip Beard, Much Marcle
Phillip Anderson, How Caple
Richard Davies, Hereford
Richard Mayo, Ross
Rita and John Sorrell, Hoarwithy
Roger Partridge, Pengethley
Roger Pye, Kington
Roger Stirling-Brown
Rosamund Skelton, Ross
Roz Lowe, Goodrich
Russell Hurley, Hoarwithy
Sherwood Keogh, Bolstone
Shirley Preece, Bridstow
Stephanie Hobbs, Hoarwithy
Sue Farr, How Caple
Sue Hubbard, Byford
Sylvia Kelly, Hoarwithy
Tom Pearson, Weston-under-Penyard
Will Lewis, Hay-on-Wye
William Bick, Newent

Illustrations – Sources

t- top; b- bottom; l - left; r - right; m - middle
All other photographs were taken by Will Lewis, Fenny Smith, P. J. Pikes, David Lovelace and
Heather Hurley for the Landscape Origins of the Wye Valley project

Chris Musson and the Woolhope Club: 30b, 31t, 32t, 39, 40t, 44t, 44b, 218

Michael Szostak: 41b, 178b

Mary Soulsby: 129

Russell Hurley: 151b

Elwyn Brooke: 78

Ron Shoesmith: 103t, 115

Sunderlands: 101tr

Sherwood Keogh: 56r

David Bick: 142tl

Ian Gwynne: 177r, 178t, 184

Geoff Gwatkin: 70, 74b, 77bl (colour coded by LOWV project)

Tim Ward Collection: 4bl, 125, 135, 172, 177l, 180t, 180b, 181t, 181b, 182t, 193t, 199

Hurley Collection: 138, 146b, 166, 167b, 179tl,179tr, 179b, 183b, 199

Aramstone Archive: 118, 222

Kentchurch Archive: 4tl, 187, 191tl, 191tr, 196t

Hereford Cathedral Archives: 53 (483), 86 (2393), 132 (5715/3/49 By permission of the Dean and Chapter of Hereford Cathedral)

Ross Recorder: 134r

Herefordshire Record Office: 59, 63tr, 63r, 67br, 92b, 102b, 120tl, 129bl, 130, 134l, 136, 142ml, 161t, 171bl,192, 196b, 198

British Library: 90 (Add.MS.36307, f.22), 186 (Add. MS. 36307, f.3)

Ordnance Survey: 141, 145, 148, 154, 159

Woolhope Naturalists' Field Club: 9t

Ross Old Books and Prints: 171t

Wye Valley Area of Outstanding Natural Beauty: 212t, 217, 224,

Hereford Museum: 14tl, 15m, 18tl, 19, 21tr, 23, 41t

Hereford City Library: vii, 77t, 124b, 128, 161bl, 167t, 171br, 158bl

Monmouth Museum: 122b (S. D. Coates collection)

English Nature: 43br, 52, 61br, 71b, 73b, 76b, 77br, 79b, 94t, 190, 197b, 207t (UK Perspectives: Licence Number UKP2005/2/108)

National Monument Record: Surveyors notes and photographs 10tl, 24bl, 30t, 31b, 69bl, 100tr, 104, 105t, 105b, 107, 109t, 109b, 112t, 114t, 114bl, 117tl. Aerial photographs 76 (mosaic of RAF/106G/UK/1652 11/7/1946 frames 4262, 4263, 5261 and 5263), 80b (RAF/106G/UK/1652 11/7/1946 frame 5147), 88b (OS/71001 2/2/1971 frame 089), 189 (RAF/106G/ UK/1652 11/7/1946 frame 3143), 191 (Aerofilms 30/4/1921 neg. no. 6050), 194 (mosaic of OS/70398 29/9/1970 frame 339, OS/71001 2/2/1971 frame 90, RAF/106G/UK 11/7/1946 frame 4262), 206b (OS/71001 2/2/1971 frame 089), 206t (OS/170398 29/9/1970 frame 344), 208 (OS/70398 29/9/1970 frame 336)

The National Archives: Documents 54 (Just1/303), 56 (C134/82), 58 (C115/96/6934), 63bl (MAF32/3/195), 65 (C115/45), 85t (C135/140), 126 (Just1/307) 205t, 205b (F22/548). Tithe Maps 60, 61tl, 72, 74t, 80tl, 123t (IR30/14/86, IR30/14/96, IR/30/14/105)

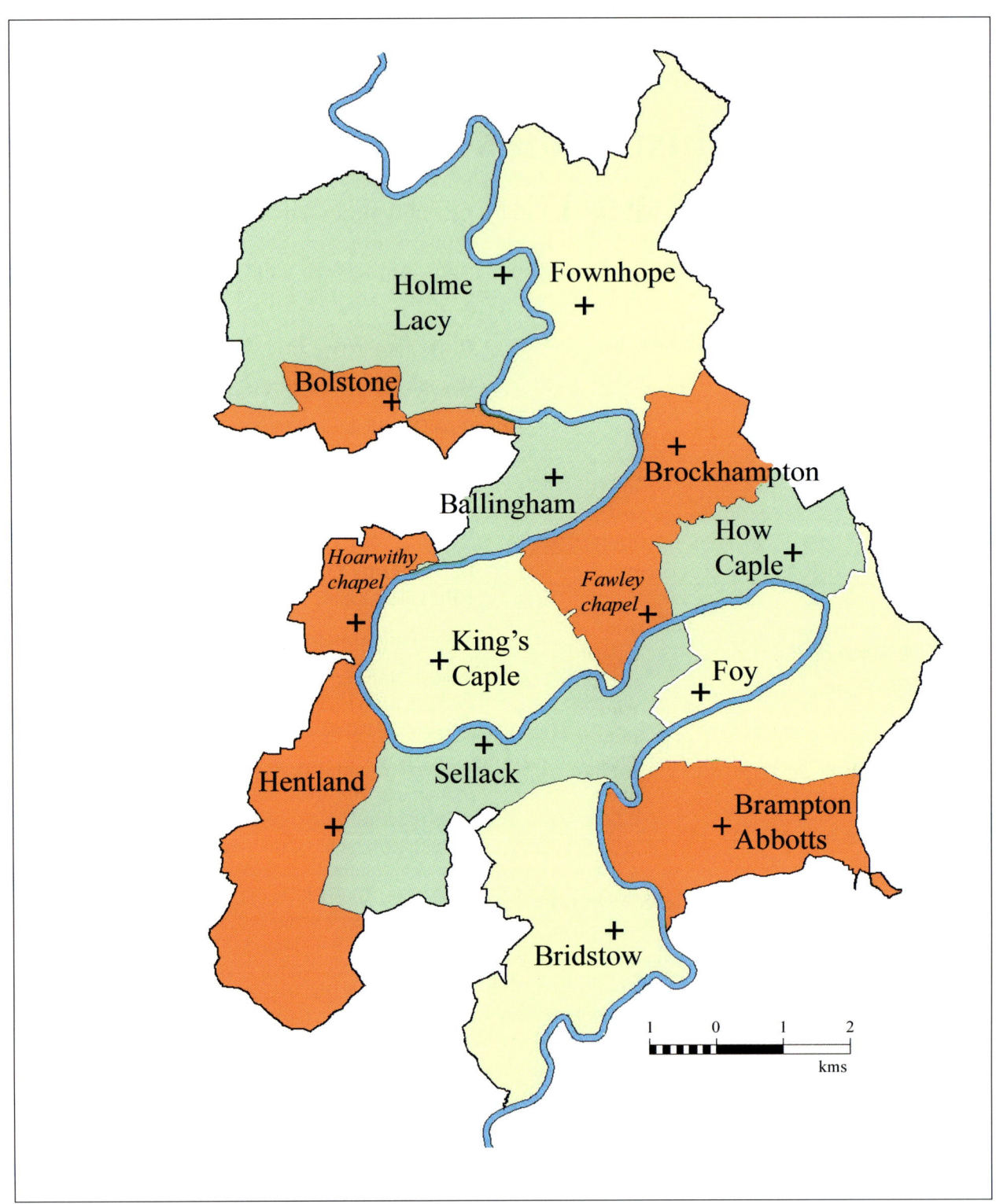

The parishes in the study area and their relationship to the River Wye

INTRODUCTION

Landscape Origins of the Wye Valley

by Heather Hurley and David Lovelace

The Landscape Origins of the Wye Valley (LOWV) was a funded project to study the history and development of the countryside in the twelve parishes which make up the northern part of the Wye Valley Area of Outstanding Natural Beauty. It was designated as an Area of Outstanding National Beauty (AONB) in 1971 for its 'internationally important protected landscape containing some of the most beautiful lowland scenery in Britain'. The twelve parishes of Ballingham, Bolstone, Brampton Abbotts, Bridstow, Brockhampton, Fownhope, Foy, Hentland, Holme Lacy, How Caple, King's Caple, and Sellack all border the River Wye in a rural area between the city of Hereford and the town of Ross-on-Wye.

The project was funded through the Herefordshire Rivers LEADER+ programme. LEADER is an acronym for *Liaison Entre Actions pour le Développement de L'Economie Rurale*, a relatively small pot of money designed to support rural communities in a variety of innovative activities from economic development to environmental protection. The '+' was to distinguish it from the earlier round of LEADER programmes. Uniquely, for European funds it was the communities who decided on the type of activities to be funded and the sort of programme that was best for each area.

In 2001 Herefordshire Council, along with all counties in the UK, facilitated a small group made up of representatives from the farming, environment, tourism and economic development sectors in the county, to draw up a funding proposal for consideration by Brussels. As the River Wye had just been designated a European site of importance for nature conservation, it seemed appropriate to develop a funding programme based around the theme of the rural environment of the Wye and its feeder rivers the Lugg, Arrow and Frome.

Acknowledging the importance of the historic dimension in appreciating and understanding the countryside, the proposed programme included an archaeology and history section. The Herefordshire Rivers LEADER+ programme was one of only two such funding programme applications to be successful in the West Midlands region. From 2002, all parishes in Herefordshire which touched the Wye or its tributaries were eligible for funding community projects which furthered the aims of the programme.

Parishes in the Arrow, Frome and Lugg valleys all had archaeology projects put forward by Herefordshire Council with matched funding from English Heritage – the Arrow and Lugg Valleys are now available as publications. The River Wye Preservation Trust (RWPT), through its local contacts, drew together a group of locally based historians to develop a community based project to study the history and development of the countryside of the parishes encompassing this section of the Wye Valley. The 12 parishes from Holme Lacy down to Bridstow were chosen as an initial project, as this tract of countryside seemed to be relatively unexplored in terms of its history and archaeology.

It is part of the conditions of the LEADER grant that projects are 'partnership' endeavours, so that the EU funding have to be 'matched' by contributions in kind and/or in cash from other sources. The Trust's proposed project – the Landscape Origins of the Wye Valley – was successful in its application for matched funding under the Heritage Lottery Fund 'Your Heritage' programme, and as the project parishes were situated in the Wye Valley Area of Outstanding Natural Beauty the Trust was also successful in securing funding from the AONB 'Finest Countryside' projects programme.

Documentary research at Caplor

The project's success has been entirely dependent upon the enthusiasm and commitment of the local people in the 12 parishes. The RWPT hopes that this project will inspire people in other parts of the Wye Valley and further afield to take a fresh look at their local countryside. Rural areas are entering a period of considerable uncertainty, with land under increasing pressure and subject to conflicting demands. Added to this, the threat of climate change, the overuse of water resources, and the degradation of land are especially acute for rivers and river valleys. This makes it more imperative that people understand the importance of their local countryside. The project hopes that this publication will help to define what makes this part of the Wye Valley so special, not just for the people who live there, but for future generations to enjoy and cherish.

This book is the result of a unique investigation into how and why the landscape of the northern section of the Wye Valley AONB developed into the countryside we see today. The project brought together an enthusiastic band of local volunteers who were advised and trained by experts in archaeology, history and analysis. This team spent two years studying the area using a huge variety of traditional and modern methods from simple field walking to the latest in geophysics; from oral history to aerial photography; from recording veteran trees to deciphering medieval manuscripts. Many new discoveries have led to a better understanding of the process of change from the remote past to the present day, and will inform everyone as to the best way of appreciating, conserving and managing this rural heritage.

Field-walking in King's Caple

In March 2005 the project was successfully launched at Sellack Village Hall, attracting 78 supporters, many who signed up as volunteers to investigate, research, and where possible excavate to establish the origins of the landscape from prehistoric times to the present day. A further public meeting was held at Brockhampton, and despite heavy rain a good audience attended to hear about the project's research of the quarries at Capler, navigation on the Wye, previously unknown crop-mark sites and the use of digital cameras at the record offices, libraries and the National Archives.

Hedgerow surveying

These early meetings were overwhelmingly successful, with excellent displays, together with an instructive tour with the funders to Bridstow Church, Backney Bridge, Pengethley Park, Hoarwithy Village, Capler Camp, and Haugh Wood, which demonstrated the beauty and variation of the Wye Valley country-side. The success led the group to organise a series of training workshops in archaeology, hedgerow surveying, researching archives, and transcribing and translating old English and Latin documents. Apart from talks and exhibitions at village halls the LOWV team also promoted the project by leading inter-pretive walks for the local community.

Guided walks during 2005 introduced the public to the geology, archaeology and history of the project area. Footpaths were followed along the Wye, through woods, fields and villages to view buildings and archaeological sites in the parishes of Brock-hampton, Sellack, Hentland, and Bolstone. From viewing these sites the team, with the help of volunteers, decided to carry out research into the barge accounts, which had been acquired from a private source; to excavate a section of a former road leading to a ford at Red Rail; and to examine the riverbed there with the expertise of the Ross Sub Aqua Club. In addition it was agreed to undertake field-walking and a geophysical survey at a cropmark site shown on an aerial photograph at Fawley.

The high profile of the project encour-aged local residents to loan previously unknown maps and archives to the project leaders. These valuable documents were

Guided walks 2005. Top – Capler Camp;
Bottom – The Wye at Sellack

Photography at Hereford Record Office

Digital photograph of maps – Bower Farm, Holme Lacy 1780

digitally photographed and studied by the group's volunteers, who were also shown how to research local history at the Hereford Record Office, the Cathedral Library and Hereford City Library. The tithe map apportionments were copied and entered onto spread sheets with all details of owner, tenant, field name, land measurement, and amount of tithe paid. This became a very useful source for the later surveys of hollow-ways, buildings, farms and the River Wye.

Above – Collecting old photographs, Hole-in-the-Wall in the early 20th century
Right – Measuring a veteran tree at Caplor Farm

As the project progressed, a collection of aerial photographs, historic maps, oral histories, Latin and English documents, old prints and photographs, and contemporary landscape photographs were digitally produced to form the LOWV archive. A sample of these were displayed on the excellent website www.wyevalleyhistory.net together with a programme of present and past events and activities. At Caplor Farm,

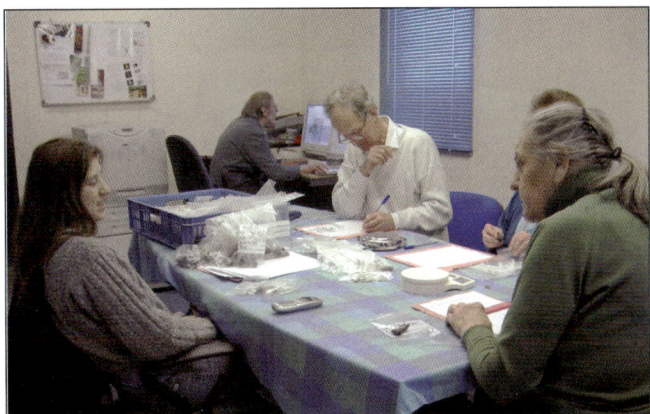

Left – Displaying the project
Above – Finds processing at Caplor Farm

two volunteers began the difficult task of digitising the tithe maps, while others searched the countryside to record veteran trees.

Before the end of 2005 the team members had contributed talks, displays and information at other events including Trackways to Remember at Overdine Farm, Fownhope Local History Group, Ross-on-Wye Civic Society, and the Brockhampton Winter Fair. Further field-walking was organised at Pengethley and King's Caple with finds processing attracting a band of volunteers to Caplor Farm. The year ended with a well-attended presentation on the history of Bolstone and local woodlands at Ballingham Village Hall.

All the volunteers and supporters, amounting to around 100, were invited to a Festive Finds, Films and Fun evening at Upper Orchard, Hoarwithy. There was a display of archaeological finds ranging from flints to clay pipes, and reproductions of documents and maps for everyone to view. The highlight of the evening was the tasting of festive food and drink made from an 18th-century recipe book from Aramstone. Group members had prepared Royal Punch, Raspberry Wine, Tunbridge Biscuits, Sugar Biskets, Cracknells, Gingerbread, Almond Biscuits, and French Bread from the recipes collected by Mary Garrett. This was followed by short films of Foy and Sellack and slides of Ballingham Station.

Showing slides of Ballingham station and bridge in the 1970s

While investigating the area with the local community, an old manuscript relating to Christmas at Caradoc was discovered. During the 18th and 19th centuries

Many old customs were kept at the Season of Christmas (both new and old days). On the twelfth the oxen were christened with ale, and the oldest servant on the estate threw the ale, after which the oxen were bountifully supplied with grain. A huge supper was held at Craddock for all classes, and all adjourned to see the ceremony. On St. Thomas' Day a bag of flour, a bottle of wine, and a large mince pie was given to every widow and widower in the parish at the door, and taken to those unable to fetch them.

At the beginning of 2006 the *Ross Gazette* reported:

members of the group have translated Latin documents, transcribed Old English archives, carried out research at the Hereford Record Office, National Archives, Hereford Cathedral Library, to discover the past history of the twelve Wyeside parishes in the project. Others have walked fields and examined aerial photographs looking for archaeological sites and finds.

This was the start of an even busier year for the volunteers and team leaders who, apart from continuing their programme of walks and talks, undertook some major projects.

Project walks 2006 – Wilton Castle   *Project walks 2006 – How Caple Church*

The walks, led by the project experts, guided groups of supporters on six occasions to investigate past historical sites at: Bridstow, to view the river, church and Wilton Castle; to Ballingham, to hear about the turnpike roads and river crossings; to Fownhope, to explore West Wood and Fownhope Park; to Holme Lacy, to investigate Tars Mill and Ramsden Coppice; to Brampton Abbotts and Foy, to learn about the past; and to How Caple Court, church and River Wye. Other walks were also led for the Wye Valley AONB programme, Ross Lecture Club, the River Wye Preservation Trust, Fownhope Local History Group, Herefordshire Walking Festival, and the Hoarwithy Club.

Further talks were held during 2006: at Holme Lacy, to discover the Archaeology and Woodland History of the Wye Valley; at Bridstow, for an illustrated presentation of Bridstow and Wilton Through the Ages; at King's Caple, to hear about the work of the Portable Antiquities Scheme in Herefordshire and Finds from the Fields; and at Brampton Abbotts, for an update on the Landscape Origins of the Wye Valley. The group also gave talks and presentations on a number of project topics at Ross-on-Wye Civic Society, Ross Lecture Group,

Fownhope Local History Group, Linton Local History Day, Monmouth Antiquarian Society, the Heritage Open Day, and at the AONB Tour of the Wye Valley. At these meetings the LOWV project team always arranged a suitable display, and by popular demand exhibitions were erected at Bridstow Church, Ross Library, St. Peter's Church in Hereford during the Three Choirs Festival, and at the Herefordshire County Fair at Caradoc.

Field-walking was arranged at regular intervals by the project leaders. At Caradoc two ploughed fields revealed a few sherds of Romano-British pottery, similar to those found at How Caple in a field where a rectangular crop-mark had been seen on an aerial photograph. Whereas at Dockhill Well Farm, recent, medieval, Romano-British pottery and prehistoric flint flakes were found. At Fownhope below Cherry Hill Iron Age camp a Neolithic flint arrowhead was discovered during field-walking, and at Llanfrother about 50 prehistoric flints including a scraper, a blade and a broken arrowhead suggested the presence of a settlement. It was disappointing not to find any artefacts that could have been associated with St. Dyfrig whose monastery was on the site in the 6th century, but an 18th-century dump revealed some bottles.

In July, one of the archaeologists took to the air to photograph some previously unknown sites in the project area, but earlier aerial photographs had indicated an interesting feature at Gillow in Hentland. A band of volunteers spent several days field-walking the site to discover a range of finds from the prehistoric to the medieval period. It was decided, with permission of the landowner, to carry out a geophysical survey before organising an archaeological excavation. The dig attracted volunteers keen to take part in this exciting project, and to learn how to excavate and identify the numerous

Investigating.   *Top – Bridstow churchyard;*
Middle – Tars Mill at Holme Lacy;
Bottom – Excavation at Gillow

finds. From 10 August to 25 September, the site was crawling with volunteers delighted to be involved in such a large archaeological project for this area.

A number of volunteers became involved with washing, weighing, marking, and identifying the finds from field-walking. They soon learnt the differences between slag, pottery, worked stone, tiles, glass, and flints – all dating from a range of periods. Once dried, marked, and identified, the finds were put into boxes ready to be deposited in the Hereford Museum.

The transcribers and researchers of the LOWV project continued to delve into the past from an assortment of archives including: 15th-century records of St. Peter's Abbey in Gloucester concerning the manor of Brampton Abbotts; the Scudamore accounts of the 1640s relating to Holme Lacy; a 1611 Marriage Settlement of John Abrahall of Ingestone; the Pengethley Rents of 1580; Fownhope Court Rolls of 1589; and 17th-century documents from the National Library of Wales. The rentals of the Benedictine Priory of St. Guthlac in Hereford revealed some interesting information about Ballingham, and many fascinating glimpses of the past were found in documents from the Hereford Cathedral Library and the National Archives. A 1448 Fownhope Charter was carefully translated for the Woolhope Club Library, where it is kept:

Top – Finds processing at Caplor
Bottom – Documentary research at Upper Orchard

Let it be known that through a petition to us by Joanna, formerly wife of Robert Falwell who recently died in our Royal College of the Blessed Mary of Eton, where he is buried, we have understood how the same Robert, in his lifetime, and the same Joanna, in her right as the heir of John Burghill (that is to say Joanna is the daughter of Agnes, who was the daughter of John Burghill) were seized of 2 carucates of land and 25 acres of meadow in Fownhope in the County of Hereford until recently when a certain John Carsy, then our escheator in the same county, by the interpretation he placed on a certain inquisition, took the buildings, lands and meadow aforesaid into our hands, to her clear destruction unless we provide a remedy.
Joanna was seized of the lands, because her grandfather John Burghill was seized of them when he died and she was his heiress. She was seized of them until the interpretation of the aforesaid inquisition.
Having considered her argument, we of our special grace have granted a licence to the said Joanna to enter the said property and have, occupy and enjoy them to her and her heirs in perpetuity.

From the Aramstone Salmon Fishing Record Books, 1887 to 1976, a volunteer entered the data onto a spreadsheet and then produced an illustrated booklet for the owner and the River Wye Preservation Society. Another volunteer transcribed a large collection of letters written during the First World War

Translating Latin – The 1448 Fownhope Charter

by members of the same family. These provide a graphic snapshot of life on the estate and at war during this tragic period.

Throughout 2006 there was training in earthwork and geophysical surveying with expert tuition, which led to a survey of sites at Hentland church, Gillow, and Capler camp. A student learned about geographical investigation systems at Caplor, and a photographer and a member of the Ross Civic Society volunteered to photograph and record the buildings that had been listed in the Royal Commission surveys of 1931 and 1932 and in the surveyor's handwritten notes of the late 1920s. Three farms were surveyed by archaeologists to produce a detailed account from cartographic and documentary material, with a walk over surveillance of the land, and a general survey of the buildings

A student at work on geographical investigation systems

Left – Surveying buildings, Ballingham church in 1927
Above and below – the River Wye Survey 2006

A hollow-way survey was suggested by an industrial archaeologist to trace a network of ancient routes, but with limited time only three parishes were completed. However, the River Wye Survey by canoe took place in the autumn and was a great success. A small team of volunteers identified, located, and photographed all the documented river crossings, weirs, wharfs, and industrial sites, and sought previously unknown sites along a 25 mile stretch of the Wye between Lucksall in Fownhope and Weirend in Bridstow.

Before the year ended a start was made on the publication of this book, with individuals contributing chapters on their specialist subjects. A few volunteers also researched and wrote certain sections which have been used in the text. In December 2006, a Project Party was held at Upper Orchard, Hoarwithy, where evidence of the LOWV achievements was on display. The *Ross Gazette* concluded:

> During 2005 and 2006 the LOWV, with the help of supporters and volunteers have undertaken a variety of activities from aerial photography to underwater investigations, from studying 13th century Latin documents to reading 20th century reports, and from surveying the Wye by canoe to investigating hollow-ways by foot.

An extension to the project had been accepted to allow for reports and dating of archaeological finds. This enabled further material to be processed at Caplor including re-assembling Roman period pots, which had been found in pieces during the excavation at Gillow. Latin translation evenings were continued and a series of archaeological seminars were held at Hereford and Ross. Presentations on 'Trackway to Turnpike', 'The River Wye' and 'Historic Wharves', were given at Fownhope, Ross-on-Wye and Monmouth, with a final walk from Wilton to Wyelea for the Wye Valley AONB programme.

Fownhope – the largest settlement in the project area

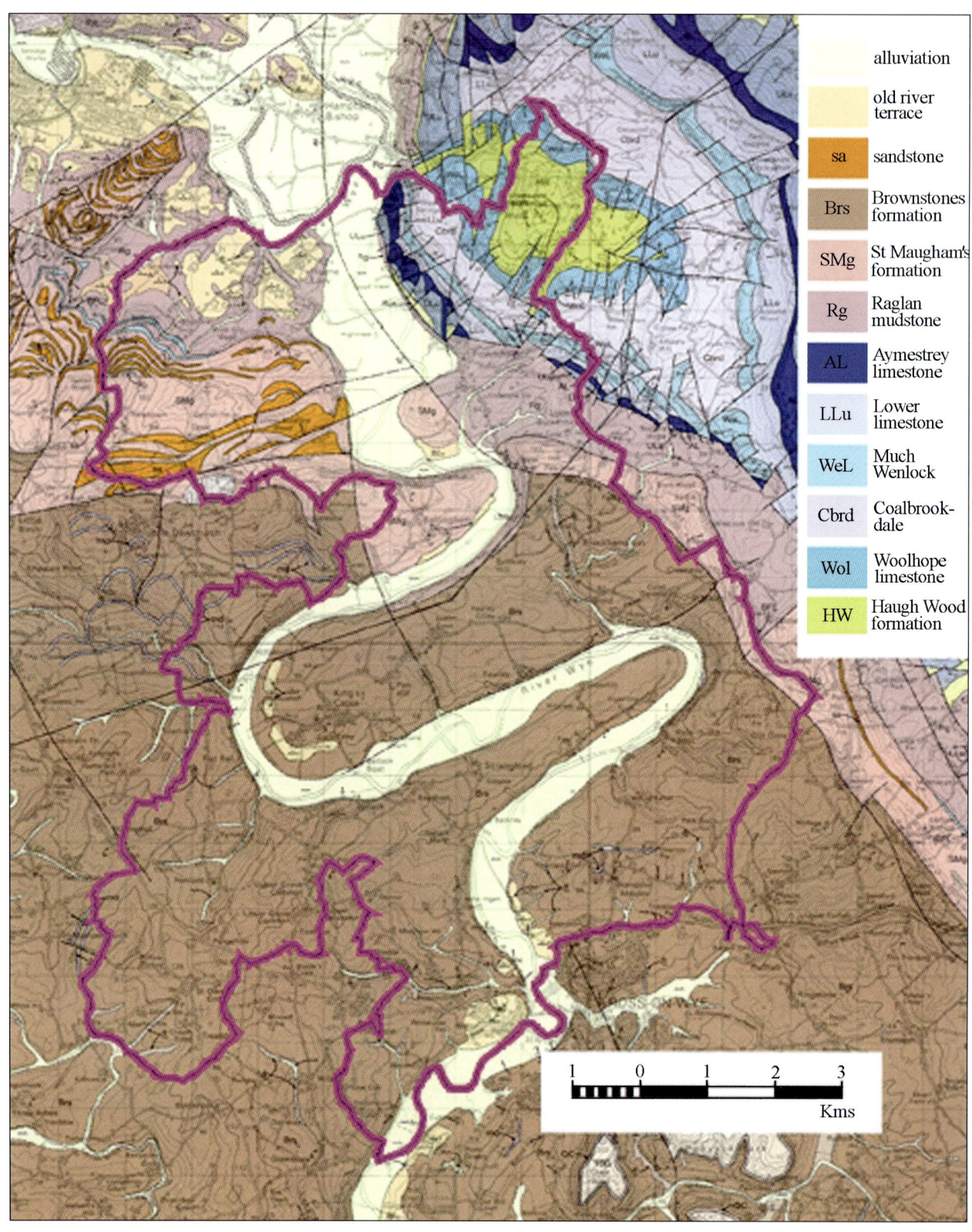

Geology map (IPR/104-58CX British Geological Survey © NERC. All rights reserved)

CHAPTER I

Geology and Prehistory

by P.J. Pikes

The Geological Background

Superficially, the landscape of the study area, like that of much of the world, is now man-made. Fields, woods, roads are all there by human design. Cottages, a few hundred years old, nestle beside roads perhaps two thousand years old or more. New roads, trees and hedges encroach on Iron Age hill-forts, which would once have dominated the surrounding areas. Parish boundaries align on Bronze Age burials. Old fords are replaced by new bridges. Churches stand in graveyards first consecrated before the English language was spoken here.

These features, constantly changing, occupy only the very surface of the land; deep below there is the mantle, a layer of viscous rock about 2,900 kilometres thick. Between, there is the crust – layers of rock, formed over eons. Most of the visible rock in the study area is the Old Red Sandstone, laid down in the Devonian period 350 to 416 million years ago.

Phanerozoic eon		
Palaeozoic era	Mesozoic era	Cenozoic era

The oldest surface rocks were formed in the Pre-Cambrian ages. This is the super-eon of geological time from the formation of the earth, around 4,500 million years ago, to the evolution of hard-shelled animals in the early Phanerozoic (meaning 'revealed life') some 545 million years ago, and covers 88% of the earth's history. Here and there, these ancient rocks are visible on the surface, such as the outcropping rocks of the Malvern Hills on the eastern edge of Herefordshire.

The Palaeozoic is the first era of the Phanerozoic eon. The word Palaeozoic means 'old animals' and this lasted from 545 to 252 million years ago and is divided into six periods – the Cambrian, the Ordovician, the Silurian, the Devonian, the Carboniferous, and the Permian – all with characteristic rocks.

Palaeozoic era					
Cambrian	Ordovician	Silurian	Devonian	Carboniferous	Permian
545m - 488m years ago	488m - 443m years ago	443m - 416m years ago	416m - 359m years ago	359m - 299m years ago	299m - 251m years ago

Trilobite fossil from the Woolhope Silurian rocks

In the area studied, the oldest rocks visible on the surface are Silurian; which are found outcropping on the Woolhope Dome above Fownhope. The sorts of creatures that lived at the time are known from similar deposits elsewhere in Herefordshire.[1] One of these deposits has produced some of the most interesting fossils ever found in the area and they are of international importance.[2] These are of a group of invertebrate animals, which were living on the bed of the ocean 425 million years ago when they were killed and buried, and finally preserved by a sudden fall of volcanic ash.[3]

Overlying the Silurian formations and covering almost the whole of the study area, is the Old Red Sandstone, which gives the characteristic colour to the local soil. Here and there, meanders of the river Wye have exposed this rock as cliffs. Elsewhere it lies just below the surface of the ground. These were laid down in the Devonian period, 400 to 350 million years ago, by rivers crossing a broad, flat, semi-arid, tropical plain to the south of the equator. The red colour is due to the presence of oxygen during the creation of these rocks – these sandstone layers have been described as the 'rust of the earth'.

The era that followed the Palaeozoic was the Mesozoic, meaning 'middle animals', and the era is sometimes known as the 'Age of the Dinosaurs'. Rocks of the Mesozoic's three periods – Triassic, Jurassic and Cretaceous –are now absent from the study area, having been eroded away.

Old Red Sandstone at Bridstow

Mesozoic era		
Triassic	Jurassic	Cretaceous
251m - 199m years ago	199.6m - 145.5m years ago	145.5m - 65.5m years ago

The Mesozoic gave way to our present era, the Cenozoic – 'new life' – 65 million years ago. The Cenozoic is divided into two periods, the Palaeogene and the Neogene. These, in turn, are sub-divided into epochs. The Palaeocene, the Eocene, Oligocene epochs form the Palaeogene while the Neogene is divided into the Miocene, the Pliocene, the Pleistocene and the Holocene. The Pliocene was characterised by a series of 'ice ages' interspersed with warmer periods – the interglacials.[4] These 'ice ages' were actually prolonged periods of

Red bank at Holme Lacy

a colder climate. Glaciation only occurred during the very coldest parts of these. The 'normal' climate of Britain was probably arctic with relatively mild summers and very cold winters: the 'normal' vegetation would have been tundra.

It is however glaciation which most affects the landscape. Although the glaciers of the most recent ice age did not cover the study area those of several previous ice ages certainly did. The glaciation of the Anglian cold period, which lasted from 478,000 to 424,000 years ago, covered most of southern Britain with an ice sheet a kilometre thick.

Gradually elements of the landscape, with which we are familiar emerged. High ground formed to the west in what is now Wales, and the Malvern Hills stood to the east. An earlier version of the River Wye, carrying more water, in braided channels, followed broadly the course it still does. Around 250,000 years ago, the River Teme, which now flows south-east from Ludlow and through Tenbury Wells

Fossilised Devonian fish –
Hemicyclaspis murchisoni

Cenozoic era						
Palaeogene			Neogene			
Palaeocene	Eocene	Oligocene	Miocene	Pliocene	Pleistocene	Holocene
65m - 56m years ago	56m - 34m years ago	34m - 23m years ago	23m - 5.33m years ago	5.33m - 1.8m years ago	1.8m -11,550 years ago	11,550 years ago - present

Pleistocene							Holocene
Beestonian glacial 680,000 - 620,000 yrs ago	Cromerian interglacials 620,000 - 455,000 yrs ago	Anglian glacials 455,000 - 300,000 yrs ago	Hoxnian interglacial 300,000 - 200,000 yrs ago	Woolstonian glacial 200,000 - 130,000 yrs ago	Ipswichian interglacial 130,000 - 110,000 yrs ago	Devensian glacial 110,000 12,000 yrs ago	Flandrian interglacial 12,000 yrs ago - present

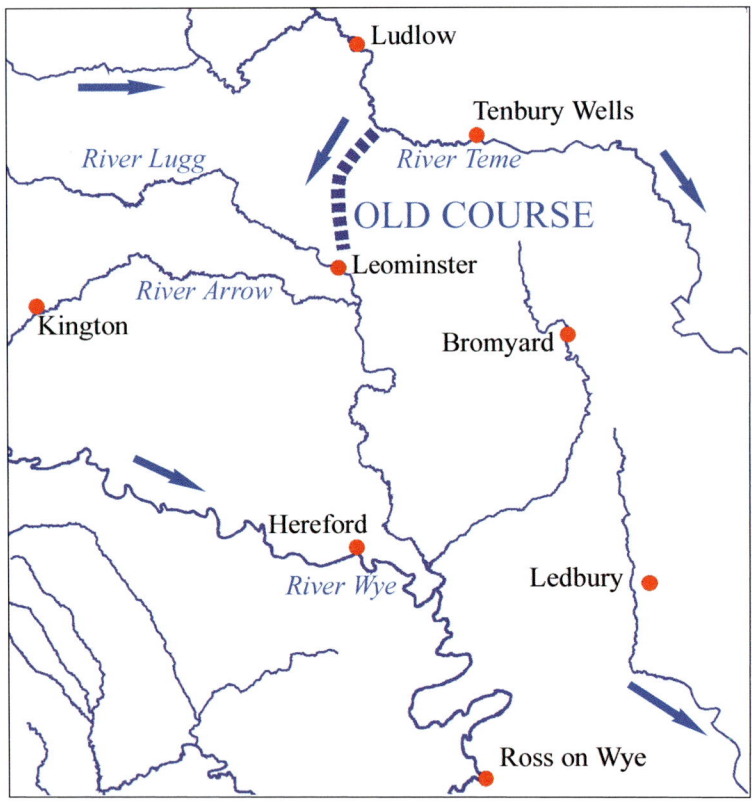

The Teme flowed into the Lugg and the Wye before the Devensian Cold Period

to join the Severn near Worcester, flowed south into the Lugg and Wye valleys. This formed a single river running to the Severn with the Arrow, the Lugg above Leominster and the Wye above Mordiford, flowing out of the high ground to the west in what is now Wales, forming tributaries of this great river.[5]

The last ice age, the Devensian, began around 32,000 years ago, and changed the drainage in the Welsh Marches. It turned the Teme eastwards, which is why the Lugg and the Wye within the study area are too small for their respective valleys. The incised meanders of the Wye around Ballingham, King's Caple and Foy run in what was once a valley over 6 kilometres wide, reflecting the width of the earlier braided river.[6] Some meanders are abandoned; a great loop once flowed east from Backney towards Weston-under-Penyard before turning south-west to rejoin the present course at Walford.[7]

Although the older ice ages must have left deposits over many parts of the landscape, subsequent erosion has removed most of this. At Much Dewchurch, there is a bed of sand and gravel, probably deposited by the Anglian glaciation. More recent glaciation has buried the sandstone of much of the parishes of Holme Lacy and Bolstone beneath layers of glaciofluvial sand and gravel.

The Wye continues to erode the bedrock over which it flows. At Hereford, the river has cut down into this by about 2 metres since glacial times.[8] Another feature of the valley is the alluviation within

The flood plain of the Wye at Holme Lacy with the Silurian hills of the Woolhope Dome in the background

the valleys of the Wye and its tributaries. At the confluence of the rivers Lugg and Wye there are extensive alluvial deposits. South of the confluence, Holme Lacy church sits on a flood plain 1.5 kilometres wide, between the Silurian rocks of the Woolhope anticline to the east and the Old Red Sandstone high ground at Holme Lacy Park to the west. South of Holme Lacy the flood plain narrows to a sinuous strip about 500 metres wide between the low sandstone hills which bound the incised course of the Wye. All of this flood plain alluviation had happened since the retreat of the Devensian glaciers.

The flood plain at Holme Lacy. On the right is the higher ground formed by the Old Red Sandstone

The Palaeolithic – the earliest humans

Palaeontology is the study of fossils, but archaeology is concerned with humans, however defined. The earliest archaeological period is the Palaeolithic – the Old Stone Age.[9] The earliest humans belong to the 'Lower Palaeolithic' and most of our knowledge of them comes from Africa. Until fairly recently there was no evidence of humans in Britain before about 250,000 years ago. However, in the last few years this has changed considerably and it is possible that early humans were in the study area over half a million years ago.

The earliest evidence of human activity in what is now Britain is from about 700,000 years ago. Around Happisburgh and Pakefield on the Suffolk coast, flint tools and cutmarks on a bone from a bison-like animal have been found.[10] At that time Britain was a peninsula of mainland Europe and these early inhabitants could have roamed across a vast plain, now covered by the North Sea. The warm climate of the time ended with the onset of the Beestonian cold period.

The Cromerian interglacial followed the Beestonian period. During the Cromerian humans were active at Boxgrove in West Sussex, where archaeologists have excavated 500,000-year-old remains.[11] The Boxgrove people were *Homo heidelbergensis* and were active in both Africa and Europe.[12] These 'hominins'[13] were

Palaeolithic		
Lower Palaeolithic	**Middle Palaeolithic**	**Upper Palaeolithic**
2,500,000-250,000	250,000-30,000	30,000-12,000
Homo antecessor Homo erectus Homo heidelbergensis	Homo sapiens neanderthalis	Homo sapiens sapiens
Oldowan culture* Acheulean culture Clactonian culture	Mousterian culture Aterian culture*	Châtelperronian culture* Aurignacian culture Gravettian culture Solutrean culture Magdalenian culture

The timing, species and cultures of the Palaeolithic, the 'Old Stone Age'. The cultures marked with an asterisk are not found in Britain

Cast of a Paleolithic hand-axe from Tupsley in the suburbs of Hereford

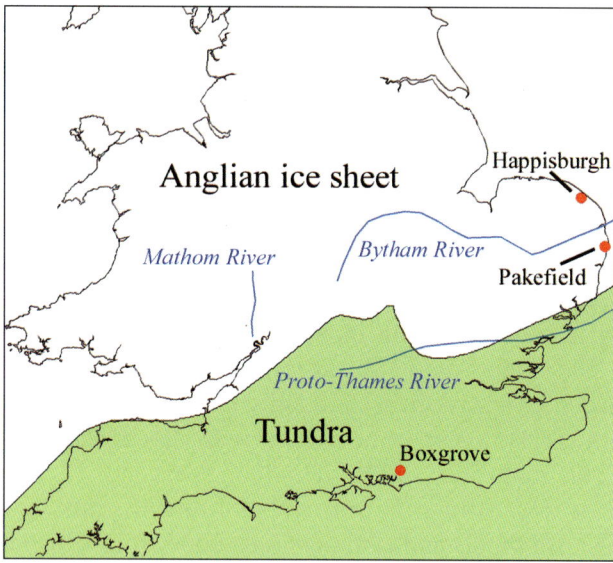

Anglian glaciation

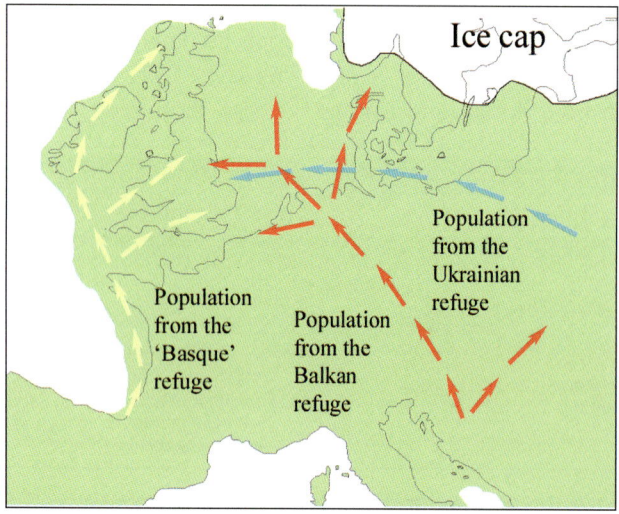

Population movement after S. Oppenheimer, 2006

probably ancestral to both Neanderthals and *Homo sapiens sapiens* and lived 300,000 before Neanderthals appeared.[14]

The dominant material culture of hominins for a very long time is named Acheulean and these tools were used by *Homo ergaster* (an early *Homo erectus*), and *Homo heidelbergensis*. Individual Acheulean hand-axes have been found at several sites in Herefordshire. Hereford Museum has one, which was found at Colwall, in the eastern part of the county, and another found in a garden in Tupsley in the suburbs of Hereford. These tools were used by hominins long before *Homo sapiens sapiens* (modern humans) arrived.

During the Lower Palaeolithic, Britain's flora and fauna changed from tundra to temperate plains and woods, then to tundra again. The coldest part of the cold spells would see glaciation over parts of Britain. Sometimes the sparse human population of the study area shared the landscape with horses, elephants, rhinoceroses, hippopotami, macaques, hyenas, and lions.[15] Our present interglacial, despite global warming, is almost certainly nearer its end than its beginning.

It was during the Devensian cold spell that *Homo sapiens sapiens* arrived, heralding the period known to archaeologists as the Early Upper Palaeolithic. One of the earliest habitation sites for modern humans was just downstream of the study area, where flint tools found in King Arthur's Cave suggest that it was periodically inhabited over 30,000 years ago.[16] The Early Upper Palaeolithic was brought to an end by the onset of the coldest part of Devensian ice advance, which brought to a temporary end human occupation of Britain.[17]

Archaeologists believe that there were no humans in Britain during the coldest part of the Devensian – about 29,000 to 20,000 BC. Average summer temperatures then were minus 10° Celsius. The ice margin is estimated to have covered western Herefordshire to a depth of over a kilometre and seems to have terminated just west of where the city of Hereford now stands. The project area, although beyond the glaciations, was under permanent snow and ice. However, in the areas away from the ice margin there would have been migratory herds of animals such as woolly mammoth, bison and reindeer.

The areas in which humans lived during the Devensian, and from which they would colonise the ice-freed lands, are known as 'refuges'. One of these refuges was in southern France/northern Spain (for convenience referred to as the 'Franco-Cantabrian' or 'Basque' refuge);[18] there were others in the Balkans and the Ukraine.[19]

As the temperature rose during the Late Upper Palaeolithic, it was from these refuges that humans moved into north-west Europe. Some 13,000 years ago, the climate was on average slightly warmer than it is today. However, within a few centuries the cold returned and persisted until about 11,500 years ago. This period is known as the 'Younger Dryas' or the 'Loch Lomond' stadial.[20]

The retreat of the ice at the end of the Younger Dryas left behind a treeless tundra landscape into which grazing animals and their predators, including humans, migrated. Although a small number of hardy ancestors of the modern British had arrived before the Younger Dryas, it was during this post-glacial period that three-quarters of the ancestors of the people of Britain and Ireland arrived from these refuges.[21] Current evidence suggests that, despite a persistent popular belief in some fictitious Iron Age 'Celtic' mass migration from central Europe, Britain received the overwhelming bulk of its population from the Basque refuge many centuries earlier.[22]

The route of this post-glacial movement of people was to become the 'Western Seaways', but in the earlier part of this period it was dry land – it would have been possible to walk from Brittany to south-west Wales. The landscape into which these new people came at the end of the last ice age was treeless grassland, rich with game. Although the temperatures were low, there was abundant food and there are indications that the population grew rapidly.

That, generally speaking, the present populations have their origins at the end of the last ice age seems to be true of most of Europe.[23] The simple explanation may be that the original hunters, who followed their prey into the lands freed of ice, simply stayed there. In the study area, they became, in turn, Neolithic, Bronze Age, Iron Age (perhaps Silures or Dobunni), Britons, Welsh, and eventually English in culture as time passed.

The Mesolithic

The 5,000 years following the last ice age is what archaeologists term the Mesolithic – the Middle Stone Age. In general, recognised Mesolithic occupation sites are rare and it is assumed that the people were largely nomadic. There is very little hard archaeological evidence from the study area to work with, although it may be assumed that the new wave of Mesolithic immigrants arrived here about 10,000 years ago

It is generally supposed that humans made virtually no impact upon the landscape during the Mesolithic period, but it is possible that even at this time people were raising structures

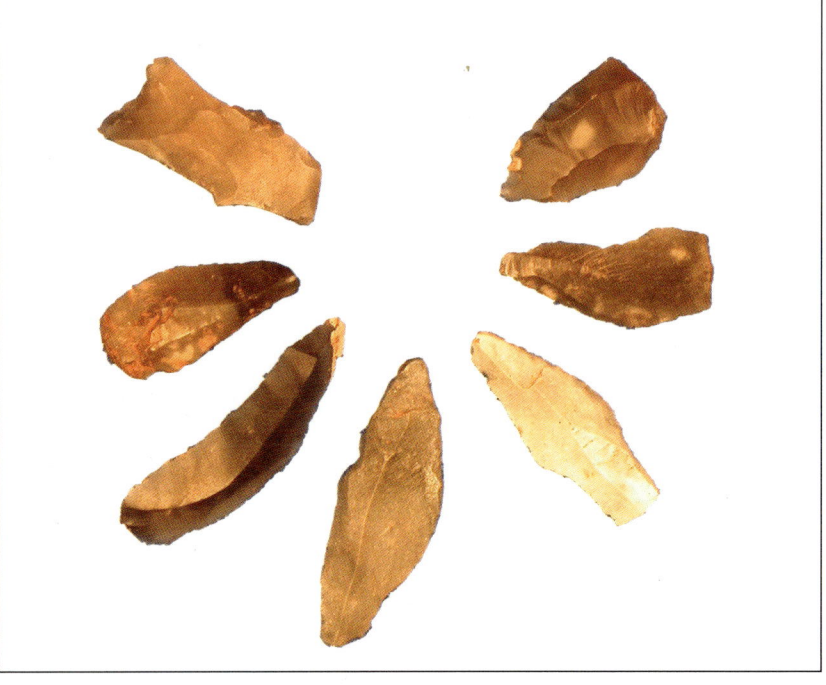

Mesolithic flints from Ross-on-Wye

19

Palaeolithic	Mesolithic	Neolithic	Bronze Age	Iron Age	Roman	Medieval
*c*700,000 - *c*8500BC	*c*8500 - *c*4000BC	*c*4000 - *c*2500BC	*c*2500 - *c*700BC	*c*700BC - *c*70AD	*c*70AD - *c*400AD	*c*400AD - *c*1500AD

intended to impress. At Stonehenge, archaeologists found four pits which had been dug to hold large posts – posts with a diameter of 60 to 80 cm, (the size of large telegraph posts). These have been radiocarbon-dated to between 8,500 and 7,650 BC. The posts must have had a ritual significance and awesomely mark Stonehenge as a special place 4,000 years before the first Neolithic monuments appear in this landscape.[24] These pits were found when construction work for visitor facilities was being carried out at Stonehenge which is, of course, a very archaeologically sensitive place.[25] The chances of pits like this being found, if they exist, elsewhere in the rural landscape, is very much less than at Stonehenge and emphasises again the truism (and it cannot be too often said) that by and large archaeological evidence is found only where archaeologists look for it.[26]

This issue of bias is particularly significant when it comes to finds from the stone ages. In recent years, the use of metal detectors has greatly increased the numbers of known metal artefacts from rural areas, discovered new sites and changed our understanding of several important aspects of early medieval archaeology.[27] But metal detectors do not find flint tools and flakes, and consequently there has been no corresponding growth in the number of known prehistoric sites. Walking carefully over ploughed fields (field-walking) is the best way of recovering them, but little of this has been done in the area. There are only 27 finds, from the whole of the long Mesolithic period, recorded in the Herefordshire Sites and Monuments record.

In the project area only two find-spots, both at Fownhope, are known.[28] At Gillow, in Hentland parish just off the A49, the project team found a 'microlith' – a very small worked flint which was attached, with many similar flints, to spear-tips by Mesolithic hunters.[29] This

Field-walking at Pengethley

Mesolithic site at Hentland

was the earliest find made during the whole of the project fieldwork, and it is apparent that the landscape in which the hunter who lost this flint lived would have been totally different from that of today.

By about 7,500 BC temperatures had risen to an average of several degrees higher than today, establishing the 'Climatic Optimum'. The River Wye had established something approaching its modern course and trees began to appear in the central Herefordshire plain. There has been a tendency to over-estimate the density of woodland in this period; it seems likely that the thick forests of popular imagination never existed and that there was always much open grassland.[30]

The Neolithic

The Neolithic period followed the Mesolithic. In the standard model there is a lot happening in the Neolithic – domesticating animals and planting crops, building major landscape monuments, making pottery and highly polished stone axes, and living in permanent settlements. All of these are commonly perceived to form one cultural package.[31] Actually they are probably better viewed as separate elements, which may appear either in numerous different combinations or in isolation.[32]

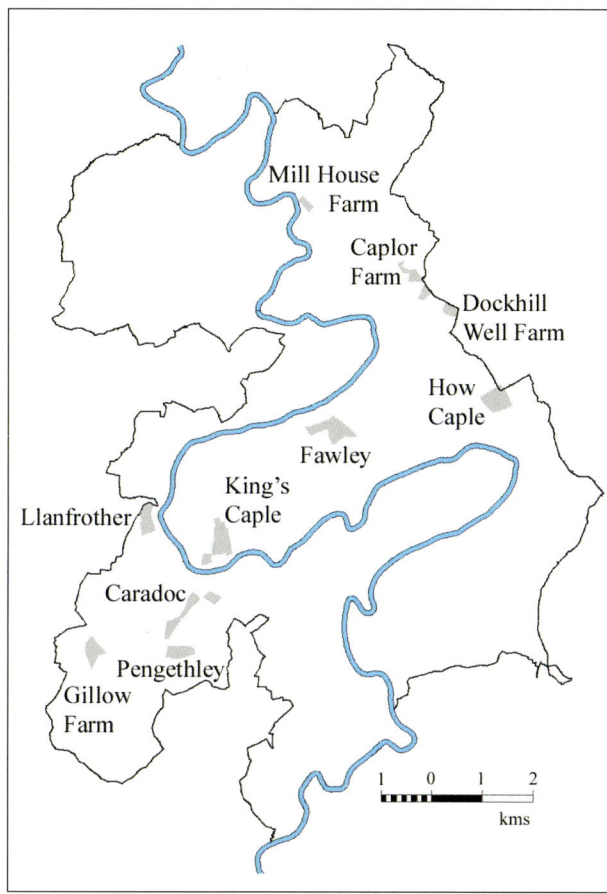

Fields walked by the project team

Neolithic axe from Harewood End in Hentland

What impact then did Neolithic people have upon the landscape of the study area? They were certainly present and archetypical Neolithic tools – polished stone axes – have been found at Fownhope, Ballingham and Harewood End.[33] At that time southern Herefordshire was probably grassland, grazed by herds of cattle, although sheep and goats may also have been present. None of these domestic animals was native to Britain.[34] As Britain was an island by the Neolithic time, these animals must originally have been imported by sea. Neolithic cattle were smaller than modern ones, but even so, transporting them by boat must have taxed the ingenuity of people of that time.[35]

The British Neolithic diet consisted mainly of animal products and gathered fruits and nuts – arable agriculture seems to have made a negligible contribution.[36] These people were not hunter-gatherers, but they were not growing crops to provide daily bread – perhaps they should be called herder-gatherers. The Neolithic people seem to have had a close relationship with cattle.[37] If the people in the study area were cattle herders, then they may well have been nomadic.

In Britain, dairying was part of the Neolithic package from the beginning and analysis of contemporary cattle bones strongly suggests that the age and sex of the animals at early Neolithic sites represent dairy herds.[38] In addition analysis of the pottery shows that much of it had contained dairy products.[39] Even now, in some communities, milk and cheese can form a major part of the human diet.[40]

The vision of Neolithic people clearing large tracts of woodland to grow crops – once an archaeological 'fact' – is no longer tenable. Woodland clearance still appears in archaeological terminology of this period but should be treated with caution. It seems improbable that herdsmen would undertake such an

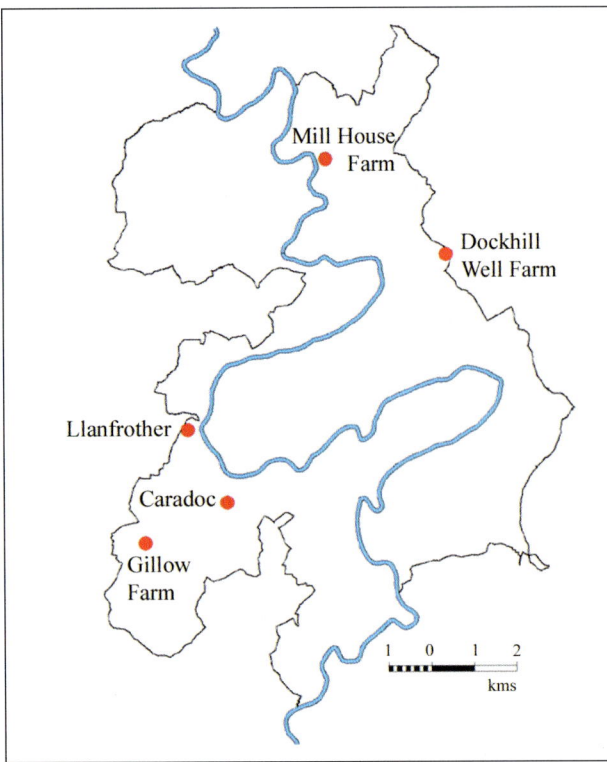

Prehistoric habitation sites discovered during the project

activity. Livestock, however, eats young shoots. In land constantly grazed, new trees can only grow if humans protect them.

Flint tools form the greater part of the evidence for the presence of prehistoric people over the greater part of post-glacial pre-history. In the Neolithic period, flint was mined by means of vertical shafts cut down thorough the chalk to the best flint-bearing strata where horizontal galleries were cut.[41] There is virtually no source of flint in Herefordshire.[42] Flint will not have come from the local rivers – they run west to east and the Welsh hills to the west have no flint in them. The flint sources are all to the east so the material must have been transported in by humans from that direction.

Field-walking by the project team considerably increased the number of flints known from the area. Altogether over 340 flints were recovered during the project, almost all of them prehistoric.[43] The number of flints found at one site probably has significance. Llanfrother, on a rise above the river, is an attractive location, and is believed to have been the site of the early medieval monastery founded by St Dyfrig.[44] It may not be fanciful to suggest that many centuries before the monks; there was a habitation site here, one of the earliest in the county.

Bronze Age thumbnail scraper from Gillow

Neolithic side scraper from Gillow

Another Neolithic occupation site, suggested by the number of flints found, is in a field opposite Mill House Farm, to the north-west of Fownhope village. This is another hillside location just above the river; other areas with concentrations of flint were near Dockhill Well Farm at Brockhampton and at Gillow Farm, a site that seems to have seen activity in all periods.

Although the arable farming component of the Neolithic may have generally been exaggerated, there was some in the area, and at an early date. At the Wellington Quarry site, just north of Hereford, during excavations in advance of gravel extraction, archaeologists discovered pits which contained pottery and carbonised material which included hazelnuts and emmer wheat. This material has been carbon-dated to 3650 – 3620 BC and indicates that, at the very least, there was some arable farming in the early Neolithic in that area.[45]

The classic Neolithic funerary monument – the long barrow – is absent from the study area, and although a feature at Gillow was identified from aerial photographs as a possible Neolithic 'henge' and targeted for excavation, in fact it was an entirely different type of structure. Recently, another Herefordshire Rivers project excavated a henge at Stapleton in the Lugg Valley and a second henge was identified nearby.[46] These are the only known features of this type in the county.

Another Lugg Valley project discovery was a Neolithic ditched enclosure at Bodenham, downstream of Stapleton and a few kilometres from the Lugg's confluence with the Wye at the northern edge of the study area. This enclosure at Bodenham is the first early Neolithic enclosure confirmed in the West Midlands.[47] Previously, this feature had been identified from aerial photographs as a probable hilltop Iron Age enclosure. Both this and the Wye Valley project's experience at the Gillow site emphasise that although aerial photography is an extremely useful tool for finding sites, it is only excavation that can provide the dating evidence for full interpretation. It is thus quite possible that some of the crop marks of enclosures in the study area, which have been interpreted as Iron Age/Romano-British, are something quite different.[48]

During 2007, a new relief road was constructed a little further to the south-east of the Causeway Farm site, and just to the north of the study area. Pits found on the course of the road suggest that occupation there began as early as about 3,500 BC and lasted for some 1,500 years. Nearby were the post-holes of a round-house dated to around 2,000 BC – the oldest house yet found in Herefordshire.

It is from this site that one of the most exciting, if enigmatic, finds ever made in Herefordshire comes. On the outskirts of the project area, the feature variously known as the Rotherwas Ribbon or Dinedor Serpent consists of a sinuous mound of fire-cracked stones about ten metres wide.[49] Environmental evidence showed that around 1,600 BC the area was open grassland with few trees.[50]

The Rotherwas Ribbon is imperfectly understood and its length is currently unknown. Its construction, however, was a large undertaking involving the heating of thousands of stones before putting them, red hot, into water. A great deal of wood would have been needed for the fires and the amount of labour cannot have been small. 'Burnt Mounds' of fire-cracked stones are well-documented prehistoric features – most belong to the later Bronze Age, although the oldest may be Neolithic.

The Bronze Age

Although the Bronze Age saw the introduction of metalworking, in fact flint tools remained extremely common and bronze finds are rare. A hoard of bronze axes was found in Foy parish in the 18th century but otherwise finds are sparse in this area.

The classic Bronze Age funerary monument is the round barrow.

*Bronze Age axes
from Pencoyd*

Possible Bronze Age ring ditch at Strangford

Although no standing barrows survive in the 12 parishes of the study area, several ring-ditches exist. After a barrow has been flattened (usually for agricultural purposes) the circular ditch which surrounded it, and from which the earth was excavated to build it, remains. These are often visible as circular crop-marks – 'ring-ditches' – in aerial photographs.

In Herefordshire, groups of barrow/ring-ditches tend to occur in valleys, with about 20 around Rowe Ditch in the Arrow Valley.[51] Other groups

Ring ditch at Hill-of-Eaton, Foy

Gillow arrowhead

are on the Teme west of Leintwardine and at various locations on the Lugg (where five new sites were discovered during the Herefordshire Rivers project).[52] On the Wye there is a small group at Walford, just downstream of the study area.[53]

These 'ring-ditches' are the earliest visible monuments in the study area and have been recorded in several parishes in south Herefordshire. A 'tumulus' (the old name for a barrow) once existed at Holme Lacy, but cannot now be found.[54] There was apparently another tumulus in Fownhope parish, but this too has now disappeared.[55] More convincingly, a pair of ring-ditches at Townsend Farm, Brampton Abbotts, stands on high ground overlooking the Wye.[56] They are directly on the parish boundary with Foy, raising the suspicion that they were used as boundary markers.

Above the Wye in Foy parish, near Hole-in-the-Wall, a bluff had long identified as the site of an Iron Age promontory fort. However, as part of the project's study of existing photographs, this feature resolved itself into one, and possibly two ring-ditches. This position is directly analogous with that of the Townsend Farm barrows, one kilometre to the south-west. In the western part of the study area, aerial photographs appear to show ring-ditches in the Gillow/Harewood End area in Hentland parish.

The Iron Age and the Romano-British

The Iron Age in Britain is, of course, associated with the term 'Celtic'. However, neither the Irish nor the Welsh are really Celts and no ancient writers referred to the inhabitants of the British Isles as Celts.[57] The name – *Keltoi* – was indeed applied to an ancient continental people, but not the ancient population of Britain. The origins of the fallacy can be traced to 1707, when Edward Lhuyd, curator of the Ashmolean Museum, first applied the term 'Celtic' to a group of languages which he identified as being closely related, including Breton, Welsh and Irish.[58] Before Lhuyd, no-one used the term 'Celt' for the Iron Age people of Britain, and the Greek and Roman writers knew that they were different – 'The men of Britain are taller than the *Celti*, and not so yellow-haired'.[59] To reiterate, the population of Britain was already in place well before the Iron Age and the material culture that we now refer to as 'Celtic'.[60]

In many parts of Europe, including the Welsh Marches, hill-forts are the characteristic Iron Age feature, although in fact they have their origins in the Bronze Age. In Herefordshire, the earliest Iron Age evidence is from the hill-fort at Croft Ambrey in the north of the county, in 700 to 650 BC. The three hill-forts in the study area – Capler, Cherry Hill and Gaer Cop – are no longer the highly visible works that they would have been 2,000 years ago. Gaer Cop has been almost levelled by road-building and ploughing, while Cherry Hill and Capler, like so many Herefordshire hill-forts, are mainly concealed by trees. Of the three, only Capler has been investigated by excavation.[61] The nearby Sutton Walls was excavated in 1948-1951 by Dame Kathleen Kenyon, who also excavated at the local hill-forts of Credenhill, Dinedor and Aconbury.[62]

Jack and Hayter's excavation on Capler in the 1920s found that the hill-fort's ditches were rock-cut. However, no evidence of occupation was found. Hayter commented:

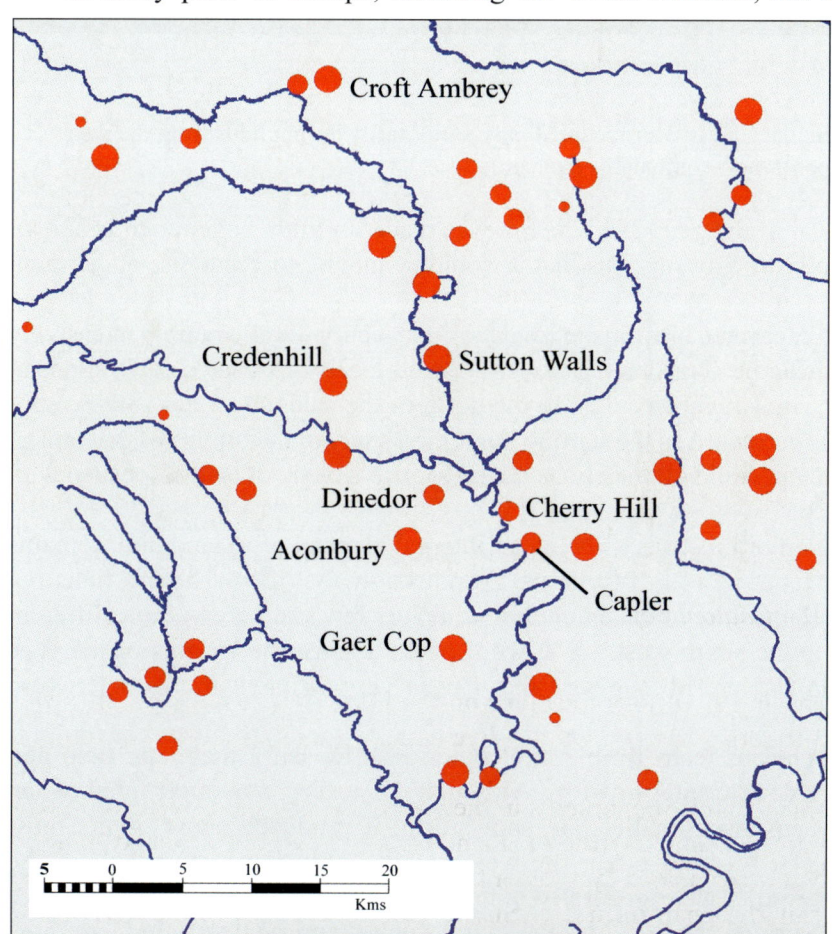

Herefordshire Iron Age hill-forts

25

Capler hill-fort

On the whole, it is a fair presumption that Capler was occupied only temporarily during raids from the west bank of the Wye, as a camp of refuge for non-combatants and cattle.[63]

This sort of interpretation is typical of the period in which it was made. In truth, not enough is known about hill-forts, but what is known now strongly suggests that it would be unwise to generalise about them in this way.

One of the most comprehensively excavated hill-forts in England – Danebury – was certainly intensively occupied in the middle Iron Age, and can be considered a 'town'.[64] More locally, extensive excavations at Croft Ambrey revealed 'streets' of square structures.[65] Just to the north of the study area, the 18th-century estate map of the manor of Marden has been used as the starting point for a study of the origins of that unit of land. The conclusion was that the land unit could ultimately be traced back to a block of land associated with the Iron Age hill-fort at Sutton Walls.[66]

The problem with the interpretation of hill-forts as being an integral element of a 'land unit' remains this – not only do we not know the function of hill-forts, we do not know that they shared a function. Excavations at Balksbury hill-fort in Hampshire found an interior with very few structures – quite different from Danebury, just 7.5 kilometres to the south-west.[67] The work of the Landscape Origins of the Wye Valley project within the hill-fort on Capler Hill suggests that it was very different in character from Danebury or Croft Ambrey.

In Spring 2006 the project geophysics team from Archaeophysica Ltd. led a magnetic field and susceptibility survey on the eastern half of Capler hill-fort. Although the survey was interrupted twice, first by the local hunt and then by an unseasonably late snowstorm, it produced some of the most significant results of the entire project. As trees cover the western half, only the eastern half of the hill-fort was examined and here the results were generally quite clear. There appeared to be evidence of at least one earlier phase of enclosure on the hill, pre-dating the ditches and rampart which are now visible.[68]

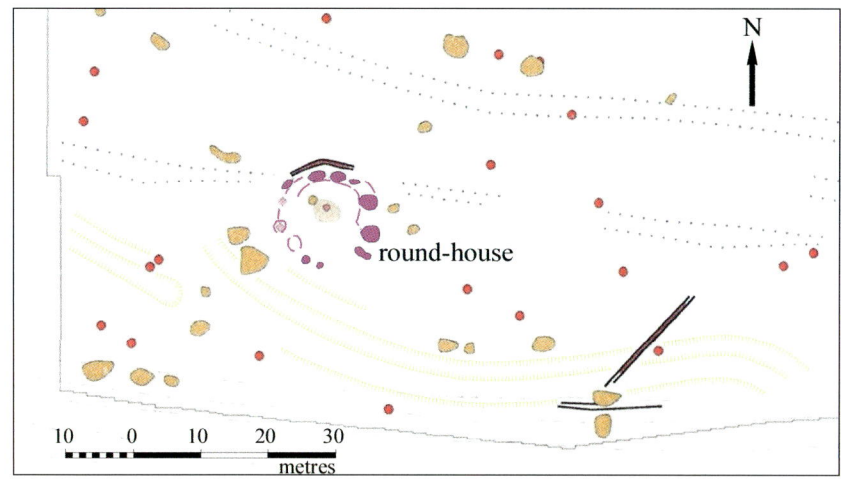

The geophysical survey of Capler hill-fort showed a single round-house (centre left) and traces of an earlier rampart with an entrance immediately to the south-west of it. Other features are likely to be pits

It is new evidence from this presumed final phase of use which has challenged previous interpretations of Capler. In the eastern half of the site there was a single, large circular post-built structure. This had all the characteristics of an Iron Age house, including a stone floor and a central hearth. The structure was 11 metres in diameter and had a 3-metre wide entrance on the east side. A pair of massive post-holes, which presumable held tall posts, marked the entrance. Such posts would be far in excess of anything required by the structure and must have had a decorative purpose, whether dictated by site status or simply style.[69] Other features, scattered around the building, are typical of contemporary rubbish pits. Although the western half of the hill-fort could not be examined, and therefore there may be other structures, this single structure standing alone is very different from groups of buildings suggestive of a settlement, which might have been anticipated if this was a 'town' like Danebury or Croft Ambrey. Was it the dwelling of a high status person, a chief or 'king', and his (or her) family?[70] Or was it perhaps some sort of temple?[71]

Cherry Hill, 2.5 kilometres to the north-west of Capler, is unusual. It has a limestone defensive circuit, which has been subjected to intense heat at some stage. There is a class of monuments, known as vitrified forts, where the defences have apparently been so treated. These are found from Ireland to Iran, with over 50% occurring in Scotland.[72] The reasons for this treatment are hard to fathom. The suggestion of earlier archaeologists that this was deliberately done to strengthen the defences fails at the first analysis, because such treatment will actual weaken the ramparts. Evidence seems to suggest that the vitrification is the result of destruction, accidental or deliberate, of these features.[73] The evidence suggests that an accidental fire so badly damaged the hill-fort at Cherry Hill that it was re-built on a slightly different alignment.[74] This is intriguing stuff, but Cherry Hill remains one of our least-known monuments.

At least some middle Iron Age hill-forts were intensively occupied, but this began to change towards the end of the first millennium BC. In south-east Britain the late Iron Age saw the abandonment of the hill-forts and the introduction of new quasi-urban centres in valley bottoms.

In the Welsh Marches, there is no unambiguous evidence in the pre-Roman Iron Age for lowland settlements larger than the farmstead/village. However, Ariconium, near Weston-under-Penyard, which was to become a nationally important 'Roman' industrial town, certainly had its origins as an ironworking settlement before the occupation. If not truly urban, Ariconium seems to have more than one iron-producing focus in the first half of the first century AD suggesting something rather more than a single farmstead.[75] Sited on the western edge of Dobunnic territory, it had trading links to the east and south-east, and may have controlled the iron industry in the Forest of Dean area.[76] Ariconium would have dominated what is now southern Herefordshire by the time it became part of Roman Britain in about 70 AD and it is likely that the important trading relationships of settlements of the study area were with this emerging centre.[77] Here too, the hill-forts had become outmoded.[78]

Whether or not they were redundant by the start of the Roman period, hill-forts were clearly major landscape features, but one of the questions addressed during the project was what other feature in the area, if any, were prehistoric. Boundaries are extremely difficult to date. To some extent, well-known techniques can be employed to date hedgerows. However, a boundary which is now formed by a living hedge may have originated in another form well before the laying of that hedge.[79] Although no direct evidence was forthcoming, it is possible that a series of 'lynchets' at Caplor Farm near Fownhope are prehistoric.[80]

These lynchets at Caplor Farm, Fownhope, are over 1^1/$_2$ m. high

Fields on the slopes of hills tend to form terraces. Ploughing on a hillside slowly moves the soil downhill, and on the upslope side of a field the effect is to cut into the hillside – this is a negative lynchet. On the downslope side of the field the moved soil builds up against the boundary – a positive lynchet. Of course, on larger hills the positive lynchet of an upper field will merge with the negative lynchet of a lower one to form quite large features. Such lynchets follow the contours of Capler Hill and there is no reason to suppose that they are not the result of a lengthy period of formation originating in the Iron Age (or even before).

Sickles found at the Herefordshire hill-forts of Croft Ambrey[81] and Sutton Walls[82] were probably used for reaping grain.[83] The grain was harvested by being cut at the top of the stalk, just the ears then being stored until required.[84] Iron Age ploughing was carried out by means of an ard pulled by oxen. Metal spikes, believed to be ox-goads, have been found at several sites on the Welsh Marches, including Croft Ambrey and, if that is what they are, would have been used to encourage oxen to greater

Ridgeway above Fownhope

effort when ploughing. The cattle of the time, probably similar to modern-day Dexters, would have therefore have been used for meat, milk and traction.

Many of the roads are likely to be prehistoric. What appears to be an archetypical ridgeway runs along the hills to the east of Fownhope and now forms part of the Wye Valley Walk. Ridgeways form part of the 'prehistoric package' handed to us by previous archaeologists. The theory derives from the old belief that thick, impenetrable woodland covered most of the country. Only the hills, it was believed, were free of trees. As has already been pointed out, it now seems likely that woodland was a lot less dominant than once had been thought. It was the river valleys which formed the natural communication routes.[85]

The roads were there when the Romans arrived, although their fascination with the Romans drew the Victorians into identifying any fairly straight piece of road or trackway as Roman. It was as if before the Conquest the native British never needed to travel anywhere or transport anything. A typical example is the alleged Roman road at King's Caple. In 1969, a paved surface on the line of a presumed road was found at Pennoxstone, but there was no dating evidence.[86]

In 2005, a team from the project excavated a trench across this road on the right bank – the Hoarwithy side – of the river. Beneath layers of flood-plain alluvium was a metalled surface of a plainly post-medieval date. This does not mean that the route was post-medieval; merely that it was being used as recently as the 18th century. But we knew that – it is marked as 'Red Rail Ford' on a 1754 map of Herefordshire by local cartographer Isaac Taylor.[87] The likelihood is that this route is ancient. Lengths of it may well have been maintained during the Romano-British period, but this does not make it a 'Roman' road.[88]

Another suggestion is that a Roman road crossed the Wye in the Hereford area and ran south through the study area, but no evidence for this has ever been produced. More plausible is a route from the north, through Fownhope towards Ariconium. The main Roman road in Herefordshire runs north to south along the Welsh Marches and ultimately joins Chester with Caerleon. Another road runs from west to east just to the north of Hereford – from the area of Clyro on the Welsh border (where there was an early Roman fort), through the Roman towns of Magnis and Stretton Grandison and on towards Worcester.

A road is likely to have run from the Chester to Caerleon road, across the east-west road and along the ridge known as Aylestone Hill, north-east of Hereford. It would then have crossed the Lugg near its confluence with the Wye at Mordiford and then run south towards Ariconium and ultimately the important centre at Gloucester. Such a route almost certainly existed in the Roman period, but there is no reason to suppose that it did not already exist when the Romans arrived.

The Roman conquest is invisible in the study area. Although, the army had campaigned into Silurian territory and may have established a fort at Monmouth by about 50 AD,[89] the annexation of Wales and the Marches did not take place until about 74 AD. It is likely that, for the local population, life mostly went on as before the conquest, although the army may have become a major consumer of agricultural produce.[90] Crop-marks of enclosure ditches, usually oval and on the sides of low hills, seem to indicate settlements of the late Iron Age/early Roman period in the area. Several of these were identified during the course of the project and plotted onto the mapping system. The distribution of these sites gives the impression of being similar to the density of modern farms. Other sites that were presumed to be of the Roman period were rectangular – the classic Roman shape that does appear in the Iron Age.

Several sites of the period were investigated during the construction of a pipeline through the area. At Winter's Cross on the A49, not far from Gillow, there were three distinct sites consisting of a Romano-British enclosure at the base of a hill, boundary ditches on the slope, and furnaces on the crest. At Hill of Eaton, on the boundary between Foy and Brampton Abbotts parishes, a multi-phase enclosure was excavated which originated in the Iron Age and continued into the later Roman period. Another Iron Age/Romano-British settlement site was found at Park Farm, in Foy parish.

The only suggestion of a villa-type structure in the study area is a crop-mark at King's Caple, which appears to show a building with two wings facing east.[91] Field-walking the area has produced quantities of very abraded Roman pottery.[92] Nearby, an excavation in 1991 produced evidence that local people adopted the new material culture from an early phase of the occupation. Pottery, trodden into the clay floor of a wattle and daub building, included both local 'Iron Age' and the new mass-produced Romano-British 'Severn Valley Ware' pottery dating from the second half of the 1st century.[93]

Further to the north-east, 500 metres north of Fawley Court was another site which produced Roman period pottery. This site was just to the south of the highest point on the King's Caple peninsula and was the location of both an enigmatic earthwork site recorded by earlier cartographers and the crop-mark of what appeared to be a large ring-ditch. This appears to be another late Iron Age/early Romano-British settlement.

Largely, field-walking on cropmark sites identified from aerial photographs produced Romano-British pottery of the 1st and 2nd centuries. Where there were no cropmarks, no such pottery was found. This was true of the fields beside the supposed Roman period road through Fownhope – the Mordiford to Ariconium road – where some roadside activity might have been anticipated.

At How Caple a field with a rectangular crop-mark was investigated. A large area in the field, which lay on the suggested Mordiford to Ariconium Roman Road, was gridded and a team of volunteers systematically walked across it. The resulting collection of finds had several sherds of Roman period pottery. Oddly these were not concentrated in the area of the cropmark itself, but a short distance to the east. Most of the sherds were small and abraded and could well have arrived where they were found because of spreading midden material from nearby habitation.

Ironworking was a major activity at Ariconium, but small-scale ironworking may have operated at a 'cottage industry' level in most or all of the contemporary settlements. Slag has been found in fields at Wilton and further north at Peterstow just to the north. Most of the fields in which Romano-British pottery was found also produced slag.

The iron industry would have been a major consumer of wood. Charcoal from Ariconium indicates that a range of species of trees were coppiced to support

Rectangular enclosure at How Caple

Crop mark in the southern part of Hentland

Gaer Cop hill-fort, Hentland; apart from one quadrant it only survives as a cropmark

Cropmarks at Harewood End and Gillow Farm

the industry and, presumably, for the everyday domestic use of the settlement. The main trees identified included maple, alder, birch, hazel, hawthorn, and oak, cut in the dormant period before leaf growth. Although there was a range of ages, 8 to 9 years predominated, indicating woodland management.[94]

Two of the oval, presumed Romano-British, sites were also field-walked and these produced excellent results. One of these, at Pengethley, had a scatter of Roman pottery over much of the area of the crop-mark. There was also quantities of slag, suggesting some level of ironworking on the site. Slag was also found at Gillow Farm, the second of these sites to be field-walked. Like the others, this site had initially been identified during the project's study of aerial photographs.

The Gillow Farm Excavation

The impressive crop marks at Gillow Farm

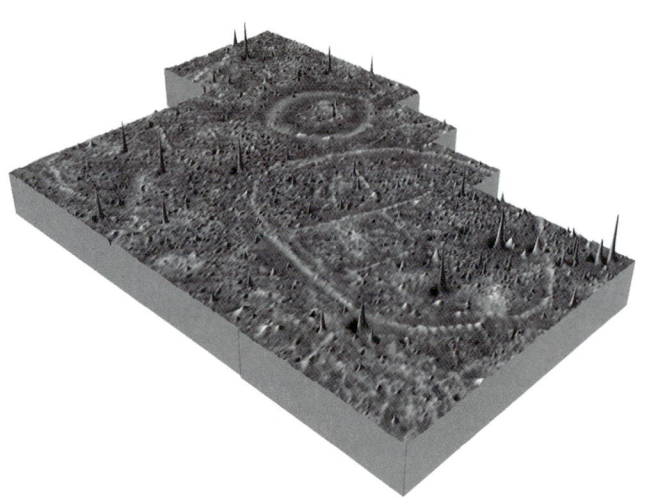

The results of the geophysical survey at Gillow Farm shown in false relief

At the field at Gillow, which had produced a Mesolithic microlith, field-walking also found a late 1st or early 2nd century brooch, a prehistoric plano-convex flint blade, and quantities of Romano-British pottery. The enclosure at Gillow was clearly worth having a closer look at, and eventually two segments of the enclosure ditch were excavated. These segments were positioned each side of the entrance.

The western segment was of considerable interest. The ditch was V-shaped, about 1.5 metres deep and cut into the natural sandstone. The base of the ditch was stepped, with a 'step' on the inside and a deeper 'gully' on the outside. These elements were likely to have been original. Such an arrangement, with an external 'sump', may have facilitated the cleaning out of the ditch. Clearly, the original intention would have been to clean out the ditch periodically – ditch maintenance has always been important. Archaeologists find disused ditches which have been filled in. Ditches are dated by finds in them, but these finds come from the period after the ditches have ceased to be used or could be residual.

Above and top right – work at the Gillow site
Right – The Romano-British ditch at Gillow

Obviously something had to be done with the rock and soil which had originally been removed when the ditch was cut. This was presumably mounded on the inside to form a bank. The total height from the top of the bank to the bottom of the ditch would have then been about 3 metres. With a palisade fence on top this must have presented a considerable barrier to anyone trying to get inside the enclosure without using the single entrance.

At some stage the enclosure ditch around the Gillow settlement ceased to be important, maintenance ceased and it began to silt up. After a few years, the now-disused ditch was used as a rubbish dump and quantities of broken pottery were thrown into it.[95] Although the ditch was no longer required for its original purpose, it remained a landscape feature for many centuries. The southern part was still serving as a curved field boundary when the Hentland parish tithe map was drawn in 1839.

The broken pottery in the ditch dated from the later 1st century, or possibly the very early 2nd century AD. The same combination of native 'Iron Age' pottery and Severn Valley ware pottery had been found trodden into the floor at King's Caple (see above). The original excavation and use of the ditch must have predated this by some years. It is difficult to tell how many – the ditch may have been scoured out any number of times. The enclosure may well have been constructed in the pre-Roman Iron Age. If so, does its use overlap with that of Gaer Cop hill-fort, three fields away to the south? Only further archaeological fieldwork can answer this question.

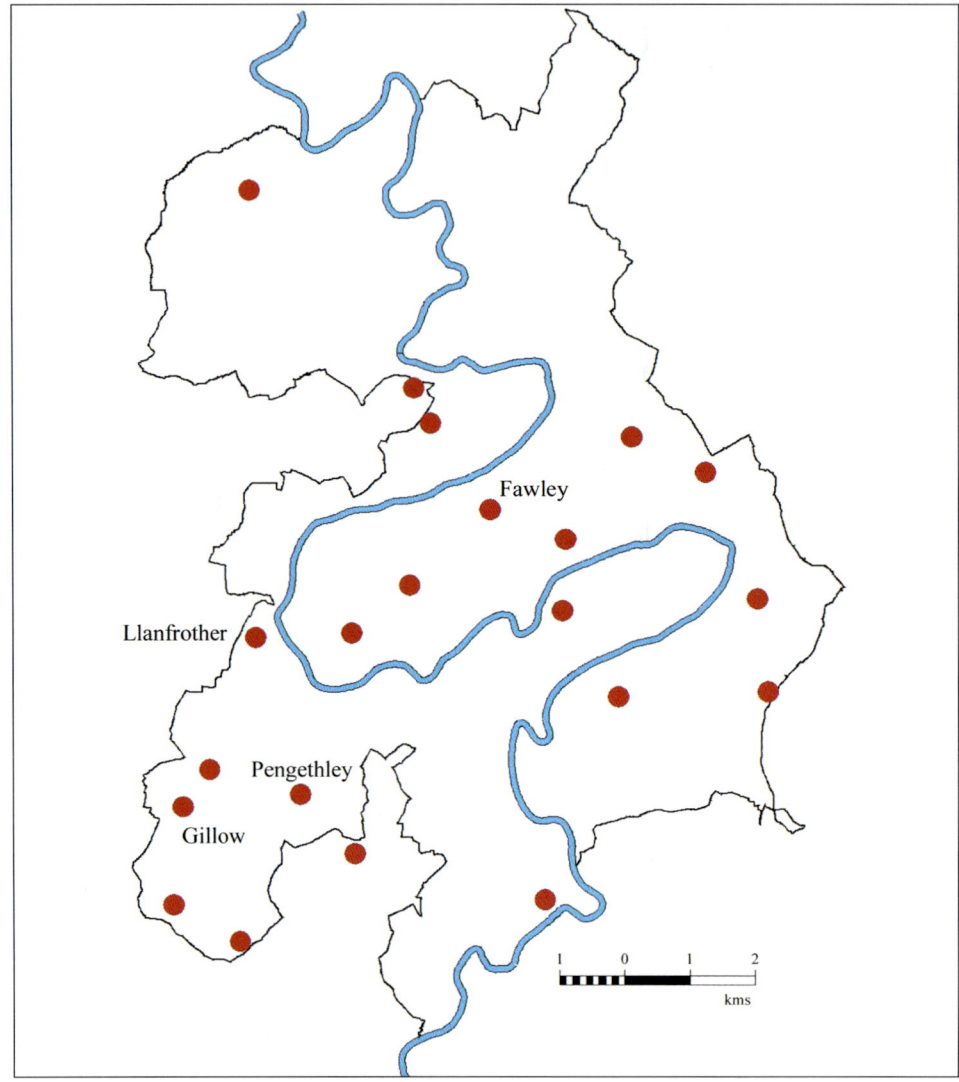

Sites which are certainly, or probably, late Iron Age/Romano-British settlements

CHAPTER II

Later Roman and Medieval

by P.J. Pikes

The Later Roman Period

The area of our study was part of the Roman Empire for almost 350 years, from about 70 AD to, traditionally, 410 AD. Nothing is known about any dramatic events during this period, but there were some, probably gradual, changes. The plough proper, with an iron coulter, replaced the ard, and so furrows were turned and heavier, wetter soils could be exploited. The warm climate of the late Iron Age (sometimes known as the Roman Warm Period) began to deteriorate in the mid-1st century AD and the new plough would have coped better with wetter conditions.[1]

It was probably in the Roman period that rye was first deliberately cultivated in the study area. It may have been only present as a weed in the Iron Age, only later being grown for its own sake. Food plants actually introduced to Britain during the Roman period included cucumbers, walnuts, celery, radish, cabbage, and lentils.[2]

A major problem with the later Roman and early medieval periods in the area is the absence of archaeological dating evidence – there is simply no pottery. The identification and dating of pottery is one of the most useful techniques available to the archaeologist. People in the area were certainly using pottery during the earlier Roman period, but in the centuries between the mid-Roman period and the arrival of the Normans there just does not seem to be any pottery at all. There is some Romano-British pottery from Ariconium and some from a 'villa' site, at Huntsham, just to the south of the study area, dating to the 4th century, and after that, nothing.[3] Considering that the technology had been developed in the Neolithic period, this is really quite curious.[4] If we judge by the pottery evidence, the settlement at Gillow went out of use before, perhaps much before, the end of the 2nd century AD.

Pottery was used for several purposes – cooking, storage and for transporting things. Presumably, these activities were still carried out in this aceramic age, and it must be supposed that something else was used for these purposes. Storage and transport could have used baskets, sacks or wooden containers – cases and barrels. Meat could have been spit-roasted or otherwise cooked by direct heat – hot stones perhaps. But it is difficult to believe that there were no cooking vessels at all. An explanation might be that they were made of metal in this period. Unlike pots, metal utensils can be repaired, and when beyond repair melted down and the material re-used.[5]

An alternative explanation for the absence of pottery might be that there were no people in the area during this period. It is probably safe to assume that this was not the case and that the study area continued to be inhabited, and farmed, much as it had been before and as it would continue to be.

Just to the north of the Romano-British settlement at Gillow, and within the same field, the project team excavated a medieval site. In the centre of the site was a layer which was composed of soil brought from elsewhere (presumably nearby). Within this soil was charcoal which has been radio-carbon dated to the 3rd or 4th centuries AD. Although this charcoal does not prove that the settlement was still occupied in the later Roman period, it certainly implies activity; this may be evidence of charcoal burning. If so, there was managed woodland. Additional evidence of activity in the area during these eight hundred years comes from documentary sources.

The Welsh

Although the withdrawal of formal Roman rule over Britain took place, conventionally, in 410 AD, it is unlikely that it had a great effect upon the way of life of the population of the study area. As central control gradually collapsed, the money economy disappeared and small kingdoms emerged throughout the country. The kingdom of Ergyng, or *Ercic*, took its name from the old iron-working town of Ariconium near Weston-under-Penyard.[6] Ergyng would continue as an identifiable entity to the present day as Archenfield – the part of Herefordshire broadly lying south of the Worm Brook and west of the River Wye.

The collection of charters and lives of saints, which comprise the *Book of Llandaff*, supplies most of the information that is known about Ergyng. The book was compiled in the earlier 12th century to support the claims of the Bishop of Llandaff to parishes which were then within the diocese of St David's and Hereford, but had in the mid-11th century been within the diocese of Llandaff. The material in the book includes many hostile references to the 'treacherous' Saxons or English who were gradually taking over the area between the 8th and the 11th century. Until quite recently many scholars dismissed most of what was in the *Book of Llandaff*,[7] but from the 1970s newer work has tended to strengthen its credibility.[8] The earliest mention of several places in the study area is in the book.[9]

Ergyng's local saint, Dyfrig (the Latin form is *Dubricius*), may have been active as early as the late 5th century.[10] Dyfrig is said to have founded a monastery at *Hennlann super ripam Gui* – 'the old church on the river Wye'.[11] This is almost certainly Llanfrother in Hentland parish, rather than the church at Hentland itself.[12] In 1334, the place was recorded as 'Hendresroudre', in 1546, 'Henfrowther'. The late medieval form of the name 'Henfresoudre' probably means 'old place of the brethren'.[13]

One of the charters in the book records that in about 620 King Gwrgan gave *Podum Sancti Badgualan* to Bishop Inabwy, together with two and a half *unciae* of land. This unit of land is in the present parish of Ballingham, but this early church here may not have been at the site of the present church and the hamlet of Carey has been suggested as a more likely location.[14] At this period all the surrounding area would have been British or 'Welsh' as the English called them. The name Carey seems to have originally applied to the Carey Brook and is almost certainly the original British one.

A re-grant of *Lann Badgualan in hostio Crican super Guy*[15] was made in the 9th century. By this time the northern part of Erging (Archenfield) had been taken by Mercia. The Taratyr brook, which flows into the Wye at the northern point of the land of *Lann Badgualan*, formed the boundary between the Welsh of Erging and the English. By this time, Fownhope, on the opposite bank from Ballingham, would have been 'English', although King's Caple, also on the east bank, was in Archenfield (and still is).

Most of the charters in the *Book of Llandaff* contain a formula granting rights in field, wood, water, and pasture. These are in Latin and imply the existence of mixed farming that presumably originated in the Iron Age. Boundary clauses in old Welsh are appended to these charters and give more detailed descriptions of individual estates. Taken together, the charters suggest a fully developed landscape with arable land and pasture, woodland, meadows, and roads. On the Wye were weirs and fish traps, but also navigation. There are many references to churches and cemeteries, but few direct references to settlements.

The hamlet of Carey is probably the site of Podum Sancti Badgualan *given to Bishop Inabwy by King Gwrgan in c.620AD*

Foy church

Sellack church

Later in the medieval period the ideal Welsh bond settlement contained about nine houses close together. This community would possess a plough, a corn-drying kiln, a churn, a cat, a cock, a bull, and a herdsman who looked after the common herd.[16] It is likely that this pattern reflects that of earlier medieval settlements, although none of these have been found in south Herefordshire. Are the cemeteries of the *Book of Llandaff* also absent? Well perhaps not – many of the churches still have churchyards – the churchyards at Bridstow, Foy, Peterstow and Sellack are still consecrated and in use and have never been excavated. But one south Herefordshire cemetery has been partially examined.

Dewsall is 7 kilometres south of Hereford. The area is now outside Archenfield, but would have been within the kingdom of Ergyng until the mid to late 8th century. In 2001 burials were unearthed during building work at Dewsall Court, just to the south of the parish church of St Michael.[17] These burials appeared to have been in a

37

now-disused part of a large cemetery, part of which is still the functioning churchyard. Bones from two individuals were radio-carbon dated – one 720 to 760 AD[18] and the other 790 to 810 AD.[19] Charcoal, recovered from within another grave was dated to the Roman period.[20] It seems entirely possible that the cemetery was in use throughout the population's evolution from Romano-Britons to Welsh to Mercians to English.[21] Judging by the evidence from elsewhere already cited, they are likely to have achieved this feat without moving.

The Welsh areas of south Herefordshire clearly had a parochial structure during the early medieval period. None of the 'English' areas in the county have records of churches as early. The English minster churches are not only later, but seem to serve large *parochia* while the churches of Ergyng seem to have a density almost as great as the modern one. Another difference is church location. In a landscape of dispersed settlement like Ergyng there was no 'central place' where a church was located. Even now, churches like Hentland, Sellack and Bridstow are not in the main settlements of their parishes.[22]

One type of early medieval monument is common in the Welsh Marches – the dyke. The various dykes are still impressive and must have been much more so when first built. The substantial dyke at Perrystone is the only such work in the study area, and was described as being equal in scale to a normal portion of Offa's Dyke.[23] If the Perrystone dyke was a territorial boundary of some sort (and it is difficult to imagine what else it could be), then the territories which it delineated are totally lost from our view. The theory that it marked a temporary limit of the Mercian expansion into Gwent/Ergyng has its attractions. At some stage the lands on the left bank of the Wye, including Walford, Cleeve, Ross, and the site of the eponymous Ariconium, were lost by the British and became manors of the English leaders who had presumably taken them.

A tree sits on top of the early medieval dyke at Perrystone

The English

Ross had been a possession of King Edmund Ironside when he died, leaving it to the church of Hereford.[24] Another royal manor was Cleeve, adjacent to, and downstream of Ross. Cleeve had been held by Harold Godwinson and had expanded into Archenfield with outliers at Wilton and Ashe Ingen on the right bank of the Wye. This intrusion into Welsh territory may have occurred at about this time. Belonging to this manor were as many Welshman as had 8 ploughs and who paid 10½ sesters of honey and 6s. and 5d. The survival of Welsh customs suggest a population in which the Welsh were a majority. Ashe Ingen had been waste in 1066 like so much of Archenfield. Also belonging to Cleeve in Domesday was a part of the forest created by William I. In King Edward's time this land had paid 6 sesters of honey and 6 sheep and 6 lambs and the Herefordshire Domesday identifies it as *Chingescaple* – King's Caple – another Archenfield vill, although on the left bank of the Wye.

The English manor of Fownhope had been a manor of Thorkell the White in King Edward's time. A man called Alric had held a place called Eatone in Sulcet hundred from Thorkell before 1066. At Domesday it was held by Hugh d'Asne, and two men there with two rendered sesters of honey. Sulcet hundred is a unique entry and is otherwise unknown. In the Hereford Domesday, the Eatone entry is annotated Strangef.[25] Strangford is in Sellack on the right bank of the Wye opposite King's Caple. This, with its Welsh render of honey, looks like another English incursion.

A manor held by Gilbert son of Thorold in 1086 also seems to have been an English acquisition in that it still had the honey render – 4 free men with 4 ploughs pay 4 sesters of honey. This, according to the annotation in the Hereford Domesday, as 'Baldinga', was Ballingham.[26] Another Archenfield vill was Baysham which had been held from King Edward by Merwin.

The present lay-out at Brockhampton is just over a century old.
The traces of the medieval landscape show as shadows

St. Cuthbert's church is almost all that is left of the old village of Holme Lacy

Looking west across the Wye from How Caple to Foy.
In the 9th century the land on the far side of the river was Welsh

These manors were, of course, economic units. Some of them were wealthy – Fownhope's value was to rise from £12 in 1066 to £16 in 1086. The sheep and honey renders emphasise that at the time the Welsh areas were not operating on a money economy.

Meadow is rare in the Domesday account of the manors of the area. Although there are 10 acres at Holme Lacy, eight at How Caple, and three at Brockhampton, there are none at Cleeve, Fownhope or Brampton Abbotts and it may be that the surveyors simply missed some out. By the early 19th century, meadows flanked the Wye along its entire course through the study area. The absence of meadow in the survey

much of this seems likely to have existed in the 11th century. The absence of meadow in the survey cannot be a reflection of reality, for it would have been an essential component of the farming economy and commonly occurs in the *Book of Llandaff*. Farming had been developing for thousands of years and had achieved considerable sophistication. The landscape of both the English and Welsh parts of the study area would have included fields and pastures, woods and meadows, lanes and houses.

The warfare of the time had a marked effect on the landscape. In the 1050s, Gryffyd ap Llewellyn had laid waste many manors, together with large swathes of Archenfield. Much of this had not recovered by the time of the Domesday Survey in 1086. At this time Osbern fitz Richard is recorded as hunting in woods that had grown up on waste land and the manor Harewood on the edge of the study area had also reverted to woodland.

The Domesday survey was carried out on the orders of William I, who had defeated and killed Harold Godwinson at Hastings. The reaction of the Welsh people of Archenfield to the events of 1066 is not recorded. The English

11th-century strap mount from Weston-under-Penyard

to this day insist on using the term 'Norman' for the invaders, but in fact many of the newcomers were not Norman. The army of William I at Hastings was a combination of 'milites' from many other lands than Normandy, and Aquitaine and Brittany were prominent among the origins of the invaders.[27] Legally, in England, subjects of the Norman kings belonged to one of two groups – French or English.[28] Those Normans who, like the late Ralph, had lived in England before the Conquest, were English; Normans who arrived with the Conqueror and after were French.[29]

But not all the French were city-dwellers; some at least of the incomers moved in among the existing rural population and farmed the land. Domesday records the tenants of the Archenfield manor of King's Caple. There were five Welshmen with five ploughs who paid a traditional Welsh due – five sesters of honey, five sheep with lambs, and ten pence.[30] There was also one Frenchman with one plough. In the reign of Edward the Confessor the tenants had been six Welshmen.[31]

With a few exceptions, Archenfield manors are not recorded in Domesday. Several places in Archenfield are recorded in the *Book of Llandaff* and others clearly existed. Hentland is a slight corruption of the Welsh *hen llan* – the old church – and must mean that the religious foundation there is of great antiquity. The site has a particular attraction for archaeologists,[32] and as one of the Landscape Origins of the Wye Valley projects, it was decided to carry out a survey of earthworks adjacent to Hentland church.

In the 11th century Strangford – the ford with the strong current – was an English settlement in Welsh lands

The Evidence in the Field

An excavation south of Hentland church in 1970 and 1971 had located remains of buildings from several periods. The earliest were wooden buildings represented by post-holes. This phase had been deliberately buried by a layer of soil before the construction of a stone building of the 13th century. This building, which was only partially within the excavated area, was represented by one wall. There was also a 15th- or l6th-century building, the end wall of which remained *in situ*. This was replaced by a 17th-century rectangular house, which was probably the manor referred to in documentary records.[33] In March 2006, members of the Landscape Origins team, under the guidance of English Heritage, carried out earthwork surveying training in the area to the north of the church and added some more medieval features to our knowledge of this site.

Landscape features most commonly associated with this period are, of course, castles. All of the known medieval earthwork sites within the study area, which might be loosely interpreted as castles or moated manor houses, were visited during the course of the project. Wilton Castle is the major medieval castle site in the area, the seat of the Longchamps, followed by the de Greys. In the *Domesday Book*, the village beside it, Bridstow, was more populous than Ross. Wilton seems to have been granted a fair and a market in the reign of King John, a generation before Ross.[34] It was the bishop's borough of Ross which was to become the major settlement of the area, but this could not have been anticipated by the Normans.

Survey work at Hentland

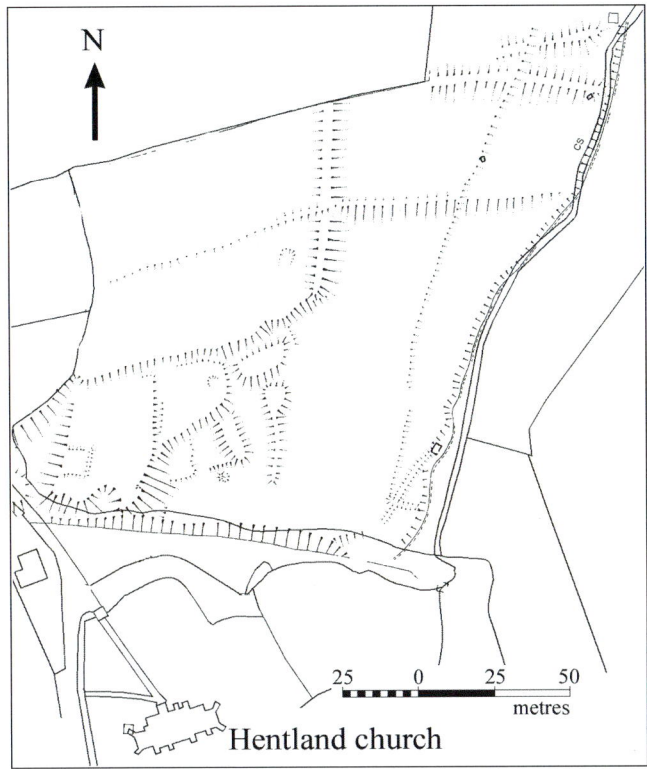

King's Caple Tump

Survey of Hentland earthworks

Chapel Tump, Hentland

At King's Caple the motte stands in isolation near the church, which may originally have been within a now-vanished bailey.[35] There is no documentary evidence whatsoever relating to this earthwork, but it is just possible that the church originated as a chapel to the castle. King's Caple church was a chapelry annexed to Sellack church, a much older foundation.

A now ill-defined medieval earthwork is Chapel Tump in Hentland parish. Cottages occupy most of this site which was a motte and bailey castle that was originally some 26 metres in diameter. Nothing is known of it and presumably the castle was abandoned at an early date. It now has the appearance of a squatter settlement. The site is best appreciated by viewing the tithe map or an aerial photograph.

In Fownhope parish the earthworks of a small moat were surveyed in 2006. It lies on sloping ground in an isolated position on pasture land. There is no documentary evidence for this feature, but it is known locally as 'the Roman burial ground'. Sherds of 12th-century pottery had been found and it has previously been recorded as a medieval homestead moat.[36]

Another odd earthwork is a feature which appears to be a moat in Trilloes Court Wood in Bolstone parish. This is currently in the middle of the wood, but this does not mean that the area was wooded at the time of the feature's construction and use. What is puzzling is that it lies on a steep slope with the top of the hill immediately above it. Whatever else it was, it was certainly not a good defensive site.[37]

Cropmark at Fawley

A further unsatisfactory feature is an apparent earthwork known as Fawley Camp in Brockhampton parish at the highest point within this bend of the Wye. This allegedly had a very wide rampart at some stage.[38] By the 1920s it consisted of nothing more than 'a slight sinking of indeterminate shape'.[39] Adjacent to this feature was a cropmark of what appeared to be a Bronze Age ring-ditch.

In September 2005, the Archaeophysica geophysicists, together with a number of project volunteers, carried out a geophysical survey on this site together with some field-walking. Unfortunately this day, Saturday, 10 September, was extremely wet

The medieval moated manor at Gillow is two fields away from the Gillow Farm excavation

and the Ross-on-Wye area had the greatest amount of rainfall in Britain, with flash flooding in the lanes, and the exercise was abandoned by 2.30pm. A reasonable quantity of Romano-British pottery was found, indicating a settlement of some sort in the area at that time.[40] However, no trace of an earthwork was visible. It was concluded that this was certainly not a medieval earthwork and possibly not an archaeological feature at all.

What can be dated to the period after the Norman Conquest is an extremely interesting but enigmatic feature at Gillow Farm in Hentland parish, which was investigated as part of the project. The selection of the site as a target for fieldwork, the geophysics, and the initial site work, have already been described in Chapter 1.

The excavation at Gillow Farm

Immediately to the north of the Gillow Romano-British settlement was a large circular feature. On the aerial photographs it looked a lot like a Neolithic henge. The geophysical survey carried out over this site provided some additional and very interesting evidence. First, there had been intensive burning within the ditch, concentrated towards the north-east. Second, the interior formed a low but distinct mound.

These attributes were characteristic of a large Bronze Age barrow. The archaeological team therefore adopted the standard strategy for excavating such features, and divided it into four quadrants with the crossing in the very centre of the monument. This method allows for linear sections to be drawn through the feature. The topsoil in the opposing north-west and south-east quadrants was removed by machine. The topsoil was then removed from the greater part of the remainder, leaving metre-wide unexcavated baulks between them and the original two quadrants. These formed two opposing L-shaped baulks running north to south and east to west across the centre of the site.

What the machining revealed was that outside the circular ditch the topsoil overlay the natural Old Red Sandstone, as it did all over the field. However, within the area of the ring, there was a solid layer of clay and stone. Was this the remains of the ploughed-down Bronze Age barrow? For a while, the team worked in the belief that this was the case, but then they began to find sherds of medieval pot sticking out of the clay and stone layer. This was not a prehistoric feature!

The work of cleaning this layer by trowel was hard, but needed to be done in order to identify any features – post-holes and the like – which might have been cut into it. Despite many hours of hard and careful work, no such features were found: one homogenous layer had been laid over whatever lay beneath.

Digging the northern ditch segment

In tandem with the excavation of the north-east quadrant within the ring, two sections were cut through the fill of the ditch itself. Standard archaeological techniques include the recording of the stratigraphy of ditch fills. Ordinarily, different layers are visible to the naked eye and archaeologists make scale drawings of them in order to record the different events during the infilling of such features. In this case, no layers were visible within the fill of the ditch. Archaeophysica Ltd, the project geophysics team, decided to attempt a new approach. Using a hand-held KT5 magnetic susceptibility meter, they took 10cm. readings over the whole exposed vertical face of the northern section through the ditch. Other members of the project team were then trained in the use of the KT5 meter and the southern section of the ditch was also recorded. These readings suggested tip-lines running in from the outside. In other words, when the ditch was cut, the spoil from the ditch was banked on the outside. This material then fell, or was pushed, back into the ditch at a perhaps very much later date.[41]

The geophysical survey had determined that the greatest anomalies were in the north-east quadrant. It was, therefore, from this area that the layer of stone and clay was removed. If cleaning down to the layer was difficult, removing it by trowel was almost wrist-breaking. Once again this was done by the team of volunteers.

Section across ditch

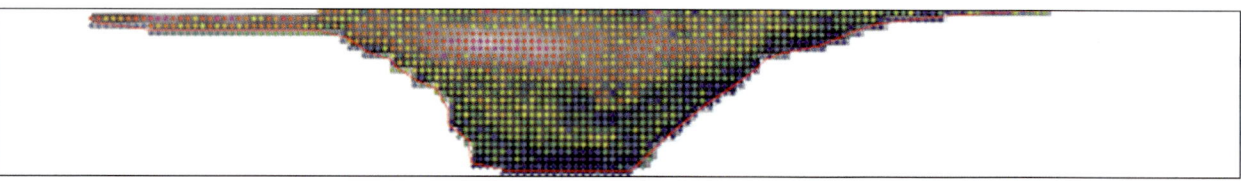
The magnetic susceptibility plot of the ditch section showing tip-lines from left to right

Left – Using the meter in the ditch
Above – Sampling the ditch fill

What was revealed was extraordinary. In front of the diggers was a spread of smashed pottery and small fragments of bone. A whole side of one pot lay where it had fallen, smashed, but clearly smashed where it lay. Archaeologists simply don't find this sort of thing – pottery and bone is found in the fills of rubbish pits and ditches, not just in a layer. Magnetic susceptibility readings by the hand-held KT5 meter indicated that the whole area had been the site of a fire and that two small areas, visible as rectangular red colourations on top of what was otherwise a darker soil, had been the location of even more intense fire. Metal finds included nails and, very tantalisingly, an arrowhead. Bone does not generally survive for long in the acidic sandy soil of the study area and the presence of bone fragments must be a consequence of the peculiar environmental conditions beneath the layer of clay. This looks like a single dramatic event, the nature of which we can only speculate about. Whatever it was, someone had gone to a great deal of trouble to bury it under the clay and stone that the team had initially found.

Beneath this spread of burning and smashed pot was a layer of dark soil. The team removed a two-metre wide strip of this running at 45° to the east-west alignment of the main baulk. It was up to half a metre thick towards the centre of the ring, and thinned towards the edge where it disappeared. This layer contained fragments of medieval pot and a few sherds of Roman-period pottery. Charcoal contained within this layer was probably residual (that is, it was lying around and does not date the layer itself). However,

Planning

Surveying

Measuring

The miniature aeroplane

The excavation of the circular medieval feature at Gillow Farm. The figures are standing by the section cut through the northern part of the ditch. The photograph was taken from the miniature aeroplane

it has been radio-carbon dated to 230 to 410 AD, confirming Roman activity in the area.[42] Beneath this layer were several features cut into the original natural soil and sandstone bedrock.

The historical sequence of events on this complex site has now been established, using radio-carbon and pottery dating to add to the excavation evidence. The first event seems to have been the excavation of a two-metre deep circular ditch into the natural sandstone bedrock. The material from this work was built into a bank on the outside of the ditch. Some of the rock fell back in quite soon after, sealing a cattle tibia below a large piece of sandstone. This was fortunate, because the clay preserved the bone. Almost everywhere else on the site, and indeed over the whole project area, the acidity of the sandstone soil destroyed bone within a few centuries (unless the bone was burnt, as were all the fragments within the ring). Although there were some technical problems with the dating of the bone from the ditch the result – 1020 to 1210 AD with a 95% probability – certainly ruled out this being a re-used prehistoric feature.

Within the central area a number of pits or post-holes were cut into the rock and presumably some sort of structure erected. The area excavated down to this level was not sufficient to determine a plan of these features, but it is likely that they are post-holes associated with some structure within the circular ditch.

It is assumed that these two events were contemporary, but in fact the sequence is not known, nor with the present state of knowledge can it be ascertained. The ditch might have preceded the post-holes by many years, or it might have been the other way round.

At a later date the posts, which are presumed to have stood originally

Top – Burnt areas
Middle – The pottery layer
Bottom – Broken pot

within these post-holes, were removed and the whole internal area of the ring, but not the ditch itself, was covered with a layer of soil brought in from elsewhere. This, presumably, was from nearby and included charcoal and pottery from the Roman period. (The site is immediately adjacent to the Gillow Romano-British settlement.) The top of this material was levelled and there were no features cut into it.

A single, apparently dramatic, event occurred at some time subsequent to the dumping and levelling. This was fire – some of it localised in rectangular, hearth-like areas, but also spread over several square metres. Neither charcoal nor other burnt material associated with this event was recovered – any such material must have been removed. Pottery and small fragments of animal bone were spread across this area; there was also a single arrowhead. No structures were associated with this phase and their causal events.

Although the total weight of bone was small, there were 285 fragments. What was surprising was the number of species represented in this small assemblage. Domestic species included cattle, sheep (or goats – but probably sheep), pigs, horses, and chickens.[43] A goose bone could belong to a wild or domestic bird, but there were three birds which were certainly wild – one was possibly a jackdaw, another was a crow or rook, and the third a buzzard or red kite. The hare was the only wild mammal found and the only certain evidence of hunting.

Rat tooth marks on part of a pig's skull found amongst the pot and bone layer at Gillow Farm

The bones showed little sign of being exposed to very much heat and it is possible that they were deposited subsequent to the burning. However, there is another possibility. It may be that the flat surface was the floor of a building. Although there would have been walls, it is possible that the evidence for these was not apparent to the excavators – being outside the area or in a form that left no trace. The floor of this building might have been covered with straw or rushes. Large animal bones, falling onto this floor, would have been removed by servants, dogs, and vermin. Small bones and smashed pottery would have remained where they fell. The floor covering may have burnt very quickly, leaving no evidence on the bones. There remains a problem though – all the geophysical evidence suggests burning at a high temperature. There was more happening at the site than is understood. As is so often true, only more excavation is likely to resolve these problems.

Under the burnt material

This spread of bone and pot lay on the burnt surface for a brief period – not long enough for plants to grow but long enough for rats to gnaw some of the bone.[44] It was then covered with a layer of clay and stone, which formed a hardened crust just below the plough-soil. This material was laid directly on the smashed pottery and bone and seemed to represent the deliberate burying of the former material. Although there were plough-marks in it, this material survived over the greater part of the feature and was hard enough to damage recent ploughs, the broken share of one of which was found during the excavation.

This excavation at Gillow Farm was the major field element of the project. Not only did it provide experience of standard archaeological methodology to the volunteer team, it also exposed them to more advanced techniques than most of those previously employed.

It would be nice to say something more positive about this very interesting site. The ring ditch had many characteristics of a prehistoric feature. It appeared to have an external bank, and the steep profile of the ditch was more typical of a Roman or prehistoric feature than a medieval one. Although prehistoric features are

Post-holes

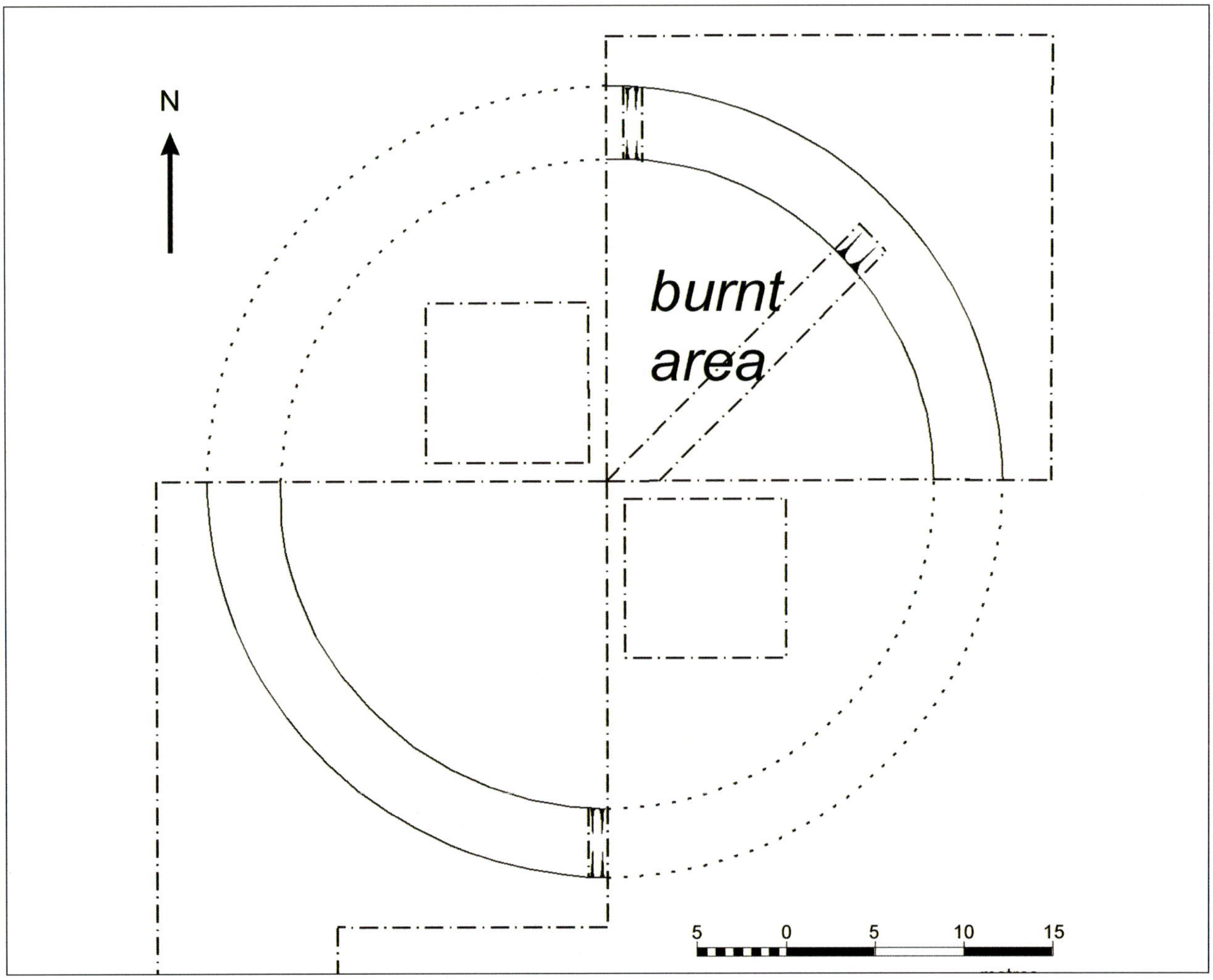

Plan of the Gillow medieval site showing areas examined

51

sometimes re-used in the medieval period, the dating of the bone from its primary fill suggests that this was constructed from scratch some time in the Norman period.

The team had briefly been attracted to the possibility that it might have been a precursor to nearby Gillow Manor. However, neither the nature of the site itself, nor the artefacts recovered from its excavation suggested that this site was a moated manor house of the sort that occurs throughout southern Britain in the medieval period. The V-shaped circular ditch is nothing like a moat and in any case had a bank on the outside. Manor house sites also tend to produce higher status finds than those recovered from this excavation.

The Gillow site is likely to have been one of the latest features of this scale without any documentary evidence. Although the early medieval period in the area is a little different, and lacks archaeological evidence to support the documentary record, generally the number of documents increases from this time onwards, and can increasingly be used to augment the study of the development of this landscape.

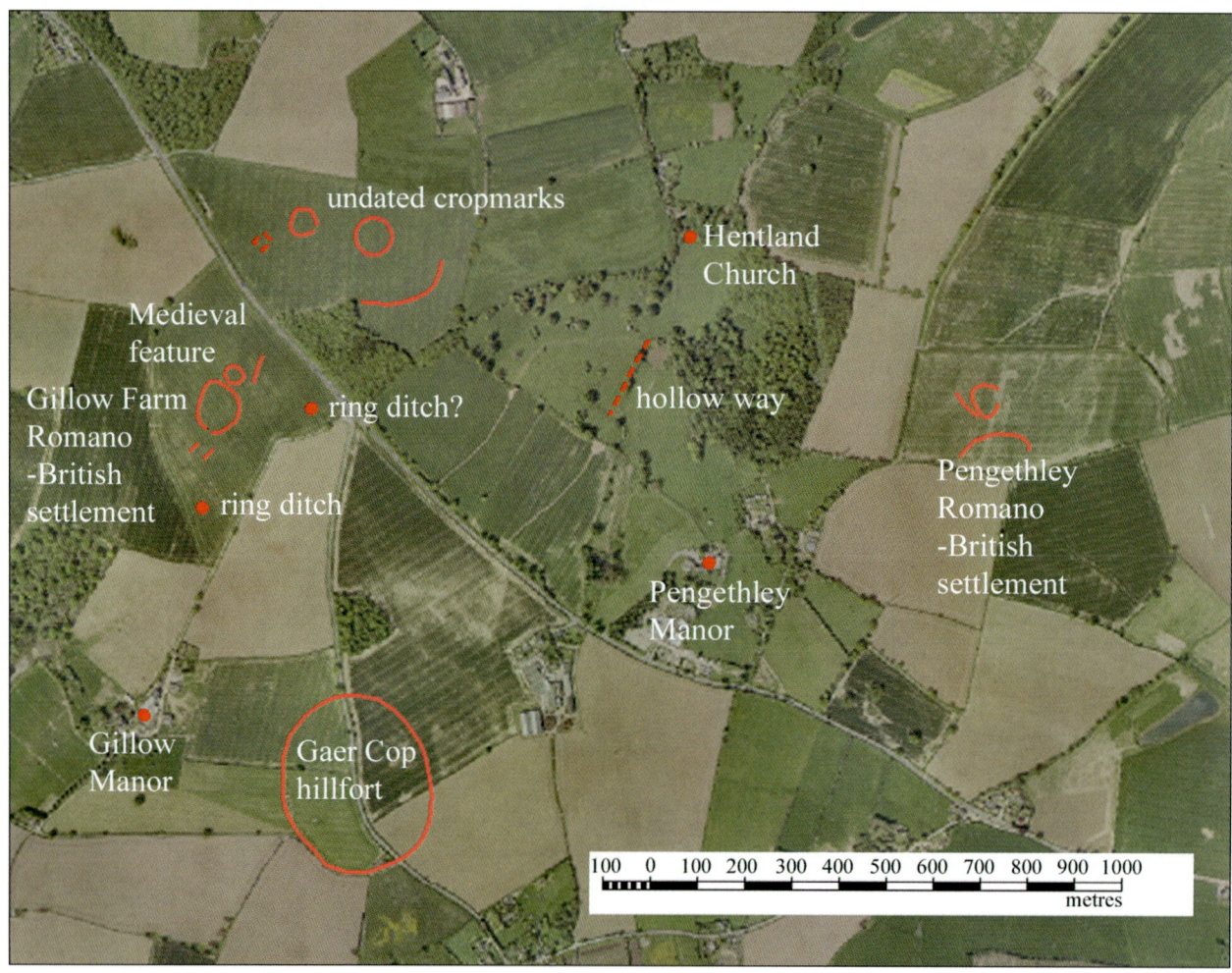

The Gillow landscape

CHAPTER III

Documentary Evidence

by David Lovelace and Heather Hurley

The project examined a wide range of original documents relating to the area, dating from the 13th to the 20th century. During the course of the project many Latin documents were translated and early English ones transcribed for the first time. All available documents were examined, some individual farms were surveyed, and estate maps in public and private collections were photographed. These records, combined with field work, provide a greater understanding of the landscape and provide the background to this chapter.

Land was used on the manor in three main ways: the lord's farm, tenanted land and marginal land. The land farmed by the lord directly for his own benefit is known as the 'demesne' – the equivalent of the 'home farm' of a modern estate. For Fownhope, at the time of Domesday, this included an area of arable land that required three plough teams (roughly 150 acres), worked by ten 'unfree' tenants bonded to the manor and the 26 slaves (of which 8 were female). Most of the land was farmed by 24 tenants, who between them had 26 plough teams working about 1,300 acres of arable land. The church, a major land owner in the county, held half 'a hide' – about 60 acres.[1] In all, 29 plough teams were recorded, which would have cultivated some 1,500 acres of the richer soils of Fownhope, equivalent to roughly half the area of the modern parish.

After the Domesday survey there is no known documentation concerning the project area until the 13th century, from which a few documents regarding land transactions survive, but they only deal with small areas of land. For example, in 1250 Walter de Lacy exchanged land with Simon de Clifford involving 3 acres of meadow in Holme Lacy.[2]

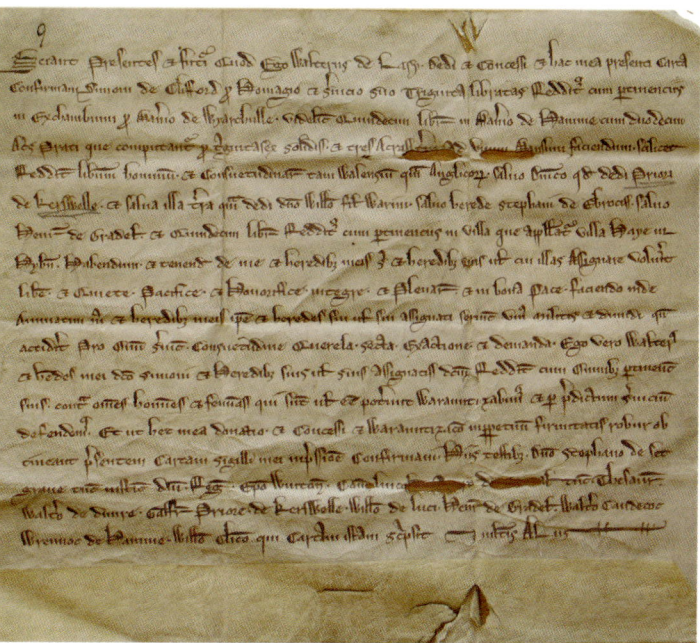

Exchange of land in Holme Lacy in c.1250

53

The Eyre Rolls

More information comes from the 'Eyre Rolls', which were court proceedings equivalent to the present circuit courts, whereby the king's official heard disputes and judged alleged crimes – especially those against the interests of the king. The earliest ones for Herefordshire date from the reign of Edward I, and provide some fleeting glimpses of life in the Wye valley from the late 13th century.

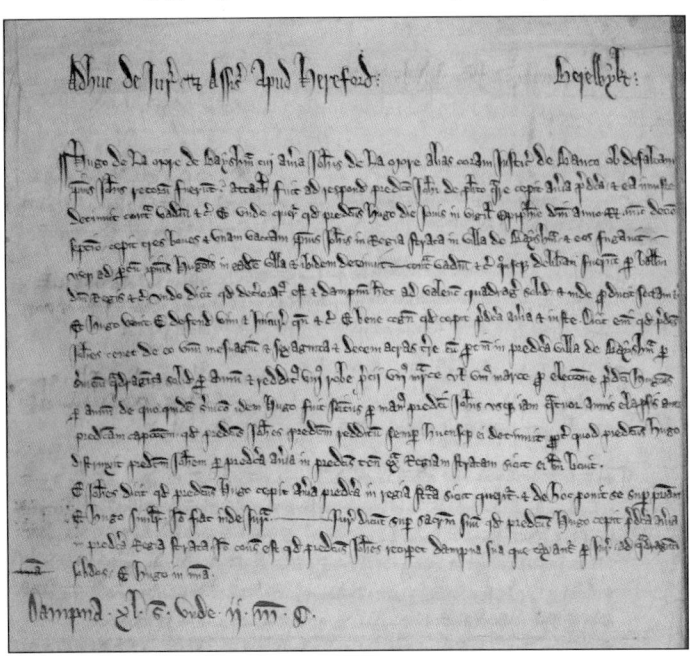

The Eyre Roll 1292 referring to Baysham in 1289

In 1289, Hugh de la More of Baysham stole 3 oxen and a cow on the public road through Baysham from John de la More who farmed 70 acres of land in Baysham. The court found Hugh guilty and assessed the damage at 40 shillings.[3]

In 1290, Williams de Chandos was in dispute with Robert Doter regarding the succession to the tenancy of a farm in King's Caple which consisted of a farmhouse, 44 acres of land, 4 acres of meadow and 4 acres of woodland.[4]

Another dispute in 1290 recorded that Roger de Grey, lord of Wilton in Bridstow, and his wife Matilda were accused of taking a virgate of land (about 30 acres) from Melisa de Longchamps in order to build a water mill. The case is interesting because it shows that Roger had acquired Wilton through marriage to Matilda de Longchamp, daughter of the previous lord of Wilton, so Melisa was being ousted by her brother-in-law. The court favoured Melisa and assessed her damages at half a mark.[5]

In 1307 the crown carried out an investigation into fishing in the Wye from Chepstow to Mordiford. The main concern was that salmon (a prerogative of the king) were being fished outside the close season and that the local gillies were incompetent or perhaps complicit. As with deer, a license was required from the king to fish for salmon. The court rolls reveal that at Foy 'Hugo Brekedent of Eton, fisherman, caught large and small salmon using a net and other devices in the Wye during the close season'. So did Robert le Pechour of Wilton, John de How Caple, Walter Boucke de Fawley and William de Grandissono 'from his pond in Eyton'.[6]

John de la More, who farmed at Baysham and whose cattle were stolen on the road a few years earlier, 'caught small salmon at Baysham in the Wye during the close season', as did Roger le Noggare of King's Caple and William Barnard, who were catching undersized salmon 'at the pond of the mill of Abercare' in Ballingham. All were found guilty by the court and John de la More had his lands at Baysham seized by the sheriff of Hereford, and was committed to Hereford gaol but ended up paying a fine of 40d. John de How Caple and le Noggare of King's Caple both had their nets burnt. The sheriff could not find William Barnard and Robert le Pescour and since they had no land to be seized they were declared outlaws.[7]

Inquisitions Post Mortem

An important source of information about the land and its people in the middle ages can be gleaned from the surveys of manors known as Inquisitions Post Mortem (IPMs) – literally meaning 'inquiries following death'. All land belonged to the king to whom the lord of a manor, as his tenant in chief, owed allegiance and duties in proportion to the value of his manors. For example, in time of war the lord was obliged to supply fully equipped knights, but by the 14th century these obligations had mostly been commuted to monetary payment. When the lord died his lands were temporarily taken over by the crown which oversaw the succession to the next generation, which involved an entry fee payable to the crown. It was important for the crown to assess the value of each estate and its individual manors. This valuation and survey was carried out by the king's representative in each county, known as an escheator, who appointed a 'jury' of local landholders. Each IPM details the lord's demesne, but usually only the rents and dues of the tenants were recorded, which means that IPMs give relatively little insight into the nature of rented land.

The earliest known IPM in the project area is for Gillow manor in Hentland for 1280. It does not detail the land, but does provide an insight into the dues peculiar to Archenfield:

> held by Henry of Pembridge deceased in Herefordshire. The jurors say he held Gillow manor in chief of the lord king by the service that he will find a man for 15 days at his own cost when the king goes to war which is called 'Latheferd' and he serves on the court of Wormelow hundred every 15 days and when he dies he gives one ox for heriot or 2s. if he hasn't got an ox according the Welsh custom in this hundred.[8]

The IPM of 1285 for lands in King's Caple and Baysham records:

> A messuage, 2 parts of 1 carucate land, 3 acres meadow, a piece of underwood, a windmill, rent of assize and pleas held of Alan Plukenet, lord of Kilpeck in chief by service of ½ Knight's fee and doing suit of court of Kilpeck.

Windmill Field, as a name, persisted to the middle of the 19th century on tithe maps for Sellack and King's Caple. The IPM shows the relationship with the important manor of Kilpeck and its castle.[9]

The 1324 IPM for the manor of Wilton (see next page) describes the demesne lands in some detail (the tenants and income from the manor court have been excluded):

> The jurors who say under oath that John de Grey was seised on the day of his death of the manor of Wilton upon Wye in the County of Hereford and that he held the said manor by the service of 2½ knights' fees of the king in chief
>
> And they say that there is a certain castle with an outer court with two gardens, one courtyard and one pigeon house which are worth per year 16s 8d
>
> Item: they say that there are there 360 acres of arable land which are worth per year £4 10s which is 3d per acre
>
> And there are 90 acres of meadow which are worth 40s per year which is 18d an acre
>
> And there are there 18 acres of pasture which are worth 9s per year [6d per acre]
>
> Item: there are there 4 acres of under-wood worth per year 3s 4d [10d per acre][10]
>
> and there are two water mills upon the Wye worth per year at 60s and there is there a third part of one water mill value per year 8s.
>
> Item: there are there two fulling mills worth per year 40s[11]
>
> and there are there two fishponds and they are worth per year 6s 8d
>
> and there are there a fishery with a weir which are worth per year 13s 4d'
>
> Item: one ferry across the Wye 100s per year'.[12]

The demesne lands described here are likely to be representative of the better land of the Wye Valley and some general conclusions may be drawn, bearing in mind that this IPM was carried out just before the Black Death when the population density was as high as at any time before the Tudor period. Woodland is very minor land use, meadow was the most valuable type of land followed by pasture and then arable, which occupied the highest proportion of a manor. The information is summarised in the following table:

The 1324 IPM for Wilton

Type of land	Acres	Percentage	Annual value, pence per acre
Arable	360	76	3
Meadow	90	19	18
Pasture	18	4	6
Woodland	4	1	10
Total	**472**	**100**	

The demesne lands of the manor of Wilton from the 1324 IPM

The following extracts concern the demesne lands of Fownhope from two 14th-century IPMs. In 1353:

> one ruined messuage worth nothing; a garden 11d, one dovecote 40d; two water mills worth nothing because they have been destroyed by the floodwater of the Wye; four carucates that contain four hundred acres, worth per year per acre 2d; 80 acres meadow worth per year per acre 12d; 26 acres pasture worth per year per acre 6d; a park whose coppice is worth nothing because of the large trees 13s. 4d; 100 acres of coppice worth per acre 4d. and no more because coppice cannot be cut for seven years; one boat; one messuage and a virgate worth 13s. 4d; one messuage and a virgate from the prior of the hospital of St John.[13]

In 1375:

> there is a ruined house which is worth nothing per year after debts have been paid. And three carucates of land which are worth per year 100s; 40 acres of meadow which are worth per year 10s. [4d./acre]; 4 acres of pasture which are worth per year 4s. [12d./acre]. And there is a water mill with a weir that is worth per year 100s. and a park whose coppice is worth per year 5s. And 50 acres of underwood which can be cut every seventh year and at that time an acre is worth 20d. but nothing this year because it was cut two years ago.[14]

Other Documents
An Early Lease
This document of 1332 details the livestock for a small holding in Holme Lacy. Draught animals were the 'tractors' of agriculture and the lease is ensuring that they remain on the farm at the end of the tenancy:

> Receipt for taking on a farm at Holme Lacy which includes twenty-four oxen and two draught-animals of the value of thirteen shillings and four pence each, one cart and four wagons hooped with iron worth ten shillings each, four ploughs and four harrows twelve pence each, in the barn there are three tables with trestles, all of the which are to be handed over at the end of the term of the aforesaid farm. Given in the church of Hereford.[15]

Bailiff accounts
These record the management of the demesne lands of a manor carried out on behalf of the lord by his stewards and bailiffs, who were also responsible for producing the annual accounts. A set of accounts for Eaton Tregoz in Foy, spanning the years 1422 to 1445, illustrate the wide range of activities of a typical manor of the area at this time. These include hay making, grazing, fishing, working in the park, selling timber, repairing weirs and barns, ditching and building a new mill. This comparatively large farm reflected the importance of the hay harvest, a job for skilled contractors.

Included was the Cames, a hay meadow on the east bank of the river Wye – a valuable field with its hay crop sold in 1426 for £5. This represents almost an eighth of the total income of £42 from the demesne manor for that year. The income from both hay and grazing was £11 9s., just over a quarter of the total. For the scything of the meadow, drying the hay in the field and taking it to the barn, the manor hired men and paid them 28 shillings. Pasturing pigs on the acorns from the oaks (pannage) in Eaton Tregoz Park earned the manor the large sum of 42s. in one year, indicating that there were a fair number of oaks in the park. Over the next few years there was no income from pannage, presumably because acorn crops (mast years) are by their nature intermittent. Four pounds was received from the sale of timber, coppice and branchwood from Lyndor Wood on the east bank of the Wye in 1445.

Expenses for maintaining boundaries included 4s. to John Bennet 'for enclosing meadows including the lord's meadow, the lord's garden and Fry meadow by custom'. Bennet and his associates were also busy 'making and repairing the pale around the park in the places where it is broken down'. For reasons unspecified 'John Gervaise was hired to construct a pit in the lords park'.

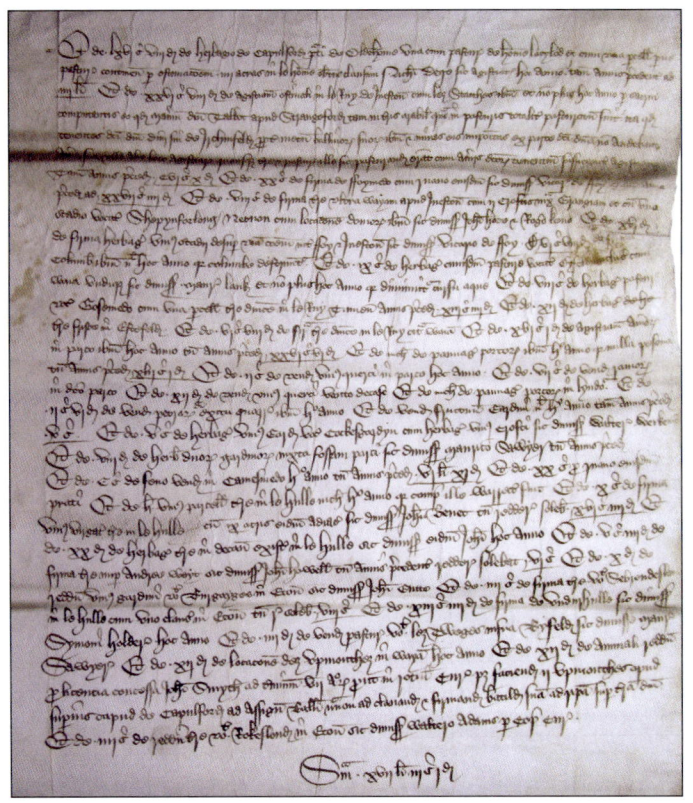

Bailiff's accounts for Eaton Tregoz, 1442-5

The water mill, with its associated weirs and fisheries, was leased for £8 a year to Henry Milward. The right to use fish and eel traps along the river earned the lord 2s. John Smyth paid 12d. a year for a seven-year license to make two 'upmouths above the head of Capulford as directed by the steward' and had to keep the lord's boat in good repair. The upmouths were woven funnel-shaped traps placed in favoured locations, in this case somewhere below Under-hill Farm, Foy.

The leats, weirs and mill ponds were in constant need of repair and rebuilding. Richard Wild was paid '2s. 2d. for mending the wall of the mill pond' and 'diverse labourers' were hired to place 'block wood to shore up weirs'. 'Transporting wood to strengthen and repair the mill and weirs' required a team of 6 oxen with 2 men and their servants working for 22 days. Then there was 'repairing the water course of the main weir as far as Inston'. In 1445 a new bank was being constructed and osiers (thin willow stems) were cut to make 'welez' to protect one of the main weirs. These may have been a kind of woven structure to shore up the banks, which would then take root to make a living bank underpinning the weir. There were also 'Two iron hooks' used in some way to control the weir. The greatest single item of expense in the accounts was £5 1s. in 1426 for 'making a mill from new as ordered by John Abraham, Thomas More the lords supervisor'.

The maintenance and repair of buildings and barns make a regular appearance in the accounts costing 33s. 6d. in 1422: 'two masons to repair the walls of the barn per 4 days each per day 5d.; 3s. 4d.', '2 dozen ridge tiles bought for the said barn 3d.' and Thomas Tiler of Ross hired for 'tiling the barn and other places as directed'. Building material was recycled from buildings which were beyond repair, so David Philips was paid 8d. for 'dismantling tiles from a house'. The manor had its own quarry and regularly sold stone and tiles – for example '12d. from the sale of cart-loads of stone tiles and round stones'.

Finally the account includes the costs of the administration with wages of the auditor being 60s. 8d. in 1446, expenses of the bailiffs attending the court of the Hundred of Greytree 5s., land measurement 9d., paper and parchment for court roles 13d., and wages of the scribes writing the accounts: 3s. 4d.[16]

Court Rolls

These were the records of the manorial court that had legal control over tenants, such as deciding succession to tenancy, fining for transgressions, setting rents and dues, commissioning inquiries, and upholding the 'custom of the manor'. The court controlled many aspects of farming such as the way the common fields were managed. It also levied fines for a range of misdemeanours; these fines were an important source of revenue for the manor. The proceedings of the manorial court provide a potential rich source of information about the tenants and ordinary villagers of the manor. The manor of Brampton Abbots was a possession of Gloucester Abbey prior to the Conquest, and remained in their ownership until the Dissolution. Entries in the court rolls between 1499 and 1518 include the following.

John Beynesham and William Vaughan, who had allowed timbers of their roofs, barns and houses to deteriorate, were ordered to repair them by the next court or forfeit 3s. 4d. Thomas a Brege and John Vaughan both sublet to others without permission, and had to get rid of their tenants. The court regulated the numbers and types of livestock that tenants could turn out on the common pastures, and were ordered to 'close up their land' between the common fields of Ox Rye and Cow Rye from the Feast of St. Trinity (the 8th Sunday after Easter) and to 'close' all sown fields until the Feast of Annunciation (25 March).

In 1504 Thomas Belamy was fined 2d. for putting more than his allocation of 4 oxen, 2 cows, 30 sheep and 6 pigs on the common meadows, while Catherine Shepherd was ordered not to put out more than 100 sheep and 16 pigs. The presence of pigs, normally associated with rooting around in rough ground or woodland, is surprising in the context of common meadows; presumably the Brampton Abbotts pigs would have been ringed and well controlled.

In 1513 Thomas Gryffiths, Walter Baton, and William Parker were threatened with a fine of 40d. because they sublet their allocation of the common or meadow 'to strangers' (meaning people outside the manor), and 'Thomas Gryffiths forfeited his penalty of 40d. because he had put piglets on the meadow more than he is allowed'. 'Tenants who have hedges and ditches around the Rise must make them good by St. Michael [29 September]', all 'tenants who have hedges leading from Whitbroke to Yarns Hill [near Monks Grove] make them well and sufficiently stockproof by Christmas', and 'Thomas Madok has not cleaned out his ditch, therefore he must do so by 1 August on penalty of 3s. 4d.'

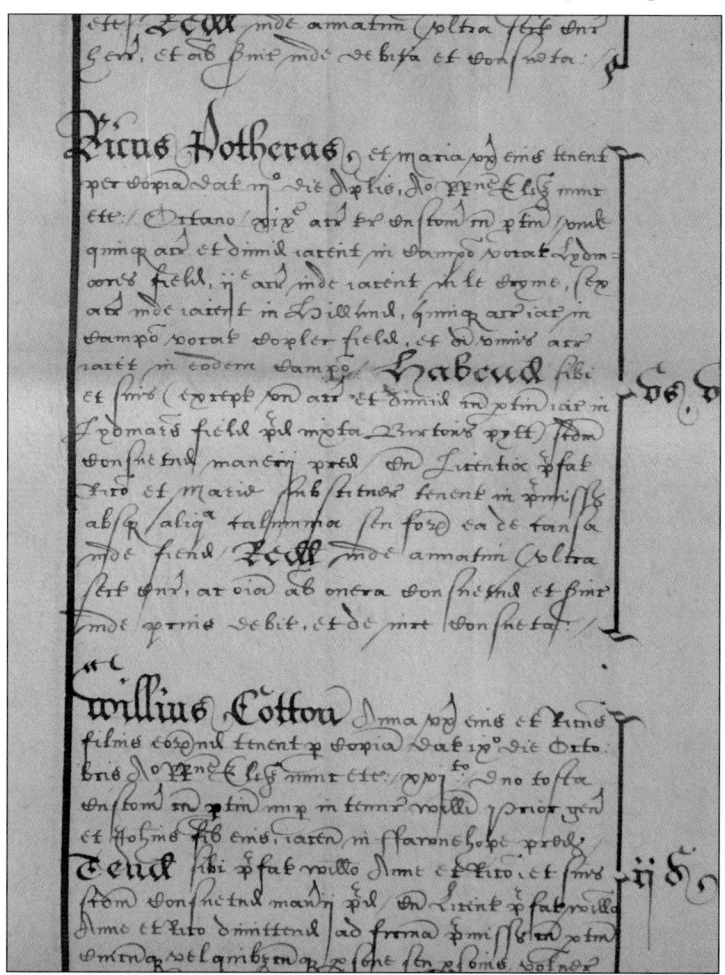

Part of the Fownhope Court Roll for 1589

Also recorded in these court proceedings are details of the expenses of the Abbey's steward and 'cellarer' in charge of provisions; both would have travelled from Gloucester. Their bread cost 10d., ale 12d., game meat 4d., butter and cheese 6d., eggs 3½d., salted fish 2d., fresh fish 12d., salted meat 2½d., and provisions for their horses 4d. A total of 4s. 7½d.[17]

In 1589 the Earl of Essex ordered an inquiry into his manor at Fownhope. All his tenants, their land, the type of leasehold, and their rents and dues they owed were detailed in the court rolls. By this date the land was not farmed by the Earl – not even indirectly – but was all let. The main residence of the manor, Fownhope Court, formerly the demesne farm, had 507 acres of land which included the remains of the medieval Fownhope Park which was leased to Thomas Lechmere of Hanley Castle.

The second largest of these tenants was the 'Vicars Choral of the Cathedral church of Hereford' who farmed 240 acres. The total acreage of the manor recorded in the court survey was 2,979 acres, very similar to the 3,081 acres of the modern parish of Fownhope.[18]

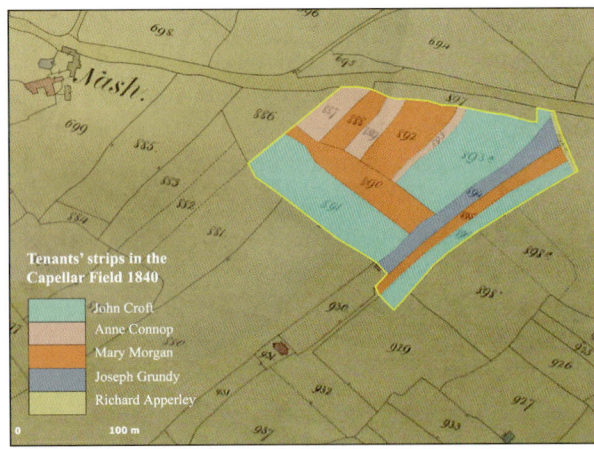

Capler Fields on the Fownhope Tithe Map of 1843

Tenants' strips in the Capellar Field 1840
- John Croft
- Anne Connop
- Mary Morgan
- Joseph Grundy
- Richard Apperley

The inquiry recorded place and field names, many of which have persisted to this day. Tenant holdings were often scattered throughout the parish, Richard Potheras had '19 acres of which 5½ are in the field called Lydmoores, 2 in Le Cryme, 6 in Hillend, 5½ in Capler field'. Some arable fields were farmed in long strips each one occupied by a different tenant. John Kydley had, amongst his other lands, '1 selion in Lydmores' where the medieval word 'selion' refers to a single ridge of arable in a common field. The Lydmores Field was farmed by seven different tenants. Capler field was another open field with strips and farmed by 5 tenants. These two open fields survived to the 1843 tithe map which shows them divided into strips. [19]

Leases

In Foy all tenants were required to take half of their arable land out of production, and this was written into their leases from 1644. For example, James Collins, who farmed at the Park Farm, 'shall not plough up any more than one half of the arable but suffer the other half to lye old and untilled for pasture and shall there spend all the fodder that shall be raised upon the premises'. Grazing livestock on land taken out of production and feeding them vegetation from elsewhere replenished soil nutrients lost by arable cropping so optimising the natural resources within the manor.

Each lease also defined the right to graze livestock in the manor's common meadow known as the Cames, located on the banks of the Wye. After harvesting the hay, the flush of new grass growth in late summer was known as the 'aftermath'. Cames Meadow was a large, undivided field, and the amount of grazing allocated to each tenant in the manor was given on basis of the number of animals that could graze. John Collins was entitled to a 'parcel of meadow lying in Cames meadow containing 6 days math' and John Cooke on the much smaller holding called Becknoll was allocated '2 days math'. Such aftermath grazing recycled nutrients into the meadow which helped ensure a strong growth of hay the following year.[20] This practice was maintained throughout the 17th century as recorded in a 1690 lease to the widow Susan Apperley of 13 acres of arable in the Hill Field which allowed '2 days math of meadow ground lying in a meadow called Crims Meadow'.[21]

Valuations and Inventories

A valuation and inventory was made by the Scudamores in 1739 of a property in Ballingham occupied by a Mr. Rogers. In his hall was a 'great table', in two rooms there were 'tapestry hangings', shelves in the pantry and dairy, and there was a 'stone cider mill of 10 foot diameter with a runner and two presses. His stock on the farm consisted of 14 oxen, 5 bullocks, 14 cows, 18 heifers, 8 Welsh cattle, 360 sheep, 40 pigs and 24 horses including yearlings, harness horses, and a stallion known as a 'stone horse'. Also recorded were '600 bushells of wheat supposed to be in the three ricks, 300 bushells of more wheat threshed in the house and barn, 500 bushells of barley or there abouts, 300 bushells of oats, 200 bushells beans and peas, seed clover, casks of all sorts'. The total value of all his possessions came to £775 5s.[22]

Sale Particulars

These usually provide detailed information of a property and its land. An early printed example dates from 1827 of Tresseck and Biblett Farms at Hoarwithy. At the Green Dragon Hotel in Hereford, the estate was offered for sale by auction as a 'convenient Farm House, with necessary Outbuildings; also situate on the

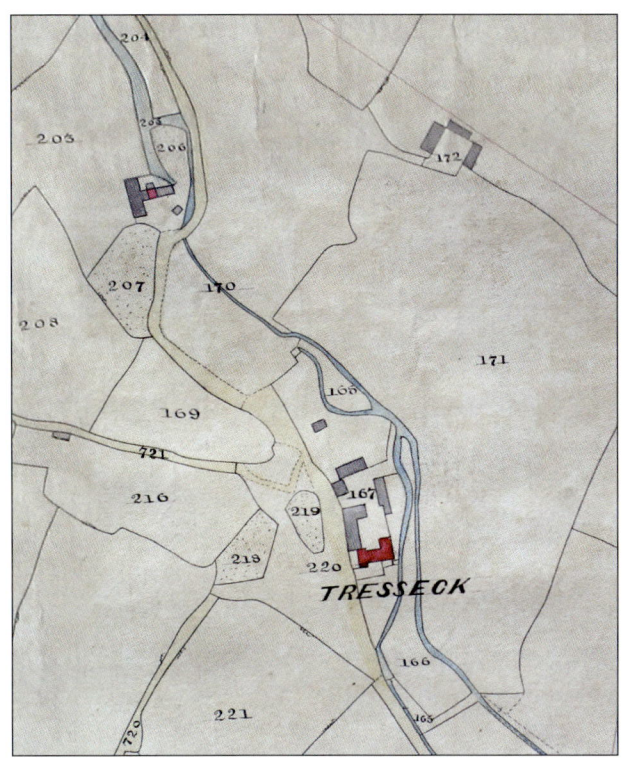

1842. Tresseck on the Hentland Tithe map

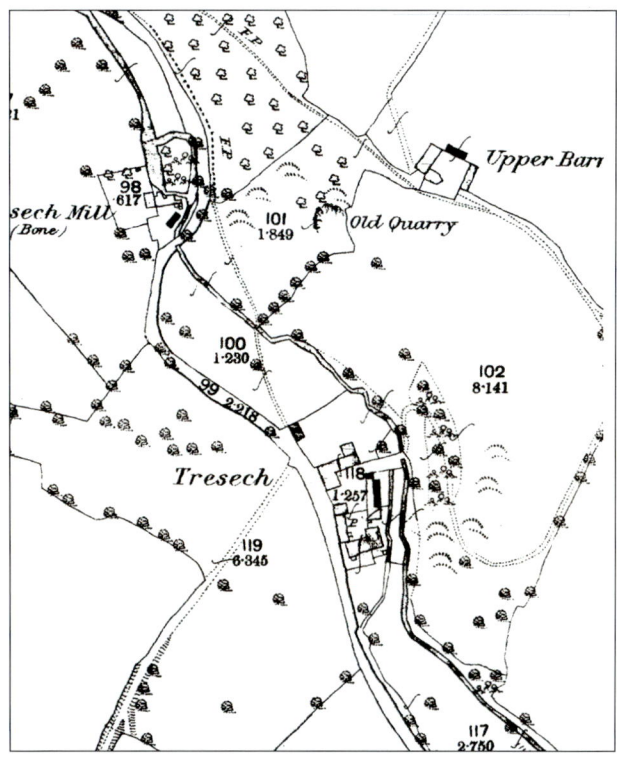

1888. Tresseck on the Ordnance Survey map

1946. Tresseck aerial photograph

2002. Tresseck aerial photograph

Tresseck Farm in Hoarwithy, 2007

banks of the river Wye, with 188a. 1r. 33p. of extremely rich and productive Arable, Meadow, Pasture, Orcharding and Woodland'. William Dobson was the tenant farmer employing workmen who lived in the 'Two Cottages and Gardens', and the 'House, Garden and Fold' at the Biblett were included in the sale.[23] The farm was later acquired by Robert Bamford Esq., an absentee landlord from Gloucestershire, who sold Tresseck in 1910 with 193 acres. There was another attempted sale in 1939, but the attractive house with dining and drawing rooms, kitchens, and 7 bedrooms together with barns, sheds, a granary and its 193 acreage did not sell. It was sold in 1943 for £4,500 to the Governors of Guy's Hospital and resold to the present owner after the war.[24]

Tithe Surveys

These mid-19th-century surveys produced the first detailed land use maps and showed that the balance of livestock and arable farming had shifted towards arable. In Fownhope, 49% of its farmland was arable, 37% grassland and 14% orchard, but by the end of the 19th century much of the previous arable had returned to grass. The First World War stimulated a brief rise in arable production, but by the end of the mid 1930s Herefordshire had the highest proportion of grassland probably since Tudor times. In the early 1940s Fownhope farmland was 22% arable, 68% grassland and 11% orchard.

Second World War National Farm Surveys

These surveys were carried out throughout the country in 1941 to target land that could be brought into arable production for the war effort. The surveys are now in the public domain and the data for Brampton Abbotts has been analysed and is tabulated on the opposite page:[25]

Land use in acres	Netherton	Pigeon House	Townsend	Overton	Gatsford
Wheat	12	16	16	11	23
Barley	52	22.5	94	104	16
Oats, rye etc	14	15	39	32	23
Potatoes	7	5	9	8	3
Turnips/Swede/Mangolds	12	5	20	26	8
Other crops		10	8	31	2
Grass (in rotation)	84		116	12	8
Grass (permanent)	112	84.5	204	148	64
Livestock in head					
Horses (working)	5	7	6	9	4
Cattle	158	47	133	118	33
Sheep	415	160	407	318	173
Pigs	27	2	70	30	2
Fowls	400	89	450	30	
Ducks		23			

Agricultural census returns for farms in Brampton Abbotts, 1941

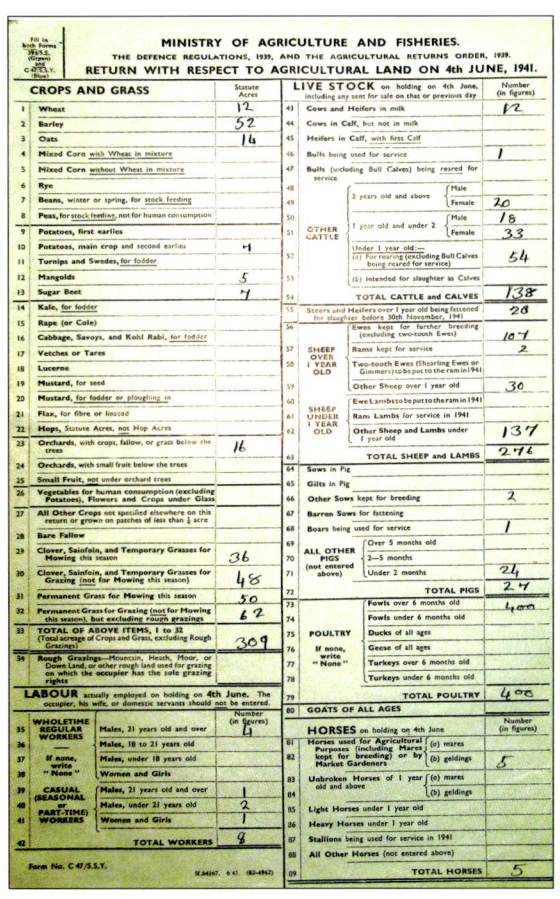

1941 census for Netherton Farm

Brampton Abbotts c.1940

The last cart horse at Brampton Abbotts

Brampton Abbotts c.1940

Land size in year	1589	1941
Less than 5 acres	28	22
5 to 10 acres	11	6
10 to 25 acres	6	10
25 to 50 acres	5	3
50 to 100 acres	6	6
Over 100 acres	6	6
Total	**62**	**53**

Number of land holdings by size in Fownhope

Fownhope was also analysed and a comparison of the information from the Elizabethan 1589 inquiry and the 1941 survey is of some interest. Over the course of three and a half centuries there has been little change in the number of farms and their sizes.

What is striking about the results of the war time survey for Fownhope farms is the variety of produce on very small holdings. Nineteen farms had pigs, many on very small holdings, the largest number being 24 on the Rise Farm. Almost every farm had chickens which were clearly not intensive, as the highest number kept on any farm was at Nash Farm with 230. 23 farms kept cattle extensively reared in small herds, the largest number of 79 being at the Tump Farm which also had the largest number of sheep – 234. Five farms had dairy units and goats, and most smallholdings had at least one cow. Every farm in Fownhope over 30 acres kept at least one working horse with six recorded at the 260 acre Tump Farm. On average there were 41 acres of farmland per horse. Tractors were being used on five of the bigger farms. The arable grew wheat, barley and oats, with root crops for winter livestock feeding. Orchards were listed on almost every farm. This pattern of self-reliant traditional mixed farming had been perfected over many centuries and was little changed since Elizabethan times.[26]

Farm Histories

The LOWV team, with the help of volunteers, researched the history and surveyed three farms in the project area. The documents, which included deeds, sale particulars, maps and plans, have produced some fascinating facts about farming and land use throughout the centuries, and shows how farms and farmland have developed and survived to form important features in the landscape of today.

Caradoc, Sellack

The de la More family were at 'Caricradok' from 1281, and in 1308 the property consisted of a messuage, garden, dovecote, 2 ploughlands of 80 acres each, pastures and woodland. During the 1440s the Abrahalls acquired 'Carrycradok', possibly through marriage, and were paying wool tithes in 1568. During the next decade 'Carycradock' was sold to Richard Mynors as an estate consisting of a messuage, toft, 2 gardens, 40 acres of land, 50 acres of meadow, 600 acres of pasture, and 120 acres of wood.

From the records it appears that John Abrahall retained an interest in the property, for in 1594 he sold

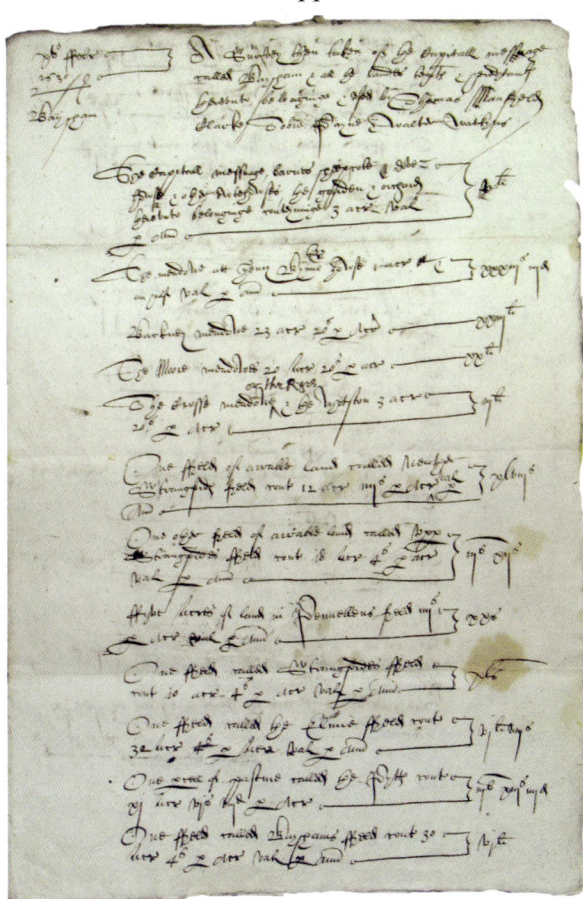

Baysham survey, 1630

'Cary Craddock' to Rowland Scudamore, the brother of Sir John Scudamore of Holme Lacy. Rowland remodelled Caradoc before his death in 1630, when an almost illegible inventory was made describing the newly-built mansion consisting of a hall, great parlour, little parlour, cellar, dairy, at least eight bed chambers, servants quarters, kitchen, an old hall, and a mill housing cider. Part of the earlier house still stood, containing a kitchen, hall and chamber, together with a barn.

In one of the barns there were 120 bushels of rye, 24 loads of hay, rye on the ground, 4 pigs, and 16 oxen, and in the Canons Barn by the church there were 80 bushels of rye, and 80 bushels of barley worth 4s. a bushel. Also recorded on the premises were 250 bushels of rye, 250 bushels of barley, 40 bushels of oats, 380 sheep, 25 loads of hay, several wains, harrows and assorted farming implements. [27] His 426 acres of meadows, fields, woods, orchards and gardens at Baysham were surveyed and valued at £168 7s. 4d., which included two houses with gardens and the 'capital messuage, barns, sheepcot, dovehouse and other outhouses'.[28]

After Rowland's death 'Cradocke' continued to be owned by the Scudamores, and during the late 17th and early 18th centuries the property was occupied by various members of the Scudamore family until John Scudamore of Cradock died in 1714. The estate then passed to his elder brother the third Viscount Scudamore, who died two years later leaving Cradock to his wife's father Lord Digby. Although Scudamore's wife was re-married to William Dew, they were allowed to remain at 'Cradock'.

The Dews leased the Caradoc estate of 322 acres from the Digbys until 1863 when it was advertised for sale and purchased by Elisha Caddick, of Leadon Court, who dramatically altered the mansion, and added the farmhouse, lodge and drive. Caddick's son inherited the estate with its 350 acres, and by 1910

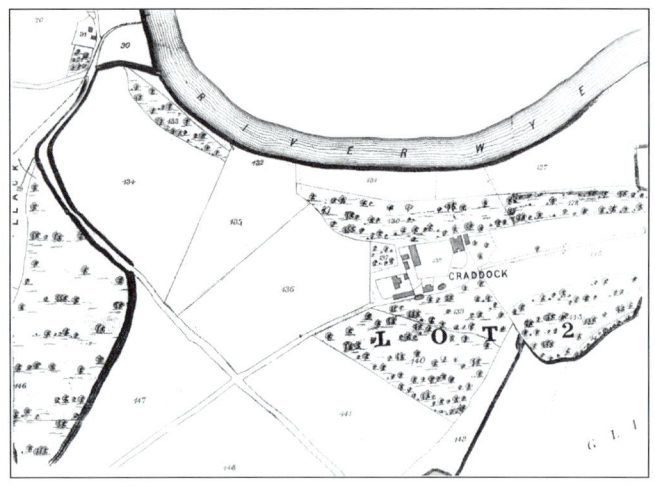

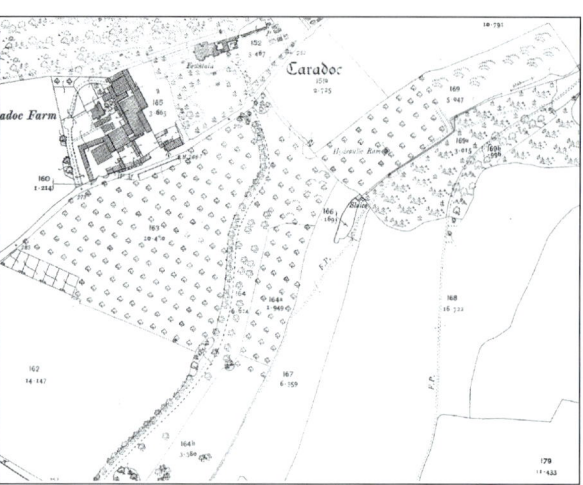

The plan of the Caradoc Estate from the 1863 sale catalogue

The 1904 Ordnance Survey showing Caradoc when it was put up for sale by the son of Elisha Caddick

Caradoc Estate
Top left: The farm house
Top right: The stable yard
Left: Barn interior

it had been purchased by Colonel Heyward. After the death of the Heywoods the property passed to their married daughter, a race horse trainer, and in 1978 it was sold to another trainer who kept the farm and the estate, but sold the mansion. It was between these sales that a fire gutted the building in 1986. The farm was sold in 1997 with 707 acres and with all facilities for training race horses and the mansion is currently being restored.[29]

Upper Pengethley, Sellack

The name Pengethley dates from a reference in the Bishop's Registers of 1334, although little is known of its early history. In the 1560s the estate passed from the Pychards to Browne who sold it to Edward Powell in 1583. Before the sale, a detailed survey was made of the 'seyte of the sayde Mannor Edyfyed with the Hall, Parlor, Buttery, Kytchyne and Chambers and all other houses, Garnars, Barnes and Stables necessary with the yards, Orchards, Gardyns', and an estate containing 247 acres.

In 1716 the estate included 'the Vineyard lying above the Barn next the Green' and fields, closes, groves and woods with names describing their use, such as the Perry Field, High Tree Field, Grove Field, the Ewe Pasture, the Brick Close, the Long Close, the Eighteen Acres, the Pitt Field, Calves Close, the Cow Lease, the Little Meadow, and Pengethley Coppice.

By 1740 the estate had been divided into three farms called Pengethley, Dason and the Grove, which were leased from Thomas Symonds of Pengethley to William Donne. He had the use of:

> Cellars, Store Rooms, Chambers and appurtenances, the Outhouses and Buildings, the Oxhouse, the Cowhouse and Stable thereto adjoining the Rye Barn, the Pease Barn, the Barley Barn, the Wainhouse and Fold and Rickyard all lying together upon the Green at Pengethley, the Great Sheepcot with the Tallets over it, the Granary lying over the Coachhouse and also over the adjoining Cellar of the said Thomas Symonds, the little Brick Stable and the Poultry House.

The land at Pengethley included 'Orchard on the Green and 10 acres of 'Vicar's Glebe' and totalled 279 acres of which 232 were arable.

Upper Pengethley Farm was traditionally known to have been built as a Dower House, possibly for Penelope, co-heir of the estate, who married Thomas Symonds. He died in 1760 but she outlived him by

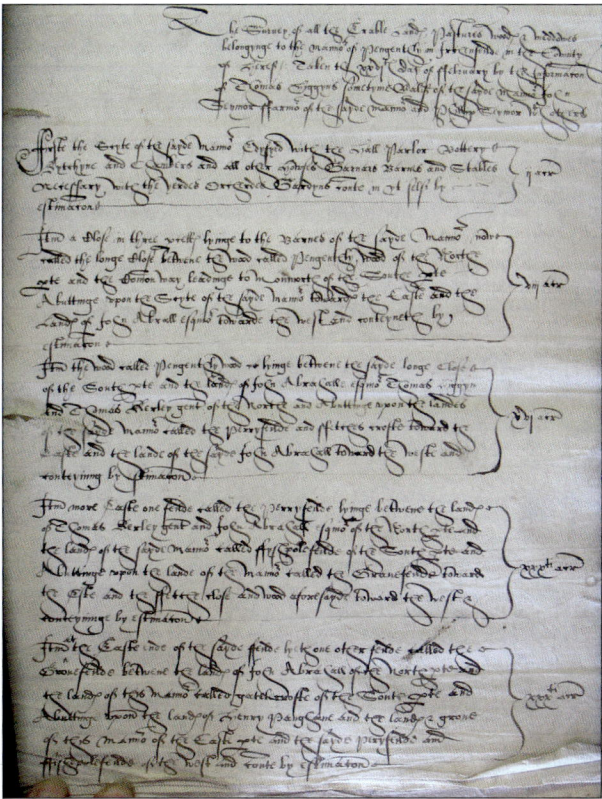

Pengethley. Top: Farmhouse; Bottom: Converted barn   *Pengethley survey, 1580*

eleven years and died at the age of eighty. The farmhouse, with its cellar, two storeys and attic, dates from the 18th century when James Partridge was the tenant from 1783 until his death in 1817. James Matthews then occupied the house and farmed 207 acres of arable, orchard and pasture, and was followed by William Prosser in 1851 and Richard Scudamore in 1877, when another survey recorded that Pengethley Farm consisted of 230 acres of pasture, wood, arable, orchard, and meadow.

The 1901 Census provides information about the family living at Upper Pengethley. The farmer was a 65 year old widower called John Miles, who employed his son Charles, a shepherd, and a waggoner on the farm, and two servants in the house. Miss Caroline E. Symonds at 35 was the head of the Pengethley estate living at the mansion with her mother and numerous servants. From 1925 Harold Partridge took over the tenancy of Upper Pengethley Farm as recorded by his son Roger in the project's oral history:[30]

This place became vacant in 1925, so father came here then. He came from Walsall; he was an accountant then a bank clerk. He fancied farming, he got a bit of tuition when he was a lad; he went to Canada just before the First World War – a lot of boys were going out there then. He went out, war broke out, he joined the Canadian army and came back in the First World War. Then he decided to get a bit more tuition and he eventually took the tenancy of this farm in 1925.

The estate was sold in 1951 – it was owned by the Symonds family. Miss Symonds, the last survivor, died in the war, in 1944, the estate went to a niece who sold it in 1951. The sitting tenants (my father was a sitting tenant) bought it, there were no other bids and my neighbour was the same. The several cottages scattered around were sold too, mostly to tenants, some went for £100. In those days farmers didn't borrow much, there was no such thing as the agricultural mortgage association and banks were very reluctant to lend much money in 1950. But a couple of his family put up a bit and they managed to buy it. Land prices then were around £100 per acre though he got it a lot cheaper than that. Cottages had no value much.

The farm consists of arable fields plus some parkland and pasture fields. The area of the farm has changed slightly because we have a bit more parkland. We have one field in Hentland, the rest is in Sellack, land is around the farm building, plus the parkland. We used to rent 50 acres and a couple of years ago we took on more, now it is 100 acres. This belongs to the National Trust. It was a mixed farm, which was typical of most farms. Apart from arable most farms had dairy or beef and a flock of sheep and pigs.

Since the farming revolution they took up hedges, panned the land. We are making amends lately in the Countryside Stewardship Scheme. My son is very keen on the scheme We have a lot of headlands now under permanent grass. We have planted new hedges to be kept bird friendly and we get a bit of payment for it. But it is reversing a trend that began after the war when no one took any notice of conservation measures until the 1980s.

Roger Partridge

Caplor Farm, Fownhope

In 1648 Edward Andrews released his claim of Caplor Farm, which was left to James Oswald in 1658, and later it was occupied by the Powell family. In 1758 John Evans, a canon at Hereford Cathedral, acquired the property, and after his death in 1772 his wife and children inherited his estates including the farm and his 'Books, Quarto Bible and Harpsichord'. His widow sold Caplor Farm to her tenant John Powell for £1,200 in 1784. John Powell died in 1797 and left a will with many bequests to his wife and family including 'my Estate called Caplor and the Camp with the Lands and premises ... one of the best Hogsheads of Cyder produced from my Estate called Buckenhill' and three dwellings 'known by the name of Tayler's, Addis's and Tandy's'.

Caplor Farm
Above: The Farmhouse
Right: The Cider Mill

John Powell's son, Francis, inherited the farm, but lived at How Caple leaving the farming of Caplor to his son John. After Francis died in 1841, his son John inherited 'Capela together with Cidermill, ½ acre in Woolhope ... also Rise with cidermill and other lands'. 'Capellar Farm' in 1843 consisted of 87 acres, but was heavily mortgaged and continued to be owned by the Powell family.

After the death of John Powell in 1896, it seemed inevitable that his 'Widow Hannah' sold Caplor with its 87 acres of pasture, orchard, arable and woodland to William Kingsbury in 1918. Within four years the farm passed to Elizabeth Greenow and was sold to Morgan T. Williams in 1922. The sale particulars describe the farm as having 87 acres of orchard, arable, pasture and wood with a farmhouse containing five bedrooms, a sitting room and a cellar. The outbuildings included a barn, granary, stables and a cider mill. Unfortunately the barn was burnt down in 1949, but the cider mill has survived. Since 1922 the holding has been farmed by the Williams family who possess a bundle of fascinating deeds, maps and notes that together with documents at the Hereford Record Office enabled its history to be traced.[31]

The barn in 1929, before it was burnt down in 1949

Village Growth and Development

The growth and development of the selected villages of Bridstow, Fownhope, Holme Lacy, King's Caple and Hoarwithy (in Hentland) can be appreciated through a sequence of maps and aerial photographs dating from the early 19th to the 21st century. Although there has been a significant expansion of housing during the 20th century the population has remained fairly constant since the mid 19th century apart from Bridstow and Hentland. In 2001 Bridstow showed an increase of 234 and Hentland a decrease of 169 which will be explained .[32]

Bridstow

1839. Copy of the Tithe Map showing field names

The parish and village of Bridstow in 1851 was described as being 'situated on the right bank of the river Wye, at the junction of the old and new roads to Hereford', and Wilton was 'a hamlet and neat village in this parish, situated on the right side of the river'.[33] The major landowners at this date were the Governors of Guy's Hospital who were lords of the manor and owned Wilton Castle. In 1951 the parish council recorded 'the evidence of a growing residential district on the rising ground overlooking Wilton and the River Wye. Houses of pleasing appearance, which harmonise with the local beauty, have been erected in Upper and Lower Bannut Tree Lane, Benhall lane, Hoarwithy Road and other places'. The Ross Rural District Council, through the efforts of the parish council, found sites to build four new houses at Green Gates and 24 semi-detached houses at Claytons.[34] In 1961 the Guy's Hospital estate was sold and the castle passed into private ownership.[35] Towards the end of the 20th century new houses were built and barns were converted providing more dwellings for an expanding population.

The maps show how the roads through Bridstow have been dramatically altered; old roads have been abandoned and new roads added. In 1960 the A40 became a dual-carriageway leading from a newly-constructed roundabout at Wilton to join the new Ross Spur Road linking the A40 with the motorway system. Further road improvements took place in 1985 which led to the downgrading of the main road through Wilton and the refurbishment of Wilton bridge in 1993.

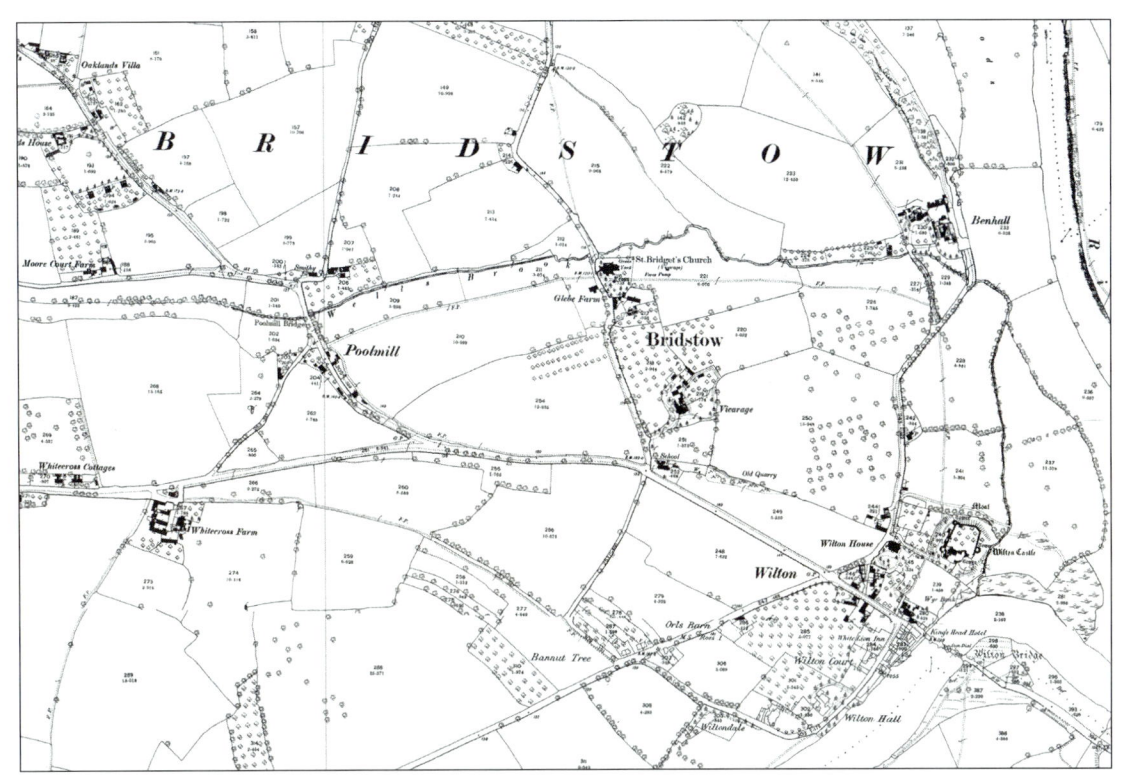

1888 1st edition Ordnance Survey 25 inch to the mile map

2002 Aerial Photograph

Fownhope

1843 Tithe Map

Fownhope is one of the larger and more populated parishes in the Wye Valley. In the mid 19th century the population of just over 1,000 were living in a self-sufficient community with employment in the local trades and industries. After 1730 the main road was improved by the Hereford Turnpike Trust from Gloucester to Hereford, and the river was navigable until the opening of the railway in 1855. In 1858 access to the Holme Lacy Railway Station was provided by a bridge that replaced the former ferry crossing at Even Pits. Guarding the entrance to the toll bridge were two inns – the Anchor and the Lucks All – which were both associated with the river. The Anchor remained open until 1972 when it was demolished to improve access to the bridge when it was rebuilt in 1973. The Lucks All had already closed, but the building remains, its former wharf now being used for canoe launching from the Lucks All Caravan Park.

Several remote cottages on Common Hill were abandoned, and a few awkwardly placed homes in the main street were demolished in the early 20th century. The Lechmere's Fownhope estate of 397 acres were offered for sale in 1921; the estate included a brick-built house, 'The Scotch Firs', with a cider mill and orchard, and the Manor Farm with its outbuildings and 65 acres of land, but appears not to have been sold until the 1960s.[36] The Scotch Firs became a housing estate of 48 dwellings, and part of Manor Farm formed Church Croft and Nover Wood Drive in the early 1970s. The impressive Fownhope Court has been converted into separate units with houses built in its grounds.

Other smaller estates have since been built and infilling has taken place within the village envelope to extend the housing in Fownhope, which is well served by a school, medical centre, memorial hall, two pubs, a general stores, a butcher's shop, a leisure centre and the church of St. Mary's. Despite this expansion of the village since the 1960s the population was only 963 in 2001 compared with 1004 in 1841. This reflects a changing lifestyle of single occupancy and a boundary change in 1986 when 130 people were transferred into Mordiford parish.[37]

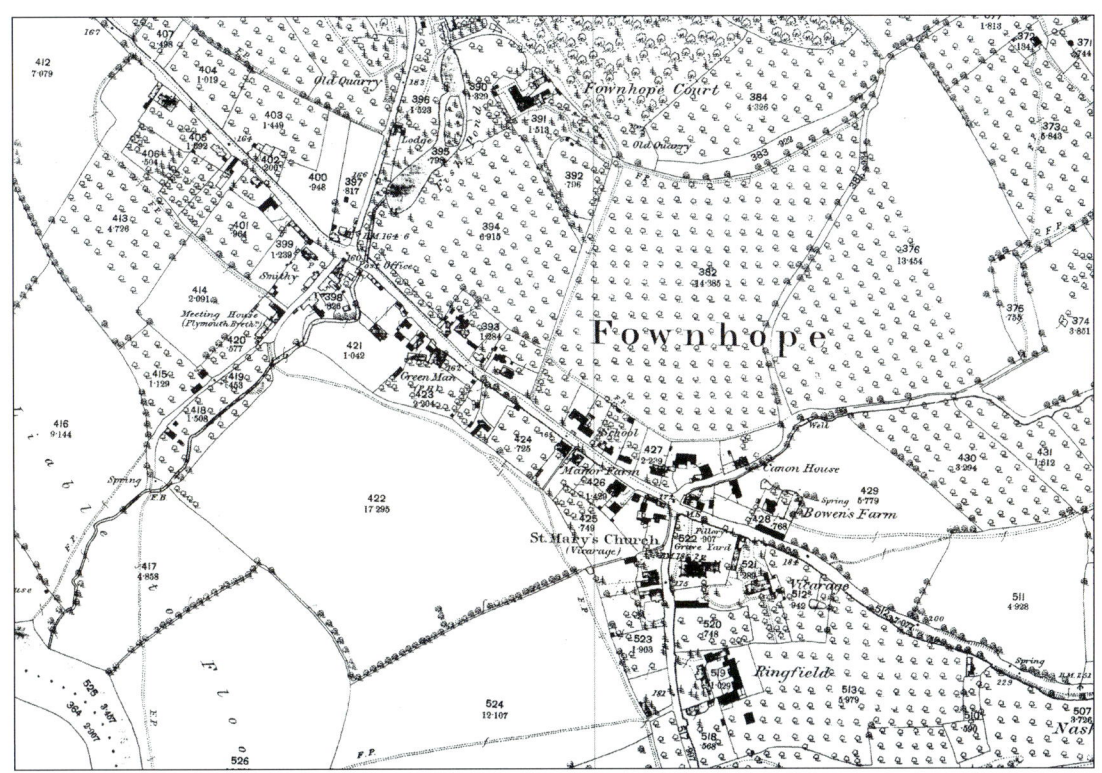

1888 1st edition Ordnance Survey 25 inch to the mile map

2002 Aerial Photograph

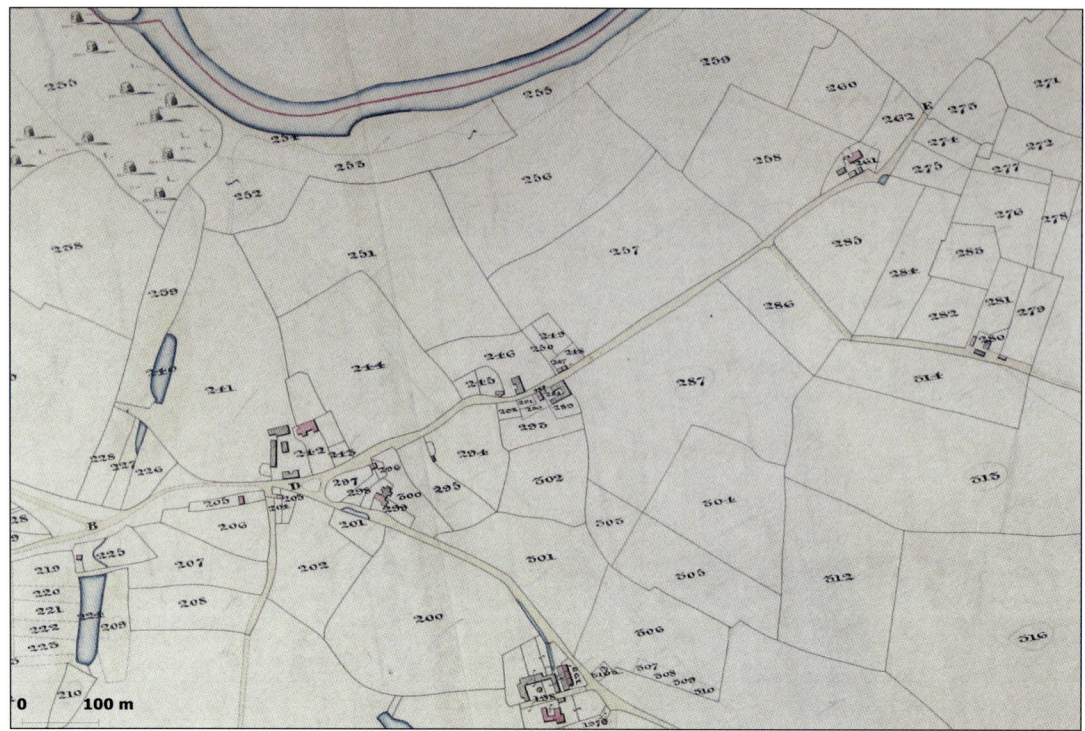

1840 Tithe Map

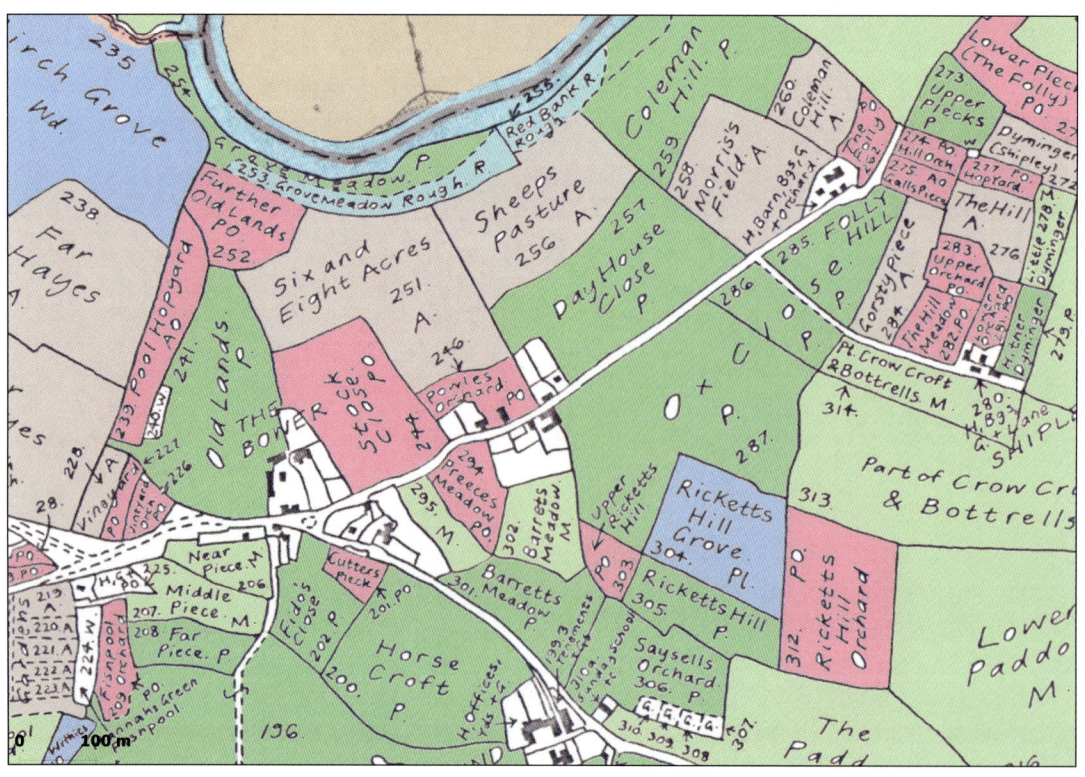

1840 Copy of the Tithe Map with field names

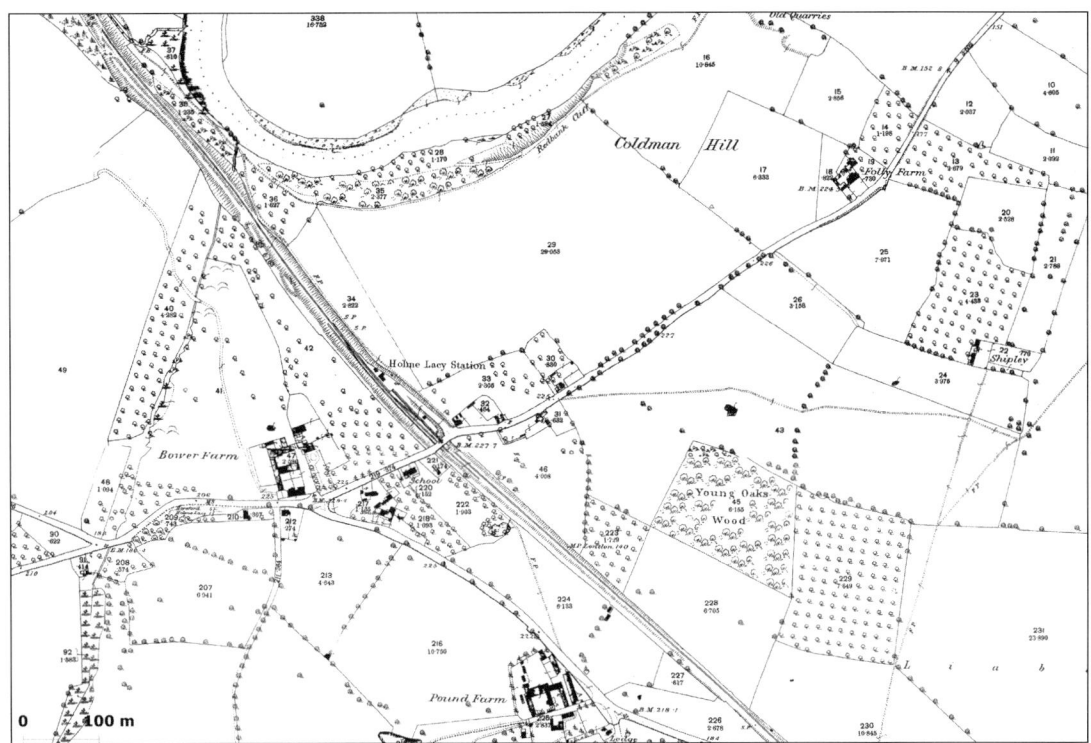

1888 1st edition Ordnance Survey 25 inch to the mile map

Although a fairly large parish, Holme Lacy has recorded a low population since its figure of 369 in the mid 19th century. 'Holme Lacy House, the seat of Sir E. F. Scudamore Stanhope, Bart., is a noble mansion surrounded by a fine park'. A transformation of the landscape began to take place in the 1850s with road and rail developments. The Hereford, Ross and Gloucester Railway went through the parish, a road was constructed from Folly Farm to the riverside, and the Holme Lacy bridge was erected.

In July 1909 'Holme Lacy with about 5,056 acres' was auctioned together with its magnificent mansion house, ancient deer park, woods and plantations, agricultural holdings, cottages and village properties.[28] Not all the properties were sold until a later sale, but the change of ownership from the once powerful Scudamores to individuals did initiate a gradual change to the landscape. From 1934 the grand mansion was used as a psychiatric hospital, eventually being sold and refurbished as a hotel in 1995. A massive extension was added to provide additional accommodation and the park is being restored.

Bower Farm in 1909 was 'an important farm in the parish of Holme Lacy ... and consists of an imposing Brick, Stone and Tiled Farm House standing well away from the road'. The yard contained 'large Barns, three-stall Nag Stable, Coach House, Harness room, Cart House, Stable for Seven Horses, Piggeries. Large Implement Shed and Root Store'. This arrangement of buildings now forms the equestrian centre of Holme Lacy College, where additional buildings include an outdoor arena, and an indoor school used by the Riding for the Disabled organisation.

Since the 1909 sale the landscape in the northern part of Holme Lacy parish has been altered with ribbon development along the road leading to Holme Lacy Bridge. The college has also expanded into a large campus offering students a variety of agricultural, forestry, rural crafts, equitation and farriery courses. The college is now part of the Herefordshire College of Technology, and in recent times numerous brick and metal-clad buildings have been constructed around Bower and Pound Farms for college use.

1946 Aerial Photograph

2002 Aerial Photograph

Holme Lacy village in 1909

Holme Lacy – The Changes from Meadow to Arable

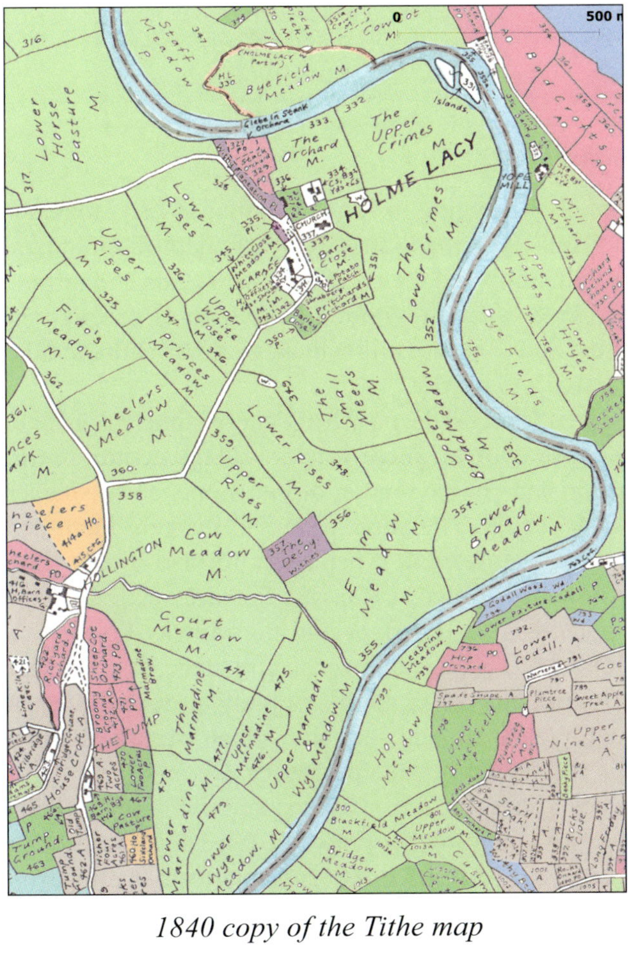

1840 copy of the Tithe map

2002 Aerial Photograph

King's Caple

1812 John Woodhouse Map

In 1812 a 'Particular of the Parish of Kings Caple ... chiefly belonging to John Woodhouse Esq.' together with a map was produced by the owner of 'Aramstone Hall'. The map (above) clearly depicts buildings, roads, field boundaries, individual trees, woods, the church, tump and the river with its islands and ferries. The river crossings were important because of King's Caple situation within a large loop of the Wye. In 1844 John Cook of Caple produced a map of 'Caple Street and Commonhill' which, together with the tithe map of 1839, shows little change since the Woodhouse map and survey.

In the 1840s King's Caple's population of 299 was spread around the parish at Pennoxstone, Poulstone, Ruxton, Penalt, Aramstone and along Caple Street near the church. There was no village centre, but in 1851 the inhabitants had a shop at Ruxton, a bread, bacon and cheese retailer at Poulstone, a dressmaker at Fish Pool, a beer retailer at Cross Trees and a national school. The population had scarcely increased by the 1870s when described as: 'a parish and small village situated in a peninsula formed by the river Wye ... From Hoarwithy the river Wye is crossed by a new iron bridge at Ruxtone ... there being no other public bridge crossing the river between Fownhope and Ross ... The river and the railway bound this parish in the shape of a horse-shoe. The church of St. John the Baptist stands on an eminence, and is a neat building with nave, chancel, porch, and square tower ... surmounted by a spire ... A pretty grove of trees on a tumulus called "Caple Tump" was formerly the scene of a festival held annually, which was attended by the inhabitants from the adjacent neighbourhood, and is still kept up by the peasantry'.[39]

At the turn of the 20th century a few cottages had been built for farm workers, and in the early 1950s a small group of council houses was built near the crossroads. In 1964 the railway ceased so the station at Fawley was later converted to a house, and in 2000 the adjacent pub closed. The most noticeable impact on the village was in the early 1970s when a development of 34 houses was built in Caple Avenue.[40] This did attract new families into the village, kept the school open and created more of a community.

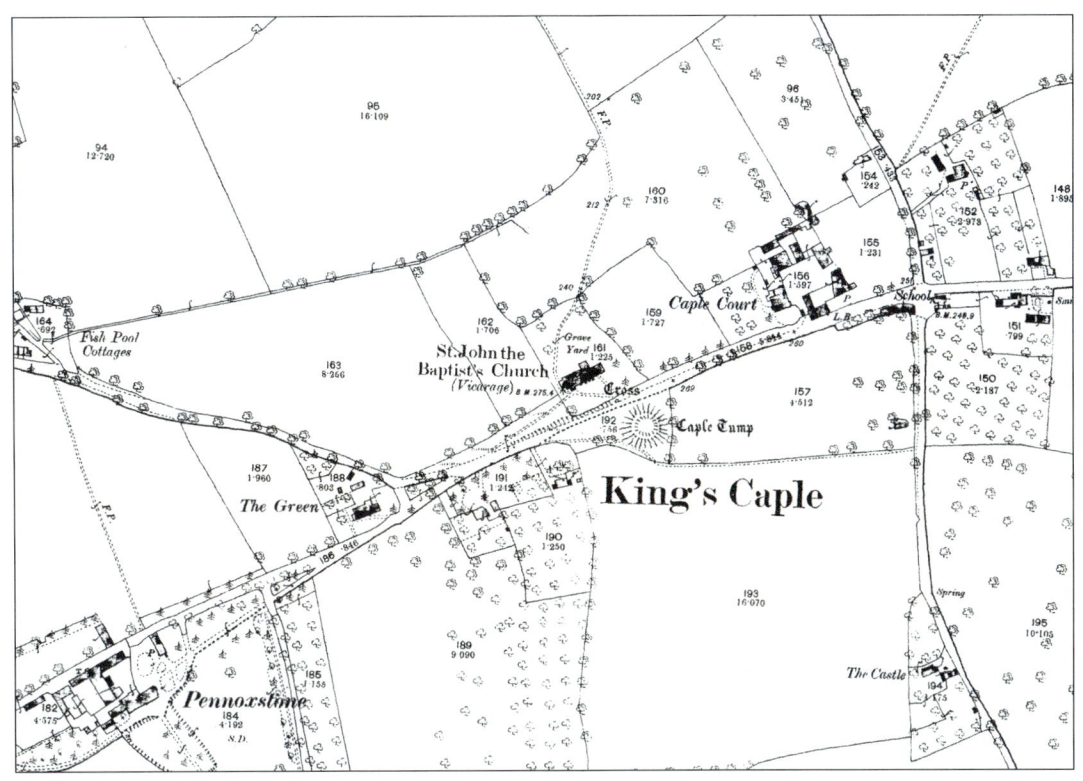

1888 1st edition Ordnance Survey 25 inch to the mile map

2002 Aerial Survey

Hoarwithy

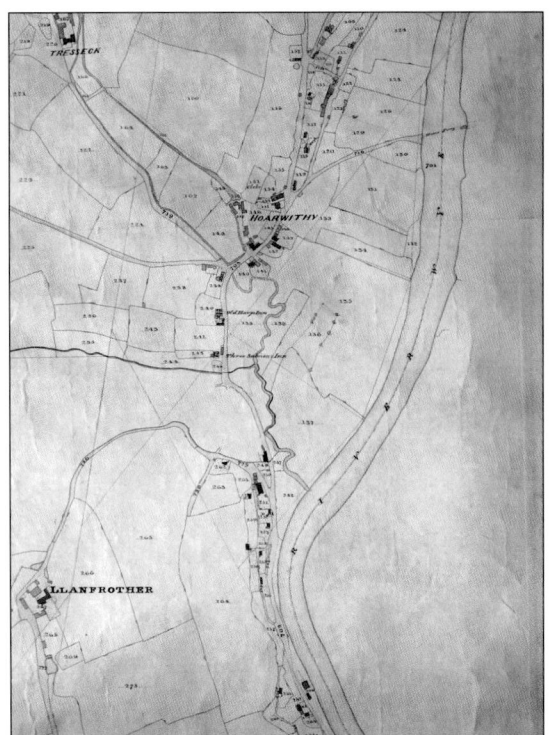

1842 Hentland Tithe Map

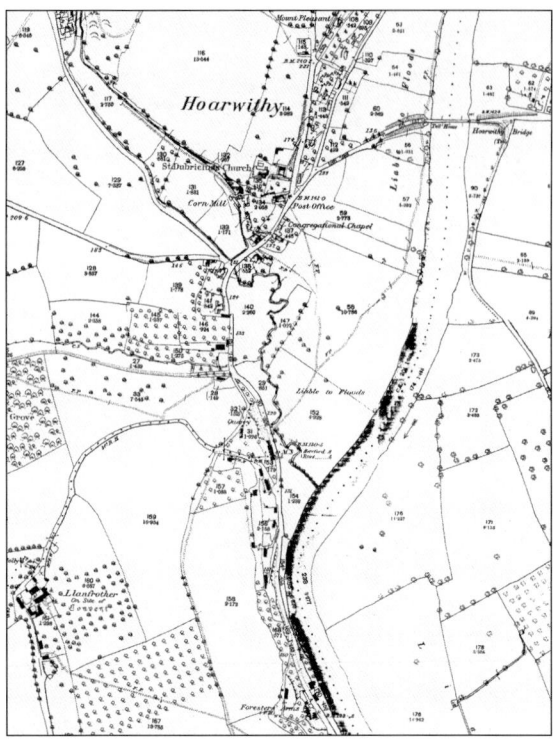

1888 Ordnance Survey 25 inch to a mile map

1946 Aerial Photograph

Hoarwithy is an attractive riverside village in the parish of Hentland. Out of a population of 612 in 1841, a third were living in Hoarwithy mainly occupying a settlement of cottages on Wye Hill. Many of these cottages have since been abandoned, and rows of two or three tenements have been incorporated into one, which accounts for the decrease of 169 shown in the 2001 census. In the mid 19th century the inhabitants of Hoarwithy were employed as agriculture labourers, carpenters, fishermen, stone masons, millers, and shopkeepers and were supplied with beer and cider from five licensed premises. The 'neat modern brick building, built in 1842' was a Chapel of Ease erected on 'an eminence overlooking the surrounding countryside'. This modest chapel was transformed during the 1880s to its present Italianate style, cleverly constructed around the earlier chapel with an additional campanile tower and cloisters. It is dedicated to St. Catherine and provides a unique landscape feature in the Wye Valley.

CHAPTER IV

Woods and Trees

by David Lovelace

In the present age woodland is seen as quite distinct from farmland, with trees forming a closed canopy and managed only occasionally. Modern legislation and policy seeks to protect woodland from change and there is an assumption that there was much more of it in the past than now. This brief study of the history of woods and trees in the project area of the Wye Valley challenges these ways of seeing things.

Early Woodland

It used to be thought that prehistoric woodland in Britain and Northern Europe was an impenetrable temperate jungle. However, it is now realised that vegetation and animals, which colonised the ground after the last ice-age, were an inter-dependent ecosystem. Populations of aurochs, the precursor to modern cattle, beavers, wild boar, deer and many other mammals reached an equilibrium with their surroundings, creating an open park-like vegetation of glades, scrub and clumps of trees preventing a continuous woodland ever forming. This is the so called 'Vera hypothesis' after the Dutch ecologist who first proposed the idea and it is consistent with what little evidence there is of the prehistoric vegetation of Herefordshire.[1] For example, hazel does not flower under a closed canopy of trees, yet its pollen is found abundantly in peat deposits from the lower Lugg Valley, which have been dated from AD 600 to before 4,500 BC. There is not yet an available pollen time-sequence for the Wye Valley, but this peat site at Wellington is just 12 kilometres upstream from the confluence of the Wye and the Lugg so should not be untypical of the Wye Valley (see next page).

The same peat analysis shows that lime trees were common in the local prehistoric woodland, but their pollen peters out around 2,000 BC and almost disappears by the Roman period.[2] This 'lime decline' is seen throughout southern Britain and is thought to have been caused by the failure of lime tree seed-lings to colonise new ground as a result of a general cooling of the climate from about 3,000 BC when Europe experienced a warm period. Since then, lime in Britain has been at the northern edge of its natural European range. Like most native trees, lime readily sends out new shoots when cut down (see next page). If a living branch or trunk of lime is in contact with the ground, perhaps having been blown down by a storm, it will also readily create roots and new shoots. Lime trees can continue growing in one place for long periods of time without ever setting seed. Where natural lime survives in present-day woodland, it is a genetic relic of these prehistoric lime populations and an indication of woodland continuity going back millennia. The wild service tree is another 'ancient woodland indicator' and like lime is found in Wye Valley woods; the presence of both tree species can be considered a kind of living fossil of the original 'wild wood'.

Lime coppice stool in Fownhope Park

The increasing number of archaeological features being found, especially from aerial photography, across Britain including the Wye Valley are an indication of the extent of human occupation dating from before the Iron Age. Settlement depends on farming and in particular farm animals which would have had an impact on whatever woodland cover there was. Two thousand years ago the Wye Valley countryside would have been settled, farmed and probably not more than a quarter wooded.[3]

Oak trees from coppice stools at West Wood, Fownhope

Domesday Woodland and Forest

William the Conqueror's manor by manor survey of 1086 includes the first systematic account of woodlands in Herefordshire. Even though the descriptions are very brief it appears that woodland was generally a minor land use in most manors. For the manor of Holme Lacy, Domesday records 'woodland ½ league long and as broad'. This is roughly 100 hectares which is 8% of the modern parish[4] – less than the current figure of 11.5%. Uniquely for Herefordshire there is another contemporary document giving more details of this woodland. In 1085 the Bishop of Hereford had granted the manor of Holme Lacy to Roger de Lacy, but reserved the right for his men from over the river at Hampton Bishop to pasture pigs in Holme Lacy's woodland and to collect fuel and timber for repairing houses on the Bishop's estates.[5] No woodland was mentioned for Fownhope, only 'waste' which was probably common grazing on the poorer soils of the manor and may or may not have had trees. Even where woodland was recorded in Domesday it would have been quite different from today.

To the west of the Wye was the old Welsh kingdom of Archenfield, which the Normans held as a separate administrative entity while respecting its Welsh customs. Half the parishes in this study, including King's Caple on the east of the Wye, were in Archenfield and their Domesday entries are less informative than those for other parishes. Domesday recorded that in Archenfield 'King Gruffydd and Breddyn laid waste this land at the time of King Edward so it is not known what it was like at this time', probably referring to the Welsh raids on Hereford in 1055.[6] It seems as if settled farming was disrupted to the extent that much of the land on the western side of Archenfield, roughly that tract of countryside bounded by Kilpeck, Holme Lacy and Kingstone, had reverted to secondary woodland by the time of the Norman invasion. There is a conspicuous blank in the distribution map of named Domesday manors just south-west of Hereford.

This was filled by the entry for the adjacent hundred of Wormelow where 'the king has 9 waste manors' and a nobleman, William FitzNorman, paid the king £15 for the 'forest' there. This was a large sum which would have reflected the value ascribed to these manors as potentially productive farmland by the Domesday surveyors. The Normans were ever on the lookout for areas of countryside that they could use as hunting reserves, hence the creation of the New Forest and the Forest of Dean which both occupy large areas of generally poor soils. Farm land which had been abandoned due to warfare and had since reverted to scrub would also have become good game habitat. To protect such habitats Norman 'Forest law' was applied over large tracts of the English countryside including ordinary settlements and farmland. Just south of Hereford, the manor of Bullingham was described in Domesday as having 'woodland which is in the king's forest'. This phrase neatly demonstrates the crucial difference between 'forest', a legal term which protected game, and 'woodland', which was an actual wood or at least wood pasture that just happened to be within the area where forest laws were applied. The area around Bullingham, between the city of Hereford and the northern boundary of Archenfield, became the royal 'Forest of Hay'.

Sometime in the 12th century, the whole of Archenfield was declared a 'forest', including those parts which were actively farmed and well settled such as King's Caple, a manor which probably had little game habitat.[7]

The majesty of the hunt and the iconic status of deer as royal quarry were important symbols of medieval power. It is unclear whether Herefordshire's Norman lords actually did much hunting in 'forests' like Archenfield or Hay, for there is little documentary evidence. It is known that forest administration became formalised as a means of raising revenue, in the form of 'fines' against a range of forest rules enforced by royal officials and these are recorded in some detail. If the locals wanted to enclose and farm a piece of heath, cut some branches off a tree, or catch deer and hares, they committed offences against forest law and risked imprisonment or banishment, but mostly they were simply fined. Forest administration had its greatest impact as a royal tax on the expansion of farming at a time of increasing population, and was loathed by tenants and lords alike. Relaxation of forest law was one of the demands of Magna Carta in 1215, but one of the least successful, as it was such a good earner for the king. The only way a group of manors could rid themselves of the burden of forest laws and interference by royal foresters, was to buy their way out. This would have been an attractive proposition for the Crown, always desperate for short term injections of cash.

So in 1253 the 'community of Archenfield' paid 200 marks to Henry III to 'disafforest' almost all Archenfield.[8] Almost, because by 1250 just three small areas of woodland had survived the expansion of farming and settlement in the 'forest' of Archenfield – Aconbury, Athelestans Wood and Harewood. These were excluded from the disafforestation agreement, so remained protected as uncultivated wild land by the Crown's forest laws. This proved effective, and 750 years later they are still enjoyed as woodland, except for Harewood ,which became a farm and parkland.

Medieval Woodland

Medieval woodland was a multi-purpose category of land, which was as important for fattening live-stock as for producing wood or timber. Such woodland often came with ancient rights, such as grazing, collecting wind-blown timber, stone, herbs, browse foliage, wild honey, fruit, and berries, and would be better described as wood pasture. Access to these resources were part of the 'internal economy' of the manor, which allowed the Lord's tenants to augment their living and pay him their dues, so optimising the use of marginal land for everyone's benefit. 'Woodland' could refer to heathland with very few trees and to wood pasture or areas dense with trees. For Fownhope no woodland is mentioned in Domesday, which states that 'from waste lands the Lord has 12s. 4d.' This is likely to refer to rough pasture or heathland occupying the thin poor soils of the area that developed into Haugh Wood during the Tudor period.

Many important sources of information about medieval land use, including the extent of woodland, are the various Inquisition Post Mortems (IPMs). All land belonged to the King so that on the death of any major landholder a county-based royal surveyor, known as an Escheator, made an enquiry or 'inquisition' into the value of their lands and who were to be the rightful successors. These IPMs are of a standard format, and include a list of local worthies as jurors who swear to the truth of the contents. The 14th-century IPMs for Eaton Tregoz in Foy, Wilton in Bridstow, Fownhope, Caradoc and Baysham (both in Sellack), and part of King's Caple have been examined and constitute a representative sample of the area:

Manor	Date	Arable	Grassland	Woodland	Park	% woodland
Eaton Tregoz (Foy)	1300	240 acres	60 acres meadow 10 acres pasture	30 acres	Yes Worth 30s.	10%
Wilton (Bridstow)	1324	360 acres	90 acres meadow 18 acres pasture	4 acres	No	1%
Fownhope	1353	480 acres	80 acres meadow 26.5 acres pasture	100 acres	Yes Worth 13s.4d.	15%
Caradoc	1293	240 acres	4 acres meadow 2 acres pasture	6 acres Worth 2s.	No	3%
Baysham and Kings Caple	1285	120 acres	3 acres meadow	3 acres coppice Worth 12d.	No	3%

Area of land by type, the presence of parks, and the estimated proportion of woodland[9]

The quantities in the IPMs are approximate and allowance must be made for the possibility of collusion to make a manor appear to the Crown to be less valuable than it actually was. The numbers in the table refer only to 'demesne' lands, those farmed directly by the Lord. Tenanted land is recorded as rental values rather than areas. There may also have been areas of marginal land which did not generate direct income to the lord. The only known medieval parks in Fownhope and Foy would have possessed some aspects of woodland and wood pasture, but their extent and character are difficult to estimate. Taking all this into account the overall proportion of land in the project area that could be defined as woodland, in the modern sense of being dedicated mainly to trees and underwood, is unlikely to have been more than 10%.

It is rare for woods to be named in IPMs, but it seems likely that the 100 acres in Fownhope refer to what is now West Wood, which occupies the steep flanks of the hill rising up from the Wye and just south of Mordiford. The 'wood worth 2s.' in Caradoc is almost certainly an early reference to Riggs Wood, which later appears in a deed for the manor of 'Cary Carddock' of 1577 as 'Wirgeswood.[10]

In 1300 at Eaton Tregoz, in the east of Foy, there were 30 acres of a 'boscus forenescus', meaning a woodland on the edge of the manor or even outside its boundary. In a later IPM the woodland of Eaton Tregoz was named 'Lyndenor' wood, where pasture was 'worth nothing because it is in common all the year'. However, the wood included some coppice which was worth 12d. This wood is almost certainly the present-day Lyndors Wood, on the banks of the Wye, confirmed by an estate map drawn up in 1780 which estimated its area to be 30 acres.

There are more details from the accounts of the bailiff of Eaton Tregoz in 1430. He recorded an income of 40s. from pasturing pigs on the acorns in the park, and from Lyndors Wood there is an income of 26s. 8d. from branch wood and bark and 8d. from 'bast' from trees.[11] The bark from oak trees was used for tanning and the bast – the stringy bark of lime trees – was used for rope making. This is the first known medieval reference to lime bark in Herefordshire and is especially significant as it shows that the tree was

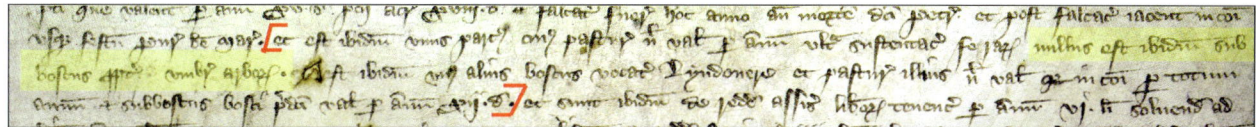

Part of the IPM that includes Lyndors Wood at Foy

Lyndors Wood from across the Wye in 2006

present in the wood with a name reflecting the Anglo-Saxon word for lime – 'linden'. Ancient limes are found today in Lyndors Wood.

The meticulous account books of the Dean and Chapter of Hereford Cathedral provide a rare insight into the relationship between a wood in Holme Lacy and mill repairs in Hereford in the late 14th century.[12] One of the most important technologies in the Middle Ages was the flour mill, supplying bread to the expanding populations of the market towns. One of the largest mills at Bartonsham near Hereford was owned by the Dean and Chapter of Hereford Cathedral. Its giant mill wheel was driven by water from a channel diverted from the River Wye and the channel was controlled by sluice gates and banks. In 1396 the Bartonsham mill suffered serious damage, probably due to that winter's floods. The main shaft, a substantial piece of timber transmitting power to a train of wooden cogs from a large mill wheel, sheared and cracked under the strain, cogs were sheared off and the bearings split. The Dean and Chapter's carpentry shop required an immediate replacement, and one John of Glasbury was paid to transport timber from Ramsden Wood in Holme Lacy to Bartonsham, a distance of some 5 miles.

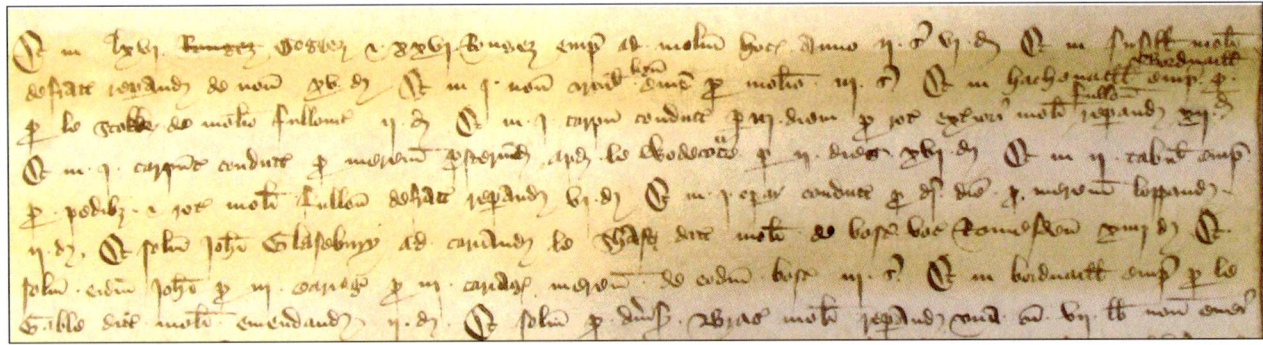

The Dean and Chapter account of the 1390s. The important section reads: John Glasebury for carrying the shaft for the mill from the wood called Ramesden 14d. and owed to the same John for three journeys carrying timber from the same wood.

Medieval Parks

Only two medieval parks – at Foy and Fownhope – are known to have existed anywhere in the twelve parishes. The earliest records of both are from the IPMs already described. There is no record of Holme Lacy Park, the best known in the area, before the Tudor period. Medieval parks were enclosed areas stocked with deer for the private pleasure of the Lord and a great status symbol. They were expensive to maintain and required the king's permission because it meant enclosing an area of 'his' land for the non-productive aggrandisement of his tenant. However, parks were not exclusively for pleasure and the Lord would let out the grass keep, if the deer had not browsed off the sward, and he would sometimes sell timber and wood. Parks included open areas where deer felt safe to browse and lie, and known by the Norman French name 'laund' meaning a glade, from which 'lawn' is derived. There was normally a lodge for the use of the hunters and visitors to view the park, store carcasses and keep weapons.

At the time of his death, John Tregoz was receiving 20 shillings a year for grazing and pannage in the park – a respectable sum. Pannage was the practice of turning pigs out to graze on acorns and beech nuts in autumn and implies the presence of mature trees. A coppice in the park was recorded but 'worth nothing on account of the shade of the trees' – the difficulty of managing coppice under a canopy of mature trees is well known to modern foresters.[13] An IPM of 1420 recorded Eaton Tregoz Park as 144 acres, but it was apparently extended by the ambitious John Abrahall to some 1,000 acres in 1440.[14]

In 1374 Roger Chandos was receiving 5s. a year from an area of coppice woodland within Fownhope Park, which would have been well fenced to prevent the coppice shoots being nibbled by livestock and deer. In 1426 the bailiff William Baker recorded that one oak was sold out of Eaton Park for 2s., and 7s. was paid for 'branch wood'. This probably refers to the practice of 'pollarding' whereby branches were cut off at a height just out of reach of nibbling deer and livestock, so that the stumps could safely re-grow to produce a future crop of branch wood. Periodic cropping of branches above the 'browse line' made pollard trees put on girth but not height. This made them unsuitable for timber and also more resistant to wind than tall trees. Both these reasons increased the chances of pollard trees surviving to become veterans in the landscape. Parks had to be permanently policed to discourage poaching by locals and damage by jealous neighbours. Both Eaton Tregoz and Fownhope Park would have been a land manager's nightmare and would have been maintained at great cost.

By Tudor times, neither Eaton Tregoz Park nor Fownhope Park existed except in name. Fownhope Park had been divided into blocks of farmland, wood pasture, and coppice which made up the home farm of Fownhope Court, the seat of the Lechmere family. 'The Old Park' was the name of a large field,[15] and there was 'summer pasture of six beasts yearly in the wood called Fownhope Park',[16] which was probably how the land had been used at Domesday, while in 1588 the quite separate Fownhope Park Coppice comprised 47 acres.[17] Fownhope Park Wood is the present name of the wood just north of Fownhope village. At Foy, Eaton Tregoz Park gave its name to the present-day Eaton Park Woods, to Old Park Cottages, to the Park Farm, and to

Fownhope Park boundary

a couple of 'lawn' field names. Vestiges of both parks remain as boundary banks and other topographical features, fragments of which are visible today in the woods where the parks were situated. Outside the woods, centuries of farming have erased most physical remains of any park.

Other medieval parks may have been created and then disappeared, leaving only 'ghost' field names as evidence of their existence. In Sellack, there is a cluster of 'Park' field names stretching east from Pict's Cross – 'Upper Park Field', 'Lower Park Field', and 'Park Wood', which were all arable fields in 1840. A survey of lands in Baysham included 'one close called the Park', an arable field 'lying in Park field', and a field called 'Launde'.[18]

Working Woodlands from 1600

People have been making iron by heating iron ore with carbon for over 2,500 years, but it was not until the 16th century that it became an industrial process being developed by investment capital. A combination of a continuous flow of water, a regular supply of large volumes of charcoal from wood, limestone for flux, and access to iron ore, were the raw materials needed to make and work iron effectively. The Wye Valley countryside had all these ingredients so was ideally suited for the development of a charcoal-iron industry. Forges and furnaces were situated by the river, which supplied the motive power for trip hammers and bellows. The light and bulky charcoal tended to fragment to dust in wagons or horse baskets, which made it difficult to transport over land in the quantities required, so coppiced woodland supplying charcoal had to be within four or five miles of a forge or furnace. By the late 1600s almost every woodland within a few miles of the River Wye was being intensively managed for the production of charcoal. The only material that travelled well on land was the iron ore and pig iron that came from the Forest of Dean. Not only wood from coppice woodland was used, but also trees in hedges, fields and parks were converted to charcoal to make iron.

In 1639 Haugh Wood was supplying wood for charcoal to the voracious forges and furnaces of John Scudamore's iron-making empire, based around the Wye Valley. Haugh and other woods in the area were repeatedly felled and regenerated in a management system that was sophisticated and sustainable. The lease of Haugh Wood from its owner, the Earl of Essex, was typical of its type to ensure that the tenant Scudamore:

A charcoal burners platform at Capler Wood

Bolstone Wood. Cropmarks in freshly-ploughed fields showing dark discs which are the remains of charcoal-burning platforms in areas of former woodland and parkland.
The red line defines the extent of Bolstone wood before parts were converted to agriculture in the 1860s.
The blue line defines the approximate southern boundary of Holme Lacy Park

shall not cut or fall in any one year of the last 20 years of the said term of one & thirty years above twenty acres of the said coppice woods ... and that all such fallages ... shall be always made & felled of such of the said coppice woods as are of oldest growth of the times at the falling thereof & shall not cut or fell any part of the said woods then standing twice in any one place thereof within the time of the last twenty years aforesaid.

Potential timber trees, known as 'standards', were required to be left within areas of cut coppice known as coupes. The lease stated that Scudamore's men:

shall leave standing and growing in & upon such parts of the woods & coppices as he shall fall from time to time, such & so many standards or young trees of 20 years growth at the time of the falling of the woods as hath been there accustomed or as the statute for preservation of woods in that case made.

The lease also required that charcoal burners' hearths should be planted after they had finished and that the tenant:

shall yearly plant upon the premises every year ... so many oaks in every place where any stubs shall be destroyed for or by reason of the making coal in the winter next following ... or as the ground is fit to contain where the coal pitts shall be so made.

Riggs Wood, Sellack

In 1642 at Riggs Wood in Sellack, Mr. Stevens was being paid the typical rate of 1s. a day for cutting and stacking 73 'cords' of wood. He was paid 6d. for every 100 faggots earning 10s. 9d. for making 2,250 of them. One hundred and forty-five perches (a perch is 5½ yards) of the boundary hedge of Riggs Wood was 'pleached' at 2d. a perch. Woodland boundaries were always well maintained to exclude any stock from damaging the young coppice.

Tenants of surrounding farmland were excluded from estate woodland, but sometimes had the responsibility of maintaining a stockproof hedge around the woods as part of their lease. In 1690 William Prosser of the Park Farm, Foy was required to:

defend and preserve the said coppice wood called Park Grove and the spring thereof from all or any hurt, trespass or destruction by cattle or otherwise ... and will & sufficiently fence mound hedge & enclose all the hedges, fences & inclosures about & belonging to the said Grove.[19]

Trees on farmland were also used for charcoal, as the following letter written in 1726 by Mr. Digby, the agent of Lady Frances Scudamore of Holme Lacy, made clear. This letter also sheds light on the use of the river for transportation, competition from other timber users, and the use of trees from Holme Lacy Park.

Lady Scudamore is now falling a considerable quantity of blockwood upon a farm at Holme Lacy which she lately took into her hand. They tell me that there will be 3 or 400 cord of 2 foot wood. Most of it, if not all oak, that is sound and good. It lies all in meadows and pastures so that she is determined to carry it to the river so as it may be conveyed away by water without damaging the grounds by coaling etc. She is informed that the maltsters and other dealers in Hereford and Ross give a much better price for such kind of wood than what she has from you in her coppices. As she gives a third more for the cutting of this wood than for that in the coppices and she is likewise at the further expense of carrying it to the water side, she expects such a price for the wood as will at least reimburse her those extraordinary charges. I am well assured that you may have this wood delivered at the next furnace upon the river for one shilling a load which, beside the saving of the waste, will come so much cheaper to you than land carriage that the price will be reduced to near the old rate, for my Lady insists upon no more than 7s. a load. You can scarce, I believe, carry a load of blockwood when coald [made into charcoal] from Hom [Holme Lacy] to Bishopswood for two & eight pence which is what the advance price and the water carriage will amount to. There is about 200 load more of blockwood now cutting in the park for which she demands 6.s a load, you coaling it up on the place.

Bowens Coppice and other woods of the Scudamore Estate in 1723 (© British Library)

Other important industries utilising wood from the Wye Valley were barrel-making, for the expanding cider industry, and tanning, which required large amounts of oak bark for curing hides into leather. Barrel makers wanted mainly ash timber of at least 12 inches in diameter, and oak older than 30 years was preferred to obtain a decent bark crop. Some coppice stems were retained after each coupe felling, to grow into medium-sized trees to supply these demands in addition to charcoal. To avoid shading the valuable coppice, trees were only allowed to grow to the minimum size necessary and then at a low density throughout the wood, typically not more than 10 per acre. This system was called 'coppice with standards'. Local people also needed wood for their domestic fuel requirements, so all the small branchwood and very young coppice was bundled into faggots. Not a twig was wasted.

For Bowens Coppice, (now called Brick Kiln Wood) in Holme Lacy, a set of complete accounts dated 1725 illustrates the way that most of the Wye Valley woods were managed at that time.[20] James Multow and Edward Drew, timber merchants of Ledbury, bought all the coppice ash for barrel-making that year. Their contract with Lady Scudamore specified that the ash coppice poles be stacked in 'cords' 8 feet by 4 feet by 4 feet containing 128 cubic feet. They paid £2 3s. a cord for ash poles called 'hoop ash' over 15 inches diameter and £2 for poles of more than 11 inches diameter. For 'worst ash' under 9 inches diameter they paid 27s. a cord.

In 1725 the merchants received over 8,000 cubic feet of timber from this wood, paying Lady Scudamore £132 under a contract which allowed them 'to carry the hoop ash from the wood to some of the nearest parts of the river Wye and likewise a proper place or places to lay the hoop ash down until it can be loaded and sent away'. Multow and Drew also bought the rest of the timber trees in Bowens Coppice marked for felling. The same year the suitably named David Tanner of Monmouth purchased 76 tons of oak bark for 40s. a ton, also shipped down the Wye, and no less than 35,750 faggots were cut from Bowens Coppice. The balance sheet for the wood during 1725 shows how profitable woodlands were:

Income	£	s	d	%	Expenditure	£	s	d	%
Timber, over 11 inches diameter	286	1	3$\frac{1}{2}$	26	Supervising	2			2
Coppice, 11 inches diameter or less	620	5	5$\frac{1}{2}$	56	Hedging	2	6	4$\frac{1}{2}$	3
Bark, 76 tons	152			14	Felling & stacking	82	9	1	64
Faggots, 35,000	44	12	6	4	Bark stripping	24	9		19
					Making faggots	17	17	6	14
Total	**1,102**	**19**	**3**	**100**		**129**	**1**	**1$\frac{1}{2}$**	**100**
Income over expenditure						973	17	3$\frac{1}{2}$	

Seven acres of Capler Wood, next to the river, were owned by the Dean and Chapter of Hereford Cathedral. Within its boundary, a quarry supplied stone for the repair of the Cathedral and other buildings owned by the Chapter. A set of leases to the Scudamore family, for the coppice of Capler Wood, covers the period from 1602 to 1834 and demonstrates the care and consistency with which the management was controlled.[21] The leases stipulated that the coppice must only be cut 'at reasonable times of year ... leaving and preserving standards' and that the fence around the coppice must be maintained at the leaseholder's expense. Daniel Williams was paid a shilling a day in 1849 for 'cutting down wood, stripping the bark and tying the faggots' in Capler Wood.[22]

Every part of every wood in the Wye Valley would have been felled at least 10 times between 1600 and 1800. The new crop of wood and timber would have re-grown either by sprouting from cut stumps (stool re-growth) or from naturally occurring seedlings. Throughout this period the only documented planting in any wood is the requirement in the Haugh Wood contract that charcoal burners hearths should be planted with oaks at the end of a tenancy. The woodlands of this period were therefore 'closed eco-systems',

Oak derived from coppice at Capler

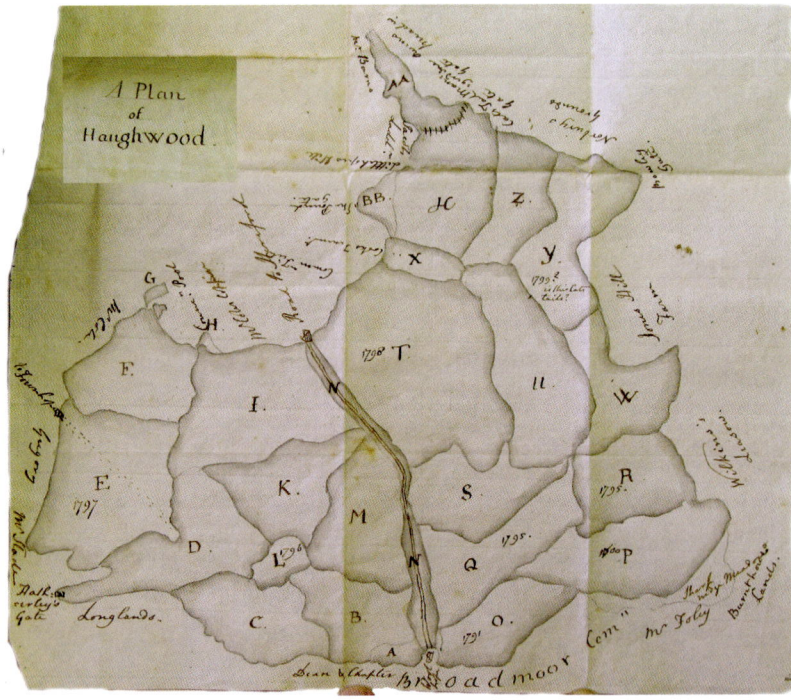

Haugh Wood coppice compartment c.1798

continually renewing themselves so that their species, composition, and genetic character was perpetuated through successive management cycles.

By the late Victorian period, the charcoal-iron industry was long gone and the railways were supplying plentiful and convenient coal for domestic heating and cooking, as well as for the blacksmiths' forges. However, the industrial revolution created new markets for coppice products. These included huge quantities of young willow and hazel wands for packing and crating crockery in the Staffordshire potteries, tent pegs for the army, and chemicals from distilled wood. In the early 19th century, land-owners were being exhorted to grow large oaks for the navy, so some coppices had been allowed to grow up and oak was favoured over other species. Oak bark was being phased out in favour of chemical means of curing leather, reducing this regular source of income, while the technology of iron shipbuilding made naval oak redundant. Timber imports from Britain's vast empire were increasing at this time. The overall result was that local woodlands lost markets for their produce and were declining in profitability. When Haugh Wood was sold in 1881 it was advertised as much for its game potential as its ability to produce wood and timber:

The principal wood or ancient forest, called Haughwood, formerly the property of the Earl of Essex is a thriving, productive and easily marketable wood, valuable, even in its present condition, as a stored coppice, but its capabilities as a game preserve cannot be well overstated. It may, with judicious management, be made one of the best and most exclusive preserves in the county.[23]

Twentieth Century

While Britain had easy access to supplies from the Empire, there was little incentive to collect statistics on the country's trees and woods so, during the First World War, there was no way of knowing how much growing timber was available for the war effort. Assuming the worst, the Government intervened, creating the state Forestry Commission in 1919 with a brief to plant trees on 'unproductive' land. Ignoring centuries of knowledge and experience the new policy of plantation forestry regarded native woodlands as being as unproductive as bare hills.

With a depressed rural economy in the early 1920s the Commission started buying up 'uneconomic' woodlands and converting them into plantations of single species of trees – often conifers. In Herefordshire the eastern part of Haugh Wood was bought in 1925 along with a number of other woodlands in the county.

Meanwhile, traditional woodland skills continued to be deployed throughout the Wye Valley. For example, coppice compartments in the western part of Haugh Wood, which remained part of the Sufton estate, were auctioned as 'coppicing and pit wood'. The sale, which was held at the Moon Inn, Mordiford, on 8 November 1935, was for 40 acres of coppice separated into 13 lots ranging from 1 to 6 acres. Nineteen of the coppice acres were in Bears Wood, part of Haugh Wood that lies north of the Pentaloe Brook, and the conditions attached to the coppice contracts included the stipulation:

> That Underwood shall be axe-felled in a good and workmanlike manner, and any Cordwood intended to be burnt for Charcoal shall be removed to such place or places, and the turf for charking the same shall be got from such land as shall be appointed by the Vendor.[24]

In the part of Haugh Wood acquired by the Forestry Commission, coppice re-growth was growing vigorously in those areas felled in order to establish plantations. The Commission had to employ numerous woodmen to cut back and suppress this re-growth in order to favour young trees of larch, Scots pine, Norway spruce and Douglas fir trees which were probably the first trees to have been planted in the wood. The outbreak of the Second World War severely curtailed the man power available to the Commission so that by peace time the natural re-growth of Haugh Wood was swamping the new plantations. Despite huge efforts by woodmen, which included many Polish and other refugees from Europe, to cut down the regenerating hardwood, the new plantations turned out to be of poor growth rate and quality. In 1953 the Sufton Estate sold all 316 acres of its part of Haugh Wood as well as the 86 acre West Wood – a total of 402 acres – to the Commission for £15 per acre.

After the War, the Forestry Commission pursued a similar policy for private woodlands, offering estate owners grants, tax incentives and advice, all aimed at encouraging the conversion of broadleaved woodland to plantation forestry – a scheme which began to be regarded by policy makers as the only viable means of growing wood and timber. Native trees were dismissed as too slow growing and traditional methods of coppice, and coppice with standards, had no place in the nation's woodlands.

By the 1960s many estates had begun the process of converting their woods according to the new orthodoxy of modern forestry. In 1971 Ramsden Coppice was clearfelled in its entirety and planted with larch. The Holme Lacy estate converted most of Bowers Wood (now Brick Kiln Wood) to plantation forestry. The western sector of Haugh Wood and West Wood, both newly acquired by the Forestry Commission, were felled and planted with blocks of larch, Norway spruce, Douglas fir, beech, and sweet chestnut, although some native broadleaved strips were left as wind breaks. In all these woods the centuries old practice of relying on natural re-growth of native species came to an end with negative consequences for the woodland ecology.

By the 1970s this coniferisation policy was coming under attack by conservationists and amenity groups. An early success was the 40 acre Trilloes Court Wood, which the Forestry Commission had acquired

Trilloes Court Wood in 2002

Discussing the future of Haugh Wood

in 1961 from Ballingham Court Farm for £265 3s. 2d. (£6 7s. per acre) who retained the right for two years to fell all the timber. The Commission's plan to plant up the felled wood with conifers was thwarted by the county branch of the Council for Protection of Rural England and Ross Civic Society who managed to persuade the Commission to scale down its plans drastically so that just a few acres ended up converted to larch.

In 1985 the Forestry Commission introduced the Broadleaves Policy, which recognised the historical and ecological importance of native woodlands and agreed to stop issuing felling licences for the conversion of broadleaved woodland to agriculture. This happened too late for the ancient Riggs Wood, half of which was allowed to be grubbed up in 1983 for 15 acres of north-facing pasture. This was the first major loss of woodland to agriculture in the project area since the grubbing up of Bolstone Wood over 100 years before.

Over the last few decades there has been increasing interest in the sustainable management of native woodland and the restoration of woodland damaged by plantation forestry. This is reflected in the current grant aid structure for private woodland and the policies of the Commission towards the woods they manage. All of Haugh Wood is now to be converted to 100% native broadleaves by 2041 reflecting its important ecology – especially butterflies and moths. The successor to the former owner of Riggs Wood has planted the grubbed half with native broadleaves.

However, there remain more insidious threats to native woodlands. The grey squirrel, introduced from America in the 1900s, poses a serious threat to young broadleaved trees, especially oak, because of its habit of bark stripping and killing off the tops of the trees making them useless for timber. The deer population in the Wye Valley woods is now many times higher than at any time in recorded history. Newly-opened areas of young coppice or broadleaved plantings have to be protected from their browsing by expensive 6 ft. high fences or by plastic tubes around the young trees. Despite these problems, native woods have the potential to produce fuel and timber in a way that is completely carbon neutral, as they have done for centuries past.

Field and Hedgerow Trees

Woods had few trees of any size because they competed with growing coppice, so most mature trees in the countryside were to be found in fields and hedgerows. These were valuable to the landowner, who retained the right to cut and carry away any trees on the farm – a right denied to the tenant except for essential repairs to buildings and for carts, ploughs and other implements. Some leases required tenants to plant trees and fill gaps in hedges. For example in 1690 John Scudamore's tenant Susan Apperley on her 42 acres in Foy was required to plant :

> 5 good & sufficient pear stocks & crab stocks in places convenient and at times & seasons convenient in & upon the said premises yearly during the said term and likewise yearly plant and set 500 of quick sets in places convenient and at times & seasons convenient in & upon the said demised premises.[25]

Groups of trees in fields and hedges were important as boundary markers. Certain arable fields at Caradoc were identified in a deed of 1621: 'lying to the south side of a row of Elms'[26].

In 1721 Holme Lacy estate workers were paid 1 shilling per tree 'for falling 107 trees in the hedges about Ramsdon'. Although hedges were principally to retain livestock as well as separating land use and ownership they were an important source of wood and timber. Apart from a high proportion of hawthorn, reflecting their primary purpose, hedges were, as now, composed of native tree and shrub species similar in composition to local native woodlands which would have included both wych elm and English elm.

Hedgerow pollard oaks, Rise Farm, Fownhope

For centuries hedges have been periodically 'laid' or 'pleached' every six to twelve years, a process which is similar to the cutting of stems in a coppice wood except the stems in the hedge, called 'pleachers', are not completely cut through, so they can be laid almost horizontally but connected to the hedge root system. The subsequent re-growth from the cut pleachers produces a dense stock-proof hedge until the process is repeated. As with natural re-growth in woodlands, the woody composition of traditionally worked hedges tends to remain unchanged through successive management cycles. A scattering of good quality stems were retained by the hedge layer to produce hedgerow timber. The hedged countryside is a lattice work of continuously worked linear 'coppice with standards'.

From the late 18th century, field trees were frequently advertised for sale in the *Hereford Journal*. In April 1773 the following advert appeared:

225 elm trees growing on the several farms called Carthage, Coles, Upper Underhill, Lower Underhill and the Court Farm in the parish of Foy adjoining to the River Wye; the trees on each farm respectively being marked with a cross and numbered with white lead and oil,

and in March 1772:

A few large elm trees, part of the Great Elm Walk at Holm Lacy; and also, a few large elm trees in Broad Meadow; and some old oaks on the banks of the River in the said parish.

Proximity to the river Wye for transport was an important selling point. On 8 March 1797 the following wee advertised for sale:

59 oaks growing upon Aramstone, Ruckstone and Carey Mill in the parish of Kings Caple and every tree standing within 100 yards of the river Wye

There were numerous field and hedgerow trees growing in the mid-Victorian period, such as 17 oaks, 24 elms and 2 ash 'standing in a field immediately adjoining Capler Quarry' auctioned in 1847.[27] This is almost certainly Caplow Meadow, a small long strip of grassland just south of the quarry between Capler Wood and the banks of the Wye not much more than 1 hectare. It was a condition of sale that the hollows in the ground left by grubbing the roots should be filled in and levelled. This indicates that many of these trees were in the field rather than in the hedgerow, because trees in a hedgerow would be felled without disturbing the hedgerow structure or root system.

Later Parks and Veteran Trees

The Tudor period was a time of constitutional and economic upheaval, which provided rich pickings for families with connections close to the centre of power. Many medieval parks in Herefordshire had disappeared by this time, but the idea of the park for pleasure and status was to see a revival. Henry VIII put John Scudamore in charge of requisitioning land from the newly-dissolved monasteries, allowing that family greatly to increase its Herefordshire land holdings. By the 1540s the Scudamores had acquired the manor of Holme Lacy and had built one of the county's finest houses. Although a park pale surrounding this house appears on Saxton's map of 1577, the first documentary evidence for a park at Holme Lacy was in the estate accounts of 1642 recording the 'red deer park'.

The park was an important source of wood and timber including the coppicing of alder, a tree of water-logged ground probably associated with the same valley as the pools, 'cutting & cording 9 cords of orle [alder] wood in the red deer park 11d. the cord'. The park was also used as source of bracken for bedding, wood for charcoal, and gravel from a quarry. As an echo of the ancient custom of pasturing pigs, an estate worker had the job of filling in the 'pigs diggings'.

Poaching and trespass was clearly a problem, and in September 1698 two estate workers were paid £1 2s. for '33 nights watching the park'. Holme Lacy Park also played its part in the family char-coal-iron business, for in 1726 Lady Scudamore's agent was telling the iron master, Mr. Faulkner, that 'There is about 200 load more of blockwood now cutting in the park for which she demands 6s. a load, you coaling it up on the place'.[28] The evidence for charcoal making in the park can be seen today in the circular dark patches of soil which become visible when the soil of the former park is ploughed.

Less is known of the origins of Pengethley Park, now managed by the National Trust. Isaac Taylor's map of 1754 shows it had a park pale alongside the main highway from Ross to Hereford. The park was apparently cleared of trees by Colonel Symonds to pay for his election expenses of 1819, and girth measurements of the remaining oaks indicate that many of the present trees date from that period.

Holme Lacy Park

However, a few are older, the largest having a girth of 8 metres, indicating an approximate age of 300 years so planted about 1700.[29]

There are several pasture areas with concentrations of open-grown broadleaved trees, such as those on the estates of How Caple Court, Perrystone Court in Foy, and along the Wye at Ashe Ingham in Bridstow. While not 'officially' parks these features make an important contribution to the landscape and will become important historic areas of parkland in the future.

Throughout the 12 parishes there are many hundreds of significant trees not just in park-like concentrations but scattered around the countryside in hedgerows, fields, churchyards and on the edges of woods. The project commissioned a systematic survey of all such trees including those considered 'veteran'. This continued the work started by the Herefordshire Nature Trust and completes an inventory of all known trees of interest in the Herefordshire part of the Wye Valley Area of Outstanding Natural Beauty. Volunteer surveyors measured the girths, recorded features of wildlife and habitat interest, photographed and located some 484 trees of which 408 were native species and 288 were oak. Many interesting trees date from the era of Victorian amenity planting as the follow table of all the trees recorded show:

Species	Number
alder	3
ash	28
beech	13
cedar	7
conifer	2
copper beech	1
field maple	6
hawthorn	1
hornbeam	1
horse chestnut	13
larch	1
lime	20
oak	288
plane	1
poplar	3
redwood	2
sweet chestnut	22
sycamore	10
wellingtonia	27
willow	30
yew	5
Total	**484**

Tree species recorded in the 12 parishes with a girth of over 3 metres

A veteran oak at Caradoc

Very occasionally, it is known when an old tree was planted. A yew tree in Hentland churchyard was planted in 1605 according to the church records. Yew readily colonises bare lime-rich ground, so the old limestone quarries in West Wood and Fownhope Park can be dated by measuring the girths of the larger yews, which are to 1.6 metres. Accounting for the slower growth rate on limestone (assume 1.3 millimetres a year) indicates that the quarries were last worked around 1800.

In 1868, when the Woolhope Club members measured the Hentland yew, it had a girth of 3.66 metres. This gives a mean ring width of 2.2 millimetres (assuming the tree was 10 years old when transplanted). It was measured as 4.27 metres in girth in 2005, giving an average radial growth rate of 1.7 millimetres a year. Using the two measurements gives a growth rate of 1.4 mm, which can be interpreted as the growth rate slowing with age due to senescence, shading by adjacent trees, and/or pollarding/pruning. These figures are consistent with the few published records.

The largest tree in the survey was an oak with a girth 9.75 metres in Holme Lacy Park, indicating an age of some 400 years. This is unlikely to be the oldest tree as girth is not a linear function of age. When trees enter their senescent phase they reduce their branch area so that the radial growth rate slows to just fractions of a millimetre per year. It is these truly veteran and very slow growing trees, almost always oaks, which are especially important for wildlife from rare beetles to bats. This is due to the variety of habitat that develops as the tree rots from the inside and many crevices are formed from dying branches. A complex biology of fungal flora and invertebrate diversity then develops which makes such trees extremely important historic and ecological features in the countryside.

A yew tee recently felled to protect the masonry at West Horsley, Surrey allowed a detailed analysis of its rings, showing a mean ring width of 2.8 mm for the first 100 years and 0.9 mm for the next 210 years (see www.tree-ring.co.uk). There is a large variation of ring width with age reported from one of the few publications on the subject – from 3.5mm for early growth down to 0.051mm for older trees, a factor of 70.[30] Given this uncertainty, the simple extrapolation from our single measurement, which extended the age from 400 to 480 years (equivalent to a 20% error) is quite reasonable.

CHAPTER V

Buildings in the Landscape

by Heather Hurley (with a contribution by Phillip Anderson)

The character and history of an area is reflected by the structure, size, shape, and position of its buildings in the landscape. Nikolaus Pevsner has described Herefordshire as

> one of the least industrialized of all counties [with its] infinite number of rivers, streams, and brooks and unusually large areas still or again covered by woods – still, where the venerable oaks and the tangled undergrowth line the serpentines of the river Wye'.[1]

In 1955 Herefordshire had 'to a large extent, escaped many modern developments, and is much more free of eyesores and the kind of ugliness we have grown accustomed to than most counties'.[2] Since these extracts in the mid 20th century, recent housing, agricultural buildings and modern farming practices have changed the traditional landscape in the Wye Valley.

The purpose of this chapter is to compare the descriptions and photographs of buildings listed by the Royal Commission on Historical Monuments (RCHM) in 1931 and 1932, with the present state of these buildings.[3] As well as the published volumes, the commissioners' handwritten notes of 1927, 1928 and 1929 were studied, as they contain more detailed descriptions, additional photographs and quite a few drawings.[4] Churches have been included, but archaeological sites such as Capler Camp and structures such as Wilton Bridge have been omitted.

The Royal Commission's Inventory of Historic Buildings only included those that in whole or in part dated from before 1714, with the purpose 'to specify those which seem most worthy of preservation'. Their findings led to the compilation of Statutory Lists of Historic Buildings under the terms of the Town and Country Act of 1947. By 1970 most authorities had compiled a statutory list, and as surveying standards and the understanding of historic buildings improved, it became clear that successive reassessments were necessary. Listed Buildings are classified as: Grade 1 – of paramount importance; Grade 11* – of outstanding interest; and Grade 11 – worthy of preserving.[5]

The Buildings

The buildings were categorised by the original type described by the Royal Commissioners and take no cognisance of later changes, when for instance a cottage was subsequently enlarged into a house, or a barn converted into a dwelling. The building types were as follows:

Ecclesiastical – churches and chapels
Great Houses – castles and country houses with estates
Houses – farmhouses and other larger dwellings
Cottages – including tenements and other smaller dwellings
Barns – including other types of outbuildings
Inns

The buildings in this chapter are also categorised by the degree of change and survival compared to the description and illustrations in the RCHM and the surveyors' notes. It must be considered that most buildings would probably have been altered between 1714 and the early 1930s when the Royal Commission's inventory was published.[6] The categories for degree of change have been based on an external view from the public road or footpath, and are as follows:

Survives largely unchanged externally with no substantial structural changes and only minor cosmetic alterations.
Survives with more substantial changes, either structural, partly demolished or with a major extension.
Does not survive.[7]

Ballingham

Ballingham is a sparsely populated parish, almost encircled by a great loop of the Wye, which had a long association with the Scudamores of Holme Lacy and has a continuous run of maps dating from the late 17th century.[8] The buildings reflect the social standing and occupations of its past inhabitants, and include farms, a great house, cottages, an inn, a former school (now a village hall), and a smithy and railway station, both of which have been converted into dwellings. The survival rate of the buildings in Ballingham has been poor; three barns, one cottage and one house listed by the RCHM surveyors have been lost. The lost cottage near the church has been replaced by a 20th-century bungalow, and while the house at Dunn's Farm does not appear to have survived, the stone house fronting the road may be a conversion of one of its outbuildings.

At Lower Ballingham Farm, now Ballingham Court, the 17th-century timber barn has been demolished, together with two barns belonging to the gracious Ballingham Hall built by William Scudamore in 1602, which appears unchanged since

Ballingham Court
Top – 1927; Bottom – 2006

1927. The church with its 14th-century tower is dedicated to St. Dubricius, one of four churches in south Herefordshire named after this saint. About a mile south of the church is the Miner's Arms Inn, now called the Cottage of Content, which dates from the 17th century, and was converted from three tenements to form a beer house that has since blossomed into a notable inn.[9] At some time after 1927 it was partly rendered and an extension built linking the pub to a former barn.

Bolstone

The smallest parish in the project area is Bolstone, lying west of the Wye and almost mid-way between Ross and Hereford. It belonged to the Knights Hospitallers from the 12th century until the Dissolution, when the manor and tithes passed to the Scudamores of Holme Lacy. Standing in the middle of a farmyard is the tiny church of St. John with its reset and blocked doorway of the 12th century. This was the only building that the 20th-century surveyors listed, although three noted farmhouses and ten cottages were recorded in the early 19th century including Bolstone Court which was said to date from the 17th century.[10]

Bolstone Church in 2006

Bolstone Court: Top – 1927; Bottom – 2008

Brampton Abbotts

The parish name, together with the field names of Monk's Grove and Abbotts Meadow, reflect its past monastic associations with St. Peter's Abbey in Gloucester. The buildings surveyed in 1928 included the church of St. Michael, dating from the Norman period with later alterations. The church with its bell turret provides an attractive landmark on approaching it by footpath from Ross-on-Wye. On the parish boundary is

Brampton Abbotts
Top – The Church; Bottom – Netherton

Rudhall, a house dating from at least the 15th century on a site long associated with the Abbey of Gloucester. At the dissolution it was granted to the Rudhalls who erected the mansion on the site of 'The Ancient Monastery of Rudhall', according to the sale particulars of Rudhall in 1825.[11] The property has not been viewed because of high fencing, but modern photographs indicate that the house survives largely unchanged externally and is in good condition. Netherton Farm was demolished around the late 1940s leaving scanty remains of the original building, which makes it impossible to make a comparison. Surviving maps of the parish date from 1780 and a photographic record of buildings, people and occupations from the 1930s and 1940s.[12]

Bridstow

Wilton is part of Bridstow parish which adjoins Ross, but is separated from the town by the river Wye. Five of the twelve listed buildings in Bridstow are in Wilton including the only remains of a castle within the project area. Wilton castle, built to defend an ancient river crossing, was originally a motte and bailey, but the stone remains that survive date from the 13th century. As Lords of the Manor, the Longchamps, were followed by the Greys, then the Brydges who made alterations and added the Elizabethan hall. During the Civil War the castle was damaged by fire and left in ruins, but in 1731 the manor and the castle were sold to the Governors' of Guy's Hospital who later built a house that incorporated the south-west tower.

Since the commissioners' photographs of the castle, the general condition of the ruins has been improved by the removal of vegetation and renovation of the stonework. Recent restoration work has made no attempt to disguise new work, which included the repair and roofing of the north-west tower, and the restoration and re-roofing of the south-west stair tower, where the Victorian house meets the medieval castle. New stone mullions and transoms have been inserted into a bay widow of the 16th-century hall, and in 2007 further restoration work was taking place on the east tower and north-east corner.

Near Wilton bridge the King's Head Inn, a shop with a dwelling together with a house were listed as one block by the surveyors. Since then the King's Head and the shop have closed and been converted to residential use, but the buildings remain substantially unchanged. The Prison House of 1600 was a cottage in 1928 but has been incorporated together with the White Lion Inn as the Old Gaol Restaurant. Apart from some alterations to the chimney the building remains unchanged. Overlooking the river and the ferry crossing is Wilton Court, built in 1600 as the Great House. It has been converted into a hotel, but otherwise appears unchanged externally. Near the Orles Barn Hotel at Wilton was a 17th-century barn, which has since been demolished.

Bridstow church, dedicated to St. Bridget, presents a pleasing scene in attractive surroundings. The church was restored in 1862, but since the 1928 report its building has remained unchanged. Just north of the church is a stone-built cottage with its inner core and projecting stack dating from around 1700. The roof has been replaced with one at a shallower pitch, allowing the dwelling to be extended, and an extension was erected on the west which has subsequently fallen into ruins. The lane from the church continues north to Ashe Farm, a substantial building dating from the 15th century with later additions. Apart from some minor alterations the farmhouse appears practically unchanged from the commissioners' photograph.

Bridstow – Wilton Castle
Top – early 20th century; Bottom – 2007

Ashe Ingham was a manor recorded at Domesday, and Ashe Ingham Court 'was built of timber late in the 16th century, rebuilt by Rev. G. Porter in 1860, burned down in 1925, and again rebuilt by Mr. T. Marshall'.[13] It was remodelled in 1928, the year that it was surveyed by the Royal Commission, and in 2006 appeared to be largely unchanged except for a small modern extension. All the outbuildings have been converted into residential use including the barn and the cider house, which also appear to have remained unchanged externally.

Two other buildings in Bridstow parish were recorded in 1928. Lane End, a 17th-century house with extensions, has now been replaced by a 20th-century house and since parish boundary changes is now in Peterstow parish. Moore Court Farm, in Wells Brook Lane, is a comfortable looking building dating from the 17th century. Since being neglected for a number of years and described as being in poor condition in 1928, the farm is now in good order and survives substantially unchanged apart from changes to the windows.

Brockhampton

Brockhampton lies on the east side of the Wye, and since the 1880s has included Fawley, previously a chapelry within Fownhope parish. Brockhampton's original church, dedicated to the Holy Trinity, was 'not in use and rapidly falling into disrepair' in 1929. This was due to a new church dedicated to All Saints that was built in 1901/2 and therefore not recorded by the surveyors. The old 14th-century church had fallen into ruin by 1969,[14] but was rescued at the beginning of the 21st century and, according to the sale particulars was 'sensitively converted into a private residence'.[15] The general outline of the building is little changed

Brockhampton – Fawley Court

except for the insertion of diamond-shaped windows and skylights. At Brinkley Hill two late 17th-century cottages were recorded; one remains little changed, whereas the other has been replaced by a larger building.

Fawley contains some impressive buildings including Fawley Court, which is a much appreciated building surrounded by delightful gardens that can be seen from the roadside. The earliest part of the Court dates from the 16th century with later extensions and alterations, but since 1929 it has survived unchanged apart from minor alterations. Its two listed barns have also survived and are largely unchanged. At Much Fawley, near the banks of the Wye, is the 12th-century Norman chapel dedicated to St. John which, despite its remote situation, is occasionally used for services. Almost adjoining the chapel is Seabournes with parts dating from the 16th century and Much Fawley with 14th-century origins. Seabournes cannot be seen from a public road, but having gained permission to view the house it appears unchanged since 1929. The same applies to Much Fawley although its 17th-century barn was not seen. It is curious that these buildings at Much Fawley were built so close together, as can be appreciated from maps of 1721.[16]

Fownhope

Fownhope is one of the larger parishes in the project area and, with a total of 29, had the highest number of buildings surveyed in 1929. Many cottages have been demolished, and some sites have been incorporated into housing developments. However, the church of St. Mary, with its graceful 14th-century spire, serves as a prominent landmark in the Wye Valley. The interior of the church includes some 12th-century remains, a tympanum, and many monuments. Fownhope Court, which is of medieval origin, is almost hidden by trees and modern houses, and although it has been converted into apartments the house survives largely unchanged externally. However the timber-framed outbuilding that stood north-east of the house, which was recorded in 1929, has not survived.

Although Fownhope vicarage was listed by the surveyors in 1929, it was the barn they were more interested in, but unfortunately it has since been demolished. There is no photograph of the vicarage in 1929, but from the description it looks as though it is largely unaltered. Opposite the church is a timber-framed house, formerly called Church Gate House, which has structurally survived but since 1929 has had an extension added and its timber-framing exposed. North of the church is Manor Farm 'probably of the early 17th century', which has survived with its timber-framing exposed to front and back, but with a small extension and decorative barge boards added.

The Green Man Inn, originally the Naked Boy, is the most prominent building in the village's main street.[17] The inn started life as an L-shaped building of 17th-century date and since 1929 has displayed a striking black and white exterior. The structure of the main building has survived largely unchanged, but it has acquired a considerable number of outbuildings. On the same side of the street four cottages were recorded. The first, called the Bark House, still has its timber-framed elevations to the street and side, but the ground-floor windows have acquired small polygonal bays, and extensions have been added to the rear. The second cottage has not survived, and it is considered that the third one has been incorporated into a house on the site.

The fourth cottage has been much altered, with a modern window at the street elevation, and the walls have been pebble-dashed, but fortunately it has survived as the West End Stores. In 1929 the Stores was kept by Harry Lloyd, a grocer who was in competition with two other grocers in Fownhope. There was also a stationer at the Post Office and a butcher's shop run by E.A. Pritchard & Sons which, under the same family name, is still supplying meat in and around Fownhope in 2008.

There were four pubs in Fownhope in 1929: the Green Man, the New Inn, the Anchor, and the Highland Home which became the Forge and Ferry. Only the first two have survived as inns to the present.[18]

On the opposite side of the village street three more cottages were described in 1929 and it appears that the existing Tump Cottage is one that has survived. It is difficult to be certain from the commissioners' photographs, as it was then almost hidden by a cottage in front which has since been demolished. The third was a mid-17th-century timber-framed

Fownhope – West End Stores
Top – 1929; Bottom – 2008

Former public house. The King's Arms, Fownhope in 1929

105

cottage which stood on the site of the present modern housing estate. It was a single-storey dwelling that was heightened in the late 18th or early 19th century, and was a public house known by the sign of the King's Arms Inn which was advertised for sale in 1863, but had closed by 1928.[19]

From the village crossroads a road leads east to Woolhope where, past the entrance to Fownhope Court, there are two houses which may incorporate some of the fabric from a building described in 1928 as a 'small barn and outbuilding attached to a cottage 200 years old' dating from the 17th century. The barn was thatched and the cottage had formerly been two tenements divided from a house occupied as one in 1843.[20] Further north-east is a house at Nupend Mill, which has survived with few changes. A small extension has been added and a timber-framed gable has been covered. The other two buildings in this valley mentioned by the Royal Commission are Horne Cottage, which once served as a public house, and Rudge End Cottage. Since 1929, the thatched roof of Horne Cottage has been replaced with slate and an extension has been added. Windows have been added to Rudge End Cottage and a former outbuilding has been incorporated into the dwelling.

Common Hill at Fownhope is a wooded hill criss-crossed by tracks and paths which once served the lime industry. The numerous houses and cottages are scattered across the hill and are difficult to locate and access. Out of the five buildings listed by the surveyors' only two were positively identified – one was dramatically altered and the other, called Little Bryalls, was easily recognised from its 1929 photograph when it was two tenements. Although the other three sites were investigated, only the remains of the Thatched Tavern, a former cider house, were barely visible.

Two barns in Fownhope were recorded by the Royal Commission. The 17th-century granary at Nash Farm was found to be structurally sound in 1929, but is now in a semi-derelict state. The other barn and granary were at Caplor Farm and dated from the 15th century with later bays added; now little remains of this large barn of six bays. Although the farms were not included in the inventory the inspector did note that Nash Farm was a 'modern building' and Caplor Farm 'an 18th or 19th century building' with reused beams and doorway. In 1963 Pevsner found Nash Farm 'clearly Late Georgian', but only mentioned the barn at Caplor, which by then had been partly destroyed by fire.[21]

At the northern end of Fownhope parish the surveyors inspected a cottage at Fiddler's Green. Described as 'Now a lodge or week-end cottage rather than a peasant's cottage', it has since been extended and had additional windows inserted. A cottage at Even Pits, called Sadler's Cottage, which stands on a bank above the road, has survived with little change; the brick infill to the timber-framing on the west front has been plastered over and the roof has acquired modern pantiles. Before reaching the original parish boundary, there is a long, low building on the roadside at Mordiford Mill, which appears unchanged from the commissioners' photograph and description.

The final two buildings listed in 1929 were on the outskirts of Haugh Wood; both are timber-framed dating from at least the early 17th century. Upper Littlehope could not be seen from a public road or path, but it is understood that few changes have been made to the building. Joan's Hill stands in a clearance of Haugh Wood about a mile from the public road, but can be viewed from a public right-of-way. It is an attractive building that has hardly been altered apart from additional windows, some timber-framing exposed on the north side and a chimney removed.

Fownhope – Mordiford Mill

106

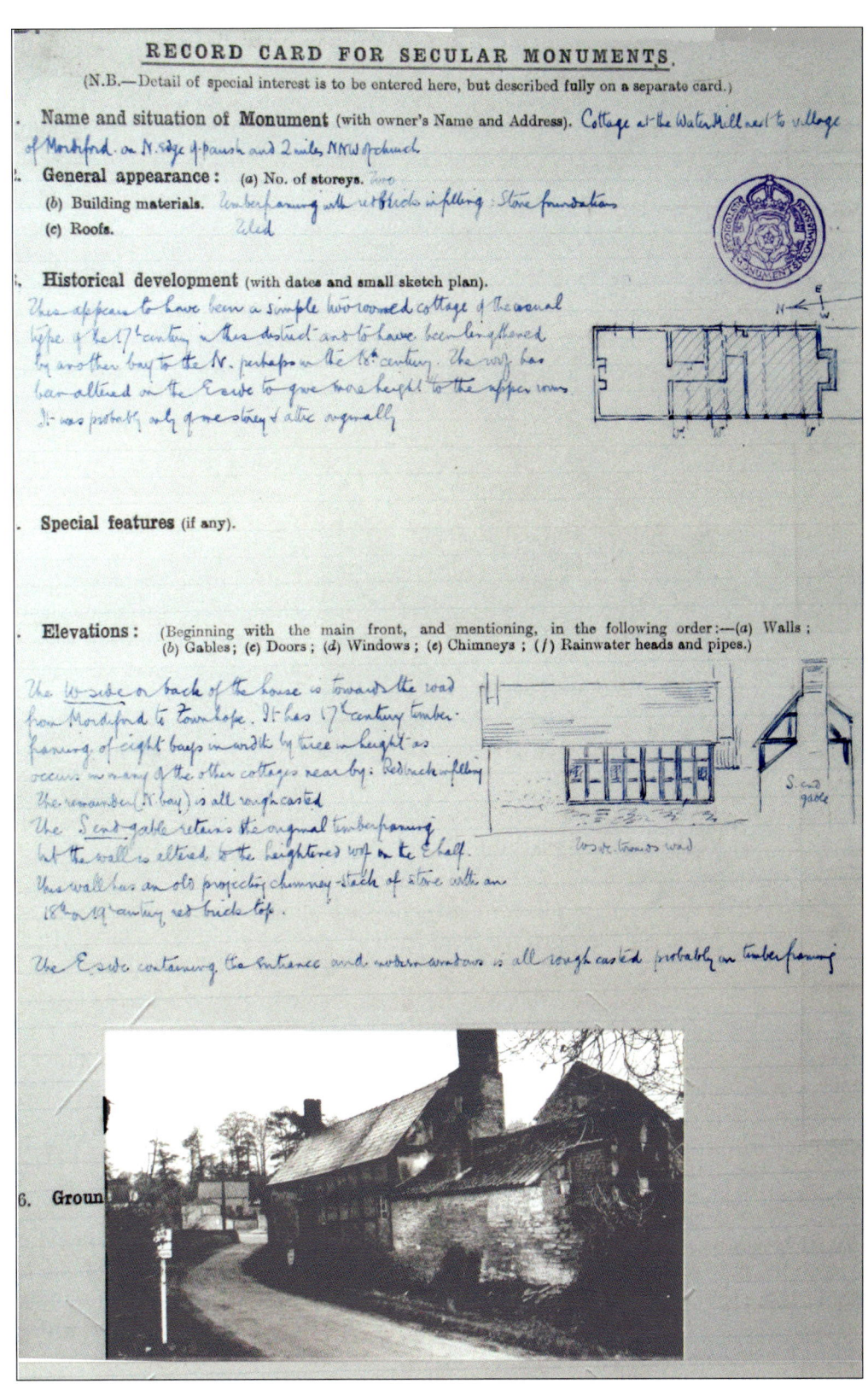

RECORD CARD FOR SECULAR MONUMENTS.

(N.B.—Detail of special interest is to be entered here, but described fully on a separate card.)

. Name and situation of **Monument** (with owner's Name and Address). *Cottage at the Water Mill next to village of Mordiford on N. edge of parish and 2 miles NNW of church*

. General appearance : (a) No. of storeys. *Two*

(b) Building materials. *Timberframing with red bricks infilling : Stone foundations*

(c) Roofs. *Tiled*

. Historical development (with dates and small sketch plan).

This appears to have been a simple two roomed cottage of the usual type of the 17th century in this district and to have been lengthened by another bay to the N. perhaps in the 18th century. The roof has been altered on the E side to give more height to the upper rooms. It was probably only of one storey & attic originally

. Special features (if any).

. **Elevations** : (Beginning with the main front, and mentioning, in the following order :—(a) Walls ; (b) Gables ; (c) Doors ; (d) Windows ; (e) Chimneys ; (f) Rainwater heads and pipes.)

The W side or back of the house is towards the road from Mordiford to Townhope. It has 17th century timber-framing of eight bays in width by three in height as occurs in many of the other cottages near by : Red brick infilling. The remainder (N bay) is all rough casted.

The S end gable retains the original timberframing but the wall is altered & the heightened roof on the E half. This wall has an old projecting chimney stack of stone with an 18th or 19th century red brick top.

The E side containing the entrance and modern windows is all rough casted probably on timberframing

6. Groun[d]

The Commissioners' record card for Mordiford Mill Cottage

107

Foy

The parish of Foy is divided into east and west Foy by the Wye, with the west side lying quite isolated in a large loop of the river. Foy has a long and fascinating history associated with Eaton Tregoz, Ingestone and the Abrahall family. The church of St. Mary dates from the 13th century and stands in a prominent position on the west side. It is linked by a footbridge to Foy east and Hole-in-the-Wall, where the buildings, apart from a barn, were listed by the RCHM. The 17th-century barn near Old Gore has been demolished, but the buildings at Hole-in-the-Wall have all survived.

Foy – Court Farm

In the past there has been much speculation about the site of Eaton Tregoz castle, but Court Farm is possibly the site either of this castle or of a fortified manor as shown on earlier maps.[22] Since 1929 Court Farm has survived largely unchanged except for modern window frames and a door made into the pent-roofed outbuilding on the roadside. Unfortunately the tall chimneys have been removed which alters its skyline. The nearby cottage was a range of three tenements featuring two gabled dormer windows, which have been replaced by modern windows, and the walls have been rendered.

The other listed building in Foy is known as Abrahall, a rectangular 17th-century building which was originally built as three almshouses 'one room up and one room down, endowed with 1s. a week for three poor pious persons by John Abrahall in 1640'.[23] In 1838 three widows were living there, each with a small garden, and in 1929 the house was described as three tenements. After weathering and floods had made the building derelict, it was restored in 1960 to form one dwelling with the date stone corrected from 1610 to 1640 – the year of John Abrahall's death.

Hentland

Hentland is a large parish in the south-west of the project area. Its name is derived from the Welsh 'hen llan' – the old church – indicating that the religious foundation is of great antiquity. The church is dedicated to St. Dubricius, the Latinised form of Dyfrig, and stands in a remote situation only reached by a single road or by footpaths along the routes of forgotten roads.[24] The most remarkable building in the parish with a long and fascinating history is Gillow Manor, which obviously impressed the commissioners who wrote copious notes and took many photographs of the premises in 1927. The moated manor dates from at least the 14th century and was associated with the Abrahall family during the 15th century. It is understood that the house has survived in good condition and substantially unchanged, but no detail could be seen, due to its distance from any public road.

Treaddow is a settlement on the southern edge of Hentland parish, where three buildings were visited by the surveyors in 1927. Great Treaddow is a handsome farmhouse, which has survived with little change apart from the appearance of the windows on the roadside elevation. The exposed cruck to the rear, which was described in 1927 as 'the cruck block on the N. side is possibly of 15th c[entury] date & represents all that remains of the original house,' remains intact. The three-bay 17th-century barn was also noted, but has

Hentland – Gillow Manor in 1927

Hentland – Treaddow in 1927

Hentland – Treaddow

since lost its later north extension. The present Little Treaddow appears to comprise only the south wing of the original larger building that existed in 1927.

At St. Owen's Cross, a makeshift sign has replaced a medieval socket stone and shaft at this ancient crossroads, which is dominated by the half-timbered New Inn. It was recorded as 'New Inne at Crosse Owen' in 1540, although the present building is of the 17th century, the name suggesting a replacement of an earlier hostelry. Since 1927, the east wall has been re-plastered to expose the timber frame and a kitchen extension has been added. The 17th-century two-storeyed barn standing by the roadside was demolished in the 1960s after Michael Foot MP was involved in a serious motor accident on the junction.[25]

The remaining buildings in Hentland are at or near Hoarwithy where the totally Italianate church, completed in the 1880s, was ignored as an important building in 1927 (see conclusions below). Llanfrother, derived from 'church of the brethren', stands above the Wye in a secluded position only accessed by an ancient track from Hoarwithy to Hentland. The place is traditionally associated with Dyfrig (Dubricius) since 1663, when Silas Taylor recorded the site.[26] Llanfrother farm dates from the 16th century, but was partly rebuilt probably by the Mynde family who were there during the 17th and 18th centuries. The south-west wing of the L-shaped building has not survived, but the remaining north-west wing is largely unchanged apart from a modern slate roof and some changes to the fenestration. The adjoining barn also survives unchanged.

Tresseck, 'a village on drained ground', is fairly unusual in having almost continuous documentation from the 13th century, and a date of building the house of '3 tie beams' in 1399.[27] The commissioners suggested a medieval origin, with later 17th- and 18th-century additions. The timber-framed house remains intact, as photographed in 1927, but with a pent-roofed addition on the south front. The barn of square timber-framing has lost its east wing, but the remainder retains its timber-framing with plank and plaster infilling.

Also at Tresseck, situated on the Wriggle Brook, was Tresseck Mill, an L-shaped timber-framed building dating from the late 16th century, but in 'bad condition and rapidly falling to pieces' in 1927. Even so, it

Hentland – Hoarwithy Church

was worthy of a plan and a description by the surveyors. The building was last used as a bone mill and then a home for agricultural labourers before it was demolished around 1960. A pair of modern cottages now occupies the site of the building, but remains of a weir and the water course are still visible.

Holme Lacy

This is a large parish, whose name is derived from Hamme, 'land in a river bend', and the de Lacy family, who held the estate in the 11th century. After the Dissolution, John Scudamore acquired the Holme Lacy estate which extended to 5,542 acres and it remained in the family until 1909. The sale particulars at that date provide a glimpse of the Holme Lacy buildings before the RCHM surveyors inspected them in 1927.[28] The church, dedicated to St. Cuthbert, is at the end of a lane beside the Wye. Due to its low-lying position and squat tower, it makes little impact on the landscape, whereas Holme Lacy House commands a prominent position overlooking the Wye Valley.

The 17th-century mansion of the Scudamores incorporates portions of an earlier house. The estate was sold and split up after the sale of 1909 and since then the mansion has been used for several purposes including a hospital and is now a hotel. The house, porch and service wing have remained intact since 1927 although there has been some internal rearrangement of rooms, and numerous modern extensions have been added to the west as part of the hotel. The Orangery is now connected to the house by a modern extension and has lost the decorative spherical vases that stood on its parapet in 1927.

Holme Lacy House
Top – 1927; Bottom – 2006

Near the church is the early 17th-century vicarage that was built on a stone plinth to enable the ground floor to be above flood level. The three-storeyed brick-built house with attics rises to a height that looks a little incongruous compared to the church. In 1776 the vicar, Gibbons Bagnall, recorded in the parish registers 'It is likewise an interest, as a great natural Curiosity, that the great Pear tree upon the Glebe, adjoining to the Vicarage house, provided this year fourteen hogsheads, each hogshead containing one hundred gallons'.[29] Apart from the ivy having been removed, the building seen between the trees and a high wall appears to have survived as described in 1927.

The Shipley Gardens, which are open to the public, are described on their web pages as 'a 17th Century Wye Valley homestead standing upon the site of previous dwellings that since Roman times have administered the adjacent ford and former ferry'.[30] The river crossing certainly existed from the 18th century, and Shipley farmhouse was recorded as 17th century with a later addition by the RCHM in 1927 when it was two tenements. Since then it has lost its thatched roof, been rendered and extended, and had modern windows inserted.

In Holme Lacy village, four cottages and one house were recorded in 1927 including one now known as The Thatch at the crossroads, with its origins dating from before the 17th century. In 1927 the building was two cottages, but it now forms one house which retains its exposed timber-framing and thatched roof. A modern cross-wing featuring a clock has been added to the west to match the rest of the property. Bower Cottage appears to be largely unchanged with exposed timber-framing to the front and modern roof tiles, and the next black-and-white cottage to the west also appears little changed. The cottage at Hannah Green has retained its timber-framing and the low addition referred to in 1927 has been heightened. Another house in this group is Primrose Bank, which had already been much altered and re-fronted before the surveyors' inspection and has since acquired timber boarding to the roadside elevation.

From the village, a road to Bogmarsh leads to further 17th-century buildings surveyed in 1927. Widow's Wood is a picturesque cottage with a thatched roof, which remains very little changed apart from the addition of a small porch. Beyond Upper Bogmarsh Farm there was a pair of cottages converted from a house, which has not survived, having been replaced by a modern house. A footpath from this road leads to Ramsden Farm where two cottages known as Ramsden Buildings have been replaced by a 20th-century house.

Billingsley is an ancient site recorded in 1055 and at a later date formed part of the Scudamore's Holme Lacy estate.[31] The farm had already been considerably altered before 1927 and is not near enough to a right-of-way to be viewed in detail, although it appears that the stone walls have been rendered. Within a quarter of a mile is Canondale, a farmhouse partly of stone and timber-framing which had been much altered by 1927. The farm buildings are almost hidden from the public road, but once again it appears that the walls have been rendered.

How Caple

How Caple is one of the smaller parishes and is almost in the centre of the Landscape Origins project area. In 1812 it was noted that 'This Parish containing 1018 acres occupies a most picturesque position on the banks of the Wye, which flows around its western boundary towards Foy'.[32] The manor belonged to the Capels from at least the 13th century until 1683 when it was sold to Sir William Gregory whose descendants sold the estate in 1894 to the present family. In the church of St. Andrew and St. Mary only the chancel is medieval, the rest dating from a rebuilding in the 1690s and the Victorian restoration of 1899.

How Caple Court stands in an enviable position overlooking the church and the Wye Valley. The house in 1929 was reported as much modernised but with parts dating from the 17th and 18th centuries. Owned by the same family since 1894, the court has survived almost entirely unchanged. The stabling and barns mentioned by the surveyors are also substantially unchanged; one was used as a garage and has now lost its external glass canopy, and another was used as a Racquet Court, whilst the third barn has recently been converted to the Concert Barn. How Caple Court Gardens are open to the public between March and October and teas are served in the courtyard.

Within half a mile from the church at How Caple is the former Rectory which in 1929 consisted of a rectangular main block dating from the late 17th century which had been modernised internally and externally. The only other building listed in 1929 was a building at Totnor on the northern edge of the parish. It was described as a 17th-century house divided into two tenements which, apart from being subsequently divided into three with an additional door and alterations to the fenestration, remains largely unchanged.

How Caple Court in 1929

King's Caple

The parish of King's Caple lies on the east bank of the Wye, where the river describes a great loop forming a peninsula which has attracted settlement from a very early date. The history of King's Caple has been written and researched from its documents,[33] and since then a private collection of archives and maps has become available.[34] The church is dedicated to St. John the Baptist, with a 13th-century nave and a 14th-century chancel and tower topped with an octagonal spire serving as a remarkable landmark in this part of the Wye Valley.

King's Caple
Left – Lower Ruxton Cottage in 1927;
Above – Remains of cottage

A cottage at Lower Ruxton dating from the late 17th century has retained its exposed timber-framing, but has lost the thatched roof of 1927 which has since been replaced by slates. It has had a modern outbuilding attached to the west end, a new door inserted on its front elevation and some other minor alterations. Eighty yards north-east of Lower Ruxton was another building described as a small, rectangular, 17th-century cottage which was in poor condition in 1927. Only a small fragment of stone walling marks the site.

At Lower Penalt the farmhouse dates from the 17th century and a barn constructed in *c*.1600 was in 'a ruinous condition' when inspected in 1927. There is no photograph for comparison with the house as it is at present, but the fine stone and brick house does not appear to have undergone any substantial changes. The barn has not survived apart from a stone base supporting weather-boarded walls. Another thatched 17th-century cottage has been replaced by a modern house situated between Mill Ditch and Sellack Boat.

Sellack

The riverside parish of Sellack was recorded as Baysham prior to the 14th century and by the 1300s almost 100 acres of land had been acquired by the Dean and Chapter of Hereford. Until boundary changes in the 1880s Strangford had been part of Fownhope. Sellack derived its name from the dedication of its church to the 7th-century St. Tysiliog. The original church was a timber structure rebuilt in the 12th century with many later additions and alterations including a major restoration in the 1840s.

The most important house in Sellack is Caradoc Court, built on a legendary site suggesting an ancient encampment. From 1594 it became home to a branch of the Scudamores who rebuilt the mansion in the 1620s, and whose descendants sold it in 1863. It was then dramatically refurbished and passed through several ownerships before a fire gutted the building in 1986.[35] It is at present being sympathetically restored, but the west wing remains unroofed and partly ruinous. The remainder of the principal front appears as in earlier photographs except that the blocked carriageway to the courtyard has been re-opened. The observation turret and its stubby spire had disappeared long before the fire.

Sellack – Caradoc Court about 1910

Caradoc Court in 2007

Towards the end of the 20th century Caradoc Court was separated from the farm, stableyard and barns which now form an attractive group of buildings. The coach house is two storeyed and was built as stables with external stairs to the first floor. In 1929 it had been converted into a garage, but since then it has been considerably altered for residential purposes. Dormers have been added, but the coach house retains its square-headed and mullioned windows. West of the Court are two large 17th-century stone barns with gabled ends. A date stone of 1634 was recorded on the larger barn, and one of 1665 on the northern one by the surveyors in 1929. The barns have remained unchanged and are used as a food store and tack room for the stableyard.[36]

At the end of the drive to Caradoc Court is the Lough Pool Inn, which takes its name from a nearby field known as 'ye Louge Poole' in 1607.[37] The building was inhabited by Richard Mynde in the 17th century and by 1839 formed part of the Guy's Hospital Estate before becoming a beer house later that century.[38] Since 1929 the inn has been extended to the south and north-east, doors have been moved and windows have been enlarged and others newly inserted, but the historic part of the inn is still broadly the same externally with its timber-framing exposed.

Two 17th-century cottages were also listed by the surveyors of 1929. Burford Cottage, which is near the church, retains its timber-frame on its north side, but dormers and an extension to the east end have been added, and its corrugated iron roof has been replaced with clay tiles. Backney Cottage, situated near Backney Common on the banks of the Wye, has been totally replaced by a building that does not appear to incorporate any fabric of the original cottage.

Sellack – The Lough Pool: Left – in 1927; Right – in 2006

Conclusions

As was perhaps expected from this survey, undertaken by the Landscape Origins of the Wye Valley project in 2006, buildings of a higher status survived better. Most churches went through 19th-century restoration but have hardly changed since. Because of the Royal Commission's cut-off date of 1714, the surveyors did not include Hoarwithy church dedicated to St. Catherine – a unique Italianate building commanding a prominent position overlooking the Wye, and All Saints at Brockhampton built in the Arts and Crafts style by Lethaby in 1902 and described as 'one of the most convincing and most impressive churches of its date in any country'.[39]

It is noticeable that the two estate villages of How Caple and Brockhampton have enjoyed a good survival rate of their buildings, whereas Ballingham has not, perhaps reflecting different priorities between the respective landowners. The overall result shows nearly a half of all buildings recorded in the late 1920s surviving largely unchanged externally, while just over a quarter have been lost. This seems quite encouraging and probably compares favourably with other regions.[40] However, smaller buildings and barns have suffered.

Great Houses

The survey area is fortunate not to have lost any of the Great Houses in the post-war period when so many were demolished country-wide. Although Aramstone House at King's Caple was demolished in the mid 1950s, it had been built soon after the cut-off date so was not included in the 1929 survey. Wilton Castle is a well preserved and consolidated ruin, and although not a noticeable landmark provides the area with an early and interesting history.

King's Caple: Armastone
Cover of Salmon Fishing Record Books
A Report by a project team member

Two great houses which have undergone more substantial changes are Caradoc Court, due to its fire, and Holme Lacy House, because of its conversion to a hotel.

Houses
The buildings categorised as houses show a good survival rate; many were or are farmhouses with few losses. Dunn's Farm in Ballingham and the divided house at Upper Bogmarsh in Holme Lacy have been replaced with modern buildings. Lane End is now in Peterstow parish instead of Bridstow due to changed boundaries, and the timber-framed mill at Tresseck has been demolished and replaced by a pair of cottages.

Cottages
The survey of cottages showed a more mixed picture of survival and change, with variations from parish to parish. Fownhope has lost the most cottages due to those situated in isolated positions on Common Hill, where unnamed properties of 1929 were difficult to locate and identify. Four others were demolished because of redevelopment or because they were obstructing the village street. Several that were recorded in poor or fair condition in the late 1920s such as a cottage at Lower Ruxton in King's Caple and a cottage near the church at Ballingham have not survived. Those that have survived have been enlarged and extended to meet modern needs.

Barns
Nearly half the barns listed in the 1920s have not survived, including three at Ballingham and four at Fownhope. It may be assumed that these losses occurred in the period after a change in farming practice before the listing system had an impact, and prior to the viability of residential conversion. The remaining barns are either quite vulnerable due to their condition, or will survive in farmyards and on estates either in their present state or converted to other uses.

Inns
All four inns that were recorded by the Royal Commissioners have survived, but have been enlarged and adapted to meet modern catering requirements. Although numerous pubs have closed in recent years it is fortunate that the Cottage of Content, the Green Man, the Lough Pool, and the New Inn are still open and offering a high standard of service.

Category	Largely unchanged		More change		Not survived		Total
Churches	12	(92%)	1	(8%)	0		13
Great Houses	7	(78%)	2	(22%)	0		9
Houses	19	(61%)	8	(26%)	4	(13%)	31
Cottages	11	(31%)	10	(29%)	14	(40%)	35
Barns	11	(42%)	3	(12%)	12	(46%)	26
Inns	0		4	(100%)	0		4
Total	**60**	**(51%)**	**28**	**(24%)**	**30**	**(25%)**	**118**

Findings 1927-1929 to 2007[41]

Hentland – New Inn

Listed Buildings in 2007

Within the twelve parishes of the project area, despite the loss of 25% of the buildings recorded in 1927, 138 buildings were listed in 2007. This number includes many additional buildings such as Lethaby's thatched church at Brockhampton, but excludes several important buildings that were in the Royal Commissioners' inventory of 1927-9. Court Farm at Foy, Ashe Ingham Court at Bridstow, Shipley at Holme Lacy, Abrahall Almshouses at Foy, and others have been omitted. The reasons explained by the National Monuments Record are that:

> The Royal Commission Inventory for Herefordshire was a project that was conducted under the terms of the Commission's Royal Charter and which had nothing to do with the listed building process. At the time the parishes were accessed for listing, the listed-building inspectors did not consider these buildings worthy of listing. The inclusion in a Royal Commission Inventory survey does not automatically mean that the building will be given listed status.[42]

Another reason according to Herefordshire Council is that:

> There may never have been a direct correlation between the pre-war RCHM research and lists. It has been pointed out that some buildings may have been victims of the deletion of the old Grade 3 category in the late 1960s and early 1970s.[43]

Brockhampton old church in 1832

Brockhampton new church in 2008

The view from Brockhampton new church 2008

CHAPTER VI

The River's Industrial Past

by Heather Hurley (with a contribution by Rebecca Roseff)

Perhaps for as long as mankind have lived near it, the River Wye (and its tributaries) has attracted a variety of industries, from its source on the Plynlimon Mountains to its mouth at Chepstow.[1] The river's constant flow of water provided the power and the valley provided the raw materials for the many industries that took place throughout the centuries on the river bank and along its tributaries. The most important ones were corn milling, iron making, tanning, brewing, paper making, lime burning, stone quarrying, shipbuilding, basket making, rope making, flax dressing, cider and perry making, tuck milling, and the rarer production of must, snuff and silk.

It is somewhat surprising that these past industries have left relatively little impression on the landscape. It is mainly through documentation, mapping and field names that sites have been identified. When a survey of the Wye was undertaken by the project team in 2006, many sites were investigated and photographed, and it was observed that remaining islands in the river appeared to coincide with early mill, weir and fishery sites. Old mill buildings add a touch of romanticism to the landscape, but only a few have survived on the Wye's tributaries, and these have been converted to residential use. The bark houses and the former brewery at Fownhope have seen many changes and the withy beds have been removed or have grown so much that they are now unrecognisable. On the wooded hills and steep escarpments of the Wye Valley, overgrown and almost forgotten lime kilns and quarries present attractive and interesting features, and together with cider orchards provide habitats for wildlife.

Water Mills

Corn Mills

Although it is known that water-mills existed before Domesday,[2] those recorded at Domesday in the project area were at Brampton Abbotts, Fownhope, How Caple, and two at Wilton, with fisheries that were often associated with mills at Fownhope and Wilton.[3] Medieval corn mills in the Wye Valley included Carey Mill and its weir of 1250,[4] which was described as 'Two water mills constructed under one building' in 1528,[5] and in need of repairing in 1589.[6] The mill at Brampton Abbotts in 1263 was probably on the Rudhall Brook,[7] but there is evidence of a mill site at Netherton.[8] The mill and fishery at Holme Lacy in 1266 was on the Wye and rented from the Dean and Chapter for '240 loads of mixtilion wheat and rye',[9] whilst the mill at Sellack was near the church and in need of repair in 1286.[10] In 1369 there were 'Two water mills worth 6s 8d' and a fishery with a weir which was worth 40s. per annum at Eaton Tregoz in the parish of Foy.[11]

During the medieval period, the upkeep of mills with their spokes, ladders, cogs, keys, spindles, hoppers, jacks, rungs, wheels, sluices etc., was an expensive and complicated business. The 14th-century mill accounts of the canons of Hereford provide some details and costs, for example:

> 66 cogs and 26 rungs bought for the mill this year 2s 6d and for renewing the broken mill wheel shaft 15d and one wooden hoop bought for the mill 3s ... for 1½ cart loads of straw bought roofing the millhouse 20d and one roofer for roofing the said mill with straw for 4½ days 18d and for 2 sawyers hired to saw 200 joists and half an oak plank for works on the said mills giving for each of the sawyers 15d ... making implements and mending the mill grinding wheel taken on day 4d.[12]

Later documentary sources reveal the existence at Bolstone of Trill Mill on a small stream and Aburtaretts Mill and weir on the Wye in 1505,[13] which was leased to Robert Hancock in 1571 with 'all the houses water courses, were gates and fyshinges'.[14] There was a mill at Poulstone in King's Caple established in the late 16th century,[15] two water corn mills at Foy in 1611,[16] and a 'Water Grist Mill called Wigley's Mill' at How Caple in 1698.[17] By the 18th century five mills had been established on the Wriggle Brook, which flows into the Wye at Hoarwithy; these included Hoarwithy Mill, Tresseck Mill, and Middle Mill in Hentland parish In other parishes, there was the Mordiford Mill on the Pentaloe Brook at Fownhope, How Caple Mill on the Totnor Brook at How Caple, and Tarrs Mill on the Tars Brook at Holme Lacy.[18] The Nupend Mill on the Tan Brook in Fownhope is probably datable to before 1817.[19]

Hoarwithy Mill was converted into a dwelling house in the late 1970s, but fortunately some of the internal machinery was preserved and the water courses can still be traced. Also at Hoarwithy, the mill and adjoining cottage of Middle Mill have been incorporated into one dwelling. The converted How Caple Mill and the buildings of Mordiford Mill are visible from the road and from the Wye Valley Walk. There are remnants of sluices and dams on the brooks that worked the water-mills, with a few scanty remains of overgrown mill ponds.

Former mill at How Caple

Hoarwithy Mill in 1983

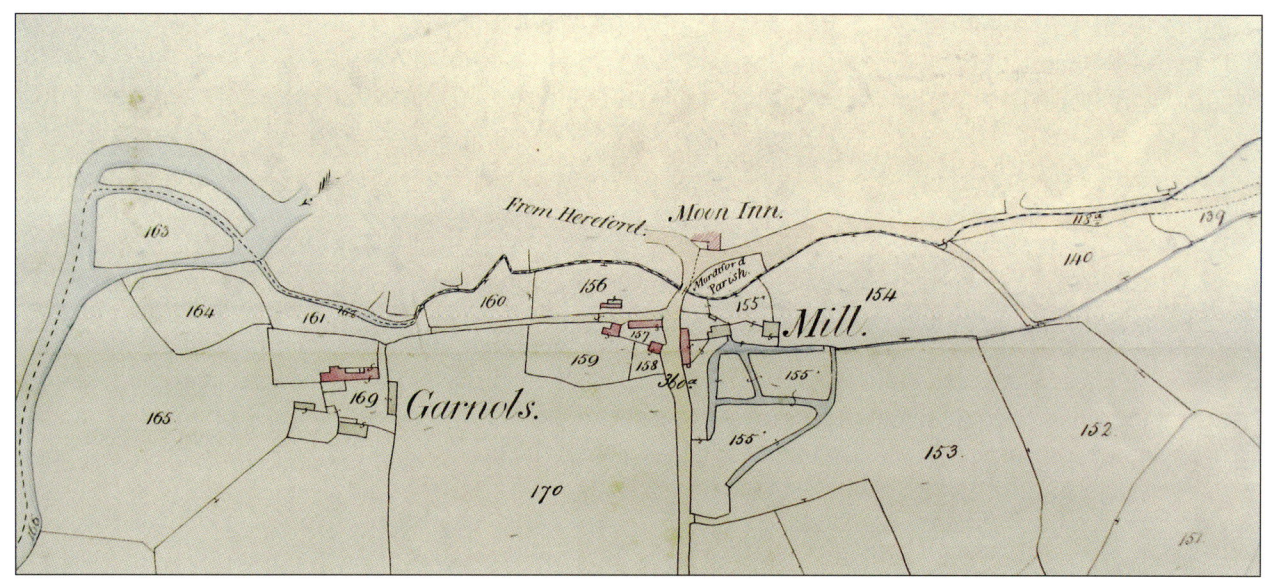

Plan of the mill at Mordiford in 1843

Iron Working

The only known iron forge on the Wye in the project area was at Carey Islands, where the earlier corn mill was either converted or rebuilt as a forge. In 1627 Sir John Kyrle of Much Marcle, Sir John Scudamore of Holme Lacy and William Scudamore of Ballingham entered into a partnership to build and run an iron forge at Carey Mills. A year later Articles of Agreement were made between the two Scudamores to erect:

> an Iron myll or forge with all howses and other necessarie buildings for the use of the same shall be with as much convenient speede as may be made ... or neere a mill called Cary Mill upon the River of Wye.[20]

The forge site on Carey Islands

The forge was completed in 1629 for the cost of £632 2s. 9d. and 'The Charge of making a ton of Bar Iron at Carey Forge' in 1630 was 15s. 8d. The iron was transported to Bristol for the smiths to produce, nails, horseshoes, tools, weapons, and agricultural implements.[21]

Further documents record the forge and include another agreement made in 1631/2 between Viscount Scudamore and William Scudamore of Ballingham, whereby the Viscount released 'all his rights title and interest of in and to the myll called Carie Mill' and 'of and in Carie Forge or Iron Worke, and all houses lands and other things thereto belonging together with all his part of all stocke of iron coale, woods and all other implements'.[22] This is the last known document referring to the iron works, so it is not known how long it was in production, but a reference to 'the boatman at Carey mill' in 1632 may serve as a clue.[23] It had probably ceased operations before the disruptive years of the Civil War and by 1679 was called Carey Mill.[24]

Paper Mills

Paper mills were located beside quick and clear running water, needed both for power and as a raw material. Early papermaking was a skilled and complicated process, sorting cotton and linen rags in water, which were placed in heaps and allowed to rot. After washing they were pulped in the stamping mill and the pulped fibres were conveyed from storage to a large vat where they were formed into sheets with the aid of a mould. These were then drained, placed in a wooded screw press and once the surplus water had been removed the sheets were taken to the drying lofts. Several paper mills existed in the Wye Valley, but only one known and one probable paper mill site were located in the project area.[25]

All that remains of the paper mill at Tresseck

The paper mill at Tresseck in Hentland parish had been converted from an earlier corn mill recorded in 1595. It was probably due to the clear and swift flowing water of the Wriggles Brook that it was converted by William Roberts in the 18th century.[26] A sale notice of 1786 of the 'Dwelling-House and Paper-Mill now in possession of Thomas White' suggests that it was also used as a 'water corn-grist-mill'.[27] In 1810 rags and junk (old ropes) were delivered by barge from Bristol to Hoarwithy for paper making and in 1810 '17 bundles' and '4 Cwt of paper' were sent to Bristol.[28] A sale particular of 1827 described the mill as a 'Dwelling House, with a Paper Mill, Drying House etc. adjoining thereto, called Tresseck Paper Mill'.[29] The paper maker was Richard Thornbury who was followed by Mary Coney an 'Independent Paper Maker' in 1841, before the mill was downgraded to a Bone Mill. Although it continued to be used for this purpose and for chaff cutting it was in a 'bad condition and rapidly falling to pieces in 1927, and the picturesque black and white timber-framed building was demolished around 1960.[30]

LOT III.

A very convenient Dwelling House, with a Paper Mill, Drying House, &c. adjoining thereto, called Tresseck Paper Mill, well adapted for carrying on an extensive business, together with 3A. 1R. 34P. (be the same more or less) of excellent Meadow, or Pasture Land contiguous, now in the occupation of Mr. Richard Thornberry.

25 Paper Mill, House, Garden, Pond, &c.	-	-	-	-	———	0	3	14
26 Sling	-	-	-	-	*Meadow*	0	1	18
27 Paper Mill Meadow	-	-	-	-	*ditto*	2	1	2
						3	1	34

Land-Tax, 7s. 6d. on this Lot.

The Sale of Tresseck Paper Mill in 1827

The other probable paper mill site is conjectural and has been listed on the basis of the names of the Paper Mill Meadow and Paper Mill Bridge shown on the Hentland Tithe Map of 1842. The bridge crosses the Luke Brook which would have provided a source of water. In earlier deeds it is referred to as 'peper Myll' in the 17th century and in 1778 'Pepper Mill' at Glewstone.[31] It may have meant a mill that was paid for by a peppercorn rent and not a paper mill at all, as no further evidence has been found to support this claim. In the Customs and Excise letters of 1816 and the list of Paper Makers in 1832, Tresseck Mill is number 147 and Bill Mills at Weston-under-Penyard is 146, but no paper mill on the Hentland boundary is listed.[32] [33]

Fulling Mills

Fulling or tuck mills, which produced woollen textiles, are well documented from early times in Ross and Hereford. There were also 'two fulling mills worth per year 40s.' at Wilton in the project area. They often had problems and the fulling mills of the Hereford canons needed constant repairs during the 14th century, with such costs as:

> repairing the broken shaft sockets and wheels of the fulling mill 6d and for one workman hired for half a day to cut timber 2d and payment to John Glasebury [for] the mill wheel shaft from a wood called Ramesden 14d.[34]

The wood now called Ramsden Coppice is at Holme Lacy, in the project area about five miles south of Hereford.

Other Mills

Snuff mills were uncommon, and apart from a record of one at Garway in 1773 no others have been discovered in this area.[35] Surprisingly, a silk mill at Fownhope was advertised for sale in 1856 with its 'Ten Horse power Steam Engine, with boiler complete. 6 Throwing Mills, 144 spindles each. 3 Winding Engines, 32 ditto. 3 Drawing Frames, 32 ditto. 2 Doubling Frames, 32 ditto,'[36] but research reveals that the mill, operated by Thomas Jennings, only existed for a very short period.[37] Silk mills were established in other parts of the country from 1721 using water power, and from the description of the Fownhope Silk Mill it was a throwing mill, involved in a process 'by which raw silk is wound from the skein, twisted, doubled and twisted again;'[38] as steam was required, a water supply was needed.

TO LET or SELL, with immediate possession, all the SILK FACTORY PLANT, situate at Fownhope, in the county of Hereford, consisting of

1 Ten Horse power STEAM ENGINE, with boiler complete.
6 THROWING MILLS, 144 spindles each.
6 WINDING ENGINES, 32 ditto.
3 DRAWING FRAMES, 32 ditto.
2 DOUBLING FRAMES, 32 ditto.

The above Machinery is entirely new and in good working condition, together with every other requisite for carrying on the above business, including a good Residence, Garden, Stabling, &c., attached.

To parties desirous of purchasing, an excellent opportunity will shortly be afforded, as this property and 5 acres of LAND adjoining, as also the *Rudgend Estate*, containing 157 Acres of LAND, the property of the late Thomas Jennings, will shortly be Sold by Auction under the direction of the Court of Chancery.

Apply to Mr. CLEAVE or Mr. SYMONDS, Solicitors, Hereford, for particulars and cards of admission.   [5424

Silk factory at Fownhope for sale in 1856

Fishing

Fish was important in the medieval period because of Friday fast days and Lent, when meat was not allowed but fish could be eaten. Rights to fishing always belonged to someone, and were jealously guarded with rent and tithe paid, but who the rights belonged to was often disputed. Challenges of ownership occurred, and the claim of 'free fishing granted from time immemorial' was a common one.[39] Normally claims by tenants that they had fishing rights in the project area of the Wye were quashed in Court[40] and the fishing allocated to the lord of the manor.

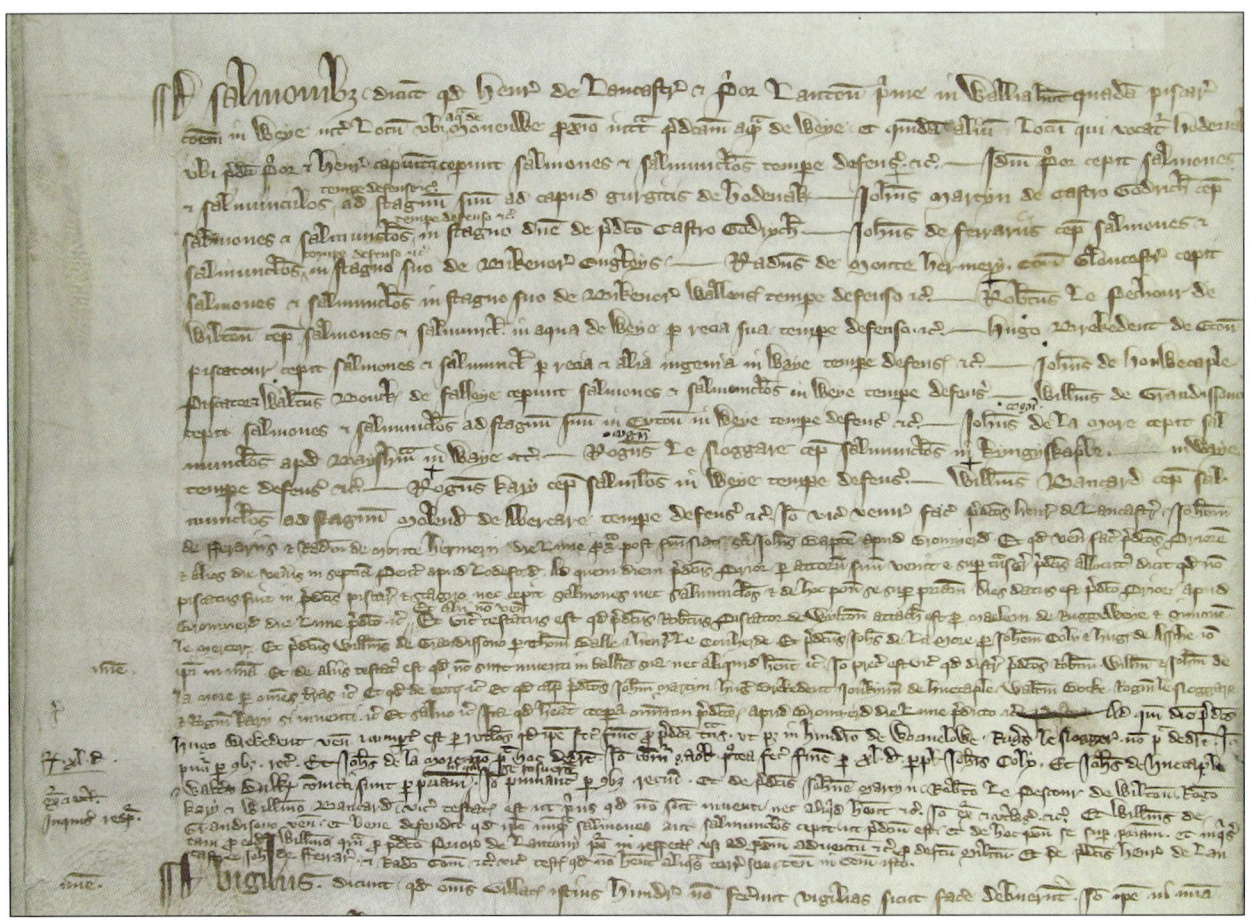

In 1307 'Robert le Pecheur of Wilton caught large and small salmon in water of the Wye using his net during the close season. Hugo Brekedent of Eton fisherman caught large and small salmon using a net and other devices in the Wye during the close season. John le Houwecaple fisherman and Walter Boucke de Falleye caught large and small salmon in water of the Wye using his net during the close season'.

At Domesday about a hundred mills were listed in Herefordshire, many of which paid rent in eels. This implies that fisheries often went with mills and also that eels were a favoured fish that could be caught comparatively easily. A number of fisheries were directly mentioned. Thus in Broadward, a fishery paid 500 eels for the rights and at Wilton a fishery paid nothing. Land held under Welsh custom in Archenfield, which included much of the study area, was not recorded in detail, so it is not known how many mills and fisheries there were. The large manor of Fownhope, to the east of the Wye, was not in Archenfield and had three fisheries which paid 300 eels.

One of the earliest descriptions of fish in the Wye comes from Gerald of Wales in his *Journey through Wales* of 1191:

> There is no lack of freshwater fish, both in the Usk and the Wye. Salmon and trout are fished from these rivers, but the Wye has more salmon and the Usk more trout. In winter salmon are in season in the Wye, but in the summer they abound in the Usk. The Wye is particularly rich in grayling, an excellent fish which some call umber.[41]

Fisheries were quite valuable. In 1369 the possessions belonging to Eaton Tregoz manor included a fishery with a weir worth 40s. per annum.[42] To compare, twenty acres of meadow were worth 30s. and two carucates of arable land 10s. The fish weir may have been near the islands at Eton Tregoz in Foy, and it is known from excavated examples elsewhere in the country that posts would have been positioned across the river in a 'V' shape, the point upstream to trap incoming fish. Between the posts would be wattle fencing which channelled fish into baskets that were fixed by means of stone weights

The bailiff accounts of Eton Tregoz between 1445-1465 describe 'upmouths':[43]

> And 12d from the location of 'upmouths' in the Wye this year. And 12d from the annual rent for the licence concessed to John Smith at the end of seven years, as in the court rolls, for making two upmouths at Upper headland of Capulford, to assign to the bailiff, also to nail and make firm the building at his river bank above the land of the demesne.[44]

Most references to 'fisheries' imply a structure often associated with mills and weirs. A weir held water back to regulate the flow on a side channel of the river leading to the mill, whilst a fishery in the form of baskets or nets was stretched over the flowing part of the river as described in 1571:

> John Scudamore of Holme Lacy and Robert Hancock of Bolston letts to RH the water mylle calle Abytarotes mylle with houses, water courses, were gates and fyshinges 4d ... and also 24 styckes of eles and 24 shotlings a year, or else to pay for every sticke 4d and for every shotlying 4d and as many stickes [more] as the said JS will have to spend in their houses for 4d the stycke, if there be as many taken at the said mill.[45]

Indeed it was considered illegal to take fish using methods other than nets. Presumably nets could be policed and taxed, while fishing lines and boats could be used to catch fish unnoticed. A Holme Lacy court roll of 1563 ordered:

> that no one henceforth shall fish with le Cruckelles otherwise lether bottes in the water there called Wye with le angles and angling Roddes. nor shall by [r]ight from henceforth in the water aforesaid with 'le Crockelles' without licence of the lords.[46]

In the same court fines for fishing without a license were ignored year after year by up to twelve offenders, very often the same ones. Their fines varied from 12d to 6s 8d and in 1622 an exasperated bailiff pronounced that henceforth the fine would be 20s., a charge which was not imposed.

The lord of the manor sometimes let the fishing rights in return for a supply of fish. For example, in 1648:

> William Scudamore of Ballingham demise grant and farme lette and sett to Thomas Dunston of Hoarwithy and John Puckmore of Biblett, Hentland one nett fishing in the river Wye in the manor and lordship of Ballingham and within all his waters belonging to his manor of Kingscapel. From 1 May last for 3 years. Yeeldinge and paying yearly to WS one seasonable salmon between March 1 and 30 April yeerely and so much good whight fish every Friday morning as shal be worth six pence.[47]

This suggests that salmon, then as now, were traditionally taken between March and April. The fish caught had to be offered to the House for sale, so while the rent (of 26s. 9d.) was not particularly high, the fresh fish was a perk for the lord. In 1637 the jurors of the Manor or Hundred of Wormelow (a large area broadly coinciding with what was termed Archenfield in the 17th century), stated that all freeholders had the right to fish in the Wye (this was later disputed) but if they caught any salmon these had to be taken to Hoarwithy and offered first for sale there before being taken to market.[48]

Fishing on the Wye in the 18th century

Tanning and the Bark Trade

Tanning

Tanyards were mainly established in the market towns, where the raw materials were readily available, but records exist of a 'Tan-House and Pitts' at Fownhope in 1787, which was probably the same as the one advertised in 1851 as a Tan-Yard with a 'A Neat Dwelling-House'.[49] The name of a house and cottages in Hentland suggests an earlier tanyard site, but no further evidence has been found.[50] The craft of tanning – converting raw hide to leather – dates from prehistoric times, progressing over the centuries into a complicated and lengthy process. From the 17th century, hides were brought to the tanyard where they were washed and then soaked in lime pits before the removal of the flesh, fat and hair, which were reused in other trades. Before tanning, the pelts were de-limed, then put through a series of tan pits full of solutions made from ground bark and water. After further washing the hides were taken to drying lofts, then to the currier who made the final touches to the leather ready for the shoe and boot makers, saddlers, harness makers, and glove makers.

The *c.*1820s sale particulars and detailed plan of the Brookend Tanyard in Ross serve as an example of a working tannery. It was described as an:

> Excellent Tanyard containing 82 Pits with Bark-mill, Drying Lofts, Store-rooms, Currier's Retail Shop, etc. in complete repair, to which the Currying Business is attached and in full work; and to which that of a Fellmonger might with convenience be added, as there is a good stream of water constantly flowing through the yard. The dwelling house is large and commodious with Vaulted Cellars, large Malthouse and Stables, and every convenience for carrying on an extensive trade,

and the advantages were that there was an abundance of the finest bark and no fellmonger within eight miles.[51] The business was unsold and advertised again in 1836 when it was sold and replaced by a new tanyard at Overross.

Bark Trade

Bark houses were situated along the banks of the Wye at Fownhope, Hoarwithy and Wilton where, in late April and May, the bark stripped from the trees was:

> made up in large stacks by the side of the river, with as much neatness as farmers make a hay rick. Here a number of women are employed, seated in the open air, to strip off the moss and outer skin, which is done with a knife about a foot long, used by them with great dexterity ... From them it is taken into the Bark house, where it is cut by men into pieces, about four inches in length, for the use of the tanners.

Bark ricks in Haugh Wood in the 19th century

The bark was then conveyed by barges, which could carry 20 to 25 tons according to the state of the river, to the tannery.[52]

The bark houses at Fownhope were at Even Pits, Lechmere Ley and in the village near the tanhouse.[53] In 1799 Bowsher, Hodges and Watkins, wine and bark merchants from Chepstow, wrote to Sir Hungerford Hoskyns requesting the use of 'a barn near the river at Hoarwithy which has not yet been finished' and 'to chop bark in for a period of three to four years, and to roof the building with straw or pantiles'. The company offered to pay '12d per Ton for the wharfing of any Bark we may send there, the quantity will be about 6 or 700 Tons in the Four Years'.[54] It appears that the bark house at Hoarwithy was used for a longer period, as it was still owned by the Chepstow Bark Company in 1842.[55]

The largest and busiest bark enterprise in the project area was at Wilton, where James Woodhouse, as agent of the Guy's Hospital Estate, kept accounts of the bark trade and the use of the wharf and warehouses at Wilton. Between 1785 and 1807 repairs were made to the coal wharf, two bark houses and an 'Old Malthouse' at Wilton. Cash was paid for 'falling and stripping bark' at £11 a ton, which appears to have sold for £12 12s. a ton plus rates for landing, warehousing and turnpikes.[56] Those involved at Wilton were William Porter, a corn factor and barge owner, and James Woodhouse, the agent, who 'proved to be more incompetent than Fortune' – the previous agent.[57]

His account (below) of bark purchased at £11 per ton in 1806 does not balance.[58] It reads:

Tons	cwt	lbs	Source
1	-	-	from Benall (Benhall)
-	19	2	from Ware End (Weirend)
-	20	-	from W Cross (Whitecross)
2	**18**	**2**	**@ 11£ £31·14·3**

The total weight should be 2 tons 19cwt 2lbs and at £11 per ton the total cost should be £32 9s 2½d

129

Stallard accounts for bark and stone in 1849

During the 18th and 19th centuries, details of bark costs and stripping are recorded in the accounts of the Holme Lacy and Brockhampton estates, and the transportation of bark by river appears in the barge accounts.[59] The great days of the bark trade were during the Napoleonic Wars, but at the end of the wars with France the trade began to decline due to a lack of demand.[60] A noticeable example of this was in 1827 when 'A Young Man of very respectable family and connexions, 13 years of age, and who has already served two years and a half of his term to a very extensive Tanner' was seeking an 'In or Out-Door Apprenticeship' in the Hereford area.[61] Other stray items referring to the bark trade have been traced in 1820, 1843 and 1850, with photographs of bark stripping in 1900.[62]

Lime Burning and Stone Quarrying

Lime Burning

Over the centuries, lime has been in demand for tanning, building, agriculture, and medicinal products. On the limestone hills of Lea and Paget's Wood, Common Hill, and at Little Hope in Fownhope, overgrown quarries and tumbling lime kilns are a reminder of the good quality lime that was produced in the past, but this lime was not used to repair the Wye Bridge at Hereford in 1684; 'baggs of Lime' and 'Seames of Lime' from Dinedor, Whitchurch and Ganarew were used.[63] The earliest known records of the lime industry at Fownhope dates from 1698, when payments were made for carrying stone and filling a kiln.[64] In 1777 'as much Lime as can be bought for five Pounds at the Lime Kilns in the Parish of Fownhope' was ordered by Lulham Farm at Madley.[65] Once the limestone had been cut from the nearby quarries, the lime burner's job was to place layers of limestone and fuel into the charge hole at the top of the kiln, and fire the furnace from below. This produced clinker which fell into the draw hole at the bottom and if slaked with water produced a fine powder of lime.

Fownhope, Common Hill – Lime kiln

Fownhope, Littlehope – Lime kiln at Scutterdine

From the late 18th century lime was in demand for agricultural improvement, and in 1794 'Lime for Sale' was supplied 'at Twelve Shillings per Load at the Kiln' from William Pritchard, who had 'caused the road through Haught, to be made commodious for single or double teams'. Orders could be taken by John Matthews, the lime burner at the kiln or on Saturdays at the Catherine Wheel in Hereford.[66] Pritchard was recorded in the Fownhope Court Rolls three years later of 'Limestone Lett on the Common Hill ... in such direction as the Veins or Seames of Lime may lead', and of another parcel at the west end of the hill at an old quarry near a 'house lately erected by Samuel Connop'.[67] This must have been the man known as King Connop who 'owned and worked most of the lime kilns' and employed parish apprentices as lime burners.[68]

In the late 18th century careful accounts were kept of an unnamed lime kiln that was associated with the Woodhouse family. The 1796 account shows the costs of '238 dozen Coal', and the burning, riddling, price of baskets and powder, labour of smith and carpenter, 8s. for '1 load Stone' and one years rent, which totalled £164 8s 1½d for producing '559 doz. Lime'.[69] At Littlehope in 1805 there was an 'excellent quarry of Lime Stone, which has for many years been worked, and well accustomed, with Four Lime Kilns, which on the average of some years, have burnt 2,000 loads annually of Lime fit for building and other purposes', and in 1811 a 'Quarry of Lime Stone sufficient for the whole of the county, with convenient and well accustomed Kilns for burning the lime' was advertised for sale.[70]

Kilns were advertised for rent in the early 1800s 'To be sold by auction ... The lease of two limekilns, now in full work, with an extensive and very valuable rock of limestone, of the first quality; situate at the Common Hill' and in 1810:

A Limestone Quarry, of excellent quality, near a good Turnpike-road, within six miles of the City of Hereford. The Lime is good either for Building or Manure, which is not the case in general. N.B. In going from the Kiln with loaded Wagons, there is no up-hill ground or dangerous roads, and, if suited a Wharf may be had for landing the Coal free of expense.[71]

In 1824 lime was conveyed by barge from Lydbrook up the Wye to Sellack, Hoarwithy, Bolstone, Holme Lacy, and other places in Herefordshire at about the same time as the large scale Radnorshire Limeworks were established,[72] which eventually superseded the local lime industry.

Stone Quarrying

From early times stone for building was quarried in the Wye Valley, where numerous overgrown quarries can be found in the escarpments and steep slopes along the river. Many quarry sites are shown on mid-19th-century maps, but few records survive of the quarries at Ballingham, Bridstow, Sellack, Hoarwithy, Capler, and Fownhope. Although the local sandstone was not an ideal stone, it was used for building cottages and farms within the project area. At Ballingham in 1804, Thomas Prosser, a stone mason from King's Caple, leased the 'stone quarry on the common or waste ground', and in 1855 stone from 'a quarry on the Aramstone Estate' was given by Admiral Ferguson for building the Hoarwithy Bridge.[73] Today the almost forgotten and overgrown quarries present an interesting feature in the landscape. A few quarries have recently been reopened for private use at Capler and Sellack.[74]

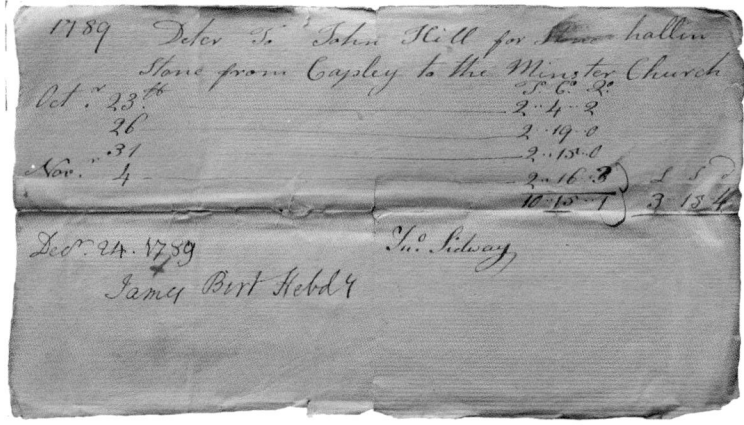

Bill for hauling stone from Capler to Hereford Cathedral in 1789

Leases of the Dean and Chapter's woods and quarries at Capler date from 1602,[75] whilst in 1789 the stone was of sufficient quality to reconstruct part of the nave and west face of the cathedral after the collapse of the west tower in 1786. The accounts show payments to John Sayer, John Hill and Edward Millard for 'raising stone', 'carriage of timber and stone' and 'haulage of stone' from Capler Quarry to the Cathedral Church.[76] Further Dean and Chapter accounts show entries of stone from Capler used for the Vicars' Choral in 1803, the tower in 1843 and the Choir in 1847. The tower contract of 1843 stated that an experienced and trustworthy quarryman must cut the letter B to indicate the bed of every stone before it left the Capler Quarry, and that the quarry was to be left in a fit and workable state. Also the contractor had to supply all the necessary chains, picks, wedges, crow-bars, trestles, planks, shovels, and barrows, and to supply carriage along the eight mile route to Hereford, which suggests transport of stone by land. [77]

Riverside Trades

Basket Making

Willow trees were grown in withy beds on the banks of the Wye to a certain length known as osiers for use by the basket makers. Hampers and baskets were made from the withy beds which grew at Wilton, Brampton Abbotts, Bolstone, and Fownhope and, although not recorded at Hoarwithy, the name and the willow trees suggest a former village industry. The withy beds of the past are hardly recognisable – at Wilton the withy bed is scarcely visible, and at Brampton Abbotts and Bolstone the willows grown to be used as osiers have matured into large trees which now grace the river bank.

The disused stone quarry at Capler is now on private land

Basket Making
Left – Brampton Abbotts; Above – Ross

At Bolstone in 1571, John Scudamore of Holme Lacy leased to Robert Hancock 'Abytarots mylle' with two closes 'lying between a close of Phillip-a-Wytherston called Withybed stretching downe upon the weye from Blakeweyes Dytche towards Wytherston', and in 1634 the Scudamores made leases to two Fownhope basket makers – one to Thomas Earsley of 'willowe twiggs coming growing or yearly renewing upon the bancks of the River of Wye' at Shiplets, and the other to Isaacke Deverox of willow twigs on the banks of the Wye growing between the 'Cryme gate unto the head of Edward Kidleys weare'. Both were required to plant the river bank with willow setts to preserve the banks, and Earsley's rent was two pence and 'as many twiggen baskets needed by Viscount Scudamore'.[78]

Before parish boundary changes, part of the riverside at Ross was in Bridstow parish, where the rope makers, flax dressers and basket makers developed their trades. John Newton and Joseph Evans were recorded as basket makers from the late 18th century in Ross, and in 1778 John Newton's 'utensils and stock' of flax dressing, rope making and basket weaving were valued at £210 for insurance purposes, whereas his house and buildings were only insured for £40. His workers would have cut and harvested the osier branches from the local withy beds before they were peeled and boiled to obtain the finished article for basket making.[79] Newton probably obtained the osiers from the Wilton Withy Bed and from 'Monks Grove Willow Bed in the Parish of Brampton Abbotts' which he rented.[80] The trade continued at Ross, Wilton and Brampton Abbotts into the 20th century.[81]

Shipbuilding

The earliest crafts used on the river were known as truckles or coracles:

> a basket shaped like the half of a walnut shell, but shallower in proportion, and covered on the outside with a horse's hide or canvas. It has a bench in the middle, and will just hold one person; and is so light, that the countrymen will hang it on their heads like a hood, and so travel with a small paddle (which serves for a stick), till they come to the river, and then they launch it, and step in'.[82]

At Foy in 1851 there was a fisherman called James Symonds, who was also recorded as a coracle maker,[83] and at Fownhope James Bailey, a wheelwright at Lechmere Ley, was also a builder of flat-bottomed boats used for netting salmon.[84] Numerous ferry boats were built on the Wye including the Hoarwithy Horse Boat and a small boat at King's Caple. In 1772 William Hudson was paid £5 15s. for making boats, which had to be replaced in 1793.[85]

Barges were built at various places along the Wye – many at Hereford, but others at a surprising number of sites along the river. The *Rival* of 17 tons was built at Wilton in 1804 by John Thomas, the *William* of 40 tons was built at Fownhope by Richard Wheatstone in 1815, and in 1824 Joseph Thomas built the *Martha* of

Coracles used for fishing

38 tons at Holme Lacy. A 37 ton trow called *Thomas* was built at Wilton in 1825 and two trows named *Ann* and *Peggy*, each of 13 tons, and the *Lady Alma* of 12 tons, were built at Fownhope for William Wheatstone in 1854 and 1855.[86] These were amongst the last of the barges to be built on this stretch of the Wye, as by this date the navigation on the river had effectively been replaced by the Hereford to Gloucester Canal which had been completed by 1845 and the Hereford, Ross, and Gloucester Railway which opened in 1855.

Brewing and Cider Making

Brewing

The age-old enthusiasm for the transformation of fermented grain into alcoholic beverages led to the establishment of brewhouses in many country mansions and inns. At the fortified manor of Eaton Tregoz in Foy, a brewery was recorded in 1420,[87] and in 1635 Robert James paid part of his rent to John Scudamore by supplying 'barme sufficient and convenient for the brewinge of beere for the said Viscount'.[88] He had a cellar holding 54 hogsheads of beer and one hogshead of ale in 1639 together with cider and wine.[89] The same year at Caradoc a lease allowed the tenant of the new house to brew in the old house when it was being remodelled. At Hoarwithy the Harp Inn of 1876 contained a 'Brew-house' where James Preece brewed for the inn which belonged to the Harewood estate.[90]

The earliest brewery of any size was established in Fownhope by Nathanial Purchas in partnership with Robert Whittlesey on former waste land, which Whittlesey had acquired. In 1771 brandy, rum, and other liquors were for sale at the 'Brew-House', which may have been extended in 1783 when Purchas acquired another 'parcel of waste' where his 'new house, Brewhouse Yard, Brewhouse Cellars Etc.' were erected. [91] The site was ideal for a brewery, having a good supply of spring water and being on the side of a turnpike road with access to the river Wye and Purchas's barges. When George Lipscomb visited the brewery in 1799 he wrote:

> Mr. Purchas conducted us through his brewery, and showed us vast repositories of wine; accompanying these attentions with an air of so great good humour, and such a pressing invitation to partake of refreshment, that we took leave of this hospitable gentleman with regret.[92]

During the 1790s Nathanial Purchas supplied his wines, spirits and beers as far afield as Kington, Bristol and Chepstow, either by barge or by land carriage. In 1793 Squire Thomas Jones recorded that he:

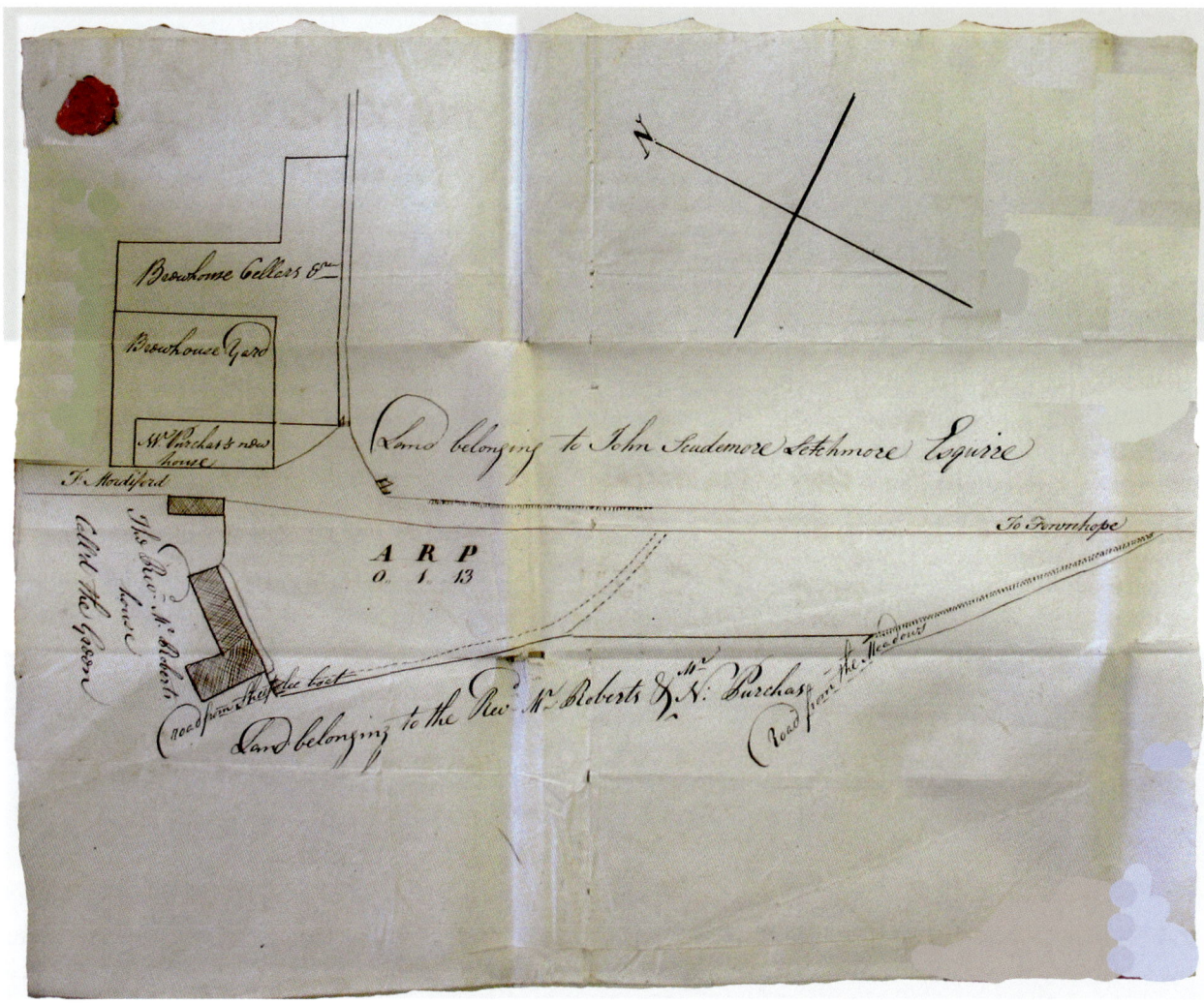

Plan of Fownhope Brewery in 1783

Sent Jack Davies & Evy with wagon to Kington to meet a cargo from Purchas of Fownhope, & the next morning they returned with a hogshead of Port wine & 20 gallons of Malt Spirits'.[93]

In his barges Purchas sent large quantities of bark, pipes of wine, hampers, baskets, and empty bottles to Bristol and, due to delays in 1797, paid five men 1s 6d a day for three days at Chepstow. His brother, Thomas, had established himself as a wine and spirit merchant in Ross and was also freighting pipes of wine and hogsheads of beer and cider on the Wye.[94]

Although Whittlesey had died, Nathanial continued brewing until his death in 1817, when his son William took over for a few years and in 1827 entered into partnership with John Reynolds under the name of 'Reynolds, Purchas and Reynolds'. By 1830 the name of Purchas had been dropped and the business gradually moved to Hereford, although in 1832 the 'Fownhope Brewery, near Hereford' was printed on the receipts of 'John Chas. Reynolds, Importer of Foreign Wines and Spirits, Brewer and Maltster'.[95] Although still known as the Brewery in 1851, when it was occupied by a carpenter, its name was later changed and in 1874 it was a residential property described as 'a commodious Dwelling-house called Rock House'.[96]

Malting

Malting is a process of converting barley grains into malt for the brewer, and in 1811 was 'coarsely ground in a mill, or, what seems to be still better, bruised between rollers; it is then fit for the brewer, in whose hands the process of making beer is completed.'[97] From the 18th century malthouses were situated at Wilton – one near the wharf owned by Guy's Hospital and others run by Charles Prosser and Charles Bullock. John Wheeler was the maltster at Hoarwithy Mill in 1833, and in 1851 Susannah Pymble occupied a row of malthouses at Hoarwithy that once overlooked the Wye.

Other malthouses were recorded in the mid 19th century at King's Caple, Brockhampton and Fownhope, but with the commercialisation of brewing maltings were established in towns adjacent to the larger breweries. These were easily recognised as 'buildings, with the long multi-windowed walls of the malting floors and the conical vents of the kilns, which form a characteristic feature of the countryside in most English barley-growing areas'.[98] These types of 19th-century maltings at Hereford and Ross were eventually superseded by modern malting factories in the larger cities.

Cider and Perry Making

During the 17th century Holme Lacy and the Ross area were renowned for good quality cider. In 1641 cider was recorded by the Scudamores at Holme Lacy, and in 1682 Thomas Baskerville wrote of :

> Hom-lacy, where my honoured uncle, the Lord Scudamore, now defunct, did live, a person to which the whole country is obliged for his worth, he being the man that brought the now so much famed redstreak cyder to perfection.[99]

Cider was made on almost every farm in Herefordshire, sometimes as a cash crop, but mainly to be drunk by the farmer's family and his labourers. Cider is made from bitter-sweet apples, which are rich in sugar but rather unpleasant to taste as they contain a lot of tannin. After crushing the apples and pressing them to extract the juice, farm cider was produced without the addition of cultured yeast, so relied upon the natural yeasts in the apples to produce a cloudy, acidic, invigorating and thirst-quenching drink. Pears were processed in the same way to produce perry.

Cider mill at Bolstone Court

The importance of cider is shown in inventories and wills. For example at Much Fawley an inventory of 1603 included a 'Mustmill house', the name for a 'Crabmill' or cider house, and at King's Caple, John Rogers of Lower Penalt had '13 hogsheads of Aple Cyder, 4 hogsheads of perry, 6 hogsheads of washing cyder' worth £14 3s. in 1704. At Fownhope John Kidley in 1714 bequeathed a great pewter flagon, a silver tumbler, and a 'Stone Cyder mill and Cyder Press at the Nash' to his eldest son, and 'twelve casks of cider' to another son.[100] In 1836 Kynaston in Hentland advertised 'A Considerable Portion of the Land is Planted into Orchards now growing into perfection, and capable of producing a Large Quantity of Cider, and it is calculated that within a Few Years, the Ordinary

Produce of Cider and Perry will be Several Hundred Hogsheads Annually', and within the mansion house there was 'Capital Arched Cellaring' for storage.[101] At Rise Farm in Fownhope there was 'choice Perry and Cider Fruit' capable of making 100 Hogsheads in 1848.[102]

In the mid 19th century the cider and perry orchards were plentiful and many cider mills stood in farmyards and beside cider-houses. The allowance of cider given to labourers in addition to wages was 'one to ten gallons a-day' in 1850, but it was recorded 'that men can not work without some drink, but that they often drink more than is probably of any advantage to them', and it was suggested that 'an allowance of money be given instead of cider, and the laborers be made to buy their drink'.[103] The removal of numerous cider orchards and the conversion of cider mills since this date has made an impact on the landscape, although cider presses are often displayed in gardens and on the roadside.

From the late 19th century, cider started to be produced commercially by several Herefordshire companies in Hereford, Much Marcle and the Golden Valley, but at the farms and on the larger estates cider was still being produced. Cider-mills were recorded at Caradoc in 1863, How Caple in 1881, and at Holme Lacy, where nearly all the estate farms had cider-mills and orchards in 1909.[104] Recently there has been a revival in traditional cider and perry making, the nearest to the project area being at Broome Farm in Peterstow, where within sight of May Hill 'the finest cider is made'.[10]

Barrel making – another Wye Valley industry

CHAPTER VII

Roads and River Crossings

by Heather Hurley (with a contribution by the late David Bick)

The investigation and development of ancient routes in the Wye Valley project area cannot be properly understood without combining the existing network of hollow-ways, tracks and roads with the known crossings of the Wye. A glance at a present day map reveals that the swift flowing Wye with its numerous and enormous meanders must have presented a formidable obstacle between settlements. Communication and trade were only made possible by crossing the river at convenient sites linked to land routes which now remain as hollow-ways, abandoned tracks and old roads. Their physical remains form historic landmarks and picturesque features in the landscape, which together with the study of early maps and documents help to provide a valuable link to the past.

> Hollow-ways are a profound enigma. The more they are pondered the more the anomalies arise, and yet at the same time the feeling grows that clues to the past lie here which no other source can reveal. It seems that the earliest tracks slowly evolved in piecemeal fashion into a network suited to the needs of a population gradually abandoning a nomadic lifestyle. Longer distance routes such as ridgeways defined by natural features, and others with a definite sense of direction often arose, but at what stage it is impossible to say. Before tarmacadam arrested their evolution, Hollow-ways resembled a living organism, forever slowly changing and enlarging, and thus the concept of age is meaningless unless measured from an agreed starting point. The ultimate aim is to discover when the route really began, whether or not first trodden by animals or man perhaps centuries or even millennia before.[1]

Hollow-ways or sunken lanes are routes that sink, through use, below the surface of the surrounding landscape and are often regarded as being of medieval origin, but there is growing evidence that many are of even greater antiquity. They were created long ago before the use of wheeled vehicles when foot travellers preferred a direct line regardless of steep gradients, rather than a longer sinuous route. The cause of sunken lanes is usually attributed to the constant wear and tear of man and animals with heavy rains washing away loose soil and stone. Deep sections often occur on hillsides where excess water flows at its fastest.[2] Hollow-ways are in great evidence within the project area and, although many have been filled in, they are still recognisable.

A track or ridgeway is defined as a high level route of a longer distance leading above water courses, but in the undulating landscape of the Wye Valley they are not so prominent. Old roads retain many features of hollow-ways and tracks but have been surfaced or tarmaced and are generally in use today. The development of roads is well researched and documented, and it is now understood that during the Roman period 'there must have been a great mileage of local tracks between settlements and fields, which had very little engineering or surfacing';[3] this applies to the study area. Alterations were made during the 18th and 19th centuries when important roads were re-aligned and improved by the Turnpike Trusts to ease the gradient for horse-drawn vehicles, whilst some routes were closed or abandoned.

The earliest river crossings were fords, which were sometimes paved and built as causeways on the river bed, and sited at wide and shallow parts of the river where it was deemed acceptable to wade across at armpit depth. Horses were ridden across up to chest height and cattle were driven across. Where the Wye was navigable a number of 'Rovings' were listed, where the tow path moved from the right to the left bank at convenient places.[4] Ferries were also used, normally sited at places called passages. Fords and ferries often complemented one another so that travellers and livestock could either wade across or use the ferry on payment of a toll. At some crossings two boats were kept, one for foot passengers and a larger horse boat for conveying goods and livestock.

As fords and ferries were found to be unusable at certain times of the year due to floods, bridges were built to provide a more convenient and dryer way of crossing. Early bridges were very temporary and makeshift, often formed from planks tied together and strung across the river, or from a row of boats joined together. Eventually stone or timber bridges were constructed, and a toll collected for their maintenance. Severe floods sometimes washed the bridges away, so they were rebuilt in a stronger design at a higher level. In modern times the weight of vehicles has caused considerable damage to bridges, and these have had to be rebuilt, replaced or strengthened.

It has been considered that the recording of hollow-ways linked to the earliest known river crossings would provide a pattern of ancient settlements and trading routes,[5] but with the limited time scale of the project it has only been possible to examine three parishes. The river crossings have been researched and investigated over a number of years, but evidence of crossings from recently researched maps and archives has led to new discoveries.[6] All known river crossing sites were surveyed, researched and photographed by those involved in the project during 2006 and 2007.[7] For ease of use, this chapter has been divided into two sections, one covering the roads, tracks and hollow-ways, and the other investigating the river crossings.

Roads, Tracks and Hollow-ways

Between 2005 and 2007 the hollow-ways in the parishes of Brampton Abbotts, Ballingham and Hentland were surveyed, researched and photographed. Over the centuries a number of past roads, tracks and hollow-ways were abandoned, and many lost their physical characteristics due to the removal of hedgerows and being filled in with earth and rubble. With the additional aid of old maps, plans and documents, together with newly-sourced archives, it has been possible to identify and record them. Some have remained as rights-of-ways, while others are waiting to be added to the definitive map either with a Modification Order or under the Discovering Lost Ways project.[8]

Brampton Abbotts
(David Bick with additional research by Heather Hurley)

Brampton Abbotts retains a network of roads linking Netherton, Townsend, Overton, Gatsford, and Rudhall at its eastern extremity. The parish lies on the left bank of the Wye and adjoins Ross which can be seen from the churchyard gate. Although Brampton church was a chapelry of Ross until 1671, the footpath heading south from the churchyard does not appear to be of any great age until it joins a deep hollow-way at Netherton which continues to the market town. North of the church is an 'area of bumps and hollows, possible site of earlier occupation – village houses or farmstead' where 'buildings no longer exist', only footpaths across the site.[9] The following routes in and around Brampton Abbotts all suggest antiquity, most being deeply sunken at one time though some have been filled in. Maps dating from the 18th century were consulted and most routes can easily be traced today, though some have virtually disappeared. Those described are mostly rights-of-way.

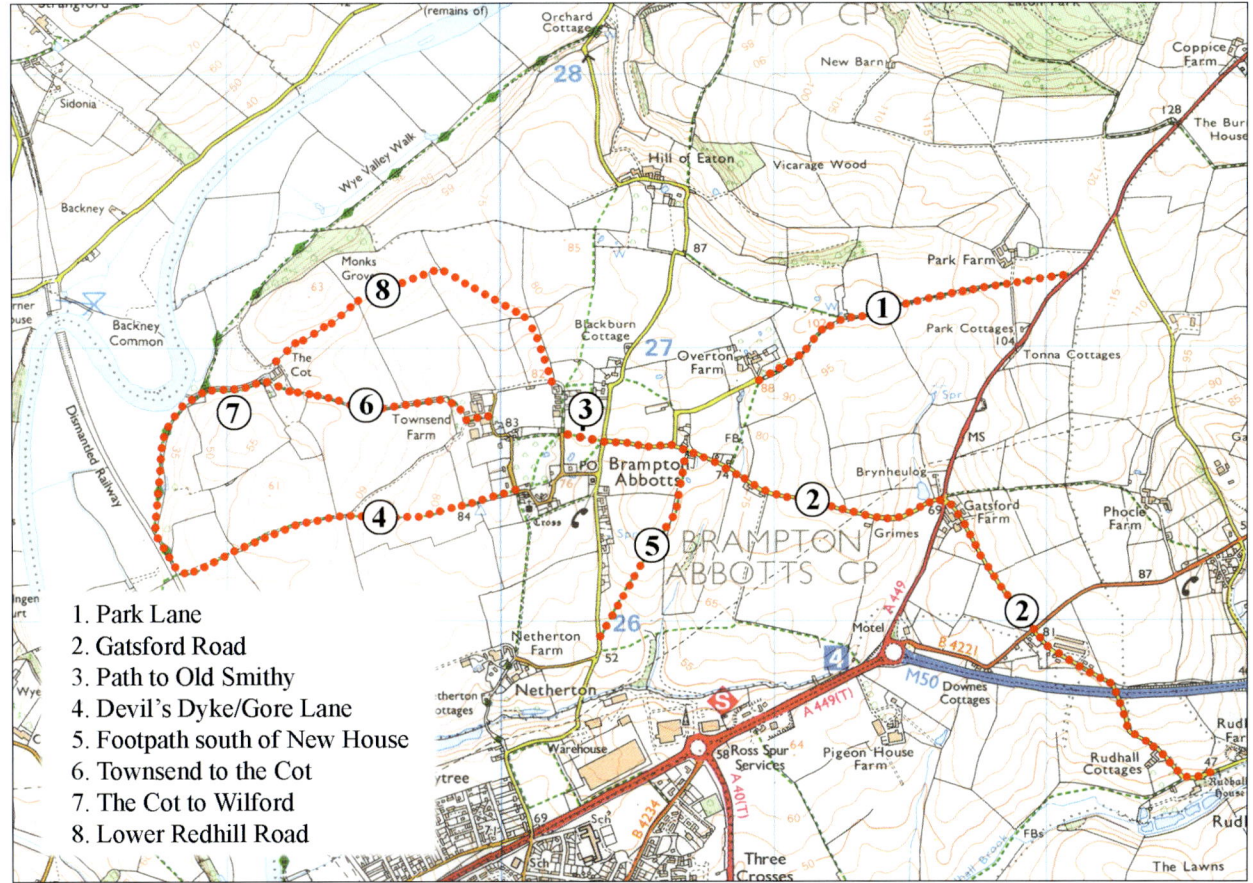

Hollow-ways in the Brampton Abbotts area
(© Crown Copyright and/or database right. All rights reserved. Licence number 100048536)

1. Park Lane
2. Gatsford Road
3. Path to Old Smithy
4. Devil's Dyke/Gore Lane
5. Footpath south of New House
6. Townsend to the Cot
7. The Cot to Wilford
8. Lower Redhill Road

1. Park Lane

Although a parish boundary north of Overton, it is perhaps at least one thousand years old but is not sunken, and in 1806 was known as Park Lane, with a Park Lane Gate still *in situ* in 1838.[10] The route is now a public footpath along a farm track.

2. Gatsford Road

The road leads from Brampton Abbotts to a place called Gatsford which was known at Domesday as Gadelsford. It is a well-used sunken road up to 3m deep in places, and appears on maps from 1754.[11]

3. Path to Old Smithy

At its junction with the main Brampton Abbotts road, steps lead up 3 metres to a field path which, although not sunken, appears to be a continuation of the Gatsford road.

4. Devil's Dyke/Gore Lane

Leading west from the church to the river was an important route called Gore Lane with a chequered history.[12] It was once an impressive hollow-way known locally as the Devil's Dyke, and in 1981 it was photographed 'in an effort to preserve some record of it, at the time what remained of the Dyke was being systematically filled in and the trees grubbed out'. It was also reported that 'with the coming of

the railway a large stretch of the Dyke was levelled and since that time much of it has been ploughed out'.[13] Even before the railway was constructed in the 1850s Gore Lane only led to the Abbott's Meadow and joined a northern route to the river crossing at Wilford. The Abbott's Meadow was one of Brampton's larger meadows held by St. Peter's Abbey in Gloucester and mentioned in 1511.[14] The route of the Devil's Dyke is preserved as a public footpath which joins the Wye Valley Walk at the disused railway track.

5. Footpath south of New House

This little used public footpath follows the course of an abandoned road that led from Overton to Netherton. At its northern end it is enclosed by overgrown hedges before entering fields and continuing as a field path.

6. Townsend to The Cot

From the farm this is a surfaced track across large arable fields, which was once a hollow-way, of which a vestige at the top end remains of hedges that once accompanied the route down to The Cot. It appears that the hedge on the south side was removed between the sales of 1890 and 1929.[15] The track is a public path, and it is interesting to note the recently replanted hedgerows.

7. The Cot to Wilford

This is a continuation of the route above leading across almost flat ground alongside a track to the river Wye and a river crossing known as Wilford. The hollow-way is an overgrown ditch some 3-4 metres

Top left – Path to Old Smithy (no. 3)
Middle left – Devil's Dyke in 1981 (no. 4)
Bottom left – Footpath south of New House (no. 5)
Above – Devil's Dyke in 2006 (no. 4)

142

The Cot to Wilford (no. 7)

deep and is quite remarkable. On level ground hollow-ways are not uncommon, and are often replaced by new roads alongside,[16] which may have evolved from a 'dry weather path'. This enabled pedestrians to avoid the hollow-ways, which would have been deeply rutted and churned-up by horses' hooves and wheeled vehicles.

8. Lower Redhill Road
A road named in 1838 which once led north-east from The Cot shown on early maps,[17] fell into disuse. It was probably a hollow-way of which only a hedge remains witness to part of the route.

Other references to the roads of Brampton Abbotts include 'the way from the Old Gore to Rosse' in 1618, the 'Green Road' of 1806 and 'Milbut cross' on the Foy boundary also noted in 1806. The most puzzling road is one of 1754 leading from Wilford to Ross alongside the Wye.[18] A few remaining hedgerows suggest a route which was either washed away by floods or destroyed when the Hereford, Ross and Gloucester Railway was constructed in 1855. Around 1860 the parish and turnpike roads of Brampton Abbotts were measured and recorded by the Vestry.[19] Their descriptions make them difficult to identify without exploring the area and studying 19th-century maps and plans. Two stretches of roads were turnpiked by the Ross Trustees in 1749, one leading to Much Marcle and the other to Upton Bishop.[20]

Ballingham
The parish of Ballingham lies within a large loop of the Wye on its right bank, and may be explored by a good network of footpaths and lanes often following the course of ancient ways. A long stretch of the riverside is not accessible, where abandoned routes once led to several river crossings. At the Dissolution, Ballingham passed from St. Guthlac's Priory to John ap Rice and then to the Scudamores of Holme Lacy who enjoyed a long association with the parish, which was surveyed for them in 1695 and 1780. These surveys, together with county maps, Ordnance Surveys and the Tithe Map provide a unique sequence of mapping.

Length of the parish and turnpike roads through the parish of Brampton Abbotts

In 2006 a survey of the Ballingham hollow-ways based on the physical characteristics of the ways and documentary evidence was organised. The Ballingham Charters of 1237-1271, which were translated in 1953, record place-names, personal names, roads and river crossings:

> The roads were as they are now – they all start from the church – from the church to Hereford, from the church to Carey, and a track which still exists from the church to Kilforge and Bolstone. Churchway, which is still so called, is the road from the church that joins the road to Carey. Two other roads are mentioned. The Lonweye may be the road leading from Seisal's farm, for there is a small piece of land called Longway in the tithe map. The track running from the church to the Deans cottage near the river is probably the Green Way.[21]

1. Church Lane
The lane leads west from the church along a surfaced hollow-way to join the Carey and Hoarwithy road at Ballingham Court, a farm previously known as Lower Ballingham. This was the Churchway of the 13th century, which was clearly depicted in 1695.[22]

2. Chapel Lane
This surfaced lane is part of a route leading northwards from the church following a sunken way to the 20th-century Ballingham chapel, where it continues as a track recently preserved as a public footpath. It joins a path that steeply descends Ballingham Hill to the site of a river crossing from Holts Meadow which is recorded in a rental of 1541.[23]

3.Ballingham Hill
The narrow sunken footpath links the cottages, some of which had been 'inclosed out of the waste of the manor of Wormelow' on Ballingham Hill near the parish boundary.[24] In 1778 it was observed that according to established custom, that if a man could raise a roof in the night and boil a pot within twelve hours unmolested he was allowed to 'inclose a sufficient quantity of land and to rebuild a more suitable cottage'.[25]

4. Ballingham Hill Path
The path across the common from Ballingham Hill is not registered as a right-of-way, but leads as a sunken grass-covered path to cottages on the hillside, many of which were constructed before the mid 19th century. The path continues down to the road understood to be the Kings Way of the 13th century which runs parallel to the river towards Holme Lacy.

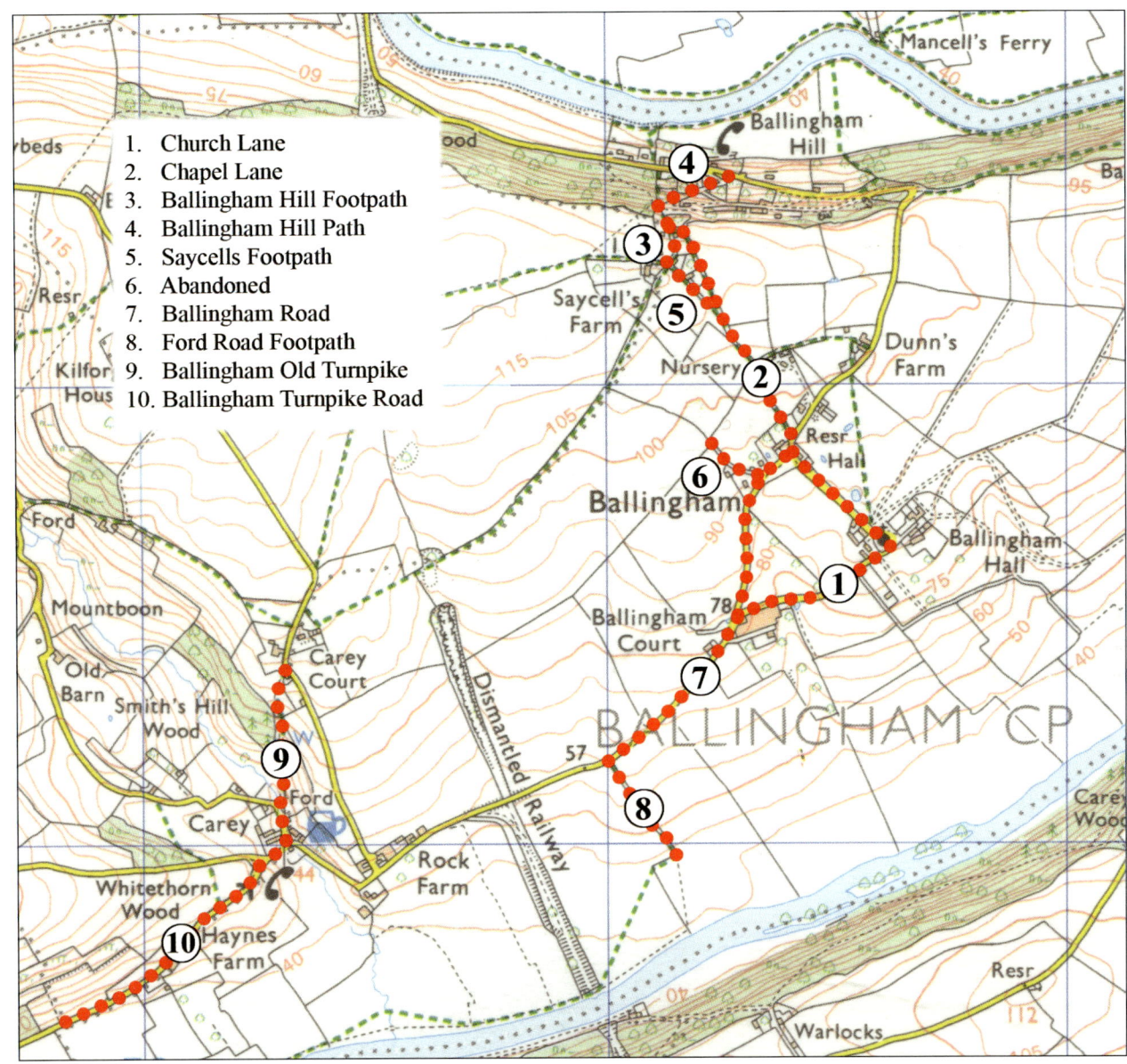

1. Church Lane
2. Chapel Lane
3. Ballingham Hill Footpath
4. Ballingham Hill Path
5. Saycells Footpath
6. Abandoned
7. Ballingham Road
8. Ford Road Footpath
9. Ballingham Old Turnpike
10. Ballingham Turnpike Road

Hollow-ways in Ballingham parish

5. Saycells Footpath

The track leads left of the chapel to Saycells Farm on the boundary of Ballingham and Little Dewchurch. It continues as a field path, and may have formed the 13th-century Longweye from Ballingham church to Kilforge. Saycells is named after a family who were recorded in Ballingham parish from at least the 13th century and in 1541 William Saychell was leasing '40 acres of free land there'.

6. Abandoned lane to Kilforge Field

There is only a suggestion of an old track leading from the village pond towards the parish boundary and Kilforge. In 1695 the track led between Quarells Close and the Little Meane and in 1839 led to the 'Half Acre or Nursery', an arable orchard owned by William Wellington.[26]

Ballingham Hill Path (no. 4)

7. Ballingham Road

This surfaced road leads between high banks from the village to Carey and in 1695 was shown as 'The Road from Cary to Ballingham', and today forms an attractive route from Hoarwithy to Holme Lacy. In the mid-19th century the road would have been altered by the construction of a bridge over the Hereford, Ross and Gloucester Railway.

Ballingham Turnpike (footpath) (no. 9)

8. Ford Road

The green lane of carriageway width known as Ford Road led down to a river crossing at Ford Meadow. The route dates from at least the 17th century, but appears to have changed its direction from the end of the enclosed section. The old lane is a public footpath and continues through fields to Careybridge and a riverside path to Hoarwithy.

9. Ballingham Turnpike (footpath)

Beyond the Cottage of Content Inn, a signed footpath follows the parish boundary along a deep hollow-way that was turnpiked in 1730 leading from Hereford to Hoarwithy Passage. In 1789 it was 'dangerous and inconvenient to Passengers and Carriages' and was abandoned as a through route. From the footpath leading above the hollow-way, the former turnpike route serves as a good example of an 18th-century road.[27]

10. Ballingham Turnpike Road
This deeply sunken road is a continuation of the turnpike road following the parish boundary before reaching Hoarwithy. Its depth suggests great antiquity, although its solid rock sides may have been made deeper by being excavated as a source of accessible stone.

Hentland
One of the larger parishes in the project area, the name Hentland is a slight corruption of the Welsh *hen llan* – the old church – and must indicate a religious foundation of great antiquity. In the parish several linear routes are apparent leading from Hentland church and from the ancient settlements at Tresseck, Altbough, Hoarwithy, Gillow and Treaddow (see map next page).

The parish has a rich collection of colourful names for its past and present lanes, including Poltrough Lane, Well Lane, Sandpit Lane, Bierless Lane, Laskett Lane, Gillow Lane, and Colys Lane,[28] all signifying ancient routes.[29] At least three deeply sunken ways are parish boundaries including 'Hell Ditch and the road traceable across Pengethley farm down to Hentland church and the road leading to Bagwy Llydiatt'.[30] It was also observed in 1822 that 'From Hentland there runs a British Trackway to the Meend, thence to Miret, thence to Wilzon, thence to Whitfield, where it falls into the Turnpike road at Pencreck, but probably went further'.[31]

1. Tresseck Bridleway
This is a steep, narrow and deep hollow-way from Tresseck, a place recorded in the 13th century, leading to another settlement at Altbough, once a common known as Hautbough Hill.[32] This path displays all the features of a hollow-way with its rocky sides and variety of hedgerows festooned with briars and ivy, and its southern end quarried for stone.

Hentland – Tresseck Bridleway (no. 1)

2. Tresseck Lane
The attractive surfaced lane leads from Hoarwithy following the Wriggle Brook to Tresseck. In the mid 19th century it was a gated road leading through the area in front of the farm then known as Tresseck Common. The road, farm, and a few fields and buildings have been identified on a map of 1695.[33]

3. Crossways
An abandoned route linking Tresseck across the parish boundary into Harewood, which has a long and fascinating history from prehistoric times to its present royal ownership.[34] From 1895 Hentland Parish Council was trying to locate a suitable piece of land for an allotment, but it was not

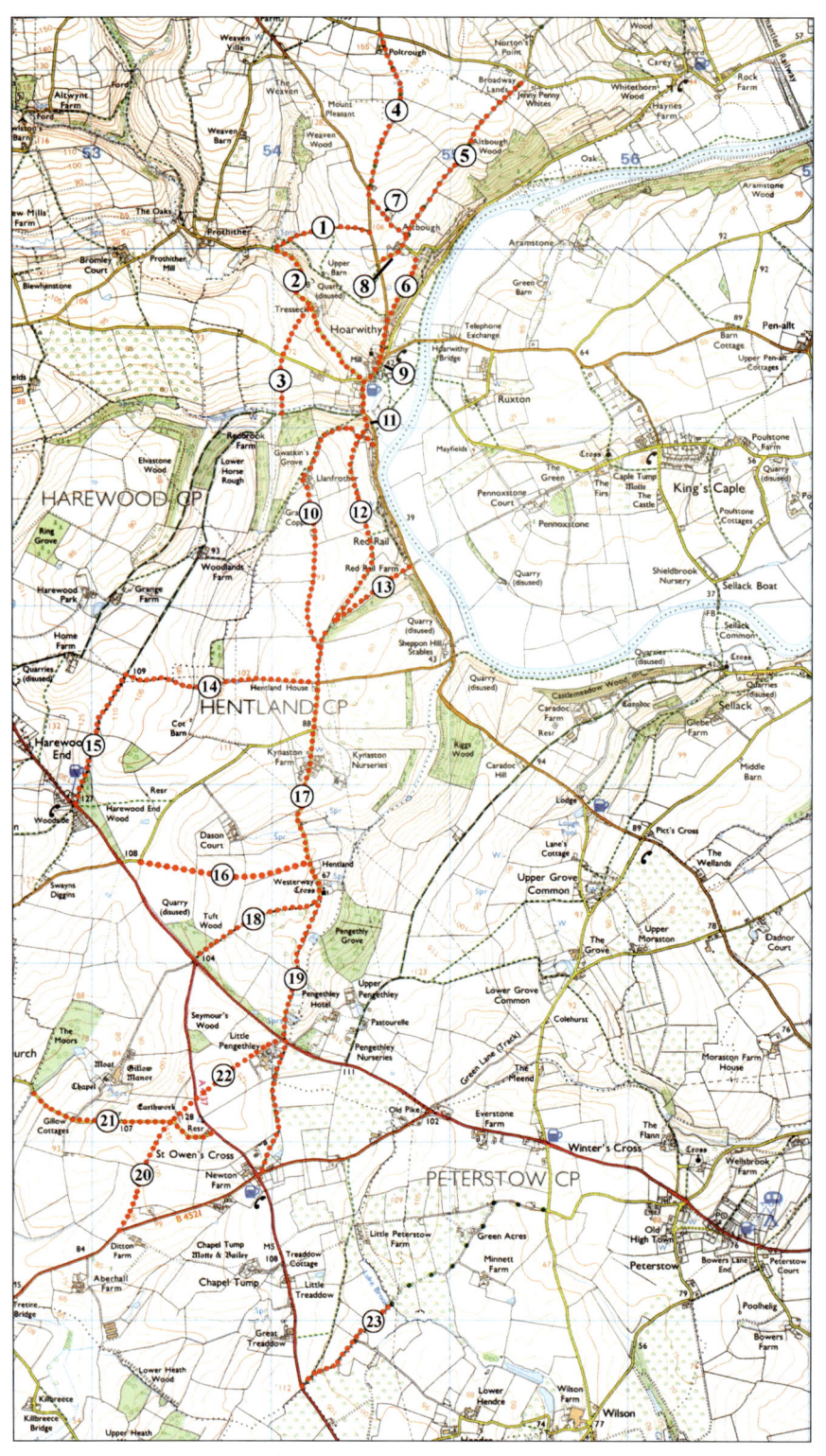

1. Tresseck Way
2. Tresseck Road
3. Crossways (abandoned)
4. Poltrough Lane
5. Green Lane
6. Well Lane
7. Altbough Lane
8. Altbough Road
9. Hoarwithy Road
10. Llanfrother Lane
11. Quarry Bank Path
12. Netherton Path
13. Red Rail Lane
14. Sandpit Lane (abandoned)
15. Harewood Way
16. Bierless Land (abandoned)
17. Hentland Road
18. Hentland to Gillow Path
19. Pengethley Park Path
20. Colys Lane (abandoned)
21. Michaelchurch Road
22. Little Pengethley Road
    (abandoned)
23. Hell's Ditch (part byway)

Hentland hollow-ways
(© Crown Copyright and/or database right. All rights reserved. Licence number 100048536)

until 1908 that the Crossway Piece was selected at 35s. an acre. The five acres were used as allotments until September 1938.[35]

4. Poltrough Lane

Poltrough Lane leads in a north-easterly direction from Altbough towards Little Dewchurch. It is a delightful unsurfaced route, and although open to all traffic, it is gated and not suitable for motor vehicles due to its narrow, sunken and overgrown state.

5. Green Lane

This wide unsurfaced lane also leads from Altbough along a Ridgeway. It is classified as a road open to all traffic, but due to its ruggedness is only used by walkers, riders and cyclists. In autumn the lane offers a seasonal choice of fruit, nuts and berries from its productive hedgerows.

6. Well Lane

The narrow path was established along the contour of Altbough Hill to the spring fed well, from where the inhabitants of Altbough and Hoarwithy could fetch their water. In 1935 the well was recorded as 'a public spring at Mount Pleasant' and was worthy of analysis.[36] Well Lane is frequently used by walkers, although not a definitive footpath, but an application has been made to add the route to the definitive map.

Top – Poltrough Lane (no. 4)
Bottom – Altbough Lane (no. 7)

7. Altbough Lane

This green lane links Poltrough Lane and Green Lane along a short attractive stretch with evidence suggesting an old road which was clearly defined in 1817.[37] An application has been made for this track to be added to the definitive map as it is not classified as a right-of-way.

8. Altbough Road

Altbough was recorded as a place in 1242, and in a charter of 1419: 'Adam of Altebough to Hugh Sayr of Porthedre; all lands etc. and goods moveable and immovable in Pothedre, Treysac and Altegwynt'. It was obviously a place of some importance with a Welsh influence and was partly in Little Dewchurch parish until 1888.

9. Hoarwithy Road

The road through Hoarwithy is an early route that formed an important thoroughfare from Ross to Hereford and to the ancient river crossing at Hoarwithy. In 1730 it was part of the road turnpiked by the Hereford Trustees 'from the said City to Hoar Withy Passage' and in 1749 the Ross Trustees turnpiked 'the road leading from the Town of Ross aforesaid, to Hoarwithy'.[39]

10. Llanfrother Lane

This ancient route winds its way along the parish boundary to Llanfrother, a legendary site associated with St. Dyfrig's monastic college of the 6th century. Since at least this date it has been in continuous use and well documented including 'bridleway' in 1870 and 'road' in 1895 and 1910, but this historic lane is still waiting to be added to the definitive map.[40]

Llanfrother Lane (no. 10)

11. Quarry Bank Path

A narrow footpath leads south from Hoarwithy village, and steeply ascends across part of Harewood parish. It passes a property known as Quarry Bank built above the disused quarries before rejoining a Hentland path. The stone for building would have used by masons such as Richard Watkins at Shepponhill in 1851 and Joseph Gunter of Rock Cottage in 1856.[41]

12. Netherton Path

The present day footpath from Quarry Bank leads above an almost unnoticeable hollow-way, which is very overgrown and partly lost. It was a sunken way to a farmstead last recorded in 1691 as 'Nethertons Farm House and land – totalling 59 ¾ acres' and had ceased to exist by 1789, but Netherton remains as a field name adjoining the former farm site.[42]

13. Red Rail

From the river crossing at Red Rail an ancient route leads in a south-westerly direction towards Hentland church. The hollow-way has been partly filled in and the public footpath follows its course. It is understood to be of Roman origin, but is probably of an earlier date. A short section of the route leading to the river was excavated by project team members in 2005, but it only revealed a paved 18th-century road which may have covered an earlier surface.[43]

14. Sandpit Lane

Sandpit Lane led from the Old School at Hentland, and was named after the soil in Sandpit Meadow next to the Brick Field on the Hentland/Harewood boundary. It has been abandoned as a lane since the mid 19th century when it was named, but some hedges were visible along its course when investigated in the 1980s.[44]

15. Harewood Bridleway
A short stretch of this bridleway at Harewood End forms the Hentland parish boundary. It is probably the 'Haroldusweye' of 1394,[45] leading from Harewood towards Pencoyd. It is very deep in places suggesting a route of ancient origin, although the continuation from its junction with Sandpit Lane to Hoarwithy is of a later date.

Harewood Bridleway (no. 15)

Hentland to Gillow Footpath (no. 18)

16. Bierless Lane
Before being closed by Quarter Sessions in 1829 Bierless Lane led from the former 'poor houses' next to Hentland church. Observed from nearby roads its course through the fields is visible to Harewood End Wood opposite a site known as David's Burial Ground. The names of lane and burial ground have led to a tradition of its having been a corpseway.[46]

17. Hentland Church Lane
The surfaced lane to Hentland church is a continuation of the ancient route from Red Rail. Together with Bierless Lane and other abandoned routes it is one of three that have survived out of at least six old roads that once led to the deserted medieval village site at Hentland. The manor with its remaining 'barn one sheepcote and Beast House lying near unto Hentland church' was last recorded in 1635.[47]

18. Hentland to Gillow Footpath
Another ancient way leading west from Hentland church starts as a field path leading above the overgrown remains of a hollow-way. It continues to Tuft Wood and over the present A49 to Gillow with its long and interesting history and intriguing archaeological sites.[48] It appears that the route once served as a stretch of 'the way to Abergavenny' in 1580,[49] The A49 from Ross to Hereford partly follows a ridgeway that was turnpiked by the Gloucester and Hereford Trust in 1726, and taken over by the Hereford Trust in 1730 with the Ross Turnpike Trust maintaining the section between Ross and Harewood End in 1749.

19. Pengethley Park

From Hentland church the Red Rail route is visible through the park, before leading across fields and over the A49 to St. Owens's Cross. In 1580 it was known as 'the common way leading to Monmouth',[50] and although it has been preserved as a public footpath, the section between Pengethley and St. Owens's Cross has been ploughed out.

20. Colys Lane

This abandoned route was noted by the Rev. John Webb as Colys Lane or Colys Road leading from Tretire to Gaer Cop, but it became 'impassable',[51] and in 1824 the Quarter Sessions considered that the highway leading from Pengethley to Aberhall was useless and unnecessary and was to be 'stopped up'. Only the line of a hedgerow suggests the line of this old road.

21. Gillow Lane[52]

This deeply sunken surfaced lane leads from Tretire and Michaelchurch to Gillow, where it follows the ramparts of Gaer Cop, an Iron Age hill fort. This earthwork was ploughed out and almost obliterated by the construction of a new turnpike road from Tuft Wood in Hentland to Old Forge in Whitchurch after the Hereford Road Act of 1819.[53]

22. Little Pengethley

From Little Pengethley there is evidence of the north-eastern section of Colys Lane, which was closed by Quarter Sessions in 1824. Earlier maps of 1787 and 1817 indicate the course of this old road, and also show the maze of lanes around Gaer Cop before the roads were rationalised by the turnpike trustees.[54]

23. Hell's Ditch

Hell's Ditch is the name of an old road at the edge of Hentland parish which forms the boundary between Hentland and Peterstow. The route through Peterstow is a byway open to all traffic, but the remaining section through Hentland parish is waiting to be claimed.[55] The route is very overgrown at its southern end and hedges have been removed in the Peterstow section, so its course today is difficult to follow.

Hell's Ditch (no. 23)

River Crossings

\From the northern edge of Holme Lacy parish, the River Wye twists and turns along a course of 25 miles through the project area ending at Weirend in Bridstow parish. Past and present river crossings were researched, investigated and photographed as part of the Wye Survey in 2006. A total of 38 fords, ferries, rovings of the tow path, crossings of the Horse Towing Path and foot, road and rail bridges were recorded. It should be appreciated that throughout the centuries the crossings were in use at different periods with later bridges replacing earlier fords and ferries. The names of the crossings found on maps, plans and documents have been taken from place-names, personal names and their usage, such as 'Holm ferry, Mancell's Ferry and Ox Ford.[56]

Due to the unpredictable state of the Wye, which rapidly varies from shallows to deep depths according to the weather, it was necessary to have places offering rest and accommodation nearby. This led to a number of riverside inns and beer houses being established for those unable to drive their cattle, carts and carriages, and for those who could not wade across by foot or on horseback because of the dangers due to swift currents and floods.

Holme Lacy to Hoarwithy (see map next page)

Working downstream from Holme Lacy, Oxford is the first known crossing, named after its use by livestock on a former 'team road from Hampton Bishop Church',[57] which passed the Holt where refreshments were available before reaching the river.[58] In the 17th century the 'fords were ways of husbandry as well as highways. When the floor of the ford was too uneven for a wain, the produce of hay or corn produce was carried over upon the back of horses'.[59]

At a place called Even Pits in Fownhope, a former ferry was replaced by a bridge built by the Fownhope and Holme Lacy Bridge Company after the Bridge Act of 1857. The company outlined the benefits to the people of Fownhope, Woolhope and Mordiford who would then be able to gain access to the 'Holme Lacy Railway Station, on the Hereford, Ross, and Gloucester Railway; thus connecting the North and South sides of the River Wye, and opening the Port of Gloucester'.[60] The original iron and stone bridge became inadequate for motor vehicles and was replaced by the existing one in 1973.

Holme Lacy bridge

Unfortunately the toll-house, where tolls ranging from one farthing for every small animal, one halfpenny for foot passengers, to two shillings and sixpence for a carriage propelled by steam had been collected until 1935 when the bridge was purchased by the County Council, was demolished at the same time.[61] In the 19th century travellers using the crossing were refreshed at either the former Anchor Inn or the Luck's All Inn, both run by the Wheatstone family of Fownhope.[62]

At Shipley on the Holme Lacy side of the Wye there was a well used ferry operating from the 'Boat Piece' and 'Net Meadow and Boat House'.[63] It was known as Shipley or Hom Ferry and conveyed goods, horses and vehicles to and from Holme Lacy House. After visiting the Fownhope Brewery in 1799, George Lipscomb wrote: 'Wishing to embrace this opportunity of seeing the Duke of Norfolk's house at Ham, we were directed to a ferry, at which a boat is kept for the purpose of conducting passengers over the Wye,

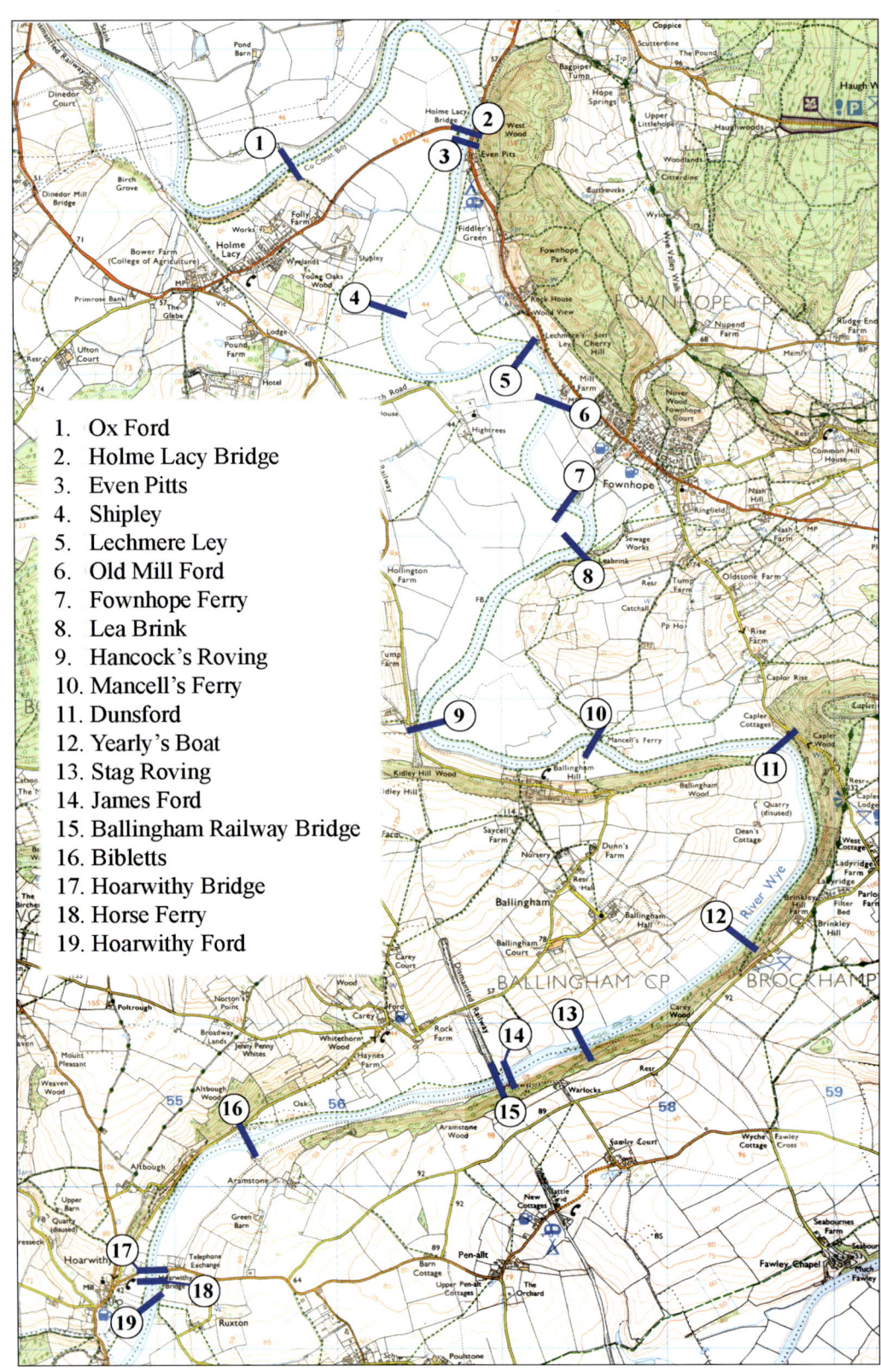

1. Ox Ford
2. Holme Lacy Bridge
3. Even Pitts
4. Shipley
5. Lechmere Ley
6. Old Mill Ford
7. Fownhope Ferry
8. Lea Brink
9. Hancock's Roving
10. Mancell's Ferry
11. Dunsford
12. Yearly's Boat
13. Stag Roving
14. James Ford
15. Ballingham Railway Bridge
16. Bibletts
17. Hoarwithy Bridge
18. Horse Ferry
19. Hoarwithy Ford

Crossings from Holme Lacy to Hoarwithy
(© Crown Copyright and/or database right. All rights reserved. Licence number 100048536)

but the wind frustrated all our efforts to make ourselves heard by the boatman, and we were therefore constrained to return by the same road to Mordiford'.[64]

On the Fownhope bank at Lechmere Ley a private boat was kept, probably at the Bark House and Yard site, to steer barges around this dangerous bend. Also at Fownhope was the Old Mill Ford, a convenient crossing for those using the mill which was described in 1920 as 'an ancient ford, in use up to about 70 years ago, connecting the left bank district with a roadway on the right hand bank, of which indications can be seen to-day, through the meadows passing Holme Lacy Vicarage, and thence through an avenue of elm and thorn trees, and across the Hereford and Gloucester Railway Line to the road to Bolston and Ballingham'.[65]

Under the terms of the Holme Lacy Bridge Act of 1857 'the Even Pitt Ferry and the Shipley Boat Ferry, both over the river between the Parishes of Holme Lacy and Fownhope, and the Ox Ford, through and across the River between the Parishes of Holme Lacy and Hampton Bishop, and the Old Mill Ford, through and across the Parishes of Holme Lacy and Fownhope, be discontinued, and that the Roads leading to these Fords respectively be stopped up'. The bridge company was empowered to purchase the ferries at Even Pit and Shipley, and could demand a toll for those fording the river within a distance of one mile from the bridge.[66]

The last ferry crossing to be used was the Fownhope Ferry, which conveyed passengers across to Holme Lacy. Its site can be identified at the end of a footpath leading from Ferry Lane, where a modest beer house became the Forge and Ferry Inn before closing a few years ago.[67] In 2000 Fownhope residents proposed building a footbridge as a millennium project that 'would bring the villages of Fownhope and Holme Lacy together. Until about 1924 the village had a ferry link which carried people back and forth, and footpaths are in place on the banks on either sides', but unfortunately the owner of the land was not in favour of this proposal.[68]

In Fownhope parish, at Leabrink, where shelves of rock are visible at low water, a boat was kept at the cottages on this sharp bend where the banks are eroding into the river. Another unlikely Fownhope crossing must have been accessed from Tump Farm along a track to riverside meadows where a private boat was operated from the Bolstone side at Hancocks Roving. This name does not appear on present maps, but the site can be identified by the remains of a railway bridge over the road below Kidley Hill Wood. In 1922 remains of Hancock's Mill and Weir, formerly Aburttaretts Mill of 1571, were visible.[69]

Mancell's Ferry operated from this bank

At the southern edge of Fownhope parish a network of footpaths lead to Mancell's Ferry, where the boatman's cottage was built on a rocky shelf, known earlier as Rocks Ferry.[70] Although the Mancells or Mansells occupied property on the left bank at Brockhampton, there is evidence to suggest that this ferry was operated from the Ballingham side. At the blacksmith's shop there was 'a large stone, which was used for mounting the horse which carried passengers through the ford. A local boat was afterwards available, and continued running up to late years, in charge of Samuel Terry'.[71]

Capler Ford

He was the parish clerk of Ballingham at the beginning of the 20th century, and the Bullock family were the blacksmiths at the forge in the mid 19th century.[72]

At the edge of Capler Woods in Fownhope parish there was an ancient crossing over the Wye which probably dated from the construction of the Iron Age hill-fort on Capler Camp. Footpaths on both banks of the river mark the site of this crossing recorded as Dunsford in the 13th century,[73] Capley Roving in 1799 and known as the boat 'in charge of Richard Alford at the time of its discontinuance' in the 19th century.[74] Around the large loop of the Wye around Ballingham were other crossings including Yearly's Boat of 1780 and the Stag Roving which was probably the same crossing place used by the Ballingham boatman 'to ferry people across to Carey Mill on the Fawley side in 1250'.[75]

The remains of Carey railway bridge

James's Ford of 1780 became known as Careyboat, and was approached by Ford Road, preserved as a right-of-way leading into Ford Meadow.[76] On the Fawley and King's Caple side of the river a small cottage was erected by the River Wye Horse Towing Path Company after they were established in 1809. No doubt the company operated a ferry which became known as Careyboat by 1835 and after the construction of the railway bridge for the Hereford, Ross, Gloucester Railway in 1855 the site was called Careybridge. The last boat used was sunk in the river, and evidence of where it sank was visible in 1922. The railway bridge was dismantled in 1964 and its piers stand as a stark feature in the landscape. Travellers using the ferry would have refreshed themselves either at the Miners Arms, now the Cottage of Content, at Carey, or at the thatched Yew Tree or Wood Inn on the King's Caple side which has since been demolished.[77]

Under the terms of the Horse Towing Path Act of 1809 the 'said Company of Proprietors shall and may keep a Ferry-Boat or Ferry-Boats at or near the places called Putteston Watering Place, and Bullingham Road, and also at or near Hoarwithy Passage and How Caple adjoining or near to the said River Wye, and moor the same to the Posts to be set up by the said Company'.[78] It has always been understood that the place chosen at Hoarwithy was at the Bibletts where the horses and the men attending them were conveyed by ferry across the river from the King's Caple side to the stables and the tow path on the right bank.[79] This is confusing as the route of the towing path is clearly defined on the plan, but a report of 1816 refers to 'The Stables and House at Carey' built by the Horse Towing Path Company,[80] which must refer to the company's cottage built at Careyboat. The Boat Meadow of 1842 between Carey and Hoarwithy was probably associated with fishing.

At Hoarwithy, the Wye is crossed by a modern steel and concrete structure supported on the original masonry piers and abutments of the iron bridge of 1876, which replaced the timber one of 1857. The first bridge had been built by the Hoarwithy Bridge Company for a cost of £2,090. It replaced an ancient ford recorded in 1347 and a horse ferry of 1581, both sited a few yards downstream.[81] At Hoarwithy it was noted that 'the lusty and strong boatman had become weak' in 1844, and 'was not likely again to cross the stream in the big horse-boat piloted by Fidoe the ferryman'.[82] The 'horse and small' boats were operated from the King's Caple bank by the traditional method using chains or cables. The horse boat conveyed livestock and vehicles, and the small boat carried foot passengers and lighter loads.

The Hoarwithy bridge company discontinued the ferries, which they purchased for £90, and stopped-up the ford, but during the rebuilding of the subsequent bridges a ferry crossing was reintroduced. On the Hoarwithy side the company built a toll house where payments were made to maintain the bridge. In 1920 William Haines was the gate-keeper followed by his daughter Mary Ann, who was the last toll collector before the bridge was purchased by Herefordshire Council in 1935 and freed of its unpopular tolls. In 2007 the toll house still belonged to Herefordshire Council, but was sold later that year.[83] The bridge company held all their meetings in the Old Harp Inn during the 1850s and 1870s, but around 1884 it was de-licensed and replaced by the present day New Harp. Earlier inns

Hoarwithy bridge and toll house

and cider houses in the village included the Oddfellows Arms, the Three Salmons, the King of Prussia and the Anchor that became the Old Harp.[84]

Within a mile downstream of Hoarwithy Bridge was the site of another ancient crossing known as Red Rail, 'the ford of the street', where the Wye flows swiftly along a narrow and deep stretch of the river, making it a dangerous crossing for both man and beast. From an excavation of 1969 it was concluded that the approach to the ford on the King's Caple side was of Roman construction, and the lime slabs found scattered in the river probably once formed a causeway or bridge across the Wye. A further excavation was carried out during the LOWV project, in 2005, on the approach to the ford on the Hoarwithy side, but only a surfaced 18th-century road was revealed within the time limit. The ford was in use during the 18th and 19th centuries but became out of use following the opening of Hoarwithy Bridge in 1856.

Red Rail Ford
Above – Excavating the track to the ford in 2005
Top left – Ross Sub-Aqua Club investigating the
river bed in 2005
Bottom left – Ford shown on Taylor's 1754 map

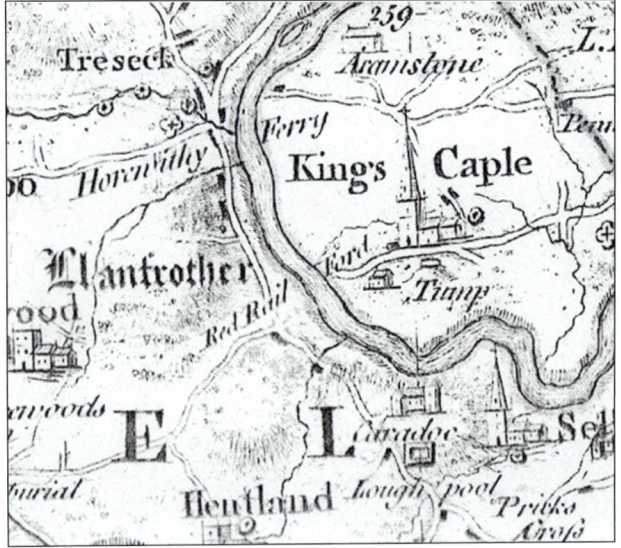

Romano-British finds and documents recording 'Caple Street' in 1453, and 'Roman Lane' in 1737 suggest a Roman route leading from Fawley to St. Owens' Cross in the project area, but the linear route is understood to pre-date the Roman period. In the 16th and 17th centuries the ford was recorded as 'Ryderdyell' and Red Rayle in King's Caple documents, and in Hentland as 'redraill' in 1608 and 'Redrayle' in 1752, but became 'Red Rail' in 1779. Unfortunately public access on the King's Caple side had been lost by the mid 19th century, but an application has been made to add the short track on the Hoarwithy side to the definitive map. [85]

Sellack to Wilton

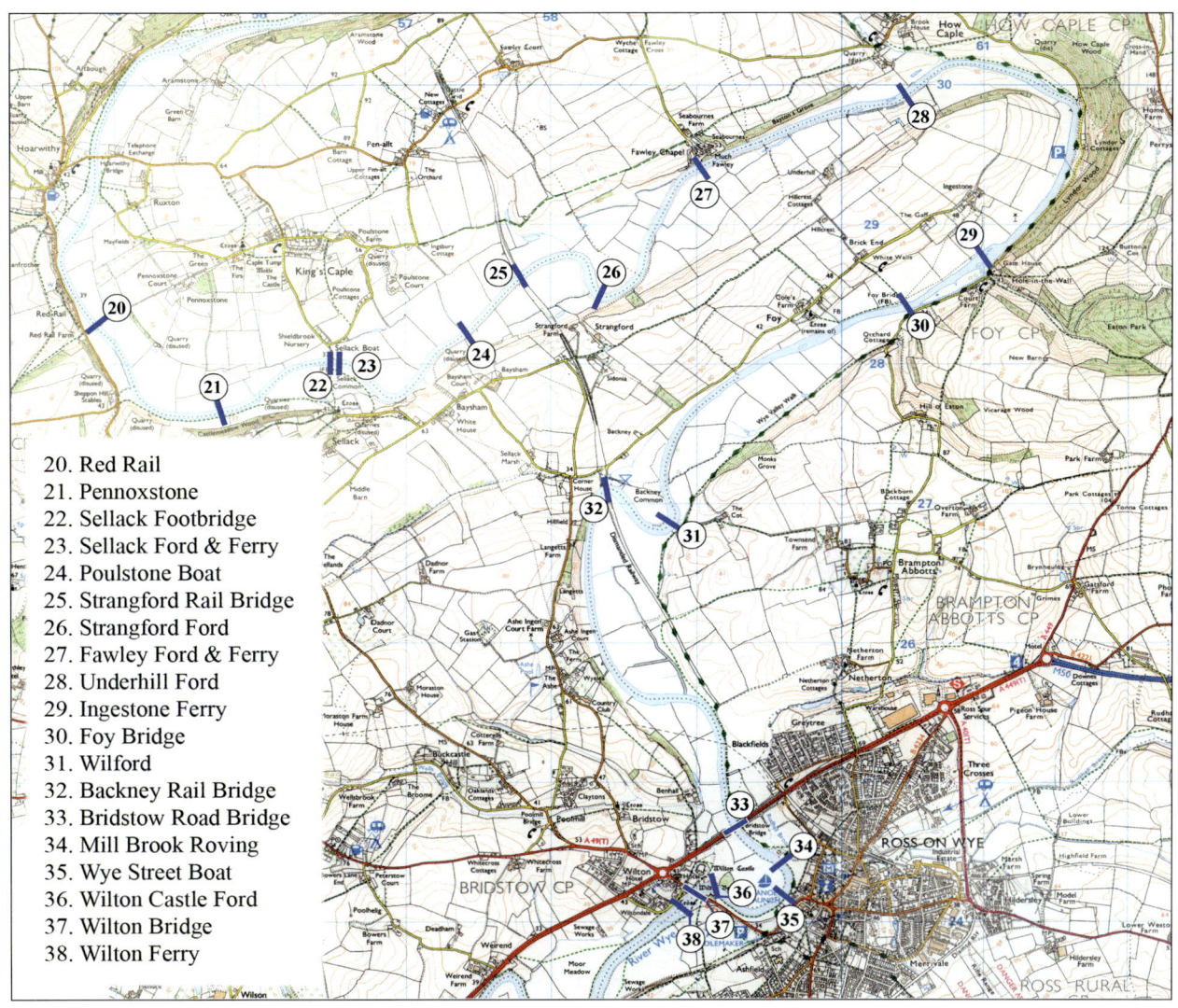

20. Red Rail
21. Pennoxstone
22. Sellack Footbridge
23. Sellack Ford & Ferry
24. Poulstone Boat
25. Strangford Rail Bridge
26. Strangford Ford
27. Fawley Ford & Ferry
28. Underhill Ford
29. Ingestone Ferry
30. Foy Bridge
31. Wilford
32. Backney Rail Bridge
33. Bridstow Road Bridge
34. Mill Brook Roving
35. Wye Street Boat
36. Wilton Castle Ford
37. Wilton Bridge
38. Wilton Ferry

Crossings, Sellack to Wilton

There is some evidence that there was a river crossing below Caradoc in Sellack to Pennoxstone in King's Caple, but the main crossing between these two parishes was at Sellack Boat where a ford and ferry were sited. 'For generations the ferry boat had been owned and operated by the Harris family of the Boat House in King's Caple. In the 1890s the fare was a halfpenny and the boat maintained by George Harris was a flat bottomed punt that could carry four or five passengers'.[86] It was mainly through the efforts of the Rev. Augustin Ley, vicar of King's Caple and Sellack, that a footbridge was erected in 1895 to enable him to have a dry and safe crossing to visit his parishioners at King's Caple.

The bridge would enable the inhabitants of Sellack to reach Fawley Station, and the petition also stated 'The river is crossed at a spot called Sellack Boat, and the passage has to be made in a small fisherman's boat, which is only occasionally available, at uncertain times, and is always dangerous in winter and during high water'.[87] A monument in King's Caple church illustrates the dangers of crossing the river. An experienced soldier, 'William Hutcheson, Captn in H.M. 76th Regt., who, after serving his country in the Peninsular at Walcheren, and in India, was drowned in attempting to cross the River Wye, at Sellack Ford, Octr. 2nd 1819. One of many lives claimed by the Wye.'

The Rev. Augustin Ley lived at Sellack Vicarage and was instrumental in setting up a Public Subscription for the cost of building a suspension bridge across the Wye. The local gentry and clergy contributed from £5 to £100, the Great Western Railway and Guy's Hospital donated £50 and £25 respectively and farmers and tradesmen gave between one and ten shillings. The total cost of constructing the bridge was £989 12s. 4d., but the donations had a shortfall of over £600 which was paid by the Rev. Ley, and the bridge was opened on St. Andrew's Day in 1895 with a 'goodly gathering to take part in the ceremony'.[88] Travellers using the ford and ferry at Sellack were able to take refreshments at a house near the church traditionally known to have been a beer house, or at the Old Boar at King's Caple, long since closed, and recently the home of the late Elizabeth Taylor, who wrote *King's Caple in Archenfield*.[89]

A short distance below Sellack Bridge was a ferry crossing in 1799 between Poulstone in King's Caple and

Sellack Bridge

The remains of Strangford railway bridge

Baysham in Sellack.[90] At Strangford the Hereford, Ross and Gloucester Railway line crossed the Wye over a stone bridge. In 1947 it collapsed almost immediately after a passenger train and a long freight train had crossed 'due to exceptional floods, which disturbed the foundations of the supports', which was reported by two young men to the staff at Fawley Station.[91] The railway closed in 1964 and the decking was removed leaving the supports striding across the Wye. The bridge was built very near the site of the Stranguard Ford recorded in 1763,[92] which crossed the river between Fawley and Strangford which were then in Fownhope parish, at a place which can be identified from the river.

At Much Fawley a hollow-way continues from the road and the chapel to a fording place known to be of great antiquity, and 'in later days it was not so much used as a ferry, as for a wharf for loading barges with farm produce'. On a map of the Fawley Estate of 1721 a ferry boat moored

1721 plan showing Fawley ford and the earliest
known image of a boat on this stretch of the Wye

to the bank is depicted, and in 1687 a lease of Much Fawley contains a curious right (with the usual legal absence of punctuation) of 'a passage for them and their servant's horses and carriages at all seasonable times between ye boat on ye river Wye at Much Fawley over and through Strangworth meadows and grounds ye Direct way by Strangworth house for ye carrying of lime and cole in their wains and carts from Howle or ye parts adjacent unto ye devised premises and for their market horses to and from Monmouth in such sort as Mr. Rodagon Oswald widdow mother of Elizabeth formerly used the same'.[93] The lime from Howle Hill was obviously of importance as certain farms were required to 'bring a waggon Load of Lime or Coal from Howell Hill to any place not exceeding 12 miles from Wilton', as part of the rent to the Governors of Guy's Hospital in 1735.[94]

In this Foy loop of the Wye there were other former crossings suggested by maps and documents including Capel Ford of 1410 later known as the Peartree Roving in 1799, and probably the same fording place leading from below Underhill across to How Caple which was intended to be used by the Horse Towing Path Company 'to keep ferries for carrying over the Draft Horses and Drivers &c'.[95] Although shown on the navigation plan of 1808, it is

Fawley ford c. *1920*

Fawley ford in 2006

known to have existed further around the bend at Ingestone, where 'a ferry was established from time immemorial, connecting with Perrystone and Sollers Hope. It was much used by all kinds of traffic and for the horses conveying the barges up the river. They had to cross the river to their stables, this being a resting point'.[96] The Boat Meadows of 1838 at Foy were probably associated with fishing.

In 1772 the vicar of Foy wrote: 'I lent unto Mrs Lloyd ye Key of ye Orchard Gate facing Carthage House to enable her & family to come with more ease & expedition to Church. As Mr. Lloyd had been so obliging to let me have ye Key & Use of his Horse Boat for myself & friends whenever I had Occasion, there being no Road on either part, but on sufferance for horses, to ye boat or thro ye orchard'.[97] In Foy east there had been several inns and beer houses associated with the river, one noted in 1844 as a 'pot-house called The Hole in the Wall … where the horse-boat was moored to the shore'.[98] The pot-house was the former Anchor and Can occupied by Sarah Hardwick, the victualler and ferry boat keeper in 1852, and there was a beer house known as the Boatman's Rest at the Gatehouse before it closed in 1858.[99]

The parish of Foy is unusual to be divided into Foy East and Foy West by the Wye, with the church on the west and the school on the east. For the convenience of the parishioners, schoolchildren and inhabitants of the parish a foot and bridle bridge was erected in 1876, replacing the ford and ferry, but there was obviously some dispute over the right of way to the bridge until 1880 when a grant of a right of way was made between Ross Highway Board and the local landowner. However, disaster

The remains of Backney railway bridge

struck the bridge in 1919 reported by the *Hereford Times* as 'Foy Bridge Swept Away'. The report continued that the crossing had been 'cut off and that some of the children were consequently unable to reach the school'. The bridge was eventually rebuilt for an estimated cost of £2,000 and was opened in 1921 as an elegant single span suspension bridge.[100]

A lengthy stretch of the river from Foy Bridge flows past the church and Monk's Grove in Brampton Abbotts before making a sharp meander around Backney Common. On the left bank is Wilford, probably named after an incident that occurred in the 12th century when Welsh raiders from across the river in Archenfield raided Brampton Abbotts.[101] Downstream are the remains of Backney Railway Bridge, the third one constructed between Ross and Hereford in the project area. The Backney Bridge Picnic Site provides a perfect view of this stretch of the river and of the railway embankment.

From Bridstow no other crossings have been discovered until reaching the modern Bridstow road bridge at the start of the famous horseshoe bend that encircles Ross. The bridge designed by Scott Wilson Kirkpatrick was completed in 1960 to link Ross and the A40 to the motorway system. The best

Wilton bridge

way to view this structure is from the Wye Valley Walk which passes beneath it on the left bank.[102] At the Ross Rowing Club the towing path of 1799 crossed the river at the Mill Brook Roving.[103] Before parish boundary alterations in 1931 a strip of land alongside the Wye on the Ross side was in Bridstow parish where, at the foot of Wye Street (formerly Dock Pitch), there was a private boat probably operated by Henry Dowell & Sons, boat builders at the Hope and Anchor during the late 19th and early 20th century.

The upstanding masonry of Wilton Castle, built to defend an important river crossing, dates from the 13th century. A ford probably existed across to the castle above Wilton Bridge, but the known ford and ferry was below the bridge marked by a 14th-century ferry cross on the Wilton bank.[104] 'The variable and seasonal levels of the Wye made this a dangerous and unreliable crossing in floods or during low water' accidents and loss of life occurring due to the overloading of boats crossing the 'furious and dangerous river', which prompted the local citizens to petition for a bridge at the end of the 16th century.

After the Wilton-upon-Wye Bridge Act was passed in 1597 the bridge was completed, by 1600, as a toll bridge but Thomas Webbe generously bought out the tolls in 1612. In 1718 the unusual sundial was erected by Jonathan Barrow from Monmouth, who originated from Bridstow.

By 1938 the bridge was 'deteriorating again due to carrying heavy loads', and the following year with the outbreak of war the bridge was widened 'in order to facilitate the passage of large indivisible loads from the Welsh ports to the Midlands'. Unfortunately the bridge was never restored to its original width, and in 1993 when the bridge was refurbished it was left standing 'uncomfortably, one half rooted in the past, and the other firmly in the present'.[105]

The 14th-century ferry cross at Wilton

The sundial of 1718 on Wilton Bridge

CHAPTER VIII

River and Rail Transport

by Heather Hurley (with a contribution by Mark Robinson)

In the past river valleys provided various means of communication, where rivers were usually navigable, roads relatively level and railways capable of being constructed along easy gradients. However, all the major roads between Hereford and Ross-on-Wye avoided the Wye Valley with its meandering river, but the railway chose a direct route crossing the Wye's irregular course and, even after closure, leaving a bold feature in the landscape. In the Landscape Origins of the Wye Valley project area there was never any competition between river and rail transport because the Hereford to Gloucester canal, completed in 1845, had already begun to take trade away from the river, some 10 years before the Hereford, Ross, Gloucester Railway opened in 1855 (see plan on next page).

River Transport

There is no direct evidence to indicate an early use of the Wye as a route for transport. A wharf was recorded near Hereford castle in 1256,[1] but it may only have been used to transport goods across the river. Other references suggest that it was the Severn for a considerable distance and the Wye only as far as Monmouth that were navigable, for in 1289 a shipment of wine was sent from Bristol to Upton-on-Severn and then by land to Hereford. Also, in 1296, a barrel of venison from Bristol was transported by river to Monmouth and then to Goodrich by road.[2] The navigation of the Wye was hindered by numerous weirs, which had been constructed to provide power for the medieval water mills and 'fish garths for breeding fish'.[3] In the study area weirs were recorded at Carey Mill in 1250, at Holme Lacy in 1266, at Wilton and Eaton Tregoz in the 14th century, and at Fownhope in 1375.[4]

It seems probable that during the 17th century, before the passing of the Wye Navigation Acts, there was no river transport above Monmouth. In 1641 an early advocate of inland waterways, the eccentric John Taylor, made a journey by boat along rivers from London to Hereford. He described his craft as a 'sculler-boate', and he was accompanied by two male servants and two boys who had to man-handle the boat where the passage was difficult. The Wye between Monmouth and Hereford was singled out by Taylor as 'debard of all passage with boates by 7 weares'. These included weirs at Wilton, Ingeston, Carey and Fownhope. Taylor commented that the people of Hereford were thus deprived of urgently needed coal. Four years later, during the Civil War, the Scottish army besieging Hereford was obliged to construct a bridge over the Wye as the Royalist garrison controlled the Wye Bridge in the city. According to a contemporary observer, the Scottish bridge was constructed on double piles sunk into the river-bed. This was an unusual way to construct a military bridge over a substantial river, for normally an army would have built a pontoon bridge; evidently at Hereford there were no suitable boats to commandeer for the construction of such a bridge.[5]

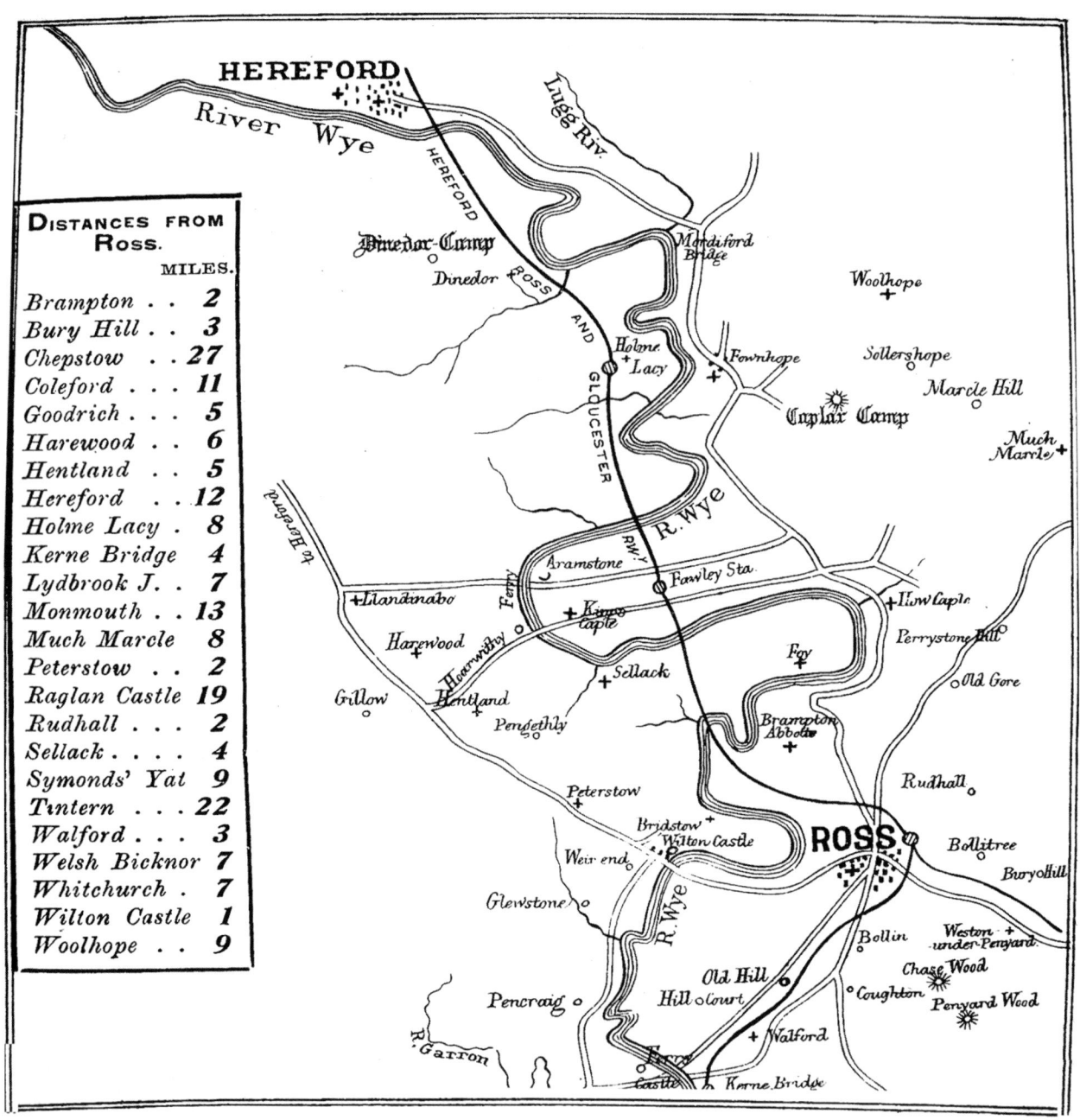

1896 map showing road, rail and river courses in the project area

Surveys

With the continual conflict between mill and fishery owners and those wishing to trade on the river, surveys were undertaken and Acts of Parliament were passed to try to resolve the situation. In 1301 a commission was appointed 'to survey the weirs, dykes and stakes in the water of Weye between Hereford and Monemuth, as it appears that ships and boats cannot pass as they were wont by reason of the erection thereof so that they extend into the channel'.[6] It is not known whether the survey took place, but a much later unofficial one was undertaken by John Taylor in 1641.[7]

166

After the Rivers Wye and Lugg Navigation Acts of 1662 and 1695, a survey attributed to Daniel Denell was ordered by the navigation trustees in 1697 of 'The Weirs, Mills, Bridges, Fords and Shallows' of the Wye and Lugg. He found two mills, a decayed lock and a 6 foot stone weir at Wilton; a decayed millhouse, floodgates and weir at Ingestone; a stone weir at Carey Mills; a decayed mill and weir with a lock in ruins at Hancock's; and a 7½ foot weir at Fownhope with a mill in good repair.[8]

At the end of the 17th century Andrew Yarranton wrote that Herefordshire 'hath a Navigable River unto the City made by Art, but imperfect at present, and ought to be mended'.[9] At this date the river was barely navigable until a further Act was passed in 1727 'for making Navigable the River Wye', and in 1763 and 1779 Isaac Taylor and Robert Whitworth produced survey plans depicting weirs, crossings and industrial sites together with proposed improvements.[10]

A barge on the Wye

With the threat of the Gloucester to Hereford canal, already constructed from the Severn to Ledbury, taking trade from the Wye, there was a growing concern at the beginning of the 19th century to improve the river navigation. It was suggested that a horse towing path should be formed between Hereford and Tintern, and the proposed route giving landowners' names was surveyed by Henry Price in 1805.[11] A 'Report on the Improvements of the Navigation of the River Wye', dated 21 August 1805 was put together by one William Jessop in which he concluded that the construction of a horse towing path would lead to 'a saving to the Public of about £4,233 per Annum, exclusive of the advantages arising from dispatch and regularity; and that of restoring about 500 Men, who are now Substitutes for Horses, to more useful Employment'.

This led to a further Navigation Act in 1809 which made provision for a 'Horse Towing-path' as shown on Price's plan of 1808.[12] When the navigation ceased between Hereford and Ross in the mid 19th century, the river was surveyed and promoted as a boating and fishing river by Edwin Stooke.[13] In 1892 a group of four undergraduates from University College, London, took a boat down the Wye and recorded their journey in a series of sketches, and in 1948 C.R. Shaw made a trip in his dinghy from Hereford to Redbrook, and produced a report on the navigability of the river with diagrams and photographs.[14] A guide for canoeists was produced in 1990 with plans and information on the river. Although running to several editions it is currently out of print.[15]

Boats on the river at Ross-on-Wye in 1905

In the autumn of 2006 the Landscape Origins of the Wye Valley project undertook a two day survey of the Wye by canoe to identify, locate and produce a photographic record of all documented crossings, weirs, islands, wharves, and industrial sites, also seeking previously unknown sites of interest between Holme Lacy and Weirend. On the first day the river was low and shallow with a few fast rapids, but on the second day the river had risen due to heavy rain and was flowing very swiftly over dark depths, This change gave the participants a much greater understanding of the problems encountered by the barges that were towed up and down stream around the large meanders and the problems of those wanting to cross the river by ford or ferry.

The Wharves

The project team located known and previously unknown wharf sites where large quantities of wheat, barley, bark, lime, poles, hoops, seeds, timber, cheese, beer, cider, flax, paper, and many other items including 'household furniture' were transported down to Wilton, Monmouth, Chepstow and Bristol. Some items even went down the Wye and back up the Severn to Stourport! Coal, bricks, rags, junk (old ropes), and wine were conveyed upstream. The various wharves were researched by the team on navigation maps and plans, in sale particulars, from contemporary descriptions, and surviving barge accounts.[16] It has been traditionally understood that every Wyeside village had its wharf and barge, and this has been confirmed by the project's investigations.

Lucksall Wharf

Holme Lacy Wharf

The wharves were numerous. At Even Pits in Fownhope parish a stone wall is a reminder of a warehouse let to John Wheatstone in 1774, while a wharf was used by William Wheatstone in 1843. A site on the opposite bank was considered to be associated with fishing.[17] Downstream, canoes are launched from the Lucksall Caravan and Camping Park at a site recorded as a wharf in 1775 when it was leased to Nathanial Purchas, the brewer in Fownhope. A few years later Purchas acquired access to 'Shiplee boat' where he sent tons of bark to Chepstow on barges which returned with pipes and casks of wine.[18] At Shipley on the Holme Lacy side of the river, a wharf was identified where a ferry was recorded in 1754. Surprisingly there was little documentary evidence of river trade at Holme Lacy, where a wharf near the church is clearly visible from the river. Only a few entries were found for goods conveyed to Holme Lacy for Hollington and Bower farms during the 1790s.[19] In the Steward's Accounts of Holme Lacy in 1632 all transport and carriage was recorded by horse, coach or packhorse. The only reference to the river was a gift paid to the boatman of Carey mill.[20] However in 1698 the accounts record a payment made for rope 'to tow Timber downe the Water'.[21]

Further downstream, on the Fownhope bank, a coalyard of 1763 was recorded at the Locking-stock – a riverside field now crossed by a footpath from the end of Ferry Lane.[22] Below Capler Camp several wharves were identified, where in the 1780s and 1790s barley was sent down to Brockweir and 'limecole' was delivered and measured.[23] Although stone was cut from the Dean and Chapter quarries at Capler for the rebuilding of the cathedral during the 1780s and '90s, the documentary evidence suggests that land carriage was used, although an effort was apparently made to seek suitable barges to carry the stone.[24] At Ballingham, grain was shipped to Wilton in 1791 from an unknown wharf.

In the past Hoarwithy has seen great activity on the riverside, with barges loading and unloading goods at four different sites. Below Hoarwithy Bridge the remains of a wharf is visible and the posts for tying up barges were identified in 1953. A 'Wharf on the river side' was mentioned but not specified in the sale particulars of Llanfrother in 1856, which may have referred to a Timber Yard there at that time.[25] From 1799 an unfinished and roofless barn was rented by the Chepstow Bark Company 'to chop our bark providing it was covered', and the site was used for 'the wharfing of any bark'.[26] At Red Rail an enclosed track leads to the fording place where wharves once existed on both banks, and at Shepponhill in Sellack parish 'The Public had a right of Wharfage for Timber paying a Toll of 1s per Ton' which was advertised in the sale particulars of Kynaston in 1863.[27]

The earliest known reference to a wharf on the Wye in the project area was at King's Caple where Daniel Kerry made a 'tying up place' for barges in 1696 at Sellack Boat. It was later known as 'Kerry's

Capler Wharf   *Hoarwithy Wharf*

Lockstock Boat Piece' , and from there cider and corn went down river to Bristol for a better price.[28] On the opposite bank and further downstream, Amos Jones was permitted 'to go through the Meadow lying by the River Wye at the Broken Bank in the parish of Sellack aforesaid with his teams to carry his Corn & Cyder to and from the said River when he shall have Occasion'.[29] Strangford is a secret place only accessible from the river, but some evidence suggests that there was a wharf where goods had been delivered by barge in the late 18th century.

At Much Fawley, a track leads down to the river to a point traditionally know as a ferry and wharf site 'for loading barges with farm produce for transit down the Wye'.[30] This was the site of the passage over the Wye to Strangworth (the Strangford) for carrying coal and lime from Howle and for taking market horses to Monmouth in 1678, and where a hundred years later grain was loaded on to barges.[31] Below How Caple Court and church a large riverside meadow called Lord's Meadow in 1763, was where tiles and coal were imported and oak and timber exported on barges in the 1790s, and was probably the site of the How Caple wharf of 1799.[32]

On the south-east side of the Foy loop is the quaintly named Hole-in-the-Wall, where the derelict Gate-house once served as an inn, stabling for the barge horses and a wharf, whilst on the opposite bank freights of apples, lime and bottles were conveyed from Ingestone in 1795. Below Foy Bridge, on the east bank, was a landing place at Cam Meadow in 1763, where Messrs. Bowsher, Hodges & Co. loaded 18 tons of timber in 1809 for their shipyards in Chepstow. The same year this company freighted bark, poles and timber from Backney,[33] and further downriver at Bridstow the remains of a stone wharf, identified by the LOWV project, was probably where Bowsher, Hodges & Co. shipped bark from Ashe to Wilton in 1795.[34]

The remains of Foy gatehouse

In the 1720s Defoe observed that Ross 'was a good old town, famous for good cyder, a great manufacture of iron ware and a good trade on the River Wye'. Most of the Ross riverside was then in Bridstow parish, including Dock Meadow and The Dock, both situated beside a premises that later blossomed into the Hope and Anchor Inn. Another dock recorded in 1753, which was located below Wilton Bridge, became the wharf of 1823 owned by Charles Jones of the Cleeve.[35] Other docks were established on both sides of Wilton Bridge where Luke Hughes, John Vaughan, William Porter, Thomas Barrow and Edward Tamplin constructed quays, wharves and warehouses to serve the river trade of the 18th century.[36] Luke Hughes was

A barge at Ash, Bridstow, in 1799 by Samuel Ireland

Wilton Wharf in 1840

also an innkeeper at Wilton until his death in 1755 and was known to have been the 'first proprietor of any barge on the river at that place, established for trading purposes'.[37]

From the end of the 18th century Wilton presented a busy riverside scene, such as when '2 Ton Coal, Frt of 6 Hampers, Bots. 39 Cheese, 2 Bags Peas & 1 Bag Hair from Wilton to Caple' was hauled upstream from the coalyard and wharf at Wilton. In 1810 William Porter conveyed 10 sacks of wheat from Hoarwithy via Wilton to Bristol, and in 1811 Henry Platt transported 12 sacks of wheat to Brockweir, and, at a later date, 30 sacks of wheat and 74 sacks of grain to the same destination. Other items shipped from Wilton included bark, pantiles, lime, and timber to various places on barges named the *Wilton*, a sloop of 65 tons, in 1791; the *Rival*, a barge of 17 tons built at Wilton, in 1804; the *Thomas*, a trow of 37 tons, in 1825; and the *Flora* and *Farmer* plying the river in 1815.[38]

At the beginning of the 19th century Wilton was described as a:

> small Hamlet, in the parish of Bridstow, about half a mile to the westward of Ross, from which it is separated by the river Wye, – and through it runs the turnpike road leading to Hereford and Monmouth, at the extremity of which it divides at different angles for those places. It might properly be called the quay or wharf to Ross, by furnishing a convenient accommodation for the shipping and landing of goods sent up and down the river. The remains of the castle are converted into a dwelling house.[39]

Barges

The flat-bottomed sloops and trows working the river were generally termed barges and had a hauling rope attached to the mast, a tarpaulin for keeping the cargo dry and an anchor. In 1763 the length of 'a common Barge from 18 to 20 tons' was '50 feet, breadth 11 feet',[40] and two barges for sale at Monmouth in 1798 were 17 and 19 tons, but the *Valiant* for sale at Hereford in 1808 was 'Thirty-two Tons Burden, well worth the attention of Timber Merchants, being capable of taking in heavy Timber'.[41] In the 1780s and 1790s timber was towed down the river, and from Canon Bridge logs were lashed together into a raft to float downstream to Chepstow.[42]

A barge at Wilton in 1755

A barge above the bridge in Hereford in 1836

Although the river barges normally carried a single square sail hung on a cross yard on the single mast, it was not always possible to use this method of propulsion. Lack of wind, breeze in the wrong direction and riverside trees sheltering the river all conspired against the sailing vessels and on many occasions the only way to progress was by towing. This service was provided by a band of men known as bow hauliers.[43]

It was tough, hard and dangerous work that required working as a team, especially when bridges had to be negotiated. Until Mr Jessop's recommendations were implemented, the barges were hauled by teams of 9 to 11 men. On approaching Wilton Bridge the hauliers would have clambered up the bank and over the road with the long tow rope attached to the top of the mast. When the barge reached the bridge the mast was lowered, the skipper released the rope and a single man hauled in the boat end from the bridge and dropped the rope back onto the barge on the opposite side of the bridge to be refastened.[44] The deeply cut grooves cut by the barge ropes were observed in 1884 and were still visible in 2007.[45]

Several incidents of drowning and barges sinking have been recorded. In one case at Foy, a bargeman was drowned in 1796; in another a man drowned when a coal barge sank at Eign, just below Hereford, in 1804. Other cases include a barge laden with cider that sank five miles from Ross in 1809, and a barge

A barge lowering its mast to get under Wilton Bridge in 1839

with 25 tons of coal on board capsized near Fownhope in 1819 when the crew of three perished.[46]

Various other documents survive which give a vivid impression of barge traffic on the Wye during the late 18th and early 19th centuries. Project team members studied several of these in some detail to provide additional background information on barge traffic and the people involved. The entries cover details of the carriage of goods, expenses associated with the barges and payments made and received. Most traffic recorded was to or from Hereford and coal was a major cargo. This was in several grades – 'firecole', 'smithcole', 'limecole', 'charkes' – and was measured by the 'tun', 'seme', 'dozen', or pound avoirdupois. Much of the coal was bought for stock and stored at Hereford on the quayside or in a two storey 'wharehouse'. The trade was often on a credit basis and purchase accounts were settled from time to time, sometimes on an annual basis.

Barge account book 1809 to 1812 [47]

In one barge account book, covering the years 1809 to 1812, the unnamed company was involved with trading in lime, bark, poles, hoops, hurdles, timber, flax, cheese, grain, seeds, paper, hops, and cider going down river, mainly from Wilton. Although less goods were freighted upstream, there were deliveries of coal, slate, iron weights, candles, soap, and pantiles. Numerous loads of timber were shipped to Bowsher & Co. at Chepstow, and time was allowed 'for loading at different Places'. Extra payments were made for 'Hauling to Trow', 'Roling the timber to the bank', 'Wharfage', and 'repairing Tarpaulin'. In 1810, the busiest months on the river were March, April and May, but the following year it was April, October and December when

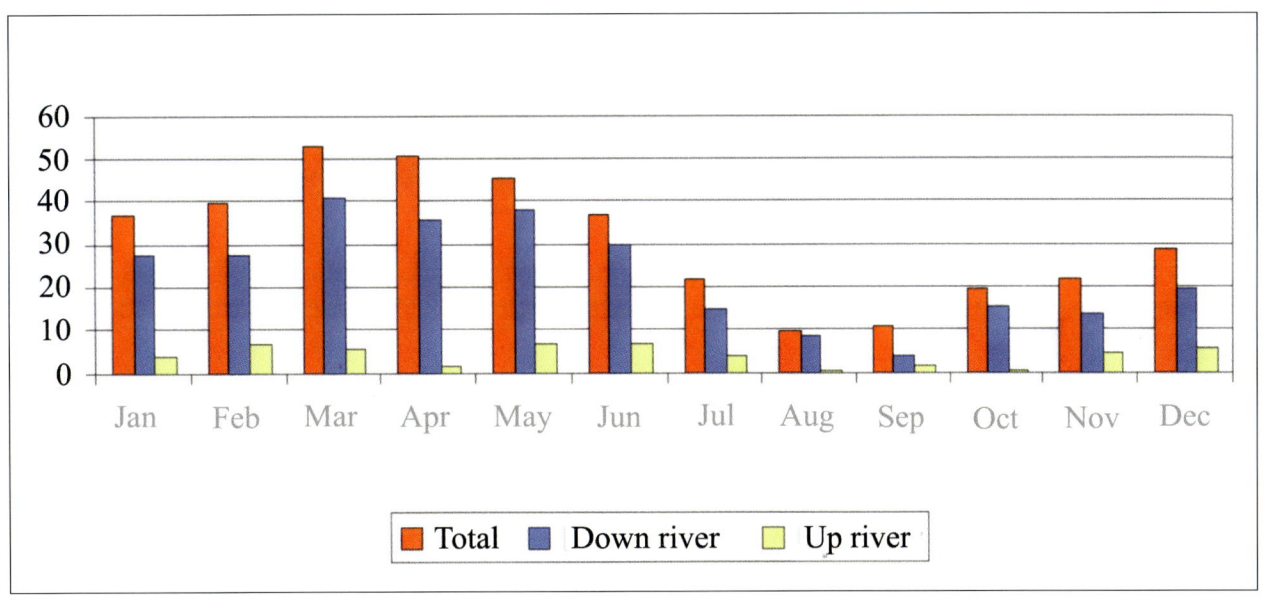

Number of shipments per month in the 1810 barge accounts

enough rain made the river swifter and deeper for barges to navigate. Although most cargo was recorded as going downstream, the barges may have continued upstream beyond the area of the account book. The quietest period was during the summer months when the river was shallow, making the Wye difficult to navigate.[48] Drink was sometimes supplied to the hauliers – usually when they were loading or unloading the cargo.

Day book 1791 to 1805[49]
The day book from 1791 to 1805 includes the following entries (amongst many others):

> 1792 September 4th agreed with phillip Hatton / for two len[g]ths of colework at the young Collers at thirty pounds the purchas / Thomas Ore & Thomas webb whiness

Phillip Hatton, together with several other people, owned and worked a level called the Young Colliers in the Forest of Dean. Coal was brought by horse-drawn wagon to the riverside where it was loaded into the barges.

A Mr. Winneat took delivery of coal, some certainly of limecole grade to be used in lime kilns at 'the hole', probably Hole-in-the-Wall, for his lime kilns at Sollers Hope, and at the Lords Meadow at How Caple.[50] In 1791 at least £54 2s. was paid for coal delivered to Hole in the Wall. Mrs. Cole was another regular customer in the early 1790s. She had coal unloaded at 'Capla' or more usually at The Mill in Fownhope, and was recorded as paying £50 on account, approximately quarterly, in 1791/2. Mr. Hinds of Sollers Hope took 'limecole', which was discharged at Lyndor above Hole-in-the-Wall, and again the bill was settled by instalments. Whilst coal provided virtually all 'imports', 'exports' included wheat and barley from Hereford, Fownhope and Hoarwithy, charged at 4d. or 6d. per bag, which was typically carried only as far as Lydbrook or Brockweir.

Some of the daybook entries for 1791-92 named the barge and the manpower on the hauling lines including 'The Fly', 'The Industry' and 'The Dick'. These boats usually had 11 men to pull them up river and in 1791 the Fly was at 'Eigng' (Eign, just below Hereford) on October 20, November 5, 9, 14, and December 8, 13, 18. Similarly the Industry was at Eign on November 14, 27, December 8, 22 and January 9 in 1792. From these and other similar figures it is evident that the same barge is listed after only three or four days' interval, having completed the journey downstream and returned. Longer periods may be explained either by the barge carrying someone else's cargo or lying idle through lack of cargo or poor river conditions. Jessop certainly assumed that Brockweir to Hereford took between 2½ and 3 days, allowing time for loading and unloading, an assumption supported by the above figures.

Jessop's report led to the creation of a towing path, although this crossed from bank to bank more frequently than he recommended. Presumably this was due to some landowners refusing to allow the towpath over their land. It would have been a temptation to allow the tow-horses to graze from the 'free' grass along the way, so the Act authorising that this path made provision for compensation for damage so caused.

Wathen's view of a barge at Capler in 1793

Day book 1811 to 1853

In this book[51] there are a few references to the barge traffic, but one important entry recorded the inaugural horse drawn traffic:

> Barges first Hauled by Horses on the River Wye Tuesday the fifteenth day of January 1811 - the first through Wilton Bridge was Jonathon Crompton's Barge the Henry, William Hoskins master with coal. Second: J. Crompton's Fanny. Thomas Jones mas[r] with two horses each.

On 26 April it was noted that: 'William Charles saw Jonathon Crompton's Son leading two horses in the Whithybed meadow much further than he ought to'. On 1 May an even more detailed note was written about straying horses – almost a witness statement. Whether compensation was paid or not is not recorded, but perhaps landowners, barge owners and masters quickly established a working relationship.

174

Ledger of the Liverpool and Bristol Company. 1825-1827[52]

This book records barge movements to and from Hereford and other places on the Wye. It covers a period starting in late 1825 – well into the horse drawn era. The entries are reasonably standardised with the name of the barge; the place of departure or arrival, but not both; the name of the master (barges tended to have regular masters); a list of consignees; and the cargo for them and its weight and/or cost of carriage. The ledger came into the possession of Chave and Jackson, chemists of Hereford, who used it as a scrapbook with the result that many pages were cut out and others damaged, before the ledger was presented to Hereford City Library. Despite these misfortunes, there is evidence of bulk cargoes of timber being exported and specialist high value timber such as mahogany arriving in Hereford from overseas. Large quantities of chopped bark were shipped out, principally in the winter months when the bark could be stripped more easily. This was destined for use in the tanning industry, especially in Ireland. Other exports were finished wooden products such as tree-nails, felloes, spokes and barrel hoops. For example timber, plank and 3,000 tree-nails were shipped on the barge *James* from Canon Bridge and Hereford on 16 January 1828.

Quantities of 'Cyder' in pipes, kilderkins and barrels went downriver, whilst the Pulling partnership in Hereford imported brandy, other spirits and wines in hogsheads, kegs and bottles. Messrs. Pullings were also substantial exporters of chopped bark and were engaged in the slate trade.[53] Other imports to Hereford included a wide range of groceries including regular chests of soap. The entries certainly show that Hereford was very dependant on the Wye for the carriage of a wide range of goods, in which trade some 50 odd barges might be engaged at any one time.

There are a number of examples of a barge spending two or three days alongside the wharf in Hereford before voyaging downstream, most likely to Brockweir or Chepstow, to return in a fortnight. Some entries show that goods from Hereford were transhipped en-route. Thus in 1828: 'Feby 29 *The Trader* to Mordiford, [where] Goods to be put into the *James & Ann* for Bristol'. Whilst the level of the river in February is unlikely to be the reason for this, at other times of the year delays and smaller, lighter loads can be explained by a low river level. Thus, in the summers of the mid-1820s, there are many entries listing goods conveyed on a variety of wagons to provide a replacement service for the barges. In 1827: 'July 10 By Old Griffiths Timber Carriage to Hereford' on which were lashed a tierce of sugar, 3 chests of soap and other goods, including 6 x 21 foot Deal planks. One 'vehicle', the '*Mordiford Trolley*', is listed on a regular basis, but it is unclear from the entries whether it was a small transhipment barge or a wagon that took goods to the riverside. At the best, river traffic was erratic and road traffic was little better. It was not until rail traffic started to take over that the difference became apparent.

A comparison of the quantity of goods that could be carried on different forms of transport is of some interest:

Method of Transport	Maximum weight of Goods
Packhorse	$1/8$ ton
Stage wagon on a soft road	$5/8$ ton
Stage wagon on a Macadam road	2 tons
Wagon on tram rails and one horse	8 tons
Barge on a river and one horse	30 tons
Barge on a canal and one horse	50 tons

Rail Transport

When the Hereford and Gloucester Canal reached Hereford in 1845, the railway network was already spreading across the nation. The former horse-drawn tramways bringing coal into Herefordshire from South Wales and the Forest of Dean were never entirely satisfactory due to underfunding and organised opposition from barge owners with a vested interest in trading in the Wye Valley.

From the 1830s various proposals were put forward for a railway to Hereford, including an ambitious plan of 1836 through Ledbury and Newent with a 'Branch from Ross'. The prospectus quoted many benefits such as:

> goods which are now shipped from thence by water to Chepstow, and forwarded by river craft or land to Hereford and Ross, will by this Company be conveyed at little more than half the present charge, with this advantage, deliveries will be made in one-third of the time now taken in the transit ,,, The farmer will have a good and cheap communication with all the Manufacturing districts of England, his produce will be within twelve hours' reach of London; fat beasts now reaching Smithfield in a lame and impoverished state, losing from eight to twelve per cent. in weight, will be brought to market in a good and wholesome condition. [54]

In the event this did not take place and Hereford was the last major city in England to be connected to the rail network, with the opening of the line from Hereford to Shrewsbury in 1853 and the line to Newport in 1854.

It was mainly due to the efforts of James Wallace Richard Hall, a solicitor and banker, that a successful meeting was held at Ross in 1849 which led to the formation of the Hereford, Ross, Gloucester Railway Company that was incorporated in 1851.[55] Plans were submitted, engineers contracted, money raised, and compulsory powers obtained for the 'short Line of twenty-three miles of Railway'.[56] In actual fact it was '30½ miles of railway from Hereford via Ross to Gloucester'.[57] Wallace Hall as solicitor and secretary of the company organised the purchase of land, and arranged a supply of gas and the provision of coal wharves at Ross Station. He undertook the setting out of footpaths to the entrance gates and booking office, and the collection of ballast from the River Wye at Backney.[58]

The Hereford, Ross and Gloucester Railway opened on 1 June 1855 amidst much celebration. The event was reported in great detail in the local papers and the *Illustrated London News* chose to focus, not on the benefits of cheaper transportation of goods, but on another angle – the fact that the railway would give 'tourists cheap and easy access to the tour of one of the finest rivers in Europe'.[59] The railway was also to provide a boost to the agricultural, timber, brewing and manufacturing industries in Ross and Hereford.

The Hereford to Gloucester line never became an important railway route, but:

> had been so well engineered that it was possible for it to carry heavily loaded trains, not just in wartime emergencies, but in peacetime, too. It was frequently used as a convenient by-pass for the north and west main line trains during engineering operations or other problems on that line.[60]

The opening of the railway between Ross and Hereford had a dramatic effect on communications between the east and west bank of the Wye. This was due to the construction of the Hoarwithy Bridge in 1856 built to enable the inhabitants of the Hentland district 'to have ready and safe access to the Fawley Station'[61], and the erection of the Holme Lacy Bridge:

> at or near Even Pitt, opposite to the Holme Lacy Railway Station, on the Hereford, Ross and Gloucester Railway; thus connecting the north and south sides of the River Wye, and opening the Port of Gloucester to the populous district lying around Fownhope, Woolhope, Mordiford, & the adjoining parishes ... The Lime Stone Quarries in the Fownhope and Woolhope Hills will be brought within reach of an abundant supply of coal, delivered at the Holme Lacy Station, while a market will thus be opened for the sale of Lime, with ready means of conveyance.

They also pressed the importance of the railway 'now that the Wye Towing Path and Navigation has (virtually) ceased to exist'.[62]

The original company was taken over by Great Western Railway in 1862 and converted from broad gauge to standard gauge in 1869, and in 1948 was taken over by British Rail. From thereon traffic and passenger services declined, and with competition from car ownership, bus transport and road haulage the line eventually closed in 1964.

The Route of the Railway

The construction of the broad gauge railway between Ross and Hereford had presented the engineers with the task of digging three tunnels, erecting four bridges across the Wye and building two stations.[63] From Ross Station the railway track followed the left bank of the Wye to its first crossing at Backney, a bridge of five masonry piers supporting six spans, originally of timber but later replaced by plate girders. In 1896 J.A. Stratford noted in *The Wye Tour* that:

> When some navvies were sent out to carry out the necessary works preparatory to the construction of a railway bridge across the river at Backney, about two miles on the Hereford side of Ross, they contemptuously laughed at the idea of having to construct a large bridge across such a poor 'little bruk'. During the previous day, however, there had been some heavy rain in the district of the upper waters, and when the navvies went to their work in the morning, they found that the angry 'little bruk' had swept away tools, piles, engineering tackle, etc., as if in revenge for the slight they had cast upon it.[64]

In 1965 the girders were removed leaving the five solitary piers striding across the Wye. Towards the end of the 20th century part of the embankment was incorporated into a picnic site known as Backney Bridge on the Sellack/Foy side of the river.[65]

A railway bridge over the Foy road has been demolished, and a deep cutting leading to Strangford has been used as a landfill site together with the halt at Backney which opened in 1933. At Strangford a small bridge over the former cutting has been retained, but the second rail crossing over the Wye has had its decking removed. In 1947 the central pier of the bridge collapsed and the spans on either side fell into the river. This damage was caused by high flood water, but was

Backney halt

Strangford railway cutting

177

The bridge over Strangford cutting

The bridge after the infilling of the cutting

The collapse and repair of the bridge across the Wye at Strangford in 1947

fortunately heard by two young men who were on their way home at the time, when they heard a terrific crash. They realised at once that it must have been the collapse of the bridge; so without the slightest hesitation got into communication with the railway staff at Fawley. They in turn promptly advised Ross-on-Wye station. Other railway officials were quickly requisitioned and the section of the line between Ross and Fawley was closed to further traffic and minutely examined.[66] While the bridge was being repaired a shuttle service of buses ran between Ross and Fawley.

Once across the Wye the railway continued over a narrow bridge across a bridleway known as the Roman Road. At Fawley a shanty camp housed the navvies, and a station was built, which was later extended with sidings, a coal depot, pens for livestock, and houses for the station master and his staff.[67] The road from

Fawley Station

179

Fawley goods yard

King's Caple crosses the railway on a bridge, and on the opposite side of the road Thomas Gatfield opened the New Inn to coincide with the opening of the railway. The inn, which eventually became the British Lion, catered for passengers, but after the railway closed its prime use was lost, and it eventually closed in the late 1990s.[68] Fawley Station was left derelict for a number of years until it was converted into a family dwelling, and the railway houses have survived.

At Fawley the railway entered a tunnel 530 yards long to reach its third crossing of the Wye at Ballingham, a bridge built in a similar style to the other two. Its tall piers remain as a reminder of its former days, and can be viewed from a riverside path leading from Hoarwithy to Ballingham. The road from Carey to Ballingham crossed the railway just before the station, originally constructed as a single-storeyed building in 1909 and rebuilt as a house in the 1980s. Beyond the station a long tunnel of 1,177 yards went through Ballingham Hill to emerge at Kidley Hill Wood. Above the tunnel a footpath passes a pile of stones which were probably left there by the navvies when constructing the tunnel.

Ballingham Station

Bridge, tunnel and goods yard at Ballingham

Holme Lacy Station

Holme Lacy goods yard

1876 advertisement

From the railway bridge below Kidley Hill the course of the railway followed a level route to Holme Lacy and crossed the lane to the church before reaching the station with its single platform, signal box and sidings built within a cutting. In 1891 Francis Charles Hayes was the stationmaster, a respected member of the community, who lived at the Station House with his wife, three children and a 20-year-old servant. Later stationmasters were renowned for their gardens which were entered in the inter-station competition. One judge commented on the 'high bank massed with yellow Rose of Sharon mingled with red roses'.[69] The station has since been demolished, and even a building used during the 1980s as a wildlife centre has vanished, Further features remain along the course of the railway as it approaches Hereford, but they are outside the project area and are not recorded here.

Goods and Passenger Services

In Hereford timber and coal merchants had been handling slates, tiles, bricks, coal, salt, timber and building materials on the Canal Wharf to be transported on the Hereford and Gloucester Canal, but the railways gradually took over the trade. In the 1860s and 1870s R.T. Smith & Co. were established in Hereford and Ross as General Carriers specialising in 'Household Furniture, Pianos, Pictures, Glass, Etc.' and Ralph, Preece & Co., at Barrs Court delivered truckloads of coal, coke and lime to 'any Railway Station in the county', Allen & Co., were dealers in 'Coal, Coke and Lime' which could be ordered from the railway wharves and John Butler who dealt in coal, coke, lime and salt had a depot at Holme Lacy Station, where cord timber from the local woods was in demand for pit-props and conveyed on the railway.

The ice house with six storeys has been converted to a most unusual dwelling

At Ross Station, William Cubitt Treen, a coal and lime merchant, dealt in 'Lime supplied direct from the Kilns at Howle Hill', and Henry Webb & Co. was transporting 'Special Bone Manures' from a depot near the railway station. Samuel Llewellyn was recorded as a 'Fish, Ice, and Coal Merchant' who guaranteed 'A Daily Supply of Best Quality Fish from the First Fisheries and Markets in the Kingdom', and was 'Contractor and Sole Agent for the Severn and Wye Valley Fisheries'[70]. In order to store the salmon he built an ice house with six floors into the cliff face between Wye Street and Wilton Road. It had sloping floors and drains where the melted ice ran out to the river.

There were six passenger trains running each day from Hereford to Gloucester, and five in the opposite direction. The first train left Hereford at 8.20am calling at Holme Lacy at 8.33 and Fawley at 8.43 to arrive in Ross at 8.55, and in the opposite direction the first train left Ross at 8.55 to arrive in

Hereford, Ross and Gloucester railway timetable for 1858

183

Hereford at 9.25am. The last trains left Ross and Hereford at 7.00 and 7.30pm respectively, and there was one train each way on a Sunday. The fare from Gloucester to Holme Lacy in 1858 was 4s. 7d. first class, 3s. 5d. second class, and 2s. 2d. for third class.

To the landowners the railway was an added attraction when they came to sell their farms and estates. Before the railway was completed the Poulstone Estate at King's Caple was for sale, and the particulars advertised that the proposed Gloucester to Hereford line 'will pass near the Estate, and it is supposed that the Parish will have in it a passenger Station'.[71] In 1881 the How Caple Estate sale particulars informed potential purchasers that it was 'Two miles from Fawley Station' on the Great Western Railway, and in 1909 the particulars of Holme Lacy mentioned 'Holme Lacy and Ballingham Railway Stations are on the Estate'.[72]

Disused railway track at Brampton Abbotts.
The spire of Ross-on-Wye church is in the background

CHAPTER IX

Landscape Changes

by David Lovelace

The 12 parishes that comprise the project cover an area of 9,380 hectares and include a population of 4,224, with an average density of 45 persons per square kilometre, but only Bridstow and Fownhope have significant village populations. In this predominantly rural area the appearance of the countryside has overwhelmingly reflected the nature of contemporary farming and woodland management over the centuries.

Apart from the Ross to Hereford railway line, completed in 1855, the area's countryside was scarcely affected by infrastructure developments until the mid 20th century. In recent decades the expansion of Ross, major trunk road improvements, and retail warehousing have eaten into the southern part of Brampton Abbotts and Bridstow. Energy transmission, in the form of pylons, power lines and, most recently, the Milford Haven to Tirley liquefied gas pipe line, have had significant impacts. Modern farm buildings often dominate the local character as is the case of potato storage units next to Ballingham church and the spread of polytunnels at King's Caple. This chapter concentrates on landscape change using the evidence of maps, aerial photographs and farming data.

Evidence of landscape change

When the vast majority of the rural population lived all their lives in the same parish, maps were unnecessary. To identify a parcel of land for the purposes of legal title or lease agreement it was usually sufficient to state the occupier, the lands adjoining and its name. This is how many parcels of land in Foy, leased to Sarah Apperley in 1690, were described: '1 other acre shoots north & south upon the Rises and lies between the lands [of] James Collins on both sides'.[1] For anyone in Foy at that time there would be no question as to exactly which strip of land was being rented, but after 400 years it is almost impossible to locate. Occasionally field names persist long enough to appear in later maps. Sometimes a boundary, such as the River Wye, the king's highway or a park pale is mentioned, helping to narrow down the location. Such was the continuity of occupancy and the strength of the community identification with places, that stewards, bailiffs and lawyers who drew up estate accounts, rent rolls, farm tenancy agreements, or adjudicated in land disputes, seldom felt the need for maps until well into the 18th century, although there were a few exceptions.

The extent and nature of historic field boundaries is also difficult to quantify, although a Royal Commission survey of Herefordshire in 1791 made the general observation that the county is 'much enclosed and has been for ages past' and there is no reason to suppose that the countryside of the project area was that different.[2] The exceptions were strips in open fields and hay meadows on flood plain grassland which were marked, if at all, by stones or stakes. What proportion of land was farmed in this way is difficult to estimate and the archaeological evidence of medieval arable strip cultivation has largely been destroyed by modern ploughing. However, past aerial photography reveals some areas to have been extensive, for example at Holme Lacy (see p. 194). By the 18th century, documentary evidence indicates that most field boundaries were live hedges and only a few open strip fields survived into the Victorian period.

Even with well documented estates it is difficult to visualise, let alone quantify, the structure and character of the countryside without the spatial clues provided by maps. Only when large scale maps became the currency of geographical information could the landscape be seen objectively, allowing changes over time to be quantified.

The earliest known maps of the project area are those of the lands of the Scudamore family, surveyed in 1695 by John Pye. These include their holdings in Ballingham, Bolstone, and Hentland, along with a schedule giving the area, field name and state of cultivation, and were commissioned shortly after John Scudamore, the 2nd Viscount, made his will in 1694.[3] By the time the map maker, Richard Frizel, had been commissioned to

The 1695 Pye map of the Scudamore holding in Ballingham (© *British Library*)

make another survey of the Scudamore estates, in 1780, their holdings had increased to include lands in Foy and Brampton Abbotts – all within the project area.[4] These maps are more detailed and beautifully hand-painted with comments on the farm buildings and the land. For example Ballingham Hall 'held by Mr. Edward Bullock is good arable, meadow and pasture ground and has a good house and offices and is beautifully situated on the river Wye and almost surrounded by it', while Gannah Farm 'Adjoins the Deer Park is good land and fit for dairy and tillage. The house which is on it is greatly gone to wreck & should be let to an occupier who would reside'. We are told that Carey Farm is 'pleasantly situated commanding a fine prospect of the county. The quality of the soil is fit for feeding, dairy and tillage and produces large crops of wheat, oats and potatoes. Has a good Farm house and orchard on it and a small copse and may be greatly improved at a small expense, it being very convenient to manure'. Evidence of earlier farming systems is recorded at Townsend Farm in Brampton Abbotts: 'This farm has a house and offices which is in good order. It has an orchard on it & about 15 acres inclosed and all the rest in common fields & lies within one mile of Ross'.

In 1780 the Scudamore estates occupied nearly 2,000 hectares (21%) of the land of the project parishes so these maps and their schedules provide a detailed breakdown of the proportion of this sample of the countryside that was woodland, parkland and farmland at this time.

The 1780 Frizel survey of the Scudamore lands in Ballingham

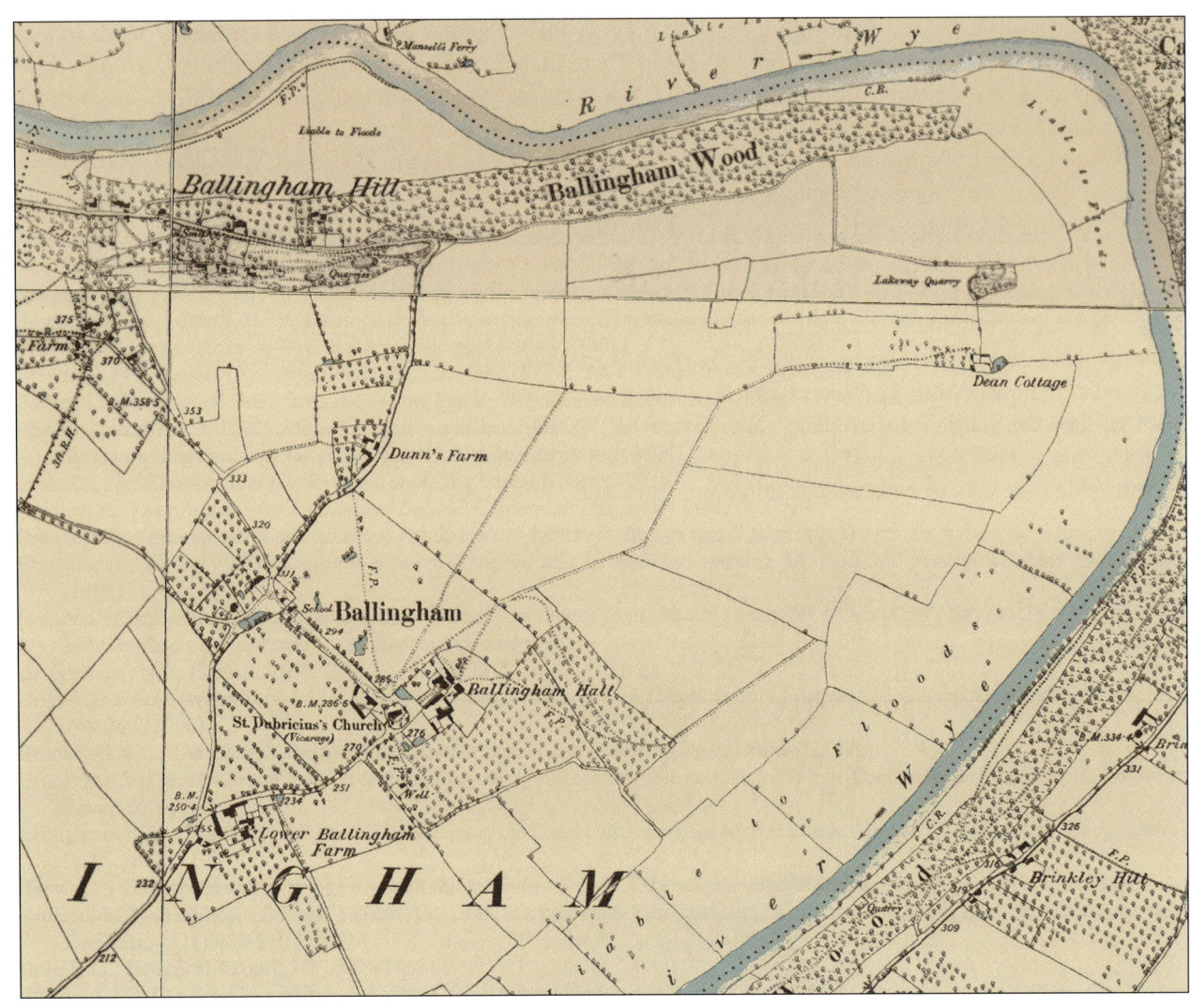

Ballingham in 1887

Land type	Hectares	%
Farmland	189	9.7
Woodland	167	8.6
Parkland (Holme Lacy Park)	1,591	81.7
Total	**1,947**	**100**

One of the woodlands, the 12 hectare Shepherds Rough in Holme Lacy, has the word 'fallen' written on it. 60 years later it is mapped as 'rough pasture' and it remains open with a scattering of trees to this day.

The Herefordshire estates owned by Guy's Hospital included most of the farmland in Bridstow which was mapped in 1755 by John Green and depicts arable, meadow, rough pasture, orchard and woodland and even distinguishes individual trees in the fields.[5] Another map by John Green made in 1788 of fields either

188

An aerial photograph of Ballingham taken in 1946

side of the River Wye at Ross is of particular interest as it plots the changes in the course of the river as it makes a loop around Wilton Castle. Between 1788 and 1814 the river bank on the Ross side had been eaten away by 10 metres, an average of half a meter per year.[6] Examination of more recent maps and aerial photographs has failed to show such a high rate of change in recent times.

Estate maps are especially revealing when analysed along with their accompanying schedules which give tenure, area and whether arable, pasture, orchard etc. When digitised and overlaid onto the modern one they can be compared with later maps and aerial photographs. A good example is the 1823 estate map of the lands of Lord Ashburton which include most of the present-day Perrystone estate in Yatton, Foy, Brampton Abbotts and How Caple.[7] Other examples are the maps of Brockhampton estate of 1832 and 1890,[8] and those of Kings Caple made for John Woodhouse in 1812 and 1844.[9] Other sources of information are sale particulars of estates which usually include a map, either made specifically by the agent or more usually modified from an existing published map. They often include a schedule with details of each field, as at Ashe Ingham Court in 1856.[10]

An aerial photograph of Ballingham taken in 2002

Tithe Surveys

The practice of 'tithing', by which a tenth of all local agricultural production was given to the church, was the formal part of the taxation system during the medieval period. After the upheavals of the Dissolution and the Civil War these tithes became increasingly unpopular and were often substituted by purely monetary payments. However, there was no organised transition from 'in kind' to cash payments and by the 19th century the nature of these dues varied enormously throughout the country. The 1836 Tithe Commutation Act standardised everyone's tithe burden on the basis of the area and value of land they occupied. The result was a large-scale mapping of the whole country, parish by parish, with an accompanying list known as the 'apportionment', which recorded every parcel of land and its owner, tenant, land use, field name, and area.[11] The tithe surveys can be considered the second Domesday survey.

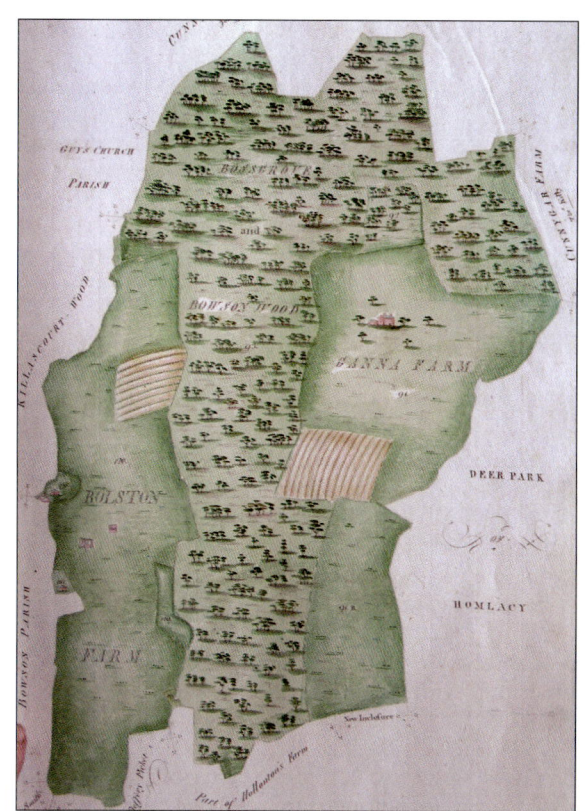

Gannah Farm in 1780

Scudamore lands in Holme Lacy and Bolstone 1780.
Composite of eight individual farm maps rectified to
the 1st edition OS 25 inch to a mile map

Wilton and the Wye from Ross 1921

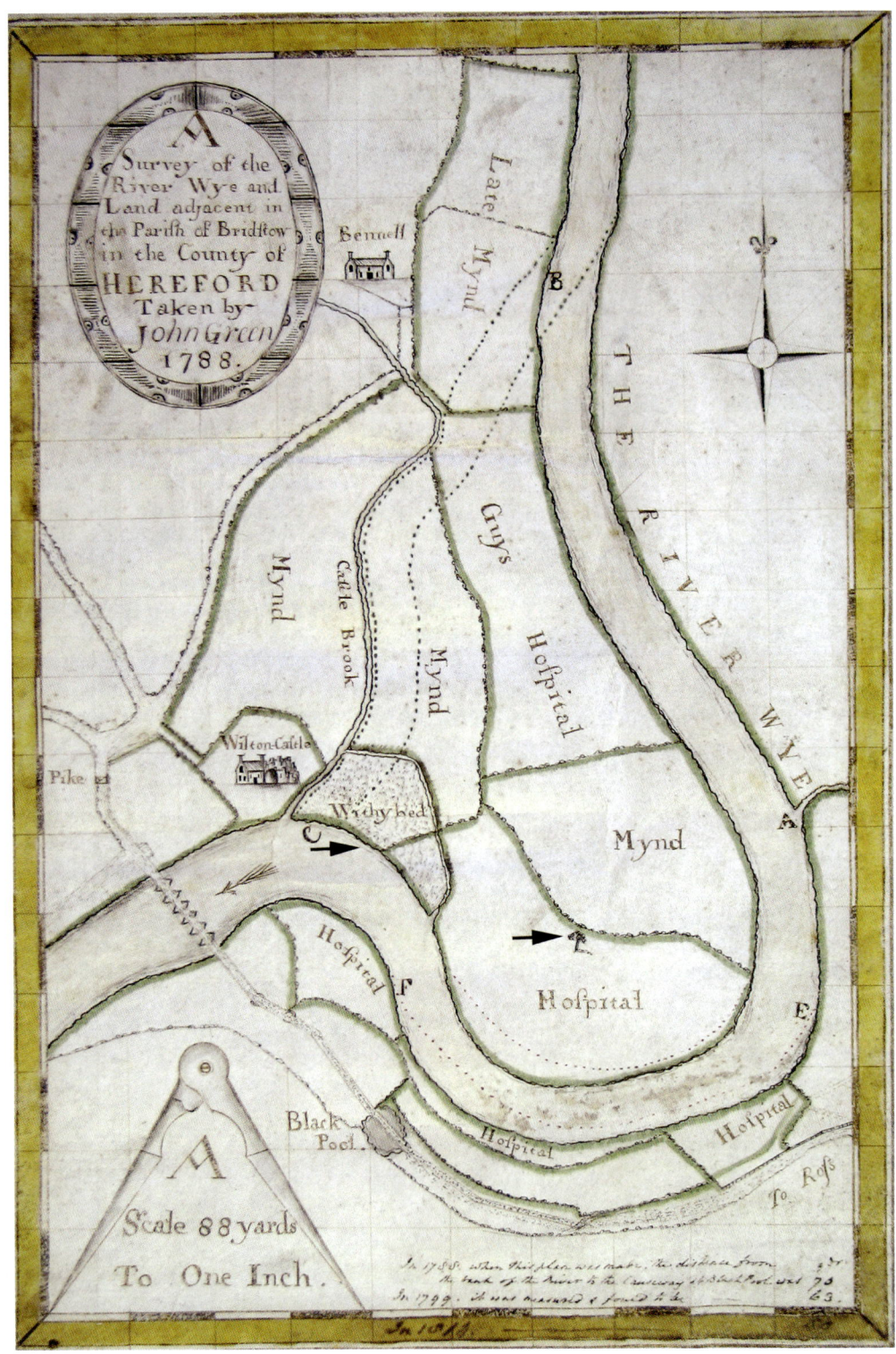

The Wilton Loop

The note at the bottom reads 'In 1788, when this plan was made, the distance from the bank of the River to the Causeway of Black Pool was 70 yds. In 1799 it was measured and found to be 63 yds'

192

Wilton – The Domesday Oak in 1912

Wilton – The Domesday Oak, 2007

Composite image of 1946, 1970 and 1971 aerial photographs of Holme Lacy showing the extent of surviving ridge and furrow features

In the 12 parishes of the project area some 6,350 individual land parcels were recorded, representing a very detailed snapshot of farming and woodland in the years between 1838 and 1843. Of particular interest is the high proportion of land in arable, which reflects the high prices for cereals in the aftermath of the Napoleonic Wars and before the Corn Laws abolished tariffs on grain imported from the colonies. In many of the parishes the proportion of land in arable was higher than at any time until the 1970s.

Tithe surveys were paid by local landowners, so the maps varied in quality, detail and scale. In the project parishes, all except Fownhope show woods with tree symbols and in some, for example King's Caple, individual trees in fields. The large scale of the Tithe Maps shows the locations of buildings clearly outlined, which is useful in comparing with later developments.

Historic County Maps

These have proved to be insufficiently detailed or not accurate enough to use for the analysis of landscape change, except for roads, parks and larger woods. The same area mapped by Isaac Taylor on his county map of 1754 may be compared with the Ordnance Surveyors drawings of 1816, Henry Price's map of 1817, and Bryant's map of 1834.[12] Taylor's map shows woods, but only very approximately by groups of tree symbols, but not their boundaries. However, both Holme Lacy and Pengethley Parks are well delineated. The map also confirms that none of the medieval parks had survived. It was not until the national First Edition of the six inch to the mile Ordnance Survey maps were published during the 1880s that field boundaries and trees were depicted in maps.

Twentieth-century Land Use Surveys

In the 1930s Professor Dudley Stamp co-ordinated a Land Utilisation Survey of how land was used in England and Wales by using supervised schoolchildren. The Herefordshire sheets were surveyed in 1934 and the results were colour-coded onto one inch maps. The main types of land were grassland, arable, woodland, orchard, and heathland. In 1999 the Herefordshire Nature Trust attempted to record the status of each land parcel in the Wye Valley on the basis of ecological criteria, to identify remaining habitats. In doing so, each field was classified according to arable, improved grassland or semi-improved grassland. Both these 20th-century surveys can be compared with the 1840 tithe surveys to show how the proportion of arable farmland has changed over 160 years. It shows the dramatic swing from the arable-dominated farming, of the early Victorian period to the pasture-dominated period of the inter-war agricultural depression and then back to the arable-dominated agriculture of today.

Aerial Photographs

Vertical photographs are made using an aircraft adapted to mount a camera pointing vertically downwards and are used as the basis of much modern map making. The first available photographs of the project area are from the Aerofilm Collection of 1921 (see next page).[13] In 1946 the RAF systematically photographed most of the county and all of the project area. In subsequent decades both the RAF and the Ordnance Survey regularly photographed the country while in recent years digital colour aerial photography has become available.

Field Boundaries from 1840

Although most hedgerow removal occurred after the 1960s, there was restructuring of holdings and field patterns on some estates in the Victorian era. For example, between 1840 and the 1890s most of the hedgerows of central Brockhampton parish were removed and replanted, roads relocated and the church replaced, such that the original field pattern is scarcely recognisable. At Brampton Abbotts, hedges were removed and Townsend Farm was rebuilt to the west of its original site. In the absence of heavy machinery

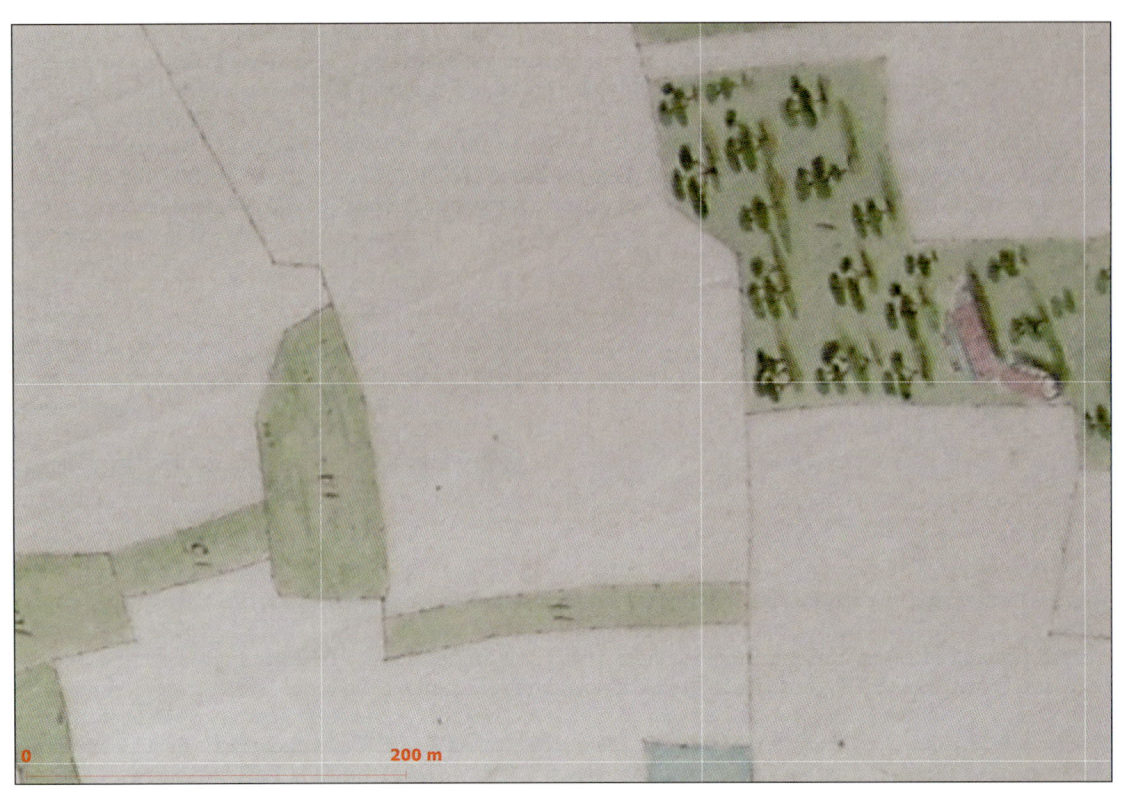

Brampton Abbotts – Townsend Farm in 1780

Townsend Farm in 1823

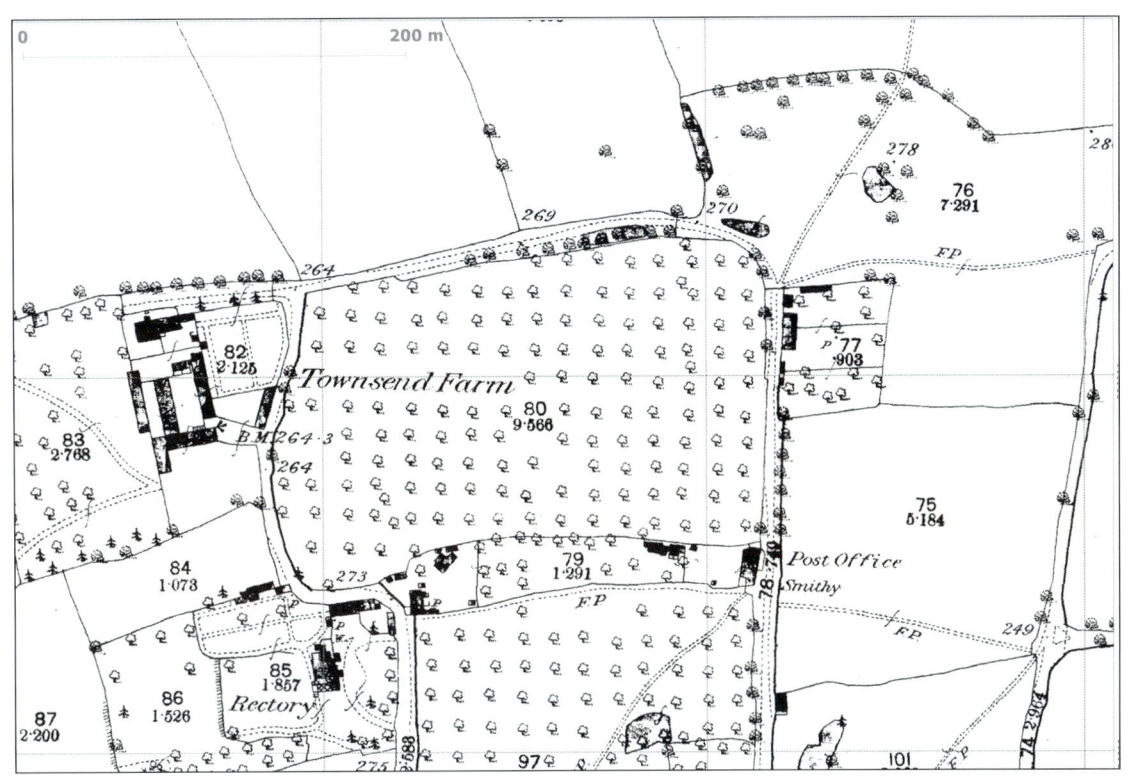

Townsend Farm on the 1888 OS map. The whole farm has moved to the west

An aerial photograph of Townsend Farm in 2002

Reaping at Brampton Abbotts in 1920

this would have been a labour intensive and expensive operation. Comparing the 1880s six inch Ordnance Survey map with the RAF 1946 aerial photographs shows how little the structure of the countryside in the project area has changed despite two world wars and emergency measures to maximise food production. The 1880s Ordnance Survey of Holme Lacy Park reveals how accurately the distribution of individual trees was plotted and identifiable 70 years later in aerial photographs.

Mechanisation, specialisation and farm subsidies, following the 1947 Agriculture Act, had a dramatic effect on large tracts of the English countryside, and the Wye Valley was no exception. The changes in the landscape have been uneven throughout the project area – field patterns in parts of Fownhope, which has remained a stronghold of smaller farms, scarcely changed in 160 years, while Brampton Abbotts has lost a large percentage of field boundaries over the same time period. In recent years a proportion of subsidy has been available for restoring or creating hedgerows as at King's Caple near Shieldbrook. Hedgerows were traditionally managed by 'laying' or 'pleaching' every 7 to 15 years, which generated new shoots from the cut stumps as a result producing variety in the hedgerow structure throughout a farm. This labour intensive method is now rarely seen and the mechanical flail is almost universal. It has severely reduced the landscape impact of hedgerows by turning them into a uniformity of square cross-section 'cut back and sides', and reducing their value as a wildlife habitat.

The transitional area between field edge and hedgerow provides an important habitat for plants, insects and birds, and being the route of many footpaths it plays a key part in the experience of many walkers and visitors to the countryside. The practice of ploughing, fertilising and spraying to the very edge of the hedgerow has further reduced the ecological value of hedgerows in arable fields.

Since the late 1980s a small proportion of agricultural subsidy has been available to fund farming methods which benefit the environment. These 'agri-environment schemes' have encouraged more traditional methods of managing hedges including allowing them to grow up for more than one year, creating uncultivated strips around arable fields, allowing wild plants to colonise, and occasionally creating new hedges.

A tractor working at Perrystone in the 1930s

Farmed Landscape 1840 to the Present Day

The farmed landscape of the 12 parishes has reflected the mixed nature of farming in the area, and the balance between pastoral and arable farming has fluctuated over many centuries. In Brampton Abbotts the proportion of farmland that was arable varied from over 60% in 1840, to 45% in 1870, just 25% in 1931 and then up again to 73% in 1988. Although the proportion of land in arable has not greatly changed between 1840 and 1988, its distribution is very different as the river-side meadows are now regularly ploughed for arable. The permanent pastures and meadow lands of the alluvial soils of the valley bottom were always highly valued, because of their excellence as livestock fattening pastures and for the quality of the hay they produced, and none appear to have been ploughed even during the trade blockade of the Napoleonic Wars when grain prices were at an all-time high. This wide tract of permanent grassland on either side of the river Wye had for centuries been an ecological buffer to the river and its ecology. The destruction of large areas of this permanent grassland by deep ploughing has been one of a number of factors which has led to a reduction in water quality and fish stocks due to the increase in run-off of eroded soils, fertilisers and pesticides.

The graph on the next page plots the proportion of farmed area for permanent grassland (PG), all grassland (AG) and arable (Ar) in the parish of Brampton Abbotts between 1840 and 1988. Note the influence of the Second World War and the subsequent agricultural policies.

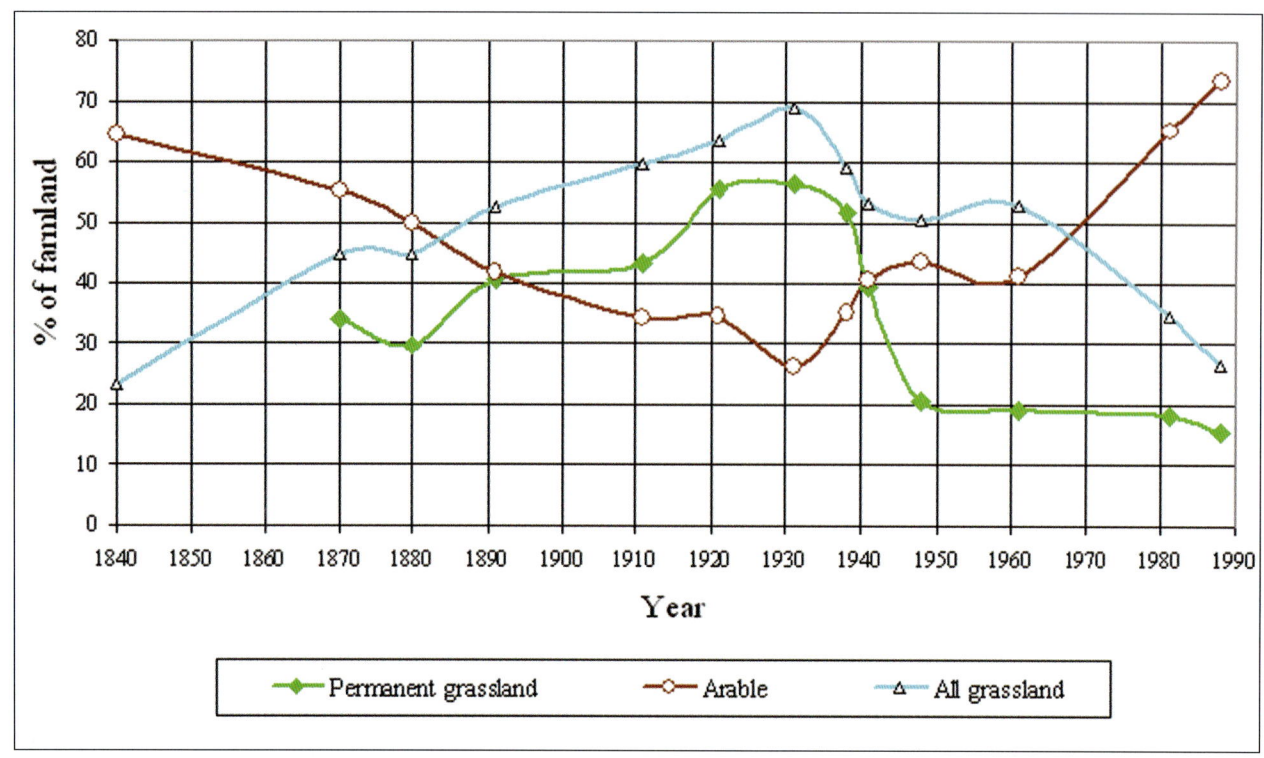

Land use in Brampton Abbotts.
1840 tithe map data and agricultural returns 1870 to 1988

The trend for increasing farm size influences the appearance of the landscape as mechanisation takes advantage of economies of scale which included hedgerow removal to enlarge fields. The table below shows the dramatic reduction of smallholdings and the concentration of land into farms of larger than 300 acres. This process has been furthered by the post-war Governments whose agricultural policies and associated subsidises have encouraged specialisation and the creation of larger farm units

The following table shows the changes in the number farms in different size ranges from 1911 to 1988.

Farm Size	1911	1921	1931	1938	1948	1961	1981	1988
Less than 5 acres	52	36	40	51	53	46	11	9
5 to 50 acres	78	70	74	73	64	62	43	40
50 to 300 acres	68	76	73	74	72	73	45	36
Over 300 acres	16	15	17	16	15	18	28	31
Total farms	**214**	**197**	**204**	**214**	**204**	**199**	**127**	**116**

Horses were the main motive power on the farm and before the First World War between 604 and 633 working horses were recorded on all the farms of the 12 parishes – an average of one horse per 13 hectares of farmland. Most farms had access to tractors during the Second World War, but even in 1948 there were still 201 working horses recorded on the agricultural census returns for the 12 parishes – an average of one horse per 40 hectares of farmland.

A major landscape change over the last 200 years has been the decline in the area of traditional orchards. The 1840 tithe maps show dense clusters of mainly small orchards in all the parishes. By the time of the agricultural census of 1891 there were 460 hectares of orchards, some 5.5% of the farmed area. This had fallen to 65 hectares in 1988, just 0.8% of the land. Only a fraction of these remaining orchards are of the traditional types, with local varieties of pear and apples and rich diversity of wildlife.

War-time Farming in the Project Parishes

The emergency regulations of the Second World War had a dramatic and lasting effect upon the farming and the landscape of the area. In 1939 the county was split up into semi-autonomous War Agricultural Executive Committee (WAEC) districts, each issued with a target area of permanent grassland to be ploughed for cereals and potatoes. All the project parishes, except Holme Lacy, Bolstone and Fownhope, were part of the Ross and Whitchurch District, which in 1940 was required to find over 4,000 acres of grassland to plough. The WAEC commissioned surveys of all farms to identify which grassland fields were to be subjected to compulsory ploughing orders.

In Brampton Abbotts, for example, 103 acres of grassland were compulsorily ploughed in 1940 and 1941. There was resistance to these regulations by the chairman of the district committee, who wrote to the county chairman that the ploughing target

represents the maximum acreage that can economically be found, as any greater contribution would entail the breaking up of highly productive young pastures and a heavy decrease in the stock carrying capacity of the district and would ultimately result in a general loss of fertility.

The regulations had an immediate and damaging effect on dairy production and the district's third largest milk producer, Mr. Perkins, who farmed at Ufton Court and Bowers Farm in Holme Lacy, appealed against an order to plough 66 acres as 'they were valuable pastures and would seriously interfere with milk production on his farm'. He also objected to ploughing 31 acres at Bowers Farm and said that in consequence 'he would have to sell his pedigree dairy herd'. His appeals were turned down, but the committee was prepared to exempt the park at How Caple on the understanding that 'steps be taken to properly graze the parkland'.

As the war progressed the demands for ploughing the remaining grassland were becoming unsustainable, and in 1944 the committee stated that 'Every piece of grassland that could not be ploughed in a single direction by a Fordson tractor was either in arable or short rotation ley. Some of this on flooding or steep land'. Seven ploughing orders had to be cancelled due to seed failures, including 10 acres at Poulstone and 16 acres at Fawley Court. Lack of available labour was also a severe problem at harvest time. On the Brockhampton estate the war time survey of available farm labour recorded that 'the chauffeur gives a hand sometimes'.

While the ecological and landscape impact of this drive to plough up grassland for arable would have been considerable, there is little evidence of hedgerow removal despite the availability of machinery. It is perhaps surprising that any grassland remained unploughed during the war, but clearly a few fields escaped unscathed, as is seen from the topography of archaeological features that only survive in permanent pasture. Such subtle undulations are destroyed or severely reduced by ploughing, but fields just north of Holme Lacy church clearly show ridge and furrow patterns which indicate medieval ploughing practice. Doubtless these features, as well as flower-rich meadows, would have been quite frequent before the start of the Second World War.

At the end of the war in 1945, Britain was economically crippled and Europe devastated. Food rationing continued for another nine years and the WAECs continued to direct and advise local farmers during that time. War-time state intervention in farming continued, but the stick of compulsion was replaced by the carrot of subsidies under the 1947 Agriculture Act. This enshrined the support for farming from taxation that continues today. Between the 1950s and 1970s the proportion of grassland in the project parishes gradually increased, but both livestock and arable farming became more specialist operations, relying on machinery and chemical inputs, as government support was directed almost solely at increasing production using high energy inputs. A large proportion of grassland was by now reseeded leys, while the remaining permanent pasture was receiving artificial fertilisers. Another landscape change during this period was the replacement of traditional breeds of cattle and sheep by high yielding but genetically uniform breeds such as Holsteins and Limousines. The traditional horned Hereford cattle grazing the rich swards of permanent pasture on the alluvial soils of the Wye Valley would have been an essential part of the pastoral scene for centuries.

Anthill Meadow, Fownhope

Unploughed grassland, which has never been sprayed or had applications of fertiliser, is now an extremely rare habitat. In Fownhope one of these meadows has many large ant-hills which are characteristic of 'unimproved' grassland. In theory, legislation exists to protect such meadows, but in practice unless these meadows have some kind of statutory protection such as a Site of Special Scientific Interest status, they are extremely vulnerable and easily destroyed.[14]

Since 1947 much agricultural development has been exempt from planning regulations, so new large-scale developments such as polytunnels and large farm buildings occupy a grey area of what is controllable under the Town and Country Planning Acts. This is proving a controversial area as economic interests are pitted against a largely powerless public and a planning system that was devised in the 1940s on the assumption that farming has top priority for rural areas.

Modern land use at Bolstone

*Above – Tump Farm
at Holme Lacy*

*Right – Potato storage
at Ballingham*

Woodlands – 1817 to the Present Day

Throughout the Victorian period most woodlands in the area were managed as coppice, as Dr. Bull observed in 1852 referring to Haugh Wood and nearby woods of the Woolhope district:

> The general botanical character of the district is wooded, the slopes and ridges being covered with underwood, consisting for the most part of oak, ash, hazel, dogwood, meal-trees,[15] elder, blackthorn, hawthorn etc, cut at regular intervals for poles, firewood etc.[16]

Victorian naturalists were much impressed by the wildlife in these woods, recording many species of orchid and also the wild lily of the valley which still persists to this day.

The vast majority of woods in the project area entered the 20th century as traditionally managed, native woodland and it was not until the Forestry Commission acquired the western part of Haugh Wood in the 1920s that any significant area of woodland was converted into plantations of non-native tree species. The influential 1947 post-war Reconstruction and Planning Survey for Herefordshire stated:

> About one-half of the woodlands [of Herefordshire] fell into the categories of 'Coppice' or 'Coppice with Standards'. Woodlands of this category make but a limited contribution to the county's economy….A quarter of the woodland area is useless from an economic point of view, for it consists of cut-over land (dating from the fellings of the 1914-18 war) which has been allowed to degenerate into a wilderness of bramble, elder and other useless growth.[17]

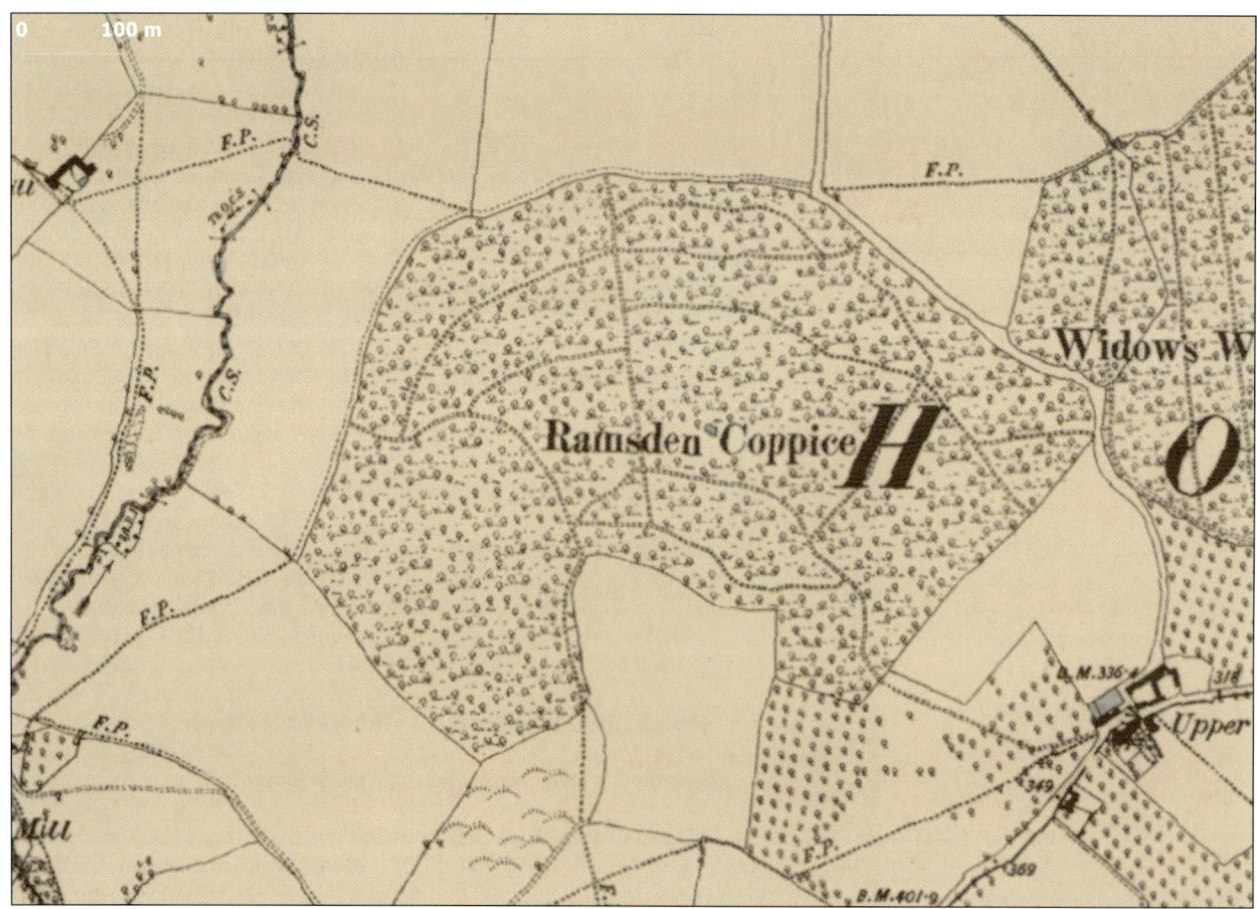

Ramsden Coppice in 1887

This comment mirrored the national post-war Forestry Commission policy, with its emphasis on fast-growing conifers and contempt for traditional methods based upon natural regeneration and native species of tree. In private woodland the process of converting woodland to plantations did not start in earnest until the 1960s. In 1953 the Forestry Commission carried out a census of all woodlands in Herefordshire and this reveals that only a very small area of private woodlands had been planted with conifers by that date. The details of canopy and underwood tree species contained in the census are useful to woodland managers who now intend to restore woods, which were coniferised after the date of the census, back to their original composition of native tree species. For example, Ramsden Coppice was recorded as a 74 acre 'coppice with standards' wood, with a standing volume of 550 cubic feet per acre and a canopy of ash, oak, sweet chestnut, and birch and the coppice made up of hazel, ash and sweet chestnut.

Between the autumn of 1970 and the spring of 1971, Ramsden Coppice was entirely clear felled and planted with conifers, mostly larch. As with many native woodlands that were treated in this manner, much of the original ecosystem survived. Native trees such as ash, hazel, field maple, birch, and oak have since re-grown naturally from seed, and shoots from cut stumps. The result is that parts of Ramsden Coppice are now a mixture of conifers and broadleaved trees. Much of the original ground flora has survived, including bluebell, dog's mercury, early purple orchids, and the rare herb, Paris. Ramsden Coppice is a good example of a wood that is a 'Plantation on a Ancient Woodland Site' that could be restored to its former broadleaved character by removing the conifers.

In 1985 the Forestry Commission introduced the Broadleaves Policy, which for the first time officially recognised the importance of both broadleaved and 'ancient' woodlands. Felling licences were no longer granted to grub broadleaved woodland for farmland, and forestry plans which converted ancient semi-natural woodland to conifers were no longer approved – grant aid was directed towards restocking felled stands with native species. In the project area a number of plantations on ancient woodland sites are being restored to native broadleaved woodland by encouraging the surviving elements of the

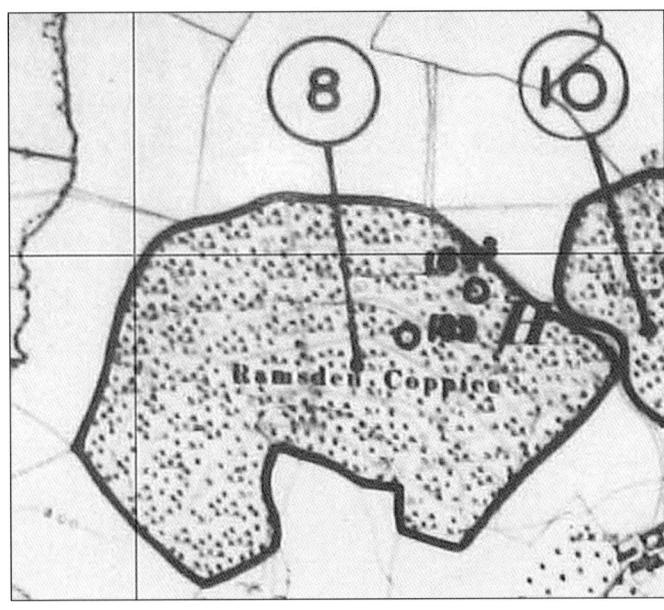

Ramsden Coppice. Forestry Commission plan and survey, 1953

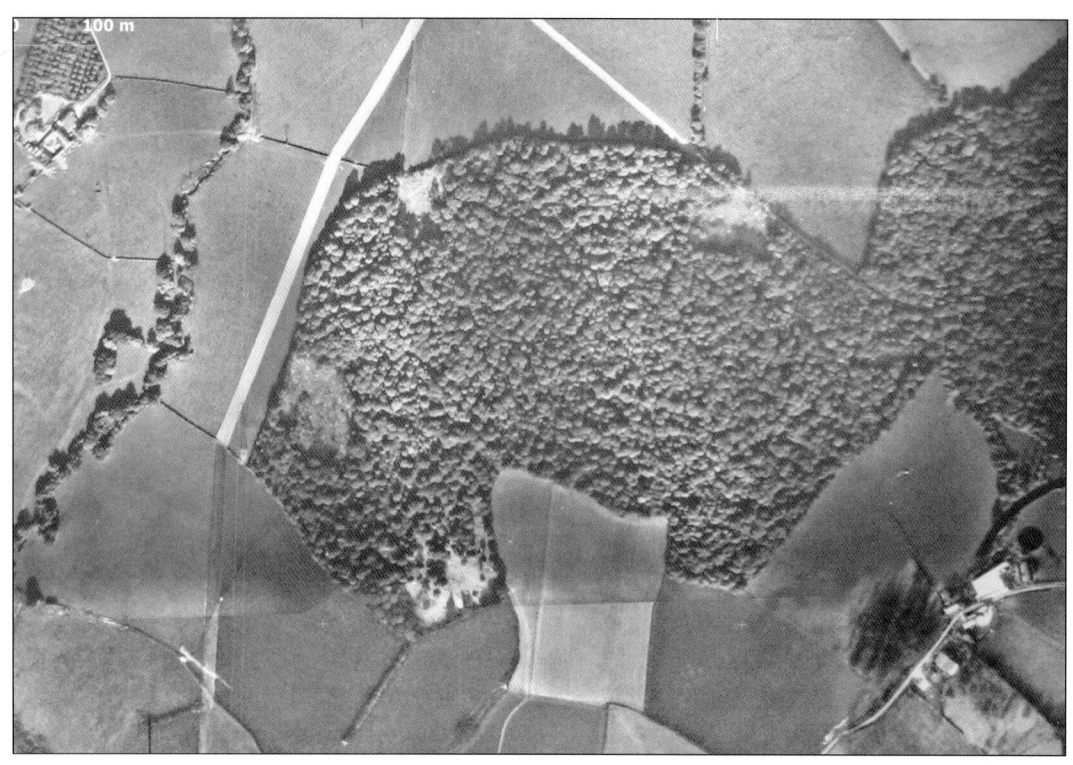

Ramsden Coppice. Top – in 1970; Bottom – in 1971

Ramsden Coppice in 2002

Ramsden in 2006

original woodland ecosystem. Important examples include Haugh Wood and Fownhope Woods, where large areas of conifers have recently been clear-felled to create the conditions for natural regeneration of native broadleaves. For Haugh Wood this restoration aims to increase the populations of rare butterflies and moths, for which the wood is nationally famous. The main problem for young broadleaved trees is browsing by deer and bark stripping by grey squirrels.

Ramsden Coppice regrowth

Haugh Wood conifer fell

Fownhope Park woods partially felled to conifer plantation in 1970

Fownhope Park Wood – Remnant broad leaves regrowing after conifer clearfell 2007

Developments in the landscape

The building of the Hereford, Ross and Gloucester Railway in 1855 had a great impact on the landscape and economy of the Wye Valley. The closure of the line in 1964 was a sad loss to the area, but the remaining embankments, bridges and tunnels are now a valued part of the valley's heritage. The railway remains have created some important wildlife refuges for bats in the old tunnels and for birds and animals in the natural woodland which has colonised parts of the abandoned line.

Pylons are a noticeable feature in today's landscape and an integral part of our modern energy-intensive civilisation. More recently an underground steel pipe carrying liquefied petroleum gas from the port of Milford Haven to Tirley in Gloucestershire has been constructed which involved making a 40 foot wide scar across the countryside scraping away all the hedgerows and meadows in its path. These features have now been restored and an archaeological survey in the path of the pipe has revealed many interesting sites.

A less obvious intrusion was noticeable during the project's River Wye survey which found a number of concrete steps, croys and the occasional pile of rubble. These structures detract from the river's natural beauty and obliterate any evidence of historic riverside features. These artificial constructions are not generally visible – they can sometimes be seen from the opposite bank, but are most apparent from the water level in a canoe.

Above – Rubble in the Wye
Right – Potato field at Widow's Wood

The Future

Pressure on the countryside is likely to increase due to globalised markets, climate change, increasing world population, incentives to grow crops for bio fuels and demands for extra house building. The effects of these developments will make the conservation of rural landscapes and habitats more difficult. Annually paid agricultural subsidies, formerly to encourage food production, are now 'de-coupled' from production to avoid international market distortion. The new 'Single Payment Scheme' in 2008 is worth about £200 per hectare of registered farmland, which amounts to £1,832,000 per year for the 8,000 hectares of farmland in the 12 parishes.[18]

Agri-environment schemes do pay for some environmental benefits, but are voluntary and remain a small proportion of overall subsidies and are likely to be reduced in the future. Crops such as potatoes and soft fruit under polytunnels can produce high returns per hectare in the short term while the economics of traditional mixed livestock farming does not compete. Non-market factors such as 'lifestyle' farming, horse and golf culture are likely to play an increasingly significant role in the rural landscape.

Capler from Kidley Hill

CHAPTER X

Agriculture Today

by Simon Dereham (with a contribution by Jon Hurley)

The pattern of the landscape of the Wye Valley today is the result of many generations of work by landowners, farmers and woodland owners. It has not come about by chance and it will not change by chance. The future landscape will reflect the outcome of decisions taken over the past five years and more, together with those changes not yet finalised in the reform of the Common Agricultural Policy which have been under debate and negotiation amongst the longer serving members of the European Community.

To some, the landscape of the countryside means mountain and moorland, rivers and streams, with a patchwork of fields, copses, woods and forests. To others it is polytunnels, broiler houses, intensive pig units, industrial-sized buildings, pack houses and dairy units with silos and slurry lagoons. Indeed, there is a world of difference between an upland farm in the Black Mountains and a 400 acre farm in the Wye Valley. Even so, the centre of Herefordshire and the Wye Valley is still considered to be one of the finest English rural landscapes and still retains many of the attractive qualities that caused John Duncumb, the 19th-century historian, to write:

> The banks of the Wye are now in great perfection, and should be visited by everyone who is pleased with rich and variegated scenery. The romantic views between Ross, Monmouth and Chepstow and the beauty and luxuriance of the prospect from Capler's Wood and the other points between the City and Ross are exceeded in very few parts of the Kingdom.

In the twelve parishes of the project area there is an enormous range of landscape features between the restored parkland at Holme Lacy and the Castle at Wilton. When travelling between these two places the woods of Fownhope Park and Cherry Hill Fort are seen above the flood plain at Fownhope. A traveller then sees the wooded escarpment, dominated by Capler Camp, which stretches from Brockhampton towards Hoarwithy. Next, the common and river meadows of Sellack, the polytunnels at King's Caple on the opposite bank, and How Caple and Foy, both with wooded escarpments and riverside fields which are often under intensive potato production. The land from Hole-in-the-Wall, past Brampton Abbotts to Bridstow is also under fairly intensive agricultural production. Field sizes have changed with the inevitable loss of hedgerows, although with the introduction of the 1997 hedgerow regulations and the encouragement of the Biodiversity Action Plan a significant mileage of new hedgerows has been planted.

The landscape of the Wyeside parishes in the study area may be explored by car on minor roads, by foot following an excellent network of footpaths, by canoe on the river, but with limited access for horses because

Aerial view of Capler, Ballingham and the Wye

Project supporters at Rise Farm, Fownhope

of a scarcity of bridleways. Throughout the project, its supporters and volunteers were guided through a variety of farmland, woodland and riverside by experts who imparted their knowledge of the history and wildlife of the Wye Valley. Improved access to the countryside and better conservation of wildlife has been due to the Wildlife and Countryside Act 1981 and the Countryside and Rights of Way Act 2000. The Department of the Environment, Food and Rural Affairs (DEFRA) continually provides information on the 'conservation of wildlife and landscape, and on countryside recreation'.

To understand the reasons behind some of the changes in land management practices that have influenced the landscape it is necessary to examine the factors that have caused these changes. In the main, farmers are forced to be reactive rather than proactive in deciding the type and scale of the farming enterprises they choose to undertake. Many find their choices about how best to get a living from their land are limited by government. Providing an example of this was the introduction, in the 1970s, of the Farm and Horticultural Development Scheme funded by the Ministry of Agriculture, Fisheries and Food and the European Economic Community.

The scheme provided a range of grants to farmers who wished to improve the productivity of their holdings, through the provision of buildings, handling systems, fencing and drainage. The result of the implementation of this scheme, particularly in the headwaters of the Wye in mid Wales, had an impact that few could have envisaged. The improvement of hill grassland by the installation of drains had a profound effect on the hydrology of the catchment area. Rainfall in the Cambrian Mountains found its way into the Wye through these new drainage systems at a dramatically faster rate than before. The sponge effect of unimproved grassland had been lost and the Wye, in a comparatively short time, became a spate river. Other drainage schemes along the Wye Valley in Herefordshire also contributed to this change in riverine behaviour.

Environmentally Sensitive Areas were introduced under the terms of the 1986 Agriculture Act to help safeguard areas where the landscape, wildlife and historic interest are of national importance, because it was recognised that agriculture can have a major influence on the conservation and enhancement of the these features. During the 1990s there were many concerned individuals in the county who felt that the disappearance of the river meadows in the Wye Valley could be reversed if a new Environmentally Sensitive Area scheme covering the vulnerable parts of the valley could be created, but despite the fact that river valley grasslands were specifically mentioned, and strong lobbying, the Minister could not be persuaded. Although there was a strong enough case, it was turned down because it had been found that Environmentally Sensitive Areas were costly to run, even though they achieved their objectives.

In 1991 the Countryside Stewardship Scheme was launched, run by the Farming and Rural Conservation Agency, which was an arm of Ministry of Agriculture, Fisheries and Food. It made payments to farmers and land managers to improve the natural beauty and diversity of the landscape with objectives to:

Sustain the beauty and diversity of the landscape
Improve and extend wildlife habitats
Conserve archaeological sites and historic features
Improve opportunities for countrywide enjoyment
Restore neglected land or features
Create new habitats and landscapes

Anyone who owned or managed land was able to apply, and the scheme was open to farmers and non-farming landowners and managers, including voluntary bodies and local authorities. A legally binding ten-year agreement was entered into between the landowner and the Ministry, but entry to this scheme has now closed as other schemes have superseded it. Many Herefordshire farms were accepted by the scheme, the project area having more than an average number of these compared to Herefordshire as a whole. The majority of these agreements are still operating as there is still time to run on the ten year period.

Rural Issues

Nationally there are many who feel that, after problems like Bovine Spongiform Encephalitis (BSE) and the fiasco of Foot and Mouth, after which the Ministry of Agriculture, Fisheries and Food was absorbed into the new super Ministry, DEFRA, Ministers have even less interest in the farming industry or in the long term future of the countryside. It is to be regretted that the Government has no clear policy for Britain's land, and seems to have a simple-minded aim to please consumers and recreational users of the countryside. Minister after Minister has stated that there is now a global market, where inefficient producers would fall out and the streamlined survivors would become profitable. This has not happened, as many farming sectors have become unviable.

In the 1970s when the European Economic Community introduced milk quotas, the UK was 85% self-sufficient and was prevented from increasing production. Twelve months ago we were 76% self-sufficient and the figure has now fallen to 68%. The import of dairy products has increased by 50% in the last two years. The Meat and Livestock Commission's 2007 figures show that red meat imports have increased by 65% since 1995. Britain gets less rural development support than any other major European country and its farmers are subjected to an ever-increasing level of regulation, almost totally of EU origin, but implemented to DEFRA's own gold-plated standards. Many question the relevance of this culture of regulation while nationally we are forced to accept imports from countries with lower standards and controls and where there is no minimum wage structure.

It does seem that the days of so-called food mountains, generated within the old European Economic Community, are over, perhaps with the exception of France, which continues to produce large surpluses of undrinkable and therefore unsaleable wine. Global production levels, coupled with the European Union Intervention regime, have dictated UK cereal prices during the past thirty years. During the 1980s feed cereal prices rose to £120 per tonne with costs of production being approximately £80 per tonne. At that time, this situation was not thought by the farming fraternity to be sustainable, even in the medium term. By the mid 1990s, cereal prices had dropped to £59 per tonne. There followed a short period during which there was a radical change in the structure of cereal farms across the country. Family farms of 200 to 600 acres in Herefordshire and the Wye Valley were no longer seen as being viable and cereal farming was reorganised into larger units, farming a much wider range of crops and achieving considerable economies of scale. This change was done in a variety of ways including share-farming agreements, farm business tenancies and, in some cases, the sale of unviable holdings. The general public were seldom aware of the degree of change that was taking place around them although they saw a significant increase in the size of tractors and equipment using the country lanes.

Farmers and landowners, when faced with diminishing returns, have always looked to diversification and the development of more profitable enterprises. Help was available through a Rural Enterprise Scheme for the promotion of farm diversification and tourism initiatives, together with a processing and marketing scheme, which formed part of The Rural England Development Plan produced by the Ministry of Agriculture, Fisheries and Food in 1999. In the project area, new agricultural activities have been introduced, such as organic production, the growing of novel crops such as hemp, rearing livestock such as llamas and alpacas and establishing agricultural and haulage contracting. Farm land and buildings have been let out, farmhouses offer bed and breakfast and outbuildings have been converted into holiday cottages. The processing, grading and packing of local produce, running farm shops and farmers markets have become popular. On the non-agricultural front, facilities for fishing, shooting, golf, forestry and a range of equestrian activities have been made available.

The majority of people living in farmhouses are no longer directly involved in farming the land, as the

Gannah Farm on the Bolstone / Holme Lacy parish boundary

former occupiers had done for centuries. Far fewer people are currently involved in arable farming, partly due to the increasing size of tractors and equipment which has led to a reduction in overhead costs. Few of the remaining farm workers still live on farms. They themselves have had to become much more mobile, some working on a variety of farm holdings, often of a large acreage and sometimes many miles apart. As the size of holdings has increased, so many farmhouses, tied cottages and farm buildings have become redundant. Houses not required by non-working farm owners, together with empty tied cottages, tend to be sold off. The redundant farm buildings are either converted to houses or turned into rural workshops, stables or light industrial units.

A barn conversion at Brampton Abbotts

On the world market the demand for food today is greater than ever. Climate change is causing droughts, some major production centres are experiencing crop failure – for instance, Australia's wheat crop in 2007 – and China and India are westernising their diet and importing food and feed grain on a scale no one ever predicted. This country may be a relatively small player on the world scene, but that is no reason for allowing issues such as food production, farming, conservation and the protection of the landscape to get out of balance. However, in the last few months of 2007 these factors combined to produce a roller coaster ride for this country's arable farmers. Prices in June 2007 for that year's crop of feed wheat were £100 per tonne and rose at record breaking speed to £185 per tonne in September 2007.

DEFRA has introduced a temporary abolition of set-aside which theoretically could free up 300,000 hectares and produce over 2,000,000 tonnes of cereals, but it remains to be seen how much of this acreage within our project area re-enters production. Farmers were not in the habit of putting their most productive land into set-aside. Arable land can still be left uncropped provided it continues to meet cross compliance requirements, which are the rules drawn up by DEFRA as a Code of Good Agricultural Practice for the Sustainable Management of Agricultural Land

Common Agricultural Policy Reform

In 1992, the system of guaranteed prices was scrapped in favour of area and headage payments, and a flat cash rate was paid per area for combinable crops such as cereals and oil seed rape on land registered as arable or in a rotation in 1991. Sheep and cattle farmers also received flat rate payments per head of their stock. The system was controlled by the Integrated Administration and Control System (IACS). Farmers sent in a map of their land use each year, and land eligible for area payments was called 'IACS registered land'. The rates had no upper limit, which meant that as prices rose between 1994 to 1998 the system became more generous than the previous intervention system. By the mid 1990s cereal prices were so high that it was worth ploughing non-IACS permanent pasture for cereals.

In 2004 the area and headage system was replaced by the Single Farm Payment (SFP) which removed all links between subsidy and land use except a bare minimum of environmental requirements. The SFP began to be paid to farmers on the basis of their historic subsidy, but it will become entirely area-based by 2013 using a taper system, and will include previously non-eligible farmland used for horticulture, soft fruit production and orcharding.

The long-awaited reform of the Common Agricultural Policy reduced the subsidies being paid directly to farmers, and through the process of 'modulation', funds became available for environmental schemes. On 3 March 2005 DEFRA introduced the Environmental Stewardship Scheme which superseded the Environmentally Sensitive Area and Countryside Stewardship Schemes. This new agri-environment scheme is run by Natural England and aims to secure widespread environmental benefits. The three elements are:

Entry Level Stewardship
Organic Entry Level Stewardship
Higher Level Stewardship

Entry Level Stewardship is a whole farm scheme open to all farmers and land managers with conventional land. Acceptance is guaranteed providing the scheme requirements are met. Organic Entry Level Stewardship is a whole farm scheme similar to the Entry Level Scheme, open to farmers who manage all or part of their land organically. Higher Level Stewardship is combined with the other Entry Level options, and aims to deliver significant environmental benefits in high priority situations and areas. This Higher Level Scheme is discretionary and concentrates on the more complex types of management, where land owners and managers need advice and support and where agreements need to be tailored to local circumstances.

Natural England set a target of 55% for the Entry Level Scheme for the West Midlands, to be achieved by December 2007. This figure was not achieved in Herefordshire. No target was set for the Higher Level Scheme and applications are only accepted if there are funds available. Natural England, together with many other government agencies and departments, has been subject to serious funding cuts, which is having a significant impact on this scheme. At the time of writing, there have been 53 Higher Level Schemes accepted within the county, with four in the project area.

Ballingham cattle in 2006

Ballingham cattle

In the early 1980s a branch of the Farming and Wildlife Advisory Group (FWAG) was established in the county. Since then, under the direction of its chairman and committee, FWAG advisors have been a great help to farmers and landowners in carrying out farm appraisals and securing entry to one or more of the environmental schemes which cover woodland management as well as farming.

Livestock farmers along the River Wye face financial hardship as a result of the reforms. The Wye Valley Graziers Group commissioned a study, the results of which showed that farmers could lose £150 for every beef cow they produce. Case studies of farms around Holme Lacy, Fownhope and Hereford looked at farm incomes under the new scheme. One showed that, after seven years, a farmer would be £20,000 worse off each year. Similarly sheep farmers are having problems with lower overall returns on their fat lamb production, due in part to the changes in livestock subsidies, and this after they had borne the brunt of the Foot & Mouth outbreak.

Without more help graziers may be tempted to turn to more profitable and intensive farming systems with increased risks of pollution to the River Wye, increased erosion, a reduction in wildlife habitat and a possible change in the character of the landscape. The Higher Level Scheme includes payments for farmers prepared to let arable land revert back to grassland, but it is disappointing that the rules do not allow supplements for farmers who are already grazing cattle and native breeds on unimproved grassland. Currently there are English Longhorn cattle being grazed in How Caple. Such a change in emphasis is overdue. Farmers in the Wye Valley will never be able to produce beef at the same costs as Argentina. If we want a landscape that is beautiful, diverse and includes grazing, livestock farmers will need to be rewarded with higher environmental subsidies.

As a part of farm diversification, there has been a welcome increase in farm shops, both on farms and in local market towns. Farmers' markets are now held on a regular basis throughout the year in both towns and villages such as Brockhampton, in our project area, and Woolhope, which is just outside. Despite the draw of cheap imported supermarket produce there is an increasing public interest in purchasing organic and sustainably produced local food. In recent years, farmers have too often found that they were not getting fair and equitable treatment from the large supermarkets and they welcome the opportunity to market their own produce and increase the return that they get.

The Wye Valley Area of Outstanding Natural Beauty (AONB) Unit management team has put together initiatives that have encouraged schools, hotels, bed and breakfast establishments, and catering outlets to use and promote locally produced food and drink. The National Farmers Union, together with the English Farming and Food Partnership, is promoting this year, 2008, as the year of Food and Farming. Part of this campaign is trying to help children reconnect with the countryside and let the next generation know why farming matters.

DEFRA recently published a paper on the future of farm support promoting 'a fair, simplified, common frame work for farmers across Europe, rather than a control system that stifles them' and also an approach 'which helps our farmers to preserve the natural heritage that we all value. That means effective, targeted schemes to protect our landscapes and wildlife'. However, before expecting this sort of action it is as well to remember that the notorious Rural Payments Agency is still not performing effectively. They have not completed payments for 2006 and there are a significant number of unresolved issues relating to 2005. The fines levied on DEFRA by the EU came directly out of the DEFRA budget and were not funded by the Exchequer. This means that all the Agencies involved in the management of the countryside such as Natural England and the Environment Agency have been faced with substantial cuts in their budgets and consequential reductions in countryside services and grants.

One piece of positive news concerns Natural England's Pilot Catchment Sensitive Farming Initiative which started in 2006 and ran through 2007 covering the rivers Dore, Gamber, Garren, Pinsley, and Arrow

The Fownhope loop

catchment areas. Advice was given to farmers and landowners on soil, nutrient and waste management, pesticide use, grazing and arable systems, and riverbank management. The promotion of good farming practice, the prevention of siltation and diffuse pollution, are the key features of this pilot. Hopefully, funding will be made available for this scheme to be rolled out into all river catchments including the rest of the Wye catchment.

Intensive Livestock Production

Chicken and turkeys, eggs and indoor pigs produced intensively in buildings are subject to stringent planning controls. Factors that are taken into account include basic siting and distance from other dwellings, feed delivery times and routes used, product collection times, cleaning out and disposal of muck and the operation of incinerators. There are few units either in or near the project area. Across the county, over recent years, there does not appear to have been much change in this type of production. These intensive units can have an impact on the landscape if they are not sited sensitively and lack adequate landscaping. They can be unpopular with the general public and problems can arise if codes of practice are not followed. The spreading of litter or muck on arable fields, down-wind of dwellings, can cause complaints unless it is ploughed in almost simultaneously.

Potato Production

Potatoes have been produced in Herefordshire since they were first introduced to England, but their production started to increase dramatically following the onset of potato diseases in the Eastern counties in the late 1980s. Growers looking for new ground on which to expand their production focussed on the river meadows, firstly of the Wye and then the Lugg, where the ground was disease-free and extremely fertile, whilst much of it had irrigation rights on either the rivers or the tributaries. Potatoes need 7 inches of rain for maximum yield and must be irrigated in dry summers, but in 2007, unlike the previous eight years, there was little requirement for irrigation. The heavy rain of 2007 did cause some damage to the crop, particularly during harvesting.

Most riverside farmers have abstraction rights from the rivers and tributaries under a variety of regulations, some of which allows them to abstract directly from the river while the more recent licences require water for irrigation to be taken from irrigation reservoirs filled over the previous winter. The pumps and pipes do not enhance the landscape, but the irrigation reservoirs, if sensitively designed and landscaped, can not only look attractive but also serve as a haven for wildlife. Some farmers have been using trickle irrigation, which does not require consent from the Environment Agency. However, all irrigation systems are being rationalised under the Catchment Abstraction Management Scheme and all users will have to be licensed and pay an annual charge.

To help achieve the better skin-set quality of potatoes required by major customers, farmers find it necessary to work the ground to a very fine, deep tilth. Contour ploughing and planting help reduce silt run-off in the event of heavy rain, and if this is not done there is a risk of polluting the ditches, streams and rivers with chemicals, nitrates and phosphates. In addition, roads and lanes are covered with mud, whilst silt discolours the river and clogs up the gravel beds on which the salmon spawn. Riverine Sites of Special Scientific Interest deserve a better level of protection than that currently afforded by Natural England, who at present have not got the necessary funds.

Orchards and Soft Fruit Production

Herefordshire has always produced a wide range of soft fruits across the county. Traditionally these crops were sold locally in towns and villages and sometimes through regional wholesale markets. During the last thirty years the level of production has increased as supermarkets became the major buyers and their requirements escalated as the number of their retail outlets increased. During this period a limited number of polytunnels were used for the production of early fruiting and autumn fruiting raspberries. In earlier days no production of this type took place within the project area, although it was used in the adjacent parish of Upton Bishop.

As the supermarkets quickly expanded their share in the retail food business, their demand for soft fruit, including early and late season fruit, increased and production in the county expanded. In more recent times the supermarkets at first recommended the use of polytunnels for the production of strawberries and then made their use mandatory if growers wished to continue supplying them. There are undoubted benefits in the use of polytunnels to both the growers and the supermarkets as it is believed that the overall quality of the fruit is superior and that the use of chemicals and pesticides is reduced. The growing season is extended and the import of soft fruit from around the world reduced. Crops can be harvested during adverse weather; without polytunnels there would have been very little available in 2007 due to the appalling weather conditions.

Although problems over run-off from large areas of tunnels have to be addressed, it is understood that the gutters and drainage ditches can channel rainwater into holding ponds so that it can then be reused for trickle irrigation. The drawback to the use of tunnels is undoubtedly the issue of their visual impact, particularly within an Area of Outstanding Natural Beauty. The growers claim that this problem is site specific and that much can be achieved through sensitive site selection and landscaping.

Polytunnels at King's Caple

Opponents to polytunnels are campaigning for their use to be subject to planning consent and lobbying for them to be outlawed within AONBs. Unfortunately the Government have resolutely refused to take the lead in this matter and appear to hope that the matter will be resolved in the Courts. However, recent cases have failed to produce definitive decisions and there are cases ongoing at the moment. Herefordshire Council has for years been guilty of prevarication on this issue, but are currently seeking the views of all concerned in an effort to reach a workable solution.

Polytunnels are also used for the production of raspberries, cherries and flowers, where the crop cycle is significantly longer than that of strawberries. In the case of these crops, growers are applying for planning consents and, by and large, these are being granted. An acceptable way forward must be found that accommodates the need to protect the landscape without compromising sustainable farming enterprises.

Cider and dessert apple orchards, together with perry pear orchards, have been a feature in the landscape of the project area since time immemorial.

The total orchard acreage reached 27,000 acres in 1883, dropped to 20,000 acres in 1936 and, at the moment, is nearly 14,000 acres and rising, due to the increasing popularity of both cider and perry. The growing of dessert apples and pears together with smaller quantities of cherries and plums continues without the acreages varying significantly. Black, white and red currants are grown on a smaller scale than previously. The majority of these cane fruits are now grown in the north of the county.

An orchard at Brampton Abbotts

Fishing

Over the centuries the fish of the Wye have offered man a valuable source of food, quiet enjoyment and sport. In the past, fishermen could use any means to land a fish, including gaffing, netting, tickling and trapping. The term 'angler' refers to the catching of fish by means of a hook, or angled pieced of steel bent to catch in the fish's mouth. It has been suggested that the 'step of making fishing into a sport, rather than just a means of catching fish for food, was the invention of the rod', but certainly fishing gradually changed from a necessity to a sport by the time it was depicted in 18th-century prints.

There have been a number of disputes between the gentry and the locals with regard to fishing the Wye. The most celebrated Wye Fishery Case of 1906 to 1911 involved George Harris and Frank Bailey, two fishermen from King's Caple and Hoarwithy, who claimed access to the river as Free Fisherman, but were charged by the Earl of Chesterfield from Holme Lacy and other wealthy land-owners for netting on private water. The fishermen lost their case.

Fishing on the Wye at Wilton

The beautiful and mysterious salmon has long been associated with the Wye and its capture once attracted fishermen from all over the world. In the halcyon days of the early 20th century, owners of the finest stretches of water with deep pools invited their friends for a day's fishing and a picnic. Tales of enormous catches were recorded, and there is no doubt that at its peak the Wye yielded some fabulous fish. On 30 March 1914 John Wyndham Smith caught a record-breaking 51 pound salmon in the Quarry Pool on a stretch of his water. Later in the afternoon he landed another large fish of 42½ pounds. His record for the two heaviest salmon caught in one day still stands and is likely to do so for a very long time.

The record salmon caught by John Wyndham Smith in the Wye in 1914

In spite of poaching, diseases and floods, huge catches were landed on all stretches of the river, especially on the Golden Mile – the stretch of river between Fownhope and Ballingham. In a 25 year period in the first half of the 20th century, records covering the length of the river record a total catch of 48,000 salmon, approximately 400 of which weighed between 35 and 50 pounds. Over the intervening 75 years the decline in the quality and health of salmon on the Wye has been devastating. Nowadays the few salmon caught have to be returned to the river, but as a large fish can take up to 25 minutes to land plus the time required to remove hooks, it is exhausted, terminally damaged and susceptible to disease by the time it goes back into the river.

The catch of salmon from the Wye diminishes year after year due to over-fishing, netting at the mouth, weeds, pollution, fertilisers containing phosphates or nitrates, acid rain, global warming, parasites, pike, cormorants, goosanders, and the otter, which is the salmon's natural predator. According to the vastly experienced General Sir Tom Pearson, who was interviewed by the oral history project in 2006:

The catch went up enormously around the 1980s. We were getting 6 to 7000. We were grossly over cropping. There was a boom in salmon fishing and people were able to buy and sell fishing rights for a profit. Estate agents advised maximising catches to keep the value up. Once it became a commercial proposition it was a free for all with the worm, prawn and the shrimp used as bait instead of the fly.

Another creature of the river has also been under threat. The common eel, too, is now endangered, as stated recently by the Minister of Fisheries. Frank Betambeau, who worked as a bailiff on the Wye, said:

Eels are caught all the year round. You can't keep taking things out, you've got to put something back. A fish living is a fish breeding. A fish dead is no good at all. We just haven't got enough fish and we have too many predators. The goosander will eat up to a hundred small fish a day, and can swallow fish of up to half a pound. A handsome and intelligent bird, it is despised by fishermen but can only be shot by permit holders.

In recent years some action has been taken to help restore life to the river. Fishing cribs have been constructed in the river to allow salmon to hide and rest. However, along the project stretch of the Wye are some hideous, crudely erected examples that should be removed by the Environment Agency. General Pearson comments:

> People now build causeways, I think this is wrong. The natural thing should be left. At Ballingham permission was given to build a causeway for canoeists. It was really done to produce cribs for salmon. It was done at the Hole-in-the-Wall but it didn't improve the fishing.

In 1993 the Wye Management Advisory Group was set up to ensure co-operation between public bodies interested in the conservation and management of the Wye for the benefit of fishermen, ramblers, bird watchers, boaters, and picnickers. The Wye's catchment area, with its generally clean water and habitat diversity, attracts at least 29 fish types, from the humble stickleback to the mighty salmon. There is also the illegally planted barbel, an inedible monster than can grow to over 15 pounds and is guaranteed to give even the most experienced fisherman all the excitement he needs. The river is also host to the tiny bleak, another recent invader that hunts in packs and strips hooks without being caught, and to the chub, dace, roach, grayling, and the fearsome pike. The Wye may be short of salmon, but is teeming with other fish for all sportsmen to enjoy, from the lad with his cane, string and bent pin, to the tooled-up serious angler with all the shiny and expensive kit, who sits hopefully under his green umbrella watching the resurgent kingfisher flash by.

The majestic salmon may be finding the Wye a bewildering and dangerous place in which to survive but the growth of coarse fishing has given the ordinary man an opportunity to share in the delights once open only to the privileged. And the besieged fishery owners are also benefiting, as explained by Lyn Cobley, gillie at Ingestone for 28 years:

> Coarse fishing is worth a lot of money and should be exploited, in a fair way. Maggots, once collected by small boys from slaughterhouses, can be purchased from tack shops. Corn, cheese, bread, worms, luncheon meat, wasp grub and halibut pellets – barbel will eat virtual anything. I've even seen them caught on jelly babies.

The days of the tweedy fisherman standing proudly by a row of enormous dead fish is a distant memory recorded only in sepia snaps on pub walls. However, all is not gloom. Over the past 20 years the Wye Salmon Fishery Owners and their supporters have spent £250,000 of their own money on anti-poaching measures, including recruiting the Gillies Association to 'provide a highly skilled and effective volunteer force'. The Wye and Usk Foundation, supported by the Environment Agency Wales, the Countryside Council for Wales, and the Forestry Commission, have removed hundreds of man-made barriers, dams and weirs, built fish passes, fenced out animal stock, cleared trees, cleaned habitats, and generally improved conditions for the juvenile fish to thrive. A spokesman said:

> The sheer scale and parlous state of the river requires a huge amount of repair to take place to bring about repopulation. There is now a reverse in the trend of falling fish stocks and numbers are on the increase for the first time in years. The comeback of trout has already been spectacular. I don't think it will be long before the big fish are back.

So all is not yet lost, the fight back to save the Wye and its most famous fish is well under way. All those who appreciate the River Wye will remember the lines written by H.A. Gilbert in 1952:

> You have a noble and glorious river – a river famous for its beauty and for its fishing. It is a river worth fighting for by everyone who loves the valley and not by the fishermen alone.

The Tirley Pipeline

The building of a 120 km gas pipeline, 1.2 metres in diameter and buried at least 1.2 metres below ground level, between Felindre in South Wales and Tirley in Gloucestershire was one of the most invasive constructions ever to have taken place across the Wye Valley AONB in our project area. Its construction involved a working width of 44 metres. A detailed Environmental Impact Assessment was carried out which comprised a series of studies, surveys and consultations that resulted in the pipeline's chosen route being one that minimised damage and disruption and ensured the successful reinstatement of the land after work was completed. Construction began in spring 2006 and finished at the end of 2007. The Wye Valley AONB Unit monitored the work as it progressed and compiled a series of photographs illustrating the 'before and after'.

Archaeological surveys were carried out before construction started and two Romano-British sites were identified close to the pipeline within our project area. The unit has been awarded funds to compensate for the loss of hedgerows and hedgerow trees, money which will be used for surgery/maintenance work on trees identified in the project's veteran tree survey.

Most of the restoration work has been completed and it will be interesting to see, in 12 months time, how apparent the line of the pipe is.

The Tirley pipeline, looking uphill towards Brampton Abbotts

The Future

Lessons can be learnt from past mistakes. The results of efforts in the 1970s and 1980s to improve agricultural efficiency through the Farm and Horticultural Development Scheme will be with us for years to come, but current and future environmental schemes could help to redress past damage to the countryside. It is relatively easy to produce a scheme, but it is much more difficult to ensure that it is properly and adequately funded. This is despite the DEFRA pronouncement that it wishes to support farming and promote 'a fair, simplified, common framework for farmers across Europe, rather than a control system which stifles them'. There is too much talk, unnecessary change and inadequate funding streams for farming and the countryside. Government departmental reorganisations and the unnecessary reorganisation of government agencies have plagued not only civil servants but farmers and countryside campaigners for the last ten years.

Ministers with responsibilities for the environment, for farming and for the countryside are too often uninterested, unconcerned and ill informed. Natural England is inadequately funded and, as a result, cannot look after and protect the integrity of Sites of Special Scientific Interest, EU Special Areas of Conservation and Special Protection Areas. Applicants for entry into HLS schemes are turned away because there is no funding available.

The Environment Agency, nationally, is unable to undertake its short and medium term responsibilities for navigation, pollution control, water quality, coastal protection, and flood defence. Locally, however, we are lucky to have flood alleviation schemes being constructed at present in Hereford and Ross-on-Wye. This rather gloomy outlook could be considered to be short term as a new administration could be

The River Wye Preservation Trust at Fawley in 2006

an improvement. It would be wrong to expect a large increase in countrywide funding. A modest increase, more intelligently applied, would do wonders for morale in the countryside.

The Herefordshire countryside continues to produce really high quality food and drink of all varieties. Cider is in the ascendancy with a large number of small producers as well as the two big ones. Local beer is available but Herefordshire now produces a fraction of the hops that it did in the past. Potato and soft fruit production has grown enormously and poultry production is still a major enterprise. The number of dairy farms has shrunk dramatically together with the size of Hereford cattle herds. However, the best of Herefordshire produce is available at farm shops and farmers' markets throughout the county.

A selection of locations in the project area are going to benefit from the £2.8m 'Overlooking the Wye' scheme with grant aid from the Heritage Lottery Fund. The scheme has had a gestation period of over nine years and it was fortunate that the bid was successful before the cut off date, after which almost the total income from the Heritage Lottery Fund is being diverted to the 2012 Olympic Games. The money will be spent on conserving and enhancing picturesque viewpoints, historic quays and industrial remains throughout the Wye Valley, taking into account both topography and land use, to make the Wye Valley more attractive and productive for many future generations.

Longhorn cattle at How Caple

Abbreviations

AA	Aramstone Archive in LOWV ARCHIVE
AONB	Area of Outstanding Natural Beauty
ARS	Archaeological Research Section WNFC
BAR	*British Archaeological Reports*
BL	British Library
CABI	Commonwealth Agricultural Bureaux International
EH	English Heritage
EIGG	Environmental and Industrial Geophysics Group
GRO	Gloucestershire Record Office
HJNL	*Hereford Journal*
HCA	Hereford Cathedral Archives
HCL	Hereford City Library
HT	*Hereford Times*
KA	Kentchurch Archive in LOWV ARCHIVE
LOWV	Landscape Origins of the Wye Valley
LOWV ARCHIVE	barge accounts, AA, KA, research notes and Wye survey (deposited at HRO)
NLW	National Library of Wales
NMR	National Monuments Record
OS	Ordnance Survey
RCHM	Royal Commission on Historic Monuments
SMR	Sites and Monuments Record, Herefordshire Council
TNA	The National Archives
TWNFC	*Transactions of the Woolhope Naturalists' Field Club*
VCH	*Victoria County History of Herefordshire*
WI	Women's Institute, Herefordshire
WNFC	Woolhope Naturalists' Field Club

Bibliography

Achilli, A., *et al,* Saami and Berbers-An Unexpected Mitochondrial DNA Link. *The American Journal of Human Genetics,* 76, 883-886 (2005)

Bannister, A.T., *The History of Ewias Harold, its castle, priory, and church.* Hereford (1902)

Barclay, W.J. and Smith, N.J.P., *Geology of the country between Hereford and Ross-on-Wye: a brief explanation of the geological map Sheet 215 Ross-on-Wye.* British Geological Survey (2002)

Barrow, J. (ed), *English Episcopal Acta, VII, Hereford 1079-1234,* Oxford University Press (1992)

Baxter, I., 'The Animal Bone from the Gillow Farm'. Unpublished Report for Archenfield Archaeology (2008)

Beech, G. and Mitchell, R., *Maps for family and local history: the records of the Tithe, Valuation Office, and National Farm Surveys of England and Wales, 1836-1943.* National Archives (2004)

Bick, D., *The Hereford and Gloucester Canal.* The Pound House (2003)

Bradley, R., *The prehistory of Britain and Ireland.* Cambridge University Press (2007)

Bradney, J., *A History of Monmouthshire, Vol. 2, Part 2.* Mitchell Hughes and Clarke (1913)

Brandon, A., *Geology of the country between Hereford and Leominster: memoir for 1:50 000 geological sheet 198.* HMSO (1989)

Brandon, A. and Hains, B.A., *Geological notes and local details for 1:10 000 sheets SO 43 NE, SO 44 SE, SO 53 NW and SO 54 SW Hereford City.* Institute of Geological Sciences (1981)

Bridgewater, N.P., Hentland, *TWNFC,* XL, 160 (1971)

Briggs, D.E.G., Siveter, David J., and Siveter, Derek J., Soft-bodied fossils from a Silurian volcaniclastic deposit. *Nature,* 382, 248-250 (1996)

Brooke, C.N.L., *The Church and the Welsh Border in the Central Middle Ages,* Boydell (1986)

Brookes, K., *et al, Historical Aspects of Ross Ross-on-Wye.* Ross-on-Wye and District Civic Society in association with Logaston Press (2000)

Broughton, M.E., *The Land of Britain. The Report of the Land Utilisation Survey of Britain, Part 64 Herefordshire.* Geographical Publications (1941)

Brown, T., Clearances and clearings in mesolithic/neolithic Britain. *Oxford Journal of Archaeology,* 16 (2) 133-145 (1997)

Bruford, M.W., Bradley, D.G. and Luikart, G., DNA markers reveal the complexity of livestock domestication. *Nature Reviews Genetics,* 4 (11) 900-910 (2003)

Bull, H.G., Botanical Report, *TWNFC,* (1852)

Butzer, K.W., The Americas before and after 1492: An Introduction to Current Geographical Research. *Annals of the Association of American Geographers,* 82 (3) 345-368 (1992)

Chandler, J., *Travels through Stuart Britain: the adventures of John Taylor, the water poet in 1641.* Sutton (1999 ed)

Charles, B.G., The Welsh, their Language and Place-names in Archenfield and Oswestry. *Angles and Britons, the O'Donnell Lectures.* University of Wales Press, 85-110 (1963)

Clark, D.M., *Fownhope Remembered: Changes in a Herefordshire Village 1919-2000,* Fownhope Local History Group (2007)

Clarke, S., Jackson, P. and Jackson, R., Archaeological evidence for Monmouth's Roman and early medieval defences. *Archaeology in Wales,* 32, 1-2 (1992)

Coates, S.D. and Tucker, D.G., *Water Mills of the Monnow,* 1978

Coates, S.D. and Tucker, D.G., *Water Mills of the Middle Wye Valley,* 1983

Coe, J., Dating the Boundary Clauses in the Book of Llandaff. *Cambrian Medieval Celtic Studies.* 48, 1-43 (2004)

Coplestone-Crow, B., *Herefordshire Place-Names.* BAR, British Series 214 (1989)

Copley, M.S., *et al,* Direct chemical evidence for widespread dairying in prehistoric Britain. *Proceedings of the National Academy of Sciences of the United States of America,* 100 (4) 1524-1529 (2003)

Cousins, J., Sustainable Farming, *Natural World,* Spring 2007

Crow, A., *Bridges on the River Wye.* Lapridge Publications (1995)

Cunliffe, B., *Iron Age Communities in Britain: An Account of England, Scotland and Wales from the seventh century BC until the Roman Conquest,* Fourth edition. Routledge (2005)

Davies, W., *An Early Welsh Microcosm; Studies in the Llandaff Charters.* Royal Historical Society (1978)

Davies, W., *The Llandaff Charters.* National Library of Wales (1979)

Denevan, W.M., The Pristine Myth: The Landscape of the Americas in 1492. *Annals of the Association of American Geographers,* 82 (3), 369-385 (1992)

Delcourt, P.A. and Delcourt, H.R., The Influence of Prehistoric Human-set Fires on Oak-Chestnut Forests in the Southern Appalachians. *Castanea*, 63 (3) September 1998, 337-345 (1998)

Di Benedetto, G., *et al*, Mitochondrial DNA sequences in prehistoric human remains from the Alps. *European Journal of Human Genetics*, 8, 669-677 (2000)

Dickau, R., *et al*, Starch grain evidence for the preceramic dispersals of maize and root crops into tropical dry and humid forests of Panama. *Proceedings of the National Academy of Sciences of the United States of America*, 104 (9) 3651-3656 (2007)

Doble, G.H., *The Lives of the Welsh Saints* (edited by D. Simon Evans). University of Wales Press (1971)

Dorling, P., *The Lugg Valley, Herefordshire: Archaeology, Landscape Change and Conservation*. Herefordshire Studies in Archaeology, 4, Herefordshire Archaeology (2007)

Dull, R.A., Evidence for Forest Clearance, Agriculture, and Human-Induced Erosion in Precolumbian El Salvador. *Annals of the Association of American Geographers*, 97 (1), 127-141 (2007)

Duncumb, J., *General View of the Agriculture of Herefordshire*. Board of Agriculture (1805)

Duncumb, J., *Collections towards the History and Antiquities of the County of Hereford, Volume 2*. Allen (1812)

Edwards, C.J., *et al*, Mitochondrial DNA analysis shows a Near Eastern Neolithic origin for domestic cattle and no indication of domestication of European aurochs. *Proceedings of the Royal Society B*, 274, 1377-1385 (2007)

Faraday, M.A. (ed), *Herefordshire Taxes in the Reign of Henry VIII.* Woolhope Club, Hereford (2005)

Farr, G., *Chepstow Ships*. Chepstow Society (1954)

Feltwell, J. and Rothschild, M., *Meadows, a History and Natural History*. Sutton (1992)

Fenn, R.W.D., Early Christianity in Herefordshire, *TWNFC*, XXXIX (II) 333-347 (1968)

Finberg, H.P.R., *The Early Charters of the West Midlands*. Leicester University Press (1961)

Fookes,C., Fears for the future of farmed landscape, *Picturesque*, AONB Newsletter, Summer (2005)

Fosbroke, T.D., *Companion to the Wye Tour. Ariconensia; or, Archæological Sketches of Ross, and Archenfield: illustrative of the campaigns of Caractacus: the station Ariconium, etc.* Ross (1822)

Fox, C., *Offa's Dyke: a field survey of the western frontier of Mercia in the seventh and eighth centuries A.D.* The British Academy (1955)

Galbraith,V.H., and Tait, J., *Herefordshire Domesday*. Pipe Roll Society (1950)

Gale, R., Charcoal from Bridgewater's 1963 excavation. In: Jackson, 2003, 145-148 (2003)

Gale, P.R., *The Great Western Railway: A record of the routes, statutes, opening dates and other particulars in 1926*. reprinted by Avon Anglia (1986)

Gange, E.F., *Fownhope: its church and its people* (1950)

Garnett, G., Franci et Angli: the legal distinctions between peoples after the conquest. *Anglo-Norman Studies*, 8, 109-137 (1985)

Garwood, P., *The Undiscovered Country: The Earlier Prehistory of the West Midlands*. Oxbow (2007 ed)

Gilbert, H.A., *The Tale of a Wye Fisherman*. Cape (1953)

Giraldus Cambrensis, *The Journey through Wales*; and, The description of Wales; translated [from the Latin] with an introduction by L. Thorpe. Penguin (1978)

Green, C*., Severn Traders*. Black Dwarf (1999)

Green, M., *The Celtic World*. Routledge (1995)

Grinsell, L.V., Herefordshire Barrows. *TWNFC*, XLVII (III) 299-317 (1993)

Hale, M.B. and Moore, L.P., The Fortress Salient in the River Wye around King's Caple, *TWNFC*, XL, 49-54 (1970)

Hart, W., Vol II, Historia et Cartularium (1863)

Haselgrove, C., Iron Age landscapes and cultural biographies. In: A. Gwilt and C. Haselgrove (eds) *Reconstructing Iron Age Societies: New Approaches to the British Iron Age*. Oxbow, 51-72 (1997)

Heath, C., *Excursion Down the Wye*. Monmouth (1828 ed)

Hey, G., Mulville, J. and Robinson, M., Diet and culture in southern Britain: the evidence from Yarnton. In: M. Parker Pearson, 79-88 (2003)

Hickling, R.E., Deserted Medieval Villages, Report of Sectional Recorder, *TWNFC,*Vol. XXXIX, part III, 488-490 (1969)

Hindle, P., *Roads and Tracks for Historians*. Phillimore (2001)

Hoverd, T., *Cherry Hill, Fownhope: A vitrified fort sequence*. Herefordshire Archaeology Report No. 47, unpublished report by Herefordshire Archaeology (2004)

Hughes, P., and Hurley, H., *The Story of Ross*. Logaston Press (1999)

Hurley, B., *Book of Trades,* 1811, 1991

Hurley, H., River Crossing at Hoarwithy, *TWNFC,* Vol. XLIV, part II, 215-226 (1983)

Hurley, H., The Forgotten Man of Ross – James Wallace Richard Hall, 1799-1860, *TWNFC,* Vol. XLV, part I, 305-311 (1985)

Hurley, H., The Brookend Tanyard at Ross. *HAN 52,* 25-26 (1989)

Hurley, H., *The Old Roads of South Herefordshire*. The Pound House (1992)

Hurley, H., The Reconstruction of Hoarwithy Bridge, *TWNFC,* Vol. XLVIII, part III, 587-588 (1996)

Hurley, H., *The Story of Bill Mills*. Logaston Press (2001)

Hurley, H., *The Pubs of Ross and South Herefordshire*. Logaston Press (2001)

Hurley, H., *The Old Mill, Hoarwithy*. Ross-on-Wye and District Civic Society Pink Publication No. 16. (2004)

Hurley, H. and J., *The Wye Valley Walk: the history and heritage*. Thornhill (1994)

Jack, G.H. and Hayter, A.G.K., Excavations on the Site of Caplar Camp, in the parish of Brockhampton, Herefordshire. *TWNFC*, XXV (II) 83-88 (1925)

Jackson, R., Pits, Pots, Places and People: approaching the Neolithic at Wellington Quarry. In: Garwood, P., (2007)

Jackson, R., Ariconium, Herefordshire: An assessment and synthesis of the evidence. Unpublished report by the Worcestershire Historic Environment and Archaeology Service, Worcestershire County Council (2003)

James, S., *The Atlantic Celts: Ancient People or Modern Invention*. British Museum (1999)

Jones, G.R.J., The pattern of settlement on the Welsh border. *The Agricultural History Review*, 8 (3) 66-81 (1960)

Jones, G.R.J., Post-Roman Wales. In: H. P. R. Finberg, *The Agrarian History of England and Wales, Volume I.II, AD 43-1042*. Cambridge University Press, 279-382 (1972)

Kain, R., and Oliver, R., *The tithe maps of England and Wales: a cartographic analysis and county-by-county catalogue*. Cambridge University Press (1995)

Kenyon, K.M., *Excavations at Sutton Walls, Herefordshire, 1948-1951*. The Royal Archaeological Society of Great Britain and Ireland (reprinted from the Archaeological Journal, Vol CX (1954)

Kissack, K. *Monmouth, the making of a county town*. Phillimore (1975)

Kissack, K., *The River Wye*: T. Dalton (1978)

Lamont, A., Fords and Ferries of the Wye, *TWNFC*, 73-94 (1922)

Latham, R.E., *Revised Medieval Latin Word-List from British and Irish Sources*. OUP/British Academy (1980)

Legge, A.J., Aspects of cattle husbandry. In: R. Mercer, *Farming Practice in British Prehistory*. Edinburgh University Press (1981 ed)

Lewis, C.A. and Richards, A.E., *The glaciations of Wales and the adjacent areas*. Logaston Press (2005)

Liddiart, R, *The Medieval Park: New Perspectives*. Windgather Press (2007 ed)

Lipscomb, G., *Journey into South Wales*. Longmans (1802)

Lloyd Jones, M., *Society and Settlement in Wales and the Marches 500 B.C. to A.D. 1100, Part i*. BAR, British Series 121 (i) (1984)

Luikart, G., *et al*, Multiple maternal origins and weak phylogeographic structure in domestic goats. *Proceedings of the National Academy of Sciences of the United States of* America, 98 (10) 5927-5932 (2001)

McLauchlan, K., Plant cultivation and forest clearance by prehistoric North Americans: pollen evidence from Fort Ancient, Ohio, USA. *The Holocene*, 13 (4) 557-566 (2003)

Marsh-Smith, S., Bringing Back the Salmon, *Herefordshire Life*, March 2008

Martin, S.H., The Ballingham Charters, *TWNFC*, Vol. XXXIV, part II, 70-75 (1953)

Matthews, J.H., *Collections Towards the History and Antiquities of the County of Hereford, Wormelow Upper Division* (1912)

Mendelsohn, O., *The Dictionary of Drink and Drinking*, 1966

Mercer, R,J., *Grimes Graves, Norfolk. Excavations 1971-2: volume 1*, DOE Archaeological Reports, 11. Department of the Environment (1981)

Miles, D., *The Tribes of Britain*. Weidenfeld and Nicolson (2005)

Miller, M, Aramstone Salmon Fishing Record Books, unpublished LOWV mss (2006)

Milles, A., Williams, D. and Gardner, N., *The Beginnings of Agriculture: Symposia of the Association for Environmental Archaeology No 8*. BAR, International Series 496 (1989 eds)

Moffett, L., Robinson, M.A. and Straker, V., Cereals, fruit and nuts: charred plant remains from neolithic sites in England and Wales and the neolithic economy. In: Milles, Williams and Gardner, 1989, 243-256 (1989)

Morgan, F.C., The Repair of Wye Bridge, Hereford 1684-5, *TWNFC*, Vol. XXXII, part II, 144-150 (1947)

Morgan, F.C., The Steward's Accounts of John, First Viscount Scudamore, *TWNFC*, Vol. XXXIII, part II, 155-184 (1950)

Noddle, B., Cattle and sheep in Britain and northern Europe up to the Atlantic period: a personal viewpoint. In: Milles, Williams and Gardner, 1989, 179-194 (1989)

O'Donnell, J., Market Centres in Herefordshire 1200-1400. *TWNFC*, XL (II) 186-194 (1971)

O'Gram, J., Single Farm Payments. Past, Present and Future, *Review of Agriculture Autumn* (2007)

Old Humphrey, *Country Strolls*, Religious Tract Society (1844)

Oliver, R.R., *Ordnance Survey Maps: a concise guide for historians*, 2nd edition.The Charles Close Society (2005)

Olmsted, F.L., *Walks and Talks of an American Farmer in England* (1852)

Oppenheimer, S., *Out of Eden: The Peopling of the World*. Constable and Robinson (2004)

Oppenheimer, S., *The Origins of the British: a genetic detective story*. Constable and Robinson (2006)

Orr, P.J., Briggs, D.E.G., *et al*, Three-dimensional preservation of a non-biomineralized arthropod in concretions Silurian volcaniclastics from Herefordshire, England. *Journal of the Geological Society*, 157, 173-186 (2000)

Parker Pearson, M., *Food, Culture and Identity in the Neolithic and Early Bronze Age*. BAR, International Series 1117. Archaeopress (2003 ed)

Parsons, D., *The Diary of Sir Henry Slingsby* (1836)

Pedrosa, S., *et al*, Evidence of three maternal lineages in near eastern sheep supporting multiple domestication events. *Proceedings of the Royal Society B: Biological Sciences,* 272 (1577) October 22, 2005, 2211-2217 (2005)

Pemberton, J.M. and Smith, R.H., Lack of biochemical polymorphism in British fallow deer, *Heredity,* 55, 199-207 (1985)

Pevsner, N., *The Buildings of Herefordshire.* Penguin (1977 ed.)

Phillips, N., *Earthwork Castles of Gwent and Ergyng AD 1050-1250.* BAR, British Series 420. Archaeopress (2006)

Porter, M., Farming and Wildlife, *Farming and Wildlife Advisory Group,* Summer (2007)

Poston, W., *A History of Bridstow and Wilton Castle.* Ross Gazette (1939)

Pryor, F., *Britain BC: life in Britain and Ireland before the Romans.* Harper Collins (2003)

Pryor, F., *Britain in the Middle Ages: An Archaeological History.* Harper Collins (2006)

Rackham, O., *Woodlands.* Harper Collins (2006)

Radcliffe-Cooke, C.C., List of Herefordshire Mills, extracted from Herefordshire Quarter Sessions Papers, 1679, *TWNFC,* XXXII, part II, 154-157 (1947)

Rake, H., The Hereford, Ross and Gloucester Railway, *Railway Magazine (*1909)

Ray, K., Iron Age Settlements in Herefordshire, *West Midlands Archaeology,* 44, 77-84 (2001)

Ray, K., The Neolithic in the West Midlands: an overview. In: Garwood (ed) (2007)

Ray, K., and Thomas, J., In the kinship of cows: the social centrality of cattle in the earlier Neolithic of southern Britain. In: Parker Pearson, 2003, 37-44 (2003)

Richards, A., 'Stratigraphy' and 'Herefordshire'. In: Lewis and Richards, 2005

Richardson, L., *The Wells and Springs of Herefordshire.* HMSO (1935)

Roberts, N., Did prehistoric landscape management retard the post-glacial spread of woodland in Southwest Asia? *Antiquity*, 76, 1002-10 (2002)

Roseff, R. Oral History, unpublished LOWV mss (2006)

Roseveare, M.J., Capler Camp, Herefordshire: Geophysical Report, Unpublished Report by ArchaeoPhysics Ltd. (2006)

RCHM, *Vol.I South-West Herefordshire* (1931), *Vol. 2 East Herefordshire* (1932)

Rouse, D., The Cattle Market (Edgar Street) Hereford: Initial Archaeological Evaluation. Hereford Archaeological Series 736, unpublished report by Archaeological Investigations Ltd (2007)

Ryle, G., *Forest Service: the first forty-five years of the Forestry Commission of Great Britain.* David and Charles (1969)

Shaw, Rev. S., *A Tour to the West of England in 1788.* Robson and Clarke (1789)

Sheppard, J.A., *The origins and evolution of field and settlement patterns in the Herefordshire Manor of Marden.* Department of Geography, Queen Mary College, University of London (1979)

Shoesmith, R., *Canoeists Guide to the River Wye.* Welsh Water Authority (1990 ed)

Shoesmith, R., *Hereford History and Guide*, Sutton (1992)

Shoesmith, R., *A Guide to Castles and Moated Sites in Herefordshire.* Logaston Press (1996)

Shoesmith, R. and Eisel, J., *The Pubs of Hereford City.* Logaston Press (2004)

Short, B., Watkins, W., Foot, W. and Kinsman, P. *The National Farm Survey 1941-43.* CABI Publishing (2000)

Sims-Williams, P., Review of W Davies 'The Llandaff Charters', *Journal of Ecclesiastical History*, 33, 124-129 (1982)

Siveter, David J., Aitchison, J.C., *et al*, The Radiolaria of the Silurian Konservat-Lagerstätte of Herefordshire, England. *Journal of Micropalaeontology*, 26, 1-8 (2007)

Siveter, David J., Siveter, Derek J., *et al*, Brood care in a Silurian ostracod. *Proceedings of the Royal Society B*, 247, 465-469.

Siveter, David J., Sutton, M., *et al*, An ostracode crustacean with soft parts from the Lower Silurian. *Science,* 302, 1749-1751 (2003)

Siveter, Derek J., Fortey, R. A., Sutton, M., *et al*, A Silurian 'marrellomorph' arthropod. *Proceedings of the Royal Society B*, 274, 2223-2229 (2007)

Siveter, Derek J., Sutton, M., *et al*, A Silurian sea spider, *Nature*, 431, 978-980 (2004)

Siveter, Derek J., Sutton, M., *et al*, A new probable stem lineage crustacean with three-dimensionally preserved soft-parts from the Herefordshire (Silurian) Lagerstätte, UK. *Proceedings of the Royal Society B,* 274, 2099-2107 (2007)

Smith, B., *Herefordshire Maps 1577 to 1800.* Logaston Press (2004)

Smith, W, *Herefordshire Railways.* Sutton (1998)

Stanford, S.C., *Croft Ambrey*, published by the author (1974)

Stevens, B., Navigation on the Wye, *Monmouth and District Field Club and Antiquarian Society, No. 5* (1955)

Stockinger, V., *The Rivers Wye and Lugg Navigation: a documentary history 1555-1951.* Logaston Press (1996)

Stringer, C.B., *et al*, The Middle Pleistocene human tibia from Boxgrove, *Journal of Human Evolution*, 34 (5) May 1998, 509-547 (1998)

Stuart, A.J., *Life in the Ice Age.* Shire Publications (1988)

Stratford, J,A., *The Wye Tour,* Stratford and Trotter (1896)

Sutton, M.D., Briggs, Derek E.G., *et al*, Methodologies for the visualization and reconstruction of three-dimensional fossils from the Silurian Herefordshire Lagerstätte, *Palaeontologia Electronica*, 4 (1) [available on internet] (2001)

Sutton, M.D,, Briggs, Derek E.G, *et al,* Silurian brachiopods with soft tissue preservation. *Nature*, 436, 1013-1015 (2005)

Sutton, M,D, Briggs, Derek E.G, *et al,* Fossilized soft tissues in a Silurian platyceratid gastropod. *Proceedings of the Royal Society: Biological Science,* 273 (1590) 1039-1044 [available on internet] (2006)

Taylor, E., The Seventeenth Century Iron Forge at Carey Mill, *TWNFC,* Vol. XLV, part II, 450-468 (1986)

Taylor, E., Mainly for Children, *Pax,* March 1989, 16, (1989)

Taylor, E., Report on the Excavation of Huntsham Romano British Villa and Iron Age Enclosure. *TWNFC*, XLVII, part II, 224-281 (1995a)

Taylor, E., Limekilns in the Woolhope Area, *HAN 63,* 49-52 (1995b)

Taylor, E., Our Bridge over the Wye, *Pax,* July 1995 (1995c)

Taylor, E., *Kings Caple in Archenfield.* Elizabeth Taylor in association with Logaston Press (1997)

Thomas, J., *Understanding the Neolithic.* Routledge (1999)

Thomas, A., and Holbrook, N., Llandough. *Archaeology in Wales*, 34, 66-68 (1994)

Thorn, F. and C., *Domesday Book: Worcestershire.* Phillimore (1977 ed)

Thorn, F. and C., *Domesday Book: Shropshire.* Phillimore (1986 ed)

Thorn, F. and C., *Domesday Book: Herefordshire.* Phillimore (1983 ed)

Tonkin, M., Mr. Guy's Hospital and its Herefordshire Estate, *TWNFC,* Vol. XLIII, part II, 91-115 (1980)

Trinder, B., *Barges and Bargemen: A Social History of the Upper Severn Navigation 1660-1900.* Phillimore (2005)

Tweed, H., *Wilton Castle: its present condition and past history.* Edward Stanford (1884)

Vera, F.W.M., *Grazing Ecology and Forest History.* CABI Publishing (2000)

Verey, D., *Herefordshire: a Shell guide.* Faber (1955)

Wainwright, G.J. and Davies, S.M., *Balksbury Camp, Hampshire: excavations 1973 and 1981,* English Heritage Archaeological Report 4 (1995)

Waters, I., *Leather and Oak Bark at Chepstow.* Chepstow Society (1970)

Watts, M., *Water and Wind Power.* Shire (2000)

Webb, J., *Memorials of the Civil War between King Charles I and the Parliament of England as it affected Herefordshire and the adjacent counties,* Vol/ I, Longmans, Green, and Co. (1879)

West Midland Group on Post-War Reconstruction and Planning, *A Planning Survey of Herefordshire,* Faber and Faber (1946)

White, P., *The Arrow Valley, Herefordshire: Archaeology, Landscape Change and Conservation:* Herefordshire Studies in Archaeology 2, Herefordshire Archaeology (2003)

Whitehead, D., and Eisel, J., *A Herefordshire Miscellany: commemorating 150 years of the Woolhope Club.* Lapridge Publications (2000)

Whitehead, D., *A Survey of Historic Parks and Gardens in Herefordshire.* Hereford and Worcester Gardens Trust (2001)

Wigan, M., Breaking Cover, *The Field*, June 2006

Willett, M., *An Excursion from the Source of the Wye in 1810,* reprinted Fineleaf Editions (2007)

Williams, A., (ed) *Great Domesday Book*, County Edition: Herefordshire (1987)

Willis, S., The Iron Age and Roman pottery. In: Jackson, 2003, 41-82 (2003)

Wood, J.G., St. Weonard's, *TWNFC,* 146-147 (1910)

Woodiwiss, S., Rotherwas Access Road, *Historic Environment Today*: Hereford Council's Historic Environment Newsletter, 10 (2) (2007)

Yarranton, A., *England's Improvement by Sea and Land*, London (1698)

Notes

Chapter I. GEOLOGY and PREHISTORY

1. A geological deposit with a variety of well-preserved fossils is known as a lagerstätte (pl. lagerstätten). They represent the life in a particular locality caught at one moment in time. Lagerstätte means 'deposit place' in German.

2. Briggs *et al* (1996). A fascinating description of the methodology used to study these fossils is published in *Palaeontologia Electronica*, on-line at http://palaeoelectronica.org/2001_1/s2/issue1_01.htm (Sutton *et al*, 2001)

3. These fossils are the subject of on-going study and among them are many previously unknown species. They are in an exceptional state of preservation, including their soft-part morphology (Orr *et al*, 2000; David Siveter, M. Sutton *et al*, 2003, 2007; David Siveter, Derek Siveter *et al*, 2007; Derek Siveter, M. Sutton *et al*, 2004; Sutton *et al*, 2005, 2006; David Siveter, J. C. Aitchison *et al*, 2007; Derek Siveter, R.A. Fortey *et al* 2007)

4. In what is known as the Quaternary Period (the last 2.4 million years) the Northern Hemisphere has experienced about 50 ice ages

5. Most of this section is derived from Richards 2005

6. Barclay and Smith (2002) p 20

7. Barclay and Smith (2001) p 18

8. Brandon and Haines (1981) p 32

9. The Palaeolithic is the period from the first use of tools by hominins to the end of the last ice age – by far the greater part of human existence. All early hominins are early, or lower Palaeolithic. Neanderthals are middle Palaeolithic and *Homo sapiens sapiens* are upper Palaeolithic onwards.

10. Tools associated with Neanderthals have been found, but not yet their bones. The Natural History Museum's Ancient Human Occupation of Britain project (AHOB) web pages (http://www.nhm.ac.uk/hosted_sites/ahob/index_2.html) [Accessed 30 July 2007] have much information about early humans in Britain and links to developing stories. Roebroeks (2005) pp 92-922

11. Boxgrove web site http://matt.pope.users.btopenworld.com/boxgrove/boxhome.htm [Accessed 31 July 2008]

12. Stringer *et al* (1998) http://www.ingentaconnect.com/content/ap/hu;jsessionid=10ukq0p84f8oe.alice

13. *Hominini* is the name given to the 'tribe' of the sub-family *Homininae* that includes, chimpanzees (*Pan*), humans (*Homo*) and their extinct ancestors. The sub-family *Homininae* includes the hominins together with gorillas. The *homininae* are part of the family *Hominidae*, which also includes orang utans. Hominids are part of the superfamily *Hominoidea*. Hominoids include humans, all the great apes and gibbons.

14. Neanderthal bones have not yet (25 May 2008) been found in Britain, but tools of what is held to be their defining culture, the Mousterian, have been. There is some dispute about how closely we should relate Neanderthals to modern humans. One view is that they form two distinct species *Homo neanderthalensis* and *Homo sapiens*, but many workers in this field believe that they should both be classified as *Homo sapiens* – as the sub-species *Homo sapiens Neanderthalensis* and *Homo sapiens sapiens*.

15. Stuart (1988)

16. George Nash, pers comm

17. Not for the first time: human occupation of what is now Britain has happened on seven occasions. Each period of occupation has been brought to an end by the onset of extremely cold weather. This period has lasted for about 12,000 years.

18. The Basque refuge provided the bulk of the ancestral stock of both the Saami of northern Scandinavia and the Berbers of North Africa (Achilli *et al*, 2005)

19. DNA analysis has revolutionised our understanding of population movements. Much of what is said in this section is derived from Stephen Oppenheimer's *The Origins of the British: A Genetic Detective Story* (2006). This continues the European part of the story of the spread of humans from his previous *Out of Eden: The Peopling of the World* (2004)

20. A 'stadial' is a period of much colder temperatures during an interglacial period. Multiple naming of the Younger Dryas Stadial causes some confusion. The term Nahanagan Stadial has been used In Ireland, while Loch Lomond Stadial is often used in Britain; the term Greenland Stadial is also used.

21. 88% of the Irish, 81% of the Welsh, 79% of the Cornish, 70% of the Scottish and 68% of the English (Oppenheimer, 2006, p 406).

22. In the *Agricola* (11) Tacitus says of the Silures of South Wales that 'the swarthy faces of the Silures, the tendency of their hair to curly hair and the fact that Spain lies opposite, all lead one to believe that Spaniards crossed in ancient times and occupied the land'. http://www.fordham.edu/halsall/ancient/tacitus-agricola.html. (Accessed 25 May 2008)

23. Until recently, this was in dispute. Many workers believed that that it was quite likely that the Neolithic population replaced that of the Mesolithic – 'this result may thus be an indication of a genealogical discordancy between Mesolithic and present-day inhabitants of Europe' (Di Benedetto *et al*, 2000, p 676).

24. Pryor (2003) pp 175-176

25. Or is it? The author has worked on two rescue excavations at Stonehenge; one in an extension to the car park, the other within the henge itself, where the trench for the new footpath by the trilithons (trilithons – three stones, in the famous Stonehenge image) was being excavated, by English Heritage workmen without any archaeological supervision.

26. Many years ago, the author saw a map of the archaeological find spots in Oxfordshire. There was a dense cluster around Oxford itself and a diagonal line of dots across the county. The latter was the line of the then-proposed M40: the former the cycling range of the Victorian don. The Oxfordshire Sites and Monuments record has improved a great deal since then though.

27. Pryor (2006) pp 39 – 43

28. As at July 2008

29. Gillow will appear again on these pages. The Landscape Origins of the Wye Valley project carried out a large field project on this multi-period site.

30. In 1997 Tony Brown suggested opportunistic exploitation of natural clearings by Mesolithic and early Neolithic people rather than deliberate clearing. F.W.M. Vera's *Grazing Ecology and Forest History* (2000) comprehensively addressed the issue of the original density of natural woodland.

31. 'The term 'Neolithic', I would argue, is still often used as being synonymous with 'mixed farming economy' (Thomas, 1999, p 7)

32. In pre-ceramic Panama, root crops and grain were being grown by 3600 BC (Dickau *et al,* 2007). In what is now the eastern USA, the domestication of plants with starchy or oily seeds dates from about 2000 BC (McLauchlan, 2003). Fire seems to have sometimes been used to prepare land for cultivation. Evidence for this practice is widespread and has been found in North America (Delcourt and Delcourt, 1998) and south-west Asia (Roberts, 2002). Although this seems to have been buried beneath terms such as 'wilderness', in the Americas, major modification to the landscape had been carried out before Europeans arrived (Denevan, 1992; Dull, 2007; Butzer, 1992)

33. SMR numbers 5747, 17316 and 8355

34. Sheep were probably domesticated about 8,000 BC. Recent DNA analysis indicated that domestications of three different populations took place at, at least, three different places and times somewhere in the area of modern-day Turkey, Iraq and Iran (Pedrosa *et al*, 2005, p 2212). Domestic goats also have their origins in at least three females from what may be a wider geographic area than sheep (Luikart *et al*, 2001). Cattle too, have been domesticated within the same period although their domestication events are much more complex and may derive from many more individual female bovines over a large area of Eurasia (Bruford *et al*, 2003). There is also a possibility that fallow deer spent some time as a domesticated species (Pemberton and Smith, 1985)

35. Although aurochs, the native wild cattle (*Bos Primigenius*), had been assumed to be ancestral to modern cattle, studies of British remains of aurochs indicate that modern British cattle are totally unrelated, having their genetic origins in Asia like sheep and goats (Edwards *et al*, 2007). This is despite the fact that aurochs were present in Britain as late as the Bronze Age (Noddle, 1989, p 182)

36. Hey, Mulville and Robinson (2003)

37. Ray and Thomas (2003)

38. Legge (1981)

39. Copley *et al* (2003) p 1528

40. In the late 20th century it was estimated that in South Darfur in Sudan dairy products provided 25% of dietary needs of some groups. It is possible for a family to live on a pure milk diet during the rainy season: in 1984/5 most families in the area did this for three months (Kerven, 1987).

41. Mercer (1981)

42. 'Rare rounded yellow-brown patinated flints' occur at Vennwood 10 km north-east of Hereford, deposited an earlier glaciation (Brandon, 1989, p 32)

43. There were a few gun-flints

44. It was the probable presence of an early medieval monastery (see Chapter 2), which led to the project team field-walking at Llanfrother. No evidence of early medieval activity was found at all (it actually seldom is). The large number of prehistoric flints was a considerable bonus.

45. Jackson (2007) p 113

46. Dorling (2007) pp 26 – 30

47. Dorling (2007) pp 20 – 25

48. 'Interpretation of crop marks is an inexact science, interpretation is by comparison and analogy with excavated sites/ Interpretation prior to excavation is sometimes wrong, how many more supposedly Iron Age enclosures date to an earlier period?' (Dorling, 2007, p 31)

49. Woodiwiss (2007)

50. Simon Sworn and Simon Woodiwiss, Fieldwork on the Rotherwas Access Road 2006 – 7, presentation at the Herefordshire Archaeological Symposium,10 November, 2007

51. White (2003) p 30

52. Dorling (2007) p 19

53. Keith Ray, pers. comm.

54. SMR number 6462

55. SMR number 6483

56. SMR numbers 7004 and 7132

57. James (1999) p 52. 'The Greeks and Romans, used the terms *Keltoi* and *Celtae*, and were, after all, contemporaries of the people they called Celts; but they never mentioned any connection with the British Isles (Oppenheimer, 2006, p 20).

58. Miles (2005) 108

59. Strabo, *The Geography*, Book 4: chapter 5.2. Available from http://penelope.uchicago.edu/Thayer/E/Roman/Texts/Strabo [accessed 14 December 2007]

60. It is of course not possible to change the view of the majority and it would be folly to try. Celtic now has a real meaning – it is just that its origins are wrong. Its utility was well appreciated by those British who attempted to re-name the Irish Sea the 'Celtic' Sea, in case there was any oil.

61. Jack and Hayter (1925)

62. Kenyon (1954)

63. Jack and Hayter (1925) p 87

64. Cunliffe (2005)

65. Stanford (1974)

66. Sheppard (1979) pp 32 – 36

67. Wainwright and Davies (1995)

68. 'One of the most enigmatic aspects of this survey has to be the possibility that the monument had an earlier phase, or even two' (Roseveare, 2006, p 7)

69. Roseveare (2006) p 9

70. Like a lesser Cartimandua or Boudicca for instance: Tacitus, in The Agricola (15) says that the Britons 'admit no distinction of sex in their royal successions'. At Hod Hill hillfort in Dorset, a house which may have been that of the chief, had been subjected to intensive ballista fire at the time of the Roman conquest (Cunliffe, 2005, pp 186; 222)

71. Structures at the centres of the hillforts at South Cadbury, Maiden Castle and Danebury have been interpreted as temples or shrines (Cunliffe, 2005, pp 561 – 2)

72. http://www.brigantesnation.com/VitrifiedForts/VitrifieedForts.htm (accessed 12 February 2008)

73. Green (1995) p 66

74. Hoverd (2004)

75. Jackson (2003) p 173

76. 'The location of Ariconium suggests that it was well positioned to develop a role as a Dobunnic tribal centre for what is now south Herefordshire. This would fill a gap on the western margins of their sphere of influence and provide a point of articulation with the Silures to the west' (Jackson, 2003, p 164)

77. The identification of Ariconium as a Dobunnic place, and therefore southern Herefordshire as Dobunnic territory, is not universally accepted – see Ray, 2001, p 78. However, its dominance of this region in the late Iron Age and Romano-British period is more difficult to dispute.

78. While Sutton Walls appears to have been occupied into the first century BC, Croft Ambrey had fallen into decline by the end of the second century (Haselgrove, 1997)

79. although living hedges as boundaries may have been used in prehistory

80. The Farm is Caplor, the hill, and the hillfort is Caplar. Spellings are sometime very recent – 'Capellar' was used on the Fownhope tithe map (1843).

81. Stanford (1974) p 168

82. Kenyon (1954) p 61

83. Lloyd Jones (1984) p 103

84. Diodorus Siculus, http://www.elfinspell.com/PrimarySource45BC.html#ref1 (accessed 4th May 2008)

85. Bradley (2007) p 16

86. Hale and Moore (1970)

87. Taylor's was the first one-inch-to-the-mile map of the county. An impressively large scale at the time (Smith, 2004, p 80) Copies are held in Hereford City Library and Herefordshire Record Office AP25/2

88. The motte at King's Caple 'is a circular mound raised by the side of the old Roman road' (Phillips, 2006, p 149)

89. Clarke and Jackson (1992)

90. The annual consumption of the army in Wales and the Marches in about 80 AD has been estimated at 401,460 bushels of wheat, 265,390 bushels of barley and 23,336,640 pounds of beef: the beef represents between 46,000 and 60,000 cattle (Lloyd Jones, 1988, p 44). These figures are a generalisation, and it is likely that in these upland areas sheep would have constituted part of the diet.

91. SMR number 30554

92. Taylor (1997) p 6

93. Taylor (1997)

94. Gale (2003) p 147

95. This rubbish tends to lie against the outside edge of the ditch, suggesting that it was thrown by someone standing on the internal bank.

Chapter II. LATER ROMAN and MEDIEVAL

1. Lloyd Jones (1984) p 107

2. Lloyd Jones (1984) p 106

3. Willis (2003) pp 41 – 82; Taylor (1995)

4. Although in fact there is very little Iron Age pottery from Wales and the Marches and it is entirely absent from many areas (Lloyd Jones, 1984, p 15).

5. Cracked pots were sometimes repaired – the author has seen rivet repairs to cracks in a Samian (early Roman period) pot in East Anglia and a medieval tripod pitcher from Hereford (now in Hereford Museum). There is a riveted Iron Age pot from Croft Ambrey in Hereford Museum. This practice should be regarded as exceptional rather than commonplace.

6. Ariconium 'would give a form Ergun in Welsh' (Charles, 1963, p 88)

7. In his *Early Charters of the West Midlands* (1961) H. P. R. Finberg marks every single Llandaff charter as spurious and in 1972 Glanville R.J. Jones (285) could write of them that 'no scholar nowadays accepts [them] at face value'. Christopher Brooke (1986, p 21) refers to 'the great collection of forgeries'.

8. Work principally by Professor Wendy Davies in *An Early Welsh Microcosm* (1978); *The Llandaff Charters* (1979). In his review of these works, although suggesting that her dates 'may be a little too early', Sims-Williams (1982) considered that Professor Davies had successfully demonstrated the likely authenticity of most of the charters: 'sufficient evidence to support the integrity of the majority of charters ... can be gleaned from both her books'.

9. The boundary clauses attached to the charters in the Book of Llandaff were written in Welsh. Analysis of the linguistic shifts in these clauses by Jon Coe (2004) (something not carried out by earlier Anglo-centric scholars) overwhelmingly supported a first millennium date for them. The dating on these grounds was unable to support the earlier dates proposed by Davies, but, as Coe says, a boundary clause as written, even in Welsh, may post-date the charter.

10. The earliest mention of Dyfrig is in the early 7th century *Vita Samsonis* – Life of St Samson, which recounts that it was Dyfrig who ordained Samson (Doble, 1971 p 54). Dyfrig's birth may have been around 440 – 450 AD (Fenn, 1968, p 334).

11. Book of Llandaff, p 80, Liber Landavensis or Book of Llandaff, National Library of Wales, MS 17110E [internet] Available from: http://www.llgc.org.uk/index.php?id=1667 [Accessed 8th August 2007] The Text of the Book of Llan Dâv, edited by J.G. Evans, Oxford (1893)

12. Llanfrother had been the site of a prehistoric settlement, see Chapter 1

13. Coplestone-Crow (1989)

14. Coplestone-Crow (1989)

15. The church of St Badgualan at the mouth of Cric (stream) on the Wye

16. Jones (1960) p 70

17. Sherlock, H. and Pikes, P. J., *The First Millennium Cemetery at Dewsall Court, Herefordshire: an interim report.* [internet] Available from the Archaeological Data Service at http://ads.ahds.ac.uk/catalogue/library/greylit/details.cfm?id=2060 [Accessed 19 June 2008] (2002)

18. 1270 ± 60 BP (before present)

19. 1240 ± 40 BP

20. 1760 ± 90 BP

21. At Llandough, Glamorgan, 858 burials were recorded in a cemetery which may have originated in the Iron Age, was in use through the later Roman period, and continued to be used through to the 10th or 11th centuries (Thomas and Holbrook 1994).

22. Hentland is often supposed to be a Deserted Medieval Village. Excavation near the church did indeed find the foundations of buildings. However, the evidence suggested a succession of single buildings on the site rather then several at any one period (Bridgewater, 1971)

23. Fox (1955) p 183

24. Finberg (1961) p 145

25. Galbraith and Tait (1950) p 71

26. Galbraith and Tait (1950) p 19

27. Garnett (1985) p 114

28. As with other waves of immigrants, the numbers were not large and this group would always have been a small minority. They are however currently not identifiable by DNA analysis of modern populations. This is probably due to the fact that the source geographic areas of this group had already been the destination of the same groups of people who had moved into England – originally Iberia and Eastern Europe, then Denmark and Norway.

29. Garnett (1985) p 118

30. Thorne (1983) 1.55

31. Thorne (1983) 1.8

32. In Henry VIII's taxation of 1523, Hentland itself does not appear. Within Hentland parish however there are five townships in three groups – Altebought (Altbough) and Tresecke (Tresseck), Trerado (Treaddow), and Kynnarston (Kynaston) and Henfrowde (Llanfrother). In 1536 there were three residents of Hentland who were taxed – John Gwyllam with land to the value of 29 pounds and Thomas Seymour and John Flanders with goods to the value of 20 pounds each. Within the parish, the townships of Llanfrother and Kynaston together had two taxed residents. (Tax assessment from Faraday, 2005) Altbough and Tresseck are near Hoarwithy; Llanfrother and Kynaston are now farms between Hoarwithy and Hentland; Treaddow is a settlement in the southern part of Hentland parish.

33. Bridgewater (1971)

34. O'Donnell (1971) p 193

35. Shoesmith (1996) p 149

36. Nicky Smith, unpublished mss. (2006)

37. Shoesmith (1996) p 53

38. VCH, Vol I p 256

39. RCHME, Vol II (1932)

40. see Chapter 1 page 30

41. This work was presented by Martin Roseveare and Anne Roseveare at the EIGG Recent Work in Archaeological Geophysics Conference, 19 December 2006

42. Dated by BETA Analytica of Miami, Florida in December 2007.

43. Baxter (2008)

44. The orbit of a pig frontal had rat teeth-marks (Baxter, 2008)

Chapter III. DOCUMENTARY EVIDENCE

1. A hide is generally interpreted as 120 acres.

2. HCA 483, an exchange of land in Holme Lacy in1250

3. TNA JUST 1/303

4. TNA JUST1/302

5. TNA JUST 1/303

6. TNA JUST 1/307

7. TNA C133/41. *Latheferd* is a local term associated with the arrangements within Archenfield which required these Welsh manors to supply soldiers to king.

8. TNA C133/41

9. Under-wood (Latin *subboscum*) implies regularly worked coppice.

10. A water-powered fulling mill processes raw sheep wool by beating it and washing it ready for making into yarn.

11. TNA C134/82

12. TNA C132/125 A carucate (Latin *caruca* a plough) is approximately the area of arable land that a plough team could manage in a year and would be equivalent to a hide. The IPM records that 1 carucate = 100 acre.

13. TNA C135/243

14. HCA 2507/9

15. TNA C115/96/6934

16. GRO GDA 1A

17. The area of land that went with Fownhope Court and that of that woodlands of the manor of Fownhope were not included

in the court inquiry. These two figures are taken from a near contemporary survey by the Crown's surveyor Robert Tressel in 1601 just after the execution of the Earl of Essex for treason against Queen Elizabeth and all his lands were confiscated. [BL Add Ch 11054 page 149]. The 13 mentions of single parcels of land where no area is given are taken to be 1 acre. Richard Kidley's pasture 'in Haugh Wood' which stretches 'from Lymburies to Sharpnage' is estimated as 50 acres.

18. HRO AB47/1/7
19. TNA C115/64/5617
20. TNA C115/7/229
21. TNA C115/69/6254
22. Tresseck Sale details 1827, HCL LC942.44
23. H. Hurley, Tresseck Farm 2005, private mss.
24. TNA MAF32/9/103
25. TNA MAF32/9/103
26. Taylor, E., Transcription of Caradoc Inventory 1630, HRO BN83/131
27. TNA C115/45/2992
28. LOWV research notes 2006
29. LOWV research notes 2006
30. LOWV research notes 2006
31. Population figures from Census 1801 – 1851, extract of census 1881, Population of Herefordshire Parishes, Hereford Council Research Team 2001, HCL 312
32. Lascelles *Directory* 1851
33. Hackett, B.C., *Bridstow* (1951) p 15
34. Guys Hospital Sale 1961, Hurley Collection
35. HRO M5/9/8, Fownhope Court Sale, 1921
36. Clark (2007) pp 21 – 27
37. HCL 914.244, Holme Lacy Sale 1909
38. Littlebury's *Directory* 1876
39. Taylor (1997) pp 325 – 327

Chapter IV. WOODS and TREES

1. Vera (2000)
2. There are two native species of lime: Small-leaved lime *Tilia cordata* and Large-leaved lime *Tilia platyphyllos*. European lime *Tilia Europea* has been planted as an amenity tree since the 18th century but rarely in woods.
3. Rackham (2006) p 110. Rackham estimates that Roman England had between 10 and 20% tree cover.
4. A Domesday league is reckoned to be about one and a half miles.
5. *The Acta of Bishop Robert of Lotharinga 1085*. Barrow (1993)
6. Williams, A. ed., *The Domesday Book*, Alecto Historical Editions (1988) .
7. Taylor (1997)
8. TNA C47/12/7
9. The amount of woodland for King's Caple, Caradock and Baysham is given in monetary terms. This is converted to areas on the basis of 4d per acre which is the value per acre known for woodland in Fownhope at this time.
10. HRO D71/1
11. TNA C115/97/6933
12. HCA 2393
13 .TNA C135/140
14. Matthews (1912) pp 140 – 141
15. Letters and Papers of Henry VIII, Vol.5 p 428, HMSO 1880. Listed under 'Grants in March 1532'.
16. WRO 1531/1/6/1/3, dated May 1567
17. TNA C66/1367 membrane 18, dated 1588
18. TNA C115/45/2992
19. TNA C115/7/228
20. TNA C115/67 item nos. 5895 to 5903
21. HCA 4810 nos. I to XX
22. HRO E88 Box 4
23. HRO AB47/1/24
24. Private Collection.

25. TNA C115/7/229

26. TNA C115/3/82

27. HCA 4810 no. XX.

28. HCL Local Collection 647.1, now transferred to HRO.

29. TNA C115/67/5919

30. Based upon measurements of a field oak blown down in Weobley 1991, which had an average tree-ring width of 4mm.

Chapter V. BUILDINGS IN THE LANDSCAPE

1. Buildings categorised by Phillip Anderson

2. LOWV map archive

3. Hurley (2001) p 139

4. J. Duncumb, Hundred of Wormelow, mss. (c.1820) HCL

5. Rudhall sale particulars 1825, HRO L50/3

6. WI History of Brampton Abbotts (1951) HRO A74/1

7. Poston (1939), p 82

8. Hickling (1969) p 489

9. Old Church Brockhampton sale particulars c2000, Hurley collection

10. Much Fawley estate map (1721) HRO K11

11. Hurley, op.cit. in note 9 pp 148 – 151

12. Kelly's *Directory of Herefordshire* (1929)

13. Hurley (2001) pp 153 – 154

14. Fownhope Tithe Map (1843)

15. LOWV research notes, 2006, Pevsner (1977) p 133

16. Isaac Taylor, New Map of the County of Hereford, 1754, A. Bryant County Map 1835, HRO F76/B241/B

17. WI History of Foy (1952 – 1977) HRO AF/79/1, p 42

18. Hurley (1992) p 15

19. Hurley (2001) pp 260 – 261

20. Silas Taylor, The History of Herefordshire, mss. (1663) HRO X8

21. H. Hurley, Tresseck Farm, private mss. (2005)

22. Holme Lacy sale particulars 1909, HCL 914.44

23. Holme Lacy Parish Registers 1776, HRO AL17/2

24. Shipley Gardens website 2007

25. LOWV research notes 2006

26. Duncumb (1812)

27. Taylor (1997)

28. LOWV map archive 2006

29. LOWV research notes 2006

30. Personal observation of the use of barns in 2007

31. Sellack Terrier 1607, 1633, HRO HD2/5/50 – 53

32. Hurley (2001) pp 127 – 130

33. Pevsner (1977) p 90

34. Comments by Phillip Anderson 2006

35. LOWV research notes 2006

36. Personal observation of the use of barns in 2007

37. Sellack Terrier 1607, 1633, HRO HD2/5/50-53

38. Hurley (2001) p 127-130

39. Pevsner (1977) p 90

40. Comments by Phillip Anderson 2006

41. Table compiled by Phillip Anderson and Fenny Smith (2006)

42. NMR letter 29 March 2007

43. Herefordshire Council letter 2 April 2007

Chapter VI. THE RIVER'S INDUSTRIAL PAST

1. Hurley H & J (1994) p 7

2. Williams (1987)

3. Thorne (1983)

4. Martin (1953) p 70

5. Elizabeth Taylor Collection, HRO BN83/105

6. Fawley Lease 1589, HRO AS58/2/16

7. Hart (1863) p 283

8. Coates and Tucker (1983) p 29

9. Holme Lacy Rental 1266, HRO AS58/2/38

10. Baysham Lease 1286, HCA 2285

11. Eaton Tregoz IPM 1369, TNA C135/209

12. Hereford Mills, 14th century accounts, HCA 2393

13. Dinmore and Garway Rental, 1505, HRO A63/111/23

14. Bolstone Lease, 1571, HRO AS58/2/15

15. Taylor (1997) p 126

16. Marriage Settlement 1611, HRO A28/25

17. How Caple Lease, 1698, HRO L38/25

18. Isaac Taylor, New Map of the County of Hereford, 1754

19. Price, Map 1817

20. Articles of Agreement, 1628, TNA C115/35

21. Taylor (1986)

22. Articles of Agreement 1631/2, HRO AS58/2/25

23. Morgan (1950) p 172

24. Radcliffe-Cooke (1947) p 154 – 155

25. Hurley (2001) p 13

26. Hurley, Tresseck Farm, private mss. 2005

27. Sale advertisement, *Her. Jnl.* 29 June 1786

28. Barge Accounts, 1809 – 1811, Tim Ward Collection

29. Sale Particulars, 1827, HCL LC942.44

30. Hurley, Tresseck Farm, private mss. 2005

31. Information supplied by Roz Lowe 2007. Glewstone Lease 1778, HRO C99/111/136

32. Birmingham Archives 1816; 1832, Birmingham Library MS2092

33. Coates and Tucker (1983) p 14

34. Wilton IPM 1324, TNA C134/82. Hereford Mills HCL 2393

35. Coates and Tucker (1978) p 40

36. Silk Mill Advert 1851, Tim Ward Collection

37. Fownhope Local History Group, Snippets 2007

38. Watts (2000) p 51

39. Richard Marnham claimed in 1293 that he and his ancestors had always been granted free fishing on the Thames; TNA SC8/127/6338

40. Wye Free Fishery Case, HRO AS58/3/33. Robert de Chandos established his ownership of fishing rights at Fownhope, the same year John de Tregoz fought off a claim for common fishing rights at Foy and elsewhere. In 1911 the Lords ruled that the Earl of Chesterfield and Mrs A. M. Foster were the owners of the fishing in the parishes of Bolstone, Ballingham, Hentland, Sellack, King's Caple, F. James, Free Fishing Case, TWNFC 1918

41. Giraldus Cambrensis (1978) p 93

43. Eaton Tregoz IPM 1369, TNA C135/209. It had reduced in value from 1300 when value of the fishery was 50s (Bannister 1902, quoting IPM extent of Ewyas Harold that included Eaton Tregoz)

43. Eaton Tregoz Bailiff's Account Henry VI, TNA C115/96/6933

44. *batilda* in the document, possible battlement, turret, but uncertain

45. Holme Lacy Lease, 1571, HRO AS58/2/15

46. Holme Lacy Court Roll, 1563, HRO AS58/2/39

47. Ballingham Lease, 1648, HRO AS58/2/26

48. Abstracts of Title, HRO AS58/3/23 – 24 & 33

49. Tan-House sale, *HJNL* 17 Jan 1787

50. Hentland Tithe Map (1842)

51. Hurley (1989) pp 28 – 30, Fellmonger – a dealer in hides.

52. Heath (1804)

53. WI History of Fownhope (1978) HRO AM26/8, pp 9 – 10

54. Bowsher, Hodges & Watkins letter 1799, HRO A29/64

55. Hentland Tithe Map (1842)

56. Guy's Hospital Estate Records, 1785 – 1807, HRO AW28/45

57. Tonkin (1980) p 98

58. Total checked by Fenny Smith 2007

59. Holme Lacy accounts, 18th century TNA C115/115. Brockhampton Accounts 1837, HRO E88 Box 4

60. Waters (1970) p 11

61. Tanners advertisement, *HJNL*. 15 Dec 1827

62. Bark references AA., HRO BN80, HRO E78/6, HRO BB/77

63. Morgan (1947) pp 144 – 150

64. Taylor (1995b) pp 49 – 52

65. Lulham Lease, 1778, HRO F37/178

66. Lime for Sale advertisement, *Her. Jnl*. 30 April 1794

67. Fownhope Court Rolls, 1797, HRO AB47/1 – 7

68. Gange (1950) p 23

69. The Lime Kiln account 1796, AA

70. *HJNL*1805, 1811 displayed at Fownhope Local History Group on April 2007

71. V. Goodbury, Herefordshire Limekilns 1992 p 15, HRO BH65/1. Advertisement, *HJNL* 5 Feb 1810

72. Lime advertisement, *HJNL* 5 May 1824

73. Lease of Stone Quarry 1894, HRO B94/3. Hurley (1983) p 220

74. Author's personnel knowledge

75. Leases of Capler 1602 – 1842, HCA 4810

76. John Leech Accounts 1788 – 1812, HCA5715/3/1 – 90

77. Dean & Chapter Registry Book 1841 – 1851 pp 100 – 101, HCA7005/7

78. Bolstone Lease 1571, HRO AS58/2/15. Fownhope Leases 1634, HRO AS58/2/43 – 4

79. Hughes and Hurley (1999) pp 138 – 139

80. Duchess of Norfolk Schedule of Estates 1829, HRO BF21

81. WI History of Brampton Abbotts (1951) HRO A71/1

82. Heath (1828)

83. Lascelles *Directory* 1851

84. Littlebury's *Directory* 1867. Gange (1950) p 22

85. Hurley (1983) p 216

86. Farr (1954)

87. Duncumb (1812) p 139

88. Holme Lacy Lease 1635, HRO AS58/2/46

89. D.R. Chapman, Scudamore Papers 1639, printed 1886, HCL 647.1

90. Harewood Sale Particulars 1876, HRO AW47/19

91. Fownhope Court Rolls 1778, 1783, HRO AB47/1 – 7. Fownhope Leases 1783 HRO AE38/1 Box 1356

92. Lipscomb (1802) p 70

93. Squire Thomas Jones Day Book, 18 May 1793, Kington Historical Society

94. AA 1795 – 1796. Hurley (2001) p 66

95. Shoesmith and Eisel (2004) p 26. Brewery Receipts 1832, HRO F60/349

96. Rock House sale particulars 1874, HRO M5/9/11

97. Hurley (1991)

98. Mendelsohn (1966)

99. Holme Lacy Accounts 1641 HCL647.1. Hurley (2001) p 15

100. Great Fawley 1611, HRO K11 LC3254. H. Hurley, Ringfield private mss. 2001. Taylor (1997) p 15

101. Kynaston Sale 1836, HLC LC942.44

102. Advertisement, *HJNL* 1848 displayed at Fownhope Local History Group in April 2007

103. Olmsted (1852)

104. Caradoc sale particulars 1863, HRO M5/15/17, How Caple Court sale particulars 1881, HRO E40/13, Holme Lacy sale
    particulars 1909, HCL 942.44

105. Hurley (2001) p 184

Chapter VII. ROADS and RIVER CROSSINGS

1. D. Bick, Holloways in the Welsh Borders, mss. 2005

2. Hurley (1992) p 6

3. Hindle (2005) p 15

4. R. Whitworth Plan 1799, HRO Q/WRn1. Stroudwater Navigation website 2007

5. Discussions between D. Bick and H. Hurley in 2005

6. H. Hurley, Herefordshire County Magazine 1981, HRO Friends Newsletter No.4 1986

7. LOWV Wye Survey 2006/7

8. Modification under the Wildlife & Countryside Act 1981. Discovering Lost Ways project arose from the CROW Act 2000, but has since been abandoned

9. SMR numbers 33632 and 33633

10. Notes on parish boundary 1806, HRO AA/15/30. Brampton Abbotts Tithe Map (1838)

11. Isaac Taylor, New Map of the County of Hereford, 1754

12. Gore Lane on A. Bryant Map 1835. D. Bick suggests that lane usually signifies an ancient route

13. WI History of Brampton Abbotts, appendix (1981) HROA59/1/1

14. Gloucester Abbey Court Rolls 1487 – 1511, GRO GDR1A

15. Ashburton Estate sale particulars, 1890, HRO M3/28/4. Townsend Farm sale particulars, 1929, HRO M5/5/40

16. Observation made by D. Bick in 2005

17. Brampton Abbotts Tithe Apportionment (1838)

18. Brampton Abbotts Glebe Terrier 1618, HRO HD2. Notes on parish boundary 1806, HRO AA15/30. Isaac Taylor, New Map of the County of Hereford, 1754

19. Brampton Abbotts Vestry Book 1850 – 1884, HRO AA/15/17

20. Hurley (1992) pp 47 – 51

21. Martin (1953) pp 70 – 75

22. J. Pye, Survey of Ballingham 1695, BL

23. St. Guthlac's Rental 1541/2, HRO BH53/1

24. Ballingham lease of 1766, HRO B94/1

25. Shaw (1789)

26. J. Pye Survey of Ballingham 1695, BL. Ballingham Tithe Apportionment (1839)

27. Hurley (1992) pp 55 – 56

28. H. Hurley, research notes 1987 – 1999. List of Roads, Herefordshire Council 1936

29. D. Bick, unpublished observations for LOWV 2005

30. Wood (1910) p 146

31. Fosbroke (1822) p 44

32. H. Hurley, Tresseck private mss., 2005. Indenture 1748, Glamorgan Deeds printed, HRO vol.4b

33. Hentland Tithe Map 1842. Tresseck map 1695, BL

34. H. Hurley in Brookes (2000) pp 181 – 210

35. Hentland Parish Council Minutes 1894 – 1955

36. Richardson (1935) p 95

37. H. Price Map 1817

38. LOWV website 2007. Additional Charters relating to Wales, printed nd, HRO83/108

39. Hurley (1992) pp 25; 55

40. H. Hurley in Whitehead and Eisel (2000)

41. H. Hurley research notes, 1997

42. A. Fleming's notes on Hentland, HRO L32

43. LOWV research notes and website 2005

44. A. Bryant Map 1835

45. The Herefordshire Field-Name Survey, Hentland Part 2, WNFC, ARS c.1990

46. Hurley (1992) p 15

47. Hentland Manor Deed 1635, HRO K61//44 LC7624

48. LOWV website 2007

49. Pengethley Survey, 1580, HRO K61/3

50. Pengethley Survey, 1580, HRO K61/3

51. Pengelly and Scudamore mss. HCL647.1

52. List of Roads, Herefordshire County Council 1936

53. Hurley (1992) pp 44 – 46

54. D. Paterson *Itinerary* 1787, H. Price Map 1817

55. Herefordshire Council letter 25 June 2004

56. A. Bryant map 1835

57. Lamont (1922) p 85

58. Information from Peter Darby in 1994

59. Webb (1879) p 9

60. Holme Lacy Bridge Company Share Application, c1857, HRO AC97/11

61. Holme Lacy Bridge Act 1857, Hurley Collection. HT 25 May 1935

62. Hurley (2001) p 155

63. Holme Lacy Tithe Apportionment (1840)

64. Lipscomb (1802) p 70

65. Lamont (1922) p 86

66. Holme Lacy Bridge Act 1857, Hurley Collection

67. Hurley (2001) p 152

68. *Ross Gazette,* 17 August 2000

69. LOWV research notes 2006

70. R. Whitworth plan 1799

71. Lamont (1922) p 87

72. Jakeman & Carver, *Herefordshire Directory* (1902). Lascelles *Herefordshire Directory* (1851)

73. Martin (1953) p 71

74. Lamont (1922) p 87

75. Taylor (1989) p 16

76. KA maps 1780, LOWV archive

77. H. Hurley, research notes for LOWV 2006

78. Horse Towing Path Act 1809

79. Horse Towing Path Act 1809. N. E. Richards, History of the Navigation of the Wye mss., HCL387

80. Horse Towing Path Report 1816, HCL387

81. Hurley (1983; 1996)

82. Old Humphrey (1844) p 79

83. Herefordshire Council personal contact 20April 2007

84. Hurley (2001) pp 130 – 135

85. LOWV research notes 2005. Taylor (1997) p 7

86. Taylor (1995c)

87. Sellack Bridge petition 1894, HRO G42 bundle 57

88. Sellack Parish Information, Archenfield Magazine, May 1896

89. Hurley (2001) p 136

90. R. Whitworth plan 1799

91. *Ross Gazette*, 3 April 1947

92. Isaac Taylor, Wye Navigation Plan, 1763

93. Fawley Lease 1687, HRO A8/11/210

94. Abstract of Leases, Guy's Hospital Estate, 1735, 1737, HRO AW/28/46/212

95. Matthews (1912) p 131. Horse Towing Path Act 1809

96. Lamont (1922) p 89

97. Foy Parish Records, HRO BH88/1

98. Old Humphrey (1844) p 73

99. Hurley (2001) pp 143 – 144

100. H. Hurley, Foy Bridge, Countryside Service Newsletter, Spring 1986

101. LOWV website 2007

102. Crow (1995) p 122

103 R. Whitworth plan 1799

104 Lamont (1922) p 90

105 H. Hurley in Brookes (2000) p 44

Chapter VIII. RIVER and RAIL TRANSPORT

1. Shoesmith (1992) pp 75 – 76

2. Green (1999) p 107. B. Stevens, Navigation on the Wye, *Monmouth & District Field Club & Antiquarian Society,* No.5, 1955

3. Stockinger (1996) p 6

4. Martin (1953) p 70. Holme Lacy Lease 1266, HRO AS/2/38. Wilton IPM 1324, TNA C134/82. Eaton Tregoz IPM 1369, TNA C135/209. Fownhope IPM 1375, TNA C135/243

5. Paragraph researched and written by Adrian Harvey from Chandler (1999) pp 191-198 and Parsons (1836) pp 163-165

6 Patent Rolls 1301 printed, HRO AL/3

7. Chandler *(*1999) pp 196 – 198

8. Wye and Lugg survey 1697, photocopy from BL, HRO AP21

9. Yarranton (1698) p 156

10 Isaac Taylor Wye Navigation plan, 1763. R. Whitworth Navigation plan 1779

11. H. Price Survey 1805, HRO AS58/9/49

12. Navigation Act 1809, HRO BC79/27/3. H. Price, Horse Towing-path map 1808, HRO Q/RWn/7

13. E. Stooke, *Tourist Map of the River Wye* 1892, Hurley Collection

14. C. R. Shaw, The River Wye, mss. 1948, HCL 387

15. Shoesmith (1990). Information on photocopy from Hereford Tourist Information Centre

16. Day Book 1744 – 1827, 1811 – 1853, AA. Barge Accounts 1790 – 1805, HRO BH58/4. Barge & Carriers Accounts 1825 – 1827, HRO CF50/204,. Barge Accounts 1809 – 1811, T. Ward Collection (the LOWV barge archive)

17. Fownhope Local History Group information displayed 2006.

18. Lease to N. Purchas 1775, HCA 3340/23. Brewery plan 1783, HRO AE38/1 Box 1356. LOWV barge archive 2006.

19. LOWV barge archive 2007

20. Morgan (1950) pp 161 – 177

21. Holme Lacy accounts 1698, TNAC115/114

22. Isaac Taylor Wye Navigation plan, 1763. H. Jnl. 1795, Fownhope Local History Group display 2006

23. LOWV barge archive 2006

24. Information from Tony Gardiner, May 2007

25. Hoarwithy History, WI 1953, photocopy, Hurley Collection. Llanfrother Sale Particulars 1856, HCL PC3344

26. Bowsher, Hodges and Watkins letter 1799, HRO A29/64

27. 'common rights of wharfage' letter c1900, HRO BN83/134. Kynaston Sale Particulars 1863, HRO M5/15/17

28. Taylor (1997) pp 232 – 233

29. A. Jones Agreement 1745, HRO AW28/31/22

30. Lamont (1922) p 88

31. Fawley Lease 1678, HRO A8/11/210. LOWV barge archive 2006

32. LOWV barge archive 2006

33. LOWV barge archive 2006

34. LOWV barge archive 2006

35. H. Hurley in Brookes (2000) p 35. Bridstow Tithe Map(1839). Wakeman's Survey photocopy 1823, Hurley Collection

36. Hughes and Hurley (1999) p 109

37. AA 1738 – 1755, HRO G87/8/4 – 17. Heath (1828 ed)

38. Farr (1954) LOWV 2006

39. Heath (1828)

40. Isaac Taylor Wye Navigation plan, 1763

41. *HJNL* 5 Sept 1798, 22 June 1808

42. John Leech accounts 1788 – 1812, HCA 5715/3. Kissack (1978) p 55

43. Monmouth Museum Display 2007

44. Information from Angus Watkins, May 2007

45. Tweed (1884) p 43

46 LOWV website 2007. J. Eisel in Whitehead and Eisel (2000) p 50. Kissack (1978) p 66

47. LOWV barge archive 2006

48. Sample from entries in 1810/1811 barge accounts, T. Ward Collection

49. Barge Accounts 1791 – 1805, HRO BH58/4

50. as named on Isaac Taylor Wye Navigation plan, 1763

51. AA 1811 – 1853, LOWV barge archive 2006

52. Barge and Carriers Accounts, HCL LC380 (since transferred to HRO)

53. Pigot's Herefordshire Directory 1835

54. Gloucester & Hereford Railway Map and Prospectus, 1836, HCL385

55. Hurley (1985) p 307

56. Hereford, Ross & Gloucester Railway notice 1851, Hurley Collection

57. Rake (1909) p 307

58. Hereford, Ross and Gloucester Railway Company Minute Books 1851 – 1855 PRO (now TNA) Rail 302 vol.1 &2

59. *Illustrated London News*, July 14, 1855, p 52 – 53

60. Smith (1998) p 10

61. Hoarwithy Bridge Company Minutes 1855 – 1875, HRO Q/RWb/1

62. Holme Lacy Bridge Company Application of Shares, c1855, HRO   AC97/11

63. Smith (1998) p 10

64. Stratford (1896) p 8

65. Crow (1995) p 120

66. *Ross Gazette*, 3 April 1947

67. Taylor (1997) p 300

68. Hurley (2001) p 137

69. LOWV website 2007. Smith (1998) p 19

70. Littlebury, *Herefordshire Directory*, 1867; 18

71. Poulstone Estate Sale Particulars 1848, HCL 942.44

72. How Caple Sale, 1881, HRO E40/13. Holme Lacy Sale, 1909, HCL 942.44

Chapter IX. LANDSCAPE CHANGES

1. TNA C115/7/229

2. 11th report of the Commissioners on the Woods Forests & Land Revenues of the Crown, 1791

3. BL, Add MS 36307 G3, G4, G49, G59 and G63

4. Private Collection

5. HRO C59/6

6. HRO A97/1, J. Green map of Wilton 1788

7. HRO BN88/11 it is BG53/15

8. HRO E88 Brockhampton Estate Map 1832, HRO M58/150/28 – 32

9. Private collection

10. HCL Pilley Collection 2344, 1856

11. Some land was exempt from tithes including land subject to Parliamentary enclosure wards, church land and some lands of ecclesiastic estates seized by Henry VIII. Harewood parish which abuts Hentland was formerly owned by the Templars who were exempted from tithes and remained so after the dissolution which is why Harewood has no Tithe survey.

12. Isaac Taylor, New Map of the County of Hereford, 1754. H. Price 1817 map HRO F76/B242, OS Drawing for South Herefordshire BL OSD21x.

13. Aerofilm Collection Film No. 13N/13 795 NMR EH

14. In February 2002 Parliament introduced the Environmental Impact Assessment regulations for semi-natural and uncultivated land which required anyone intending to subject such land to 'agricultural intensification' to apply for a permission and a 'screening survey'. In practice the legislation was proved unworkable and only few meadows in England have been successfully protected using this legislation or its successor.

15. The Wayfaring Tree *Vibernum lantana*.

16. Bull (1852) p 18

17. West Midland Group on Post-War Reconstruction and Planning, (1946)

18. University of Cambridge Farm, The Rural Business Unit, Farm Business Survey West Midlands Region, 2006/07. www.farmbusinesssurvey.co.uk

Index